The Presidency of
WOODROW
WILSON

AMERICAN PRESIDENCY SERIES

Donald R. McCoy, Clifford S. Griffin, Homer E. Socolofsky
General Editors

George Washington, Forrest McDonald
John Adams, Ralph Adams Brown
Thomas Jefferson, Forrest McDonald
James Madison, Robert Allen Rutland
John Quincy Adams, Mary W. M. Hargreaves
Martin Van Buren, Major L. Wilson
William Henry Harrison & John Tyler, Norma Lois Peterson
James K. Polk, Paul H. Bergeron
Zachary Taylor & Millard Fillmore, Elbert B. Smith
Franklin Pierce, Larry Gara
James Buchanan, Elbert B. Smith
Andrew Johnson, Albert Castel
Rutherford B. Hayes, Ari Hoogenboom
James A. Garfield & Chester A. Arthur, Justus D. Doenecke
Grover Cleveland, Richard E. Welch, Jr.
Benjamin Harrison, Homer E. Socolofsky & Allan B. Spetter
William McKinley, Lewis L. Gould
Theodore Roosevelt, Lewis L. Gould
William Howard Taft, Paolo E. Coletta
Woodrow Wilson, Kendrick A. Clements
Warren G. Harding, Eugene P. Trani & David L. Wilson
Herbert C. Hoover, Martin L. Fausold
Harry S. Truman, Donald R. McCoy
Dwight D. Eisenhower, Chester J. Pach, Jr., & Elmo Richardson
John F. Kennedy, James N. Giglio
Lyndon B. Johnson, Vaughn Davis Bornet

The Presidency of

WOODROW WILSON

Kendrick A. Clements

UNIVERSITY PRESS OF KANSAS

For my parents

Alling Mackaye Clements
(1890–1957)

Jean Kendrick Clements
(1898–1990)

© 1992 by the University Press of Kansas
All rights reserved

Published by the University Press of Kansas (Lawrence, Kansas
66049), which was organized by the Kansas Board of Regents and is
operated and funded by Emporia State University, Fort Hays State
University, Kansas State University, Pittsburg State University,
the University of Kansas, and Wichita State University

Library of Congress Cataloging-in-Publication Data

Clements, Kendrick A., 1939–
The presidency of Woodrow Wilson / Kendrick A. Clements.
p.   cm. — (American presidency series)
Includes bibliographical references and index.
ISBN 0-7006-0523-1 (alk. paper). — ISBN 0-7006-0524-X (pbk. :
alk. paper)
1. United States—Politics and government—1913-1921.   2. Wilson,
Woodrow, 1856–1924.   I. Title.   II. Series.
E766.C44   1992
973.91′3′092—dc20   91-30591

British Library Cataloguing in Publication Data is available.

Printed in the United States of America
10 9 8 7 6 5 4 3 2 1

The paper used in this publication meets the minimum requirements of the
American National Standard for Permanence of Paper for Printed
Library Materials Z39.48-1984.

CONTENTS

FOREWORD

The aim of the American Presidency Series is to present historians and the general reading public with interesting, scholarly assessments of the various presidential administrations. These interpretive surveys are intended to cover the broad ground between biographies, specialized monographs, and journalistic accounts. As such, each will be a comprehensive, synthetic work which will draw upon the best in pertinent secondary literature, yet leave room for the author's own analysis and interpretation.

Volumes in the series will present the data essential to understanding the administration under consideration. Particularly, each book will treat the then current problems facing the United States and its people and how the president and his associates felt about, thought about, and worked to cope with these problems. Attention will be given to how the office developed and operated during the president's tenure. Equally important will be consideration of the vital relationships between the president, his staff, the executive officers, Congress, foreign representatives, the judiciary, state officials, the public, political parties, the press, and influential private citizens. The series will also be concerned with how this unique American institution—the presidency—was viewed by the presidents, and with what results.

All this will be set, insofar as possible, in the context not only of contemporary politics but also of economics, international relations, law, morals, public administration, religion, and thought. Such a broad approach is necessary to understanding, for a presidential administration is more than the elected and appointed officers composing it, since its work so often reflects the major problems, anxieties, and glories of the nation. In short, the authors in this series will strive to recount and evaluate the record of each administration and to identify its distinctiveness and relationships to the past, its own time, and the future.

The General Editors

PREFACE

"In many ways," said Harry Truman, "Wilson was the greatest of the greats," and historians and the public alike have agreed, ranking him among the half-dozen greatest American presidents.[1] Remembered by the public chiefly for his success in guiding the nation during its first great modern war and for his dream of ending forever the threat of future wars through the League of Nations, Wilson is also admired by professional historians for his domestic successes, which represented the culmination of the Progressive Era of reform and brought to a close what one historian has labeled "the second golden age of American political leadership."[2]

In 1912 Wilson became the standard-bearer of a Democratic party that during the previous twenty years had changed fundamentally, moving from the conservative, passive philosophy of Grover Cleveland to a reformist commitment to make industrialization and its effects the servants rather than the masters of the American people. Wilson not only shared that commitment but also brought with him a conviction reinforced by long study that the president must be the dominating force within the government and the spokesman of the nation's aspirations for reform. Riding the crest of a wave of national zeal for change that had been building during the terms of his two immediate predecessors, he proposed and guided to passage a strong reform program, strengthened and enlarged the executive branch as the administrator of that program, and made the White House the focus of national political attention more than it had ever been before.

Among the most notable domestic achievements of the Wilson administration was the Federal Reserve Act, which modernized the nation's banking and currency systems and laid the basis for federal management of the economy. The Underwood Tariff of 1913 significantly reduced the tariff for the first time in many years and reflected a new awareness that American businesses were now powerful enough to compete in the markets of the world. The law's inclusion of a federal income tax under the provisions of the recently approved Sixteenth Amendment provided a replacement for lost tariff revenue and created a powerful tool for the redistribution of income. The Clayton and Federal Trade Commission acts gave federal authorities new powers to supervise business practices, and the passage of the first federal child-labor law and other laws regulating hours and working conditions for other groups pioneered new territory in social reform. A new Department of Labor worked energetically to achieve a fairer balance between labor and capital, and an activist Department of Agriculture greatly expanded services to farmers. Some other reforms, most notably women's suffrage and the adoption of national Prohibition, were thrust upon Wilson more than sought by him.

One of the most remarkable aspects of Wilson's presidency, at least during his first administration, was his ability to dominate the government without antagonizing Congress. A number of experts have pointed to his administration as a model of presidential leadership that avoids the paralysis seemingly built into the constitutional separation of powers. There is no great mystery to how Wilson managed this, though a number of his successors did not profit from his example. He set definite priorities, made absolutely clear the basic principles he wanted legislation to embody, consulted regularly and extensively with legislative leaders on the details and timing of proposals, compromised on nonessentials when necessary, and conducted effective campaigns to publicize issues and to mobilize public opinion behind what he wanted to accomplish. In so doing he discovered that the members of Congress, like other Americans, seemed eager to have the president emerge as a single, national leader.

Not all of this increased importance of the presidency was Wilson's doing, of course. After a long period of congressional domination of the government during the late nineteenth century, the Spanish-American War and Theodore Roosevelt's discovery of the "bully pulpit" in the White House had given the executive new importance. Wilson benefited from these recent events, but even more he rode on the shoulders of thousands of progressive reformers and publicists who had popularized the idea that the rise of giant corporations had created a national problem that could be addressed only at the national level. It was they, more than he, who had broken down a traditional American preference for local over national government and who had won public acceptance of new levels of federal intervention in daily life. Wilson consolidated and built on these changes, largely because he was so successful in convincing Americans that he, as their direct agent in the government, would supervise the growing federal bureaucracy and keep power responsible to the people's will.

In an effort to show readers how reforms were administered and how the government actually operated below the level of the White House, I have discussed in some detail the operations of the Agriculture and Labor departments in chapters 4 and 5. Wilson does not appear on every page of these chapters, as he does in most others; obviously he delegated a great deal of authority to his subordinates. Yet readers will be struck by the degree to which he participated in important decisions and set basic policy directions. If Wilson was, as he said, "in the hands of his colleagues" in the administration, he was not a passive, unaware president. I apologize to readers if details sometimes seem a bit overwhelming in these chapters but ask them to remember, as Wilson pointed out as early as 1890, that those who administer policy on a day-to-day basis are in an important sense as much legislators as those who pass the original laws. In the long run, an administration's impact is measured less by the length of its legislative record than by the actual effect of its daily activities.

There is of course a good deal in the administration's record that is controversial. The expansion of segregation in the federal bureaucracy and the suppression of civil liberties during and after the war were deeply regrettable. I have tried to confront these events honestly while demonstrating that the issues involved and the application of the policies were complex. Although it is easy to condemn these aspects of the administration righteously, the historian's obligation is to understand the issues as the participants saw them and to explain the real, not the ideal, alternatives open to policymakers.

Equally controversial, at least among historians, is the question of the purpose and effect of Wilson's reforms. Was he a trust-busting "rural Tory," as Theodore Roosevelt called him, or was he an exponent of what some recent historians have described as "corporate liberalism?" That is, did he seek to break up monopolies and restore competition, or did he create a partnership between government and corporate leaders in the interest of greater efficiency and progress? One might think that the answer to this question would be obvious, but as readers will see, intentions and results are often very different; and extraneous, unexpected factors (in this case the war and the collapse of Wilson's health) often affect outcomes in unpredictable ways.

The impact of the war on the Wilson administration and upon the evolution of the presidency is one of the central topics of this study. Raising, training, supplying, transporting, and supporting an enormous military force presented challenges for which neither the nation nor the government was prepared in 1917. The job was done extraordinarily well, considering the circumstances, and in the process the country was transformed permanently. The government doubled in size and more than doubled in its functions, reaching out to touch individuals in unprecedented ways. It drafted more than two million men, took over the railroads, regulated the price of wheat, ran a national employment service, acquired a fleet of merchant vessels, and undertook hundreds of other tasks that before the war would have been unthinkable. Its relations with big business and big labor became more intimate than ever before, and its control over even the nation's individualistic farmers grew immensely. Although at the end of the war the president's illness as well as the administration's commitment to dismantling most of the special wartime programs and surrendering emergency powers prevented the expansion of authority from becoming permanent, precedents had been created that could be used in future crises.

If, then, the Wilson administration had an enormous and lasting impact upon the development of the institution of the presidency, upon the role of the federal government in our daily lives, and upon the fulfillment of the agenda for progressive reform, it certainly had an equally vital role in the development of American foreign policy. Even if that role had been confined merely to fighting the First World War that would be the case, but in fact that is only a part of the story.

The Underwood Tariff of 1913 is a convenient symbol for one aspect of the new role Wilson proposed for America in the world. The willingness of American corporations to face world competition without the artificial protection of a high tariff is evidence that not only did the United States have one of the strongest economies in the world by the early twentieth century but also that American leaders were well aware of the nation's new power. Ironically, Wilson advocated tariff reduction to weaken the so-called "trusts" by exposing them to foreign competition, not to further the growth of an "open-door empire" of indirect economic domination of other parts of the world; but he too welcomed the idea that American influence would be felt all over the globe. His goals were more moral and political than economic, but he understood that the power that made the achievement of his goals conceivable rested upon economic strength and upon the military might that depended upon economic power.

One of the great myths about Wilson is that he was uninterested in foreign policy and unprepared to conduct it when he became president. In fact from the day he entered office, Wilson assumed more personal control over foreign policy than over any other aspect of the administration. He was convinced that freedom and democracy were universal aspirations, and he was determined that the United States would do everything possible to advance those aspirations.

And it was clear by 1913 that the United States could do a great deal. In Asia it lacked the strength to do much more than to lead by example, but in the Western Hemisphere it had the power to act; and so in Mexico, in Haiti, in the Dominican Republic, in Nicaragua, and elsewhere around the Caribbean basin, it did. Wilson explicitly renounced any materialistic goals in these interventions (though he did everything possible to facilitate "investments") and assumed therefore that American assistance would be welcomed. Gradually, painfully, he began to discover that he was wrong, that American interference was usually unwelcome, that accomplishing democratization at the point of a bayonet was difficult if not impossible, and that disentangling oneself from an intervention was harder than beginning it. By 1917 he seemed to have learned many of these lessons, however, and on the basis of earlier experience he staunchly opposed Allied intervention in Siberia in 1918 and tried to minimize American involvement when it came. Other Americans seemed to learn less. The most frequent criticism of his Latin American policy was not that it was too interventionist but that he spoke too softly and did not wield a sufficiently large stick. Benevolent interventionism would have a long and controversial history in subsequent years.

A second important Wilsonian legacy in foreign policy was the erosion of traditional American political isolationism. Although many Americans did not accept his contention, expressed in his second inaugural address, that they had become "citizens of the world," most people did agree that the nation's increasing economic and military power obligated and permitted it to play a larger political role in the world. They also agreed that the nation's purpose should be to foster democracy, international order, and economic growth throughout the world. Many of the most seemingly isolationist senators who helped to defeat the Treaty of Versailles disagreed with Wilson not over ultimate goals but over the necessity of giving up any part of national sovereignty to achieve them. To a considerable extent, the treaty debate was misleading. In contention was not isolationism versus internationalism but methods for wielding the world power that almost everyone wanted. In proclaiming that America would take its place among the great powers of the world, Wilson spoke for most Americans of his and subsequent generations.

Wilson's third great legacy to American foreign policy is represented more fully in the Fourteen Points than in the Treaty of Versailles. In that January 1918 speech he set out aspirations for a world order that have exerted great appeal for Americans ever since and that at least in part have influenced other peoples all over the world. Open diplomacy, freedom of the seas, the removal of economic barriers among nations, reduction of armaments, the ending of imperialism, self-determination for national groups, the inclusion of Russia in the world community, and the creation of an association of nations to assume collective responsibility for maintaining peace are all goals upon which most Americans have continued to agree. When these broad principles were reduced to specific clauses in a treaty, consensus dissolved in disagreement over details; but what we may call the Wilsonian program has continued to influence American foreign policy and may in a post–cold war era again become dominant.

The issue of Wilson's health and its part in the defeat of the Treaty of Versailles in the Senate has been a contentious issue among historians for several years. Recently, however, the editors of *The Papers of Woodrow Wilson* have recovered medical records of the specialists who treated the president after his October 1919 stroke. These records, analyzed by modern experts, make it clear that Wilson, though severely weakened by his illness, was more crippled psychologically than physically. Physicians at the time, however, had little knowledge of the psychological effects of strokes and so failed to recognize the degree of his incapacitation, although their medical diagnosis seems to have been extremely precise. The question of whether Wilson would have been able to steer the treaty to victory in the Senate if he had been well may never be resolved unequivocally, but the new evidence used here for the first time seems to point strongly in that direction.

Finally, I think the reader deserves a word about my personal relationship with Wilson. "Speak of me as I am," says Othello, "nothing extenuate, nor set down aught in malice."[3] I hope that has been the spirit in which I have approached Wilson. His skill in making the government work effectively, his ability to penetrate to the heart of an issue and enunciate its basic principles in powerful, precise language, and the fact that his eight years in office, including the extraordinary buildup of the war, passed without a significant scandal seem to me to place him in a special category. Above all, he challenged Americans—and the world—to recognize and deal with an international order where old relationships had broken down and new forces were rising. In all of this he showed himself a leader of remarkable intellect and character. Yet there blind spots in his leadership. A warm, human side of his personality that he showed to family and friends was seldom demonstrated in public, and those with whom he had official relations sometimes saw an uglier side: arrogance, self-righteousness, and petulance. Many people shared French premier Clemenceau's suspicion that Wilson thought himself a new messiah predestined to set the world right. Nor is it possible to ignore the contradiction between Wilson's awareness of the aspirations of subject and colonial peoples and his overbearing Latin American policy as well as his insensitivity to racial issues in the United States. Questions also must be raised about the efficacy of his domestic program for curing the evils of industrialization and about the possibility that his international program, even if it had been fully implemented, might not have produced the peaceful, orderly world he promised. These questions, however, should not obscure the fact that Wilson, far more than any other world leader of his generation, raised issues that needed to be confronted and set an agenda for future domestic and international debate. That he remains, almost three-quarters of a century after his death, a man whose proposals still have the power to inspire dreamers and to stir debate is evidence that he deserves his high place in the regard of Americans.

I am grateful to the American Philosophical Society and to the University of South Carolina Committee on Productive Scholarship for grants that enabled me to complete the research for this book. I am also indebted to series editors Donald McCoy, Clifford Griffin, and Homer Socolofsky, who went through the manuscript with the greatest care, made a great many constructive suggestions, and saved me from a number of errors; to Niels Thorsen for reading and making helpful comments on the first chapter; to Manfred Boemeke for his suggestions about where to find materials on Wilson's labor policy; and to an anonymous reader for *Agricultural History*, who read and made very perceptive criticisms of an earlier version of what is now chapter 4. The editors of the *The Papers of Woodrow Wilson*, particularly Arthur Link, David Hirst, and Manfred Boemeke, have always made my visits to Princeton fruitful and pleasant. I also gained enormously from hearing and talking with a large number of other Wilsonian scholars during a conference at Princeton in spring 1989 that was organized by John Milton Cooper, Jr., and Charles Neu; I thank them for inviting me to participate. The staff of the National Archives, especially Don Jackanicz and Richard Crawford in the Division of Scientific, Economic and Natural

Resources, provided invaluable advice and assistance as I worked my way through the Wilson administration's records. An old friend, Richard Rempel of McMaster University and the Bertrand Russell Editorial Project, generously spent hours talking about Wilson with me, led me to materials and viewpoints about which I would not otherwise have known, and helped me to formulate and clarify key points. Fred Woodward, Susan McRory, and Claire Sutton at the University Press of Kansas have encouraged and gently prodded me through the process of writing and preparing the manuscript. At the University of South Carolina, the late chair of the History Department, Thomas L. Connelly, and the vice-chair, Peter Becker, provided travel money for research and shifted teaching loads so that I could finish writing. My wife, Linda, has, as always, supported and encouraged me at every point.

1

THEORY AND PRACTICE,
1856–1912

When Woodrow Wilson was born on 28 December 1856 the United States was on the verge of civil war.[1] His earliest memories were of sectional conflict, and like most Americans of his generation, he dreaded any repetition of that catastrophe. As an adult student of American history and politics and as a political leader, he sought ways to build patriotism and to reshape the federal government to govern the reunited nation more effectively.[2]

Wilson's first and in many ways most important teacher was his father. A prominent southern Presbyterian minister of wide-ranging interests and strong personality, Joseph Ruggles Wilson encouraged his son to develop oratorical skills and stressed precision in speech and writing. Although Dr. Wilson also bequeathed to his son a strong religious faith and would have liked to see the young man follow him into the ministry, both believed that service to others was a Christian duty that could be fulfilled in political life as well as in the church. As Wilson said, "It seems to me that religion connects itself with patriotism, because religion is the energy of character which, instead of concentrating upon the man himself, concentrates upon a service which is greater than the man himself."[3]

Although it is certainly true that religion greatly influenced Wilson's public life, it was a broad "civil religion," not a specific theology, that he followed. In his argument that patriotism is "the duty of religious men," in fact, he turned orthodox Calvinism, which sought a political order that would protect true religion, upside down. Believing that Christianity required service to others, Wilson shared the convic-

1

tion common among late nineteenth-century American Protestants that God's kingdom was evolving on earth, especially in the United States. "We are to be an instrument in the hands of God to see that liberty is made secure for mankind," he said in 1917, and he believed that his own role was to be an evangelist of that plan, both at home and around the world.[4]

Wilson's mother, Janet Woodrow Wilson, was an intelligent and rather shy woman who hated her public duties as the wife of a prominent minister and lavished boundless love on her children. Wilson counted on his mother for her uncritical support, in contrast to his father's perfectionism, and throughout his life sought that acceptance from his family and from female friends. With three daughters and a number of women friends who sometimes joined the family for lengthy visits, he enjoyed himself as he seldom did with men, joking, singing, mimicking political rivals, reading aloud from his favorite romantic poets, or attending comedies or musicals at the theater. His lengthy and intimate letters to the two women who became his wives showed him to be a passionate, ardent lover, and only slightly less romantic letters to Mary Peck suggest that he was at least severely tempted outside of marriage as well. Yet neither of Wilson's wives nor his daughters were passive, subservient women. They were devoted to him and always sought to advance his career, but especially his first wife, Ellen, and his daughters were also strong-minded and independent, and they clearly helped to add an awareness of social issues to his interest in political and economic reform.[5]

The experience of the Civil War influenced much of Wilson's later political thought, but the influence was more intellectual than personal. During the war the Wilsons lived in Augusta, Georgia, and their church and its yard sometimes served as a campground and hospital for Confederate soldiers, but they experienced no fighting. Six years after the end of the war the family moved to Columbia, South Carolina. The city had burned during Sherman's occupation but was being rebuilt by the time the Wilsons got there, and their relative affluence allowed them to build and live comfortably in a solid new house for the three years before Woodrow left for Davidson College in North Carolina.

Yet if Wilson did not suffer during the Civil War, in later years he came to regard the conflict as marking the point at which the nation's original constitutional structure, with its balance between the states and the national government, became unworkable.[6] Although the balance had been challenged before the war by expansionism and by such federal policies as Hamilton's economic programs and internal improvements, Wilson believed that the war, with its centralization of power in

Washington, had dealt the old structure a deathblow. In the postwar period new realities, especially broader political participation and the rise of corporate industry, necessitated a stronger and more efficient federal government if the United States was to continue to progress. As Niels Thorsen has pointed out, historians who depict Wilson as "a nostalgic man who longed for the return of a political state of innocence or an economic state of Jeffersonian yeomanry" have missed his stress upon progress and his conviction that "overcoming of the past, not its repetition," was the key to maintaining that progress.[7]

Wilson's active analysis of American political structures began in 1876 when he was a sophomore at Princeton, having left Davidson in spring 1874 and spent the next year at home. In November 1876 the Hayes-Tilden presidential election ended in a deadlock that was resolved only by sordid bargaining among politicians in an atmosphere of crisis similar to that which had preceded the Civil War. Before the election Wilson had seemed pessimistic about the United States and predicted that "the American *Republic* will . . . never celebrate another Centennial," but after it was over he seems to have concluded that the system could be saved.[8] Drawing ideas from his reading of English writers and testing his proposals in conversations with friends, he wrote an essay in 1879 proposing the introduction of cabinet-style parliamentary government in the United States that was published in the *International Review*.[9]

Wilson's argument in his article and later in his first book, *Congressional Government* (1885), was not primarily that Congress was corrupt but rather that Congress, which then supervised administration as well as legislating, was trying to do too much. Enmeshed in routine administrative tasks, Congress had neither time nor inclination to debate the great issues before the nation, and therefore the national government did not attract the interest and support of most citizens. Unlike many conservatives, Wilson did not blame the problems of Congress on universal suffrage; its problems, he thought, could be rectified by reorganization, and universal suffrage would then become an asset because it would guarantee broad loyalty to the national government. His central goal was to assure that major issues really were debated "in the presence of the whole country," so that leaders would have widespread support for effective action.[10]

When the Constitution was written in the eighteenth century, its authors feared that power would corrupt its holders; thus they deliberately created a structure that balanced power against power and interest against interest in such a way that governmental threats to liberty would be minimized. Wilson concluded at the end of the nineteenth century, however, that the Founders had done their work too well. The

3

federal government was not only safe, it was paralyzed. A cabinet system, he argued, could break this deadlock by creating a government capable of acting effectively on pressing national problems yet that would still be safe because of being constantly under the supervision of the voters, whose own prejudices and whimsies could be expected to cancel each other out in so large a nation.[11]

A crucial question about Wilson's proposed reform, of course, was who was to lead the nation. He recognized that direct democracy was impossible. In a *modern* democracy," he wrote, "the people who are said to govern are . . . a vast population which never musters into any single assembly, whose members never see each others' faces or hear each others' voices," and government must therefore be through representatives.[12] Yet Wilson did not share either the conservatives' belief that only men of wealth and standing should lead nor the liberal view that anyone could operate the machinery of government. Leaders, he believed, must combine "ordinary ideas" with "extraordinary abilities" to produce "a power to conceive and execute the next step forward and to organize the force of the State for the movement."[13] In a psychological or even mystical way leaders must have "divine insight into human nature" and "deep sympathy with all the efforts and strivings of the common mind" but must also have the expertise necessary to implement the public will vigorously and efficiently. "It is only by the action of leading minds that the organic will of a community is stirred to the exercise of either originative purpose or guiding control in affairs," he explained.[14] Neither the conservative notion of a permanent elite nor the liberal ideal of everyman his own governor could guarantee such leaders.

Wilson's solution to the problem of where to get leaders was hardly surprising, given his career in college teaching and administration, which he began after completing his Ph.D. in history and political science at Johns Hopkins University in 1885. The new leaders would be "college-bred men," trained in a tradition of service and given the expert knowledge of politics and economics necessary to modern leadership. Although their skills would give them the "advantage . . . professional athletes have over amateurs," they would not be an aristocracy but a constantly renewed elite.[15]

Unlike the conservative Social Darwinists of his era, Wilson did not believe that business success made industrialists natural political leaders. He had enormous admiration for the achievements of businessmen within their own fields, but he also believed that the demands of business were so great that businessmen were forced to narrow their interests. Few of them, he declared, "can be said to have any [political] opinions at all."[16] He frequently liked to shock alumni audiences while he

4

was president of Princeton by telling them that the goal of the college should be to make sons as *unlike* their fathers as possible, "to make them forget the interests of their fathers and to see how the interests of all the people are linked together."[17]

Nor did he believe that average citizens were qualified to lead. "The bulk of mankind is rigidly unphilosophical," he wrote, and "a truth must become not only plain but also commonplace before it will be seen by the people who go to their work very early in the morning"; a situation "must involve great pinching inconveniences before these same people will make up their minds to act."[18] The leader's task was partly to sense the wishes of the people, but it was also to mold their ideas and to act where they would naturally be inert. A leader, he wrote, must "communicate the thoughts of the great mass of the people as to impel them to great political achievements."[19] Thus the leader must be sensitive to the dynamic needs and forces of business but not limited by its myopia; he must reflect public opinion but not be paralyzed by public inertia. Only the liberally trained college graduate, Wilson argued, had the vision and dedication necessary to guide a modern democracy and the sympathy with the people necessary to be elected.

As president of Princeton from 1902 to 1910 Wilson reached the pinnacle of his academic career and rejoiced in the opportunity to make the university a training ground for future leaders. His inaugural address, "Princeton for the Nation's Service," revealed the central theme of his presidency. The nation, he declared, needed "efficient and enlightened men," and "the universities of the country must take part in supplying them"; but these future leaders must not be narrowly trained technicians. "The managing minds of the world," he said, "even the efficient working minds of the world, must be equipped for a mastery whose chief characteristic is adaptability, play, an initiative which transcends the bounds of mere technical training."[20] Driven by this vision of liberal education, Wilson subsequently developed and secured a reformed curriculum; proposed and won faculty support for a tutorial system that emphasized close relations between teachers and students, in which students were encouraged to read widely and develop their own ideas; urged the establishment of a graduate college in the heart of the campus where its scholarship could inspire undergraduates; and fought to do away with eating clubs, which in his opinion distracted undergraduates from intellectual interests. He lost these last two battles to the influence of alumni and wealthy donors, but he never doubted that his concept of the university had been right, nor did he ever doubt that he had a personal obligation to put his own liberal education at the nation's service if an opportunity arose.

Wilson's academic battles made him a well-known public figure and his books popularized aspects of his thought, but what was perhaps his most important intellectual achievement came before he was a celebrity and was never published in book form. In *Congressional Government* and earlier writings Wilson had sought to free Congress for intelligent debate on policy by suggesting that all administration be turned over to professional civil servants. That proposal naturally led him to investigate what administration was and ought to be in the modern state, and during the ten years from 1886 to 1896 he began the first serious study of administration in the United States through a notable article and a series of lectures at Johns Hopkins.

Pointing out that laws did not enforce themselves and must be given meaning "by the administration and obedience of men," Wilson argued that society was growing organically toward more intricate economic, political, and social relationships and that the functions of government were becoming "more complex and difficult" and "vastly multiplying in number." Given the growing power of modern business, only efficient administration could make the government the "master of the masterful corporation."[21] It was therefore essential to study administration rationally and thoroughly with the goal of making it as good as possible.

Wilson was well aware that Americans were suspicious of administration as something associated with European absolutism, and he sought to break this prejudice by arguing that strong administration could make the democratic state more rather than less responsive to the people. To that end he downplayed the independence of administrators and stressed the idea that administration would be an essentially mechanical process of carrying out political decisions. In *Congressional Government*, for example, he suggested that Congress could free itself of administrative burdens by transferring such functions to a professional civil service that would carry out the laws in a mechanical, nonpolitical fashion.

As he thought further about the matter, however, Wilson was compelled to recognize that unless Congress spent all its time drafting minutely detailed laws, administrators must be given great discretion. At first he tried to avoid this problem by suggesting that it was only a matter of detail; drawing a sharp line between political and administrative responsibilities, he wrote, was unnecessary "without entering upon particulars so numerous as to confuse and distinctions so minute as to distract."[22]

Within a few years, however, Wilson realized that by recognizing frankly that administrative decisions actually created what amounted to

6

law, he might actually find a route to the reinvigorated national government that he had long sought. In 1890 he abandoned the argument that administration derived automatically from legislation and suggested instead that it was in fact a "subject in *Public Law.*" Administrative actions, he now admitted, were themselves "*a source of Law*" that went beyond legislative action.[23] When he then added that administration should become an *executive* rather than a legislative duty, the effect of Wilson's admission that administrators had significant discretionary powers was to enhance the role of the executive. In *Congressional Government* Wilson had argued that the president's duties were "*mere* administration" and suggested that he might, "not inconveniently, be a permanent officer; the first official of a carefully-graded and impartially regulated civil service system."[24] Once he eliminated the adjective "mere," he became much less interested in further study of administration and much more concerned with the office of the presidency, as he demonstrated when in June 1913 he refused to support an extension of a federal Commission on Economy and Efficiency appointed by President Taft to study administrative reform.[25]

In addition to the conclusions forced upon him by his own study of administration, Wilson's ideas about the presidency were reshaped by events. The Spanish-American War of 1898 reminded him of the president's extensive powers over foreign relations and suggested that those powers might be enhanced in other areas as well. In a preface to the 1900 edition of *Congressional Government* he wrote that the war had made foreign policy important once again and given the president "greatly enhanced power and opportunity for constructive leadership."[26]

By 1908, after his own experience of executive power at Princeton and after seven years of Theodore Roosevelt's vigorous national leadership, Wilson was ready to find in the presidency the possibilities of leadership and national unification that he had so long sought. "We have grown more inclined," he said that year in a series of published lectures delivered at Columbia University, "to look to the President as the unifying force in our complex system, the leader both of his party and of the nation."[27]

The president's leadership of his party gave him influence over Congress, Wilson argued in 1908, but more importantly his standing as the interpreter of the country's instinctive wishes and desires made him a unique national figure:

> The President represents not so much the party's governing efficiency as its controlling ideals and principles. He is not so much part of its organization as its vital link of connection with the thinking nation.

7

. . . If he rightly interpret the national thought and boldly insist upon it, he is irresistible; and the country never feels the zest of action so much as when its President is of such insight and calibre. It is for this reason that it will often prefer to choose a man rather than a party. A President whom it trusts can not only lead it, but form it to his own views.[28]

The president, in Wilson's view, thus had extraordinary potential power deriving from his triple functions as party leader, symbol of national unity, and interpreter of the wishes of all the people.

This glorification of the presidency was a remarkable change from Wilson's earlier belief that leadership should be lodged in the legislature and was a slightly ominous foretaste of the "imperial presidency" of half a century later. So much did Wilson assume that the president could become the sole voice of the nation that he suggested that members of the cabinet were "not . . . political officers at all" and should not advise the president on political issues but only relieve him of the burden of daily administration. If they did their jobs properly, he wrote, their departments "may proceed with their business for months and even years without demanding [the president's] attention." Thus "duties apparently assigned to [the president] by the Constitution have come to be . . . less important," and his power to inspire, shape, and lead public opinion had become central.[29]

In his earlier work Wilson had spoken of the president's veto and his control over foreign policy as his greatest powers, but in *Constitutional Government* he discussed those functions almost as afterthoughts. The president's "means of compelling Congress . . . through public opinion" were so great, he warned, that chief executives must be careful never to stoop to "illegitimate means" of gaining their will, such as bargaining with members of Congress or using their influence in local elections. Such behavior, he declared, would be "deeply immoral" and "destructive of . . . constitutional government."[30]

Although Wilson's dramatically enhanced vision of the presidency had evolved within his own political thought and resulted largely from his constant search for ways to secure national unity and leadership, he believed it met needs felt strongly by most Americans. Because all existing institutions were under suspicion of corruption, because the Spanish-American War had inspired a nationalism that needed a single focus, and because people in a complex modern society hungered for a sense of community that could be satisfied through common loyalty, the president became "the natural trust or depository for civic urges and republican instincts that had nowhere else to go in the modern constitutional system." Unlike most political analysts of his time who saw society as made up of self-confident economic men happy in their individualism, Wilson realized that most people felt helpless amid gigantic forces over which they had no control and yearned for somewhere to place their trust.[31] The president, he argued, could restore a sense of belonging to Americans by offering them control over their government, their society, and their lives.

It is important to understand that Wilson saw the president's role as leading the government in mastering complexity, not in destroying it. Before 1908 he usually spoke of himself as a conservative, and by that he meant a deep respect for law, existing social structures, and patriotism; he did not share the outrage some reformers felt about poverty and social injustice. On the other hand, his admiration for businessmen was limited to the economic sphere, and he certainly did not have the conservative belief that government must keep its hands off the workings of the economy. "To society alone can the power of dominating combinations belong," he wrote in *The State* in 1889; "and society cannot suffer any of its members to enjoy such a power for their own private gain independently of its own strict regulation or oversight." That meant, he said explicitly, that government could legislate to protect workers' welfare and to regulate corporations.[32] It was impossible, he concluded, for a man to seek only his selfish advantage and yet be a patriot, for patriotism required "a certain energy of character acting outside the narrow circle of self interest."[33]

To Wilson, politically controlled and directed economic development was the basis of progress. Capitalists, he believed, sought power and profit for purely selfish reasons; but "the irresistible energy and efficiency of harmony and cooperation" produced by their "vast combinations" could carry the whole society forward, provided they were regulated and guided in the public interest.[34] Without such controls, selfish competition would produce conflict and violence, on international as well as on national or private levels.

Two conclusions followed logically from Wilson's belief that economic growth must be under political control. First, although he believed that the frontier had stimulated American development, he did not think that unlimited physical expansion was essential to progress; real growth required politically shaped and directed economic development more than unlimited resources. Second, he thought that overseas imperialism after the Spanish-American War was at best a mixed blessing. It could bring the benefits of rationally directed economic growth to the world, but its potential for increasing conflict was very great.

Like William Jennings Bryan, with whom he shared more than he at

9

first realized, Wilson was seeking fundamental change in the Democratic party in the early twentieth century. At first Wilson distrusted Bryan because he thought the Commoner's populism would revive sectionalism and his radical language would disrupt national unity, but in their mutual desire to have a strong federal government control economic development the two men had much in common. Both, it gradually became clear, sought to break the Democratic party out of its mold of sectionalism and laissez faire and to recast it as a national party making use of federal power for the benefit of the nation as a whole.[35] Whether one chose to describe the program as "conservative" because of its emphasis upon controlled, orderly progress or as "progressive" because of its stress upon having government serve the masses rather than the elite, the terminology indicated a change in the meaning of political labels more than a fundamental difference between Bryan and Wilson.

When Wilson began to emerge as a national political figure about 1908 it was in his interest to emphasize rather than to minimize his differences with Bryan, however. The Nebraskan was then in the process of losing his third presidential campaign, and many influential Democrats, especially in the East, were interested in finding leaders who would be distinctly different. Although Wilson had earlier tried to reconcile himself to being only an "*outside* force in politics" through his writing and teaching, he leaped at an opportunity to become a participant rather than an observer, particularly since his ambitious program of reform at Princeton was then running into serious opposition.[36] To the prominent Democrats who began to seek him out, he stressed his commitment to "conservative reform . . . in the spirit of law and of ancient institutions" and expressed a wish that "we could do something, at once dignified and effective, to knock Mr. Bryan once for all into a cocked hat!"[37]

While Wilson thus reassured Democratic conservatives, his unsuccessful struggle to do away with exclusive clubs at Princeton made him appealing to reformers. Hence in late spring 1910 Democratic bosses in New Jersey, seeking a malleable man who could attract broad support, approached Wilson as a possible gubernatorial candidate. Knowing nothing about his political thought, they believed that the naive college professor would be a convenient figurehead behind whom they could continue to manipulate the state government for their own selfish purposes.

They soon realized their mistake. After a vigorous campaign during which he strongly affirmed his support of every reform plank in the Democratic platform and promised to crush the "boss system," Wilson won a substantial victory and brought with him Democratic majorities in both houses of the state legislature. Promising to be an "unconstitutional governor" who would keep pressure on the legislature in the interests of the people, he gave new dynamism and excitement to the state government. Even before his inauguration he proved he would not be a tool of the bosses by fighting and defeating the machine candidate for the United States Senate. His success in this first crucial battle made him a hero in New Jersey and awakened lively interest in him across the country.[38]

Following up quickly on this success, in January 1911 Wilson placed before the legislature a series of reform proposals embodying the promises of the platform. These included the replacement of party caucuses with open primaries for nominating candidates, the reform of election mechanics, the creation of a board of public utilities commissioners, a workmen's compensation law, and an act authorizing cities to adopt the commission form of government. All of these measures passed by the time the legislature adjourned on 22 April, and suddenly New Jersey, long regarded as a bastion of bossism, vaulted into the front ranks of reform. Governor Wilson's record, gushed a leading Republican reformer, was "the most remarkable record of progressive legislation ever known in the political history of this or any other State."[39]

Although Wilson and other reformers overestimated the importance and long-term effect of his reforms, his success made him a front-runner for the 1912 Democratic presidential nomination. During the remainder of 1911 and for most of 1912 he concentrated on that and gave state affairs only partial attention. In January 1912 he recommended to the legislature a series of administrative reforms that derived largely from his previous study of administration, defending them as having "no flavor of party feeling"; but Republicans and machine Democrats, eager to embarrass him, defeated them anyway.[40] Other reform proposals, made to the legislature in January 1913 while he was president-elect but before he resigned the governorship in March, fared better but proved in the long run to have little importance.

In striking contrast to what the bosses had expected when they chose Wilson as the Democratic gubernatorial nominee, he had proved that he could be a leader and that state government could meet the challenges facing it. Before Wilson, New Jersey's governor had been a largely ceremonial figure, the state had lacked machinery to deal with industrialism, and a majority of the people were being victimized by a privileged minority. He showed that the governor could become a dynamic force for reform and that state institutions could be modernized to meet new needs.

Wilson proved to be a strong leader while governor, but there is some question about other aspects of his performance. The administrative reforms that he proposed in 1912 suggest his concern about improving the efficiency of state government, yet his failure to follow up on his proposals that year or to repeat them the following year cast some doubt on the depth of his commitment. Fragmentary surviving records give us no clear picture of how well he actually administered the state either. He seems to have taken a keen interest in appointing able officials (including several Republicans) and in seeing that laws were well enforced, but we cannot reconstruct his activities in this area in detail. It is clear that from summer 1911 he was too absorbed in the national campaign to give state administration his full attention. Like many other progressive reformers of the time, Wilson seems to have believed that passage of structural reforms and good laws would ensure the permanence of reforms, underestimating, despite his own convictions about the importance of leadership, the necessity of ensuring that able successors would take up where he left off. In the end, Wilson's heart was never in being governor; as he had said in 1910, he regarded the position as a "mere preliminary" to a more important national role.[41] From his youth he had believed that state and sectional interests must be transcended and power and loyalty focused in the national government if modern problems were to be solved. With the lure of the presidency drawing him, state issues dwindled to insignificance.

In many ways besides his long intellectual analysis of the problems of government Wilson was well qualified for the presidency in 1912. Although his academic work had showed that he was not a profound thinker or a great intellectual, he had a rare ability to see the essentials of issues and to delegate authority to others to handle details. While considering issues he was open-minded, undogmatic, and eager for practical suggestions about how to achieve a goal; and once he had made up his mind he was firm and consistent.[42]

Wilson had also trained himself thoroughly in the skills of political leadership. From the time when as a boy he had practiced orations in his father's empty church on quiet afternoons until his governorship, he had studied and polished his speaking abilities. In contrast to the flamboyancy of Theodore Roosevelt, Wilson's style was restrained and undramatic, giving him a deceptive impression of being more conservative than he actually was, but his skill at putting issues on the broadest possible basis made him very successful in appealing to large numbers of people.[43] At the same time, however, the very quality that gave his speeches broad appeal also sometimes left audiences wondering after the first thrill had worn off exactly what he meant to do; and his insistence on speaking of principles rather than about details could infuriate individual politicians whose interests were practical and specific.

One of his greatest strengths as an administrator was his ability to

12

focus on a single issue, identifying its essential points and dealing with it quickly and efficiently. This talent allowed him to get through an enormous amount of work swiftly so that even during the war years he was able to work through the morning, adjourn for an hour's lunch at one, and then finish up the day's work in an hour or two more, leaving time in the late afternoon for golf or an automobile ride and the evening free to attend a musical or a light play or to read and sing with his family. The other side of this quality was an unfortunate tendency to be "one-track minded," as he and his friends frequently noted. That meant that he did not switch easily from subject to subject, and once he had made up his mind on a topic, he could be rigid and stubborn.[44]

Even though Wilson liked to talk about "common council," he was essentially a shy man who loved privacy and preferred to make his decisions alone, not in discussion with his advisers. He had broad interests and welcomed information from all sources while considering an issue, but once he had reached a conclusion he was not interested in either new arguments or new facts; and anyone who tried to repeat old arguments was likely to receive a chilly reception indeed. Supremely—and properly—confident in his own intellect, he did not suffer fools gladly and expected those around him to defer to him. Anyone who did not, and especially those who disagreed publicly with him, became a permanent enemy. He could cut off a close friend who crossed him and never see that person again, yet at the same time he hated personal confrontation and frequently endured incompetent subordinates for years rather than face and fire them.

Physically and psychologically Wilson was ready for the challenges of the presidency. His health had been delicate in the past, with chronic stomach problems and a history of untreated high blood pressure, but in 1912 he felt and looked perfectly fit. Mentally, he was extremely stable. His deep and untroubled religious convictions gave him confidence in himself and in his cause. He enjoyed holding power and looked forward enthusiastically to life in the White House. Simple in tastes and unpretentious in his interests, he was in no danger of becoming vain or being manipulated by flattery. His clothes bespoke the man: few in number, conservative in cut, and of the best possible quality. If his preference for the familiar over the new in books, poetry, recreation, and friends suggested a mind that was sometimes unadventurous, it also demonstrated self-confidence and stability.

To those who worked for him and to the members of his family, Wilson was unfailingly kind and considerate. Over the years he and Ellen took in many of their relatives, making them part of the family, and they could always be counted upon to help a troubled relative or a friend financially. His delight in children, his pride in their achievements, and his desire for their happiness were quiet but unlimited. He loved children and after Ellen's death in 1914 took great consolation in seeing the grandchildren who soon began to be born. At Christmas 1914 he suppressed his own grief and put up a Christmas tree in the White House just for them.

In all the positions Wilson had held before 1912, from his first faculty post at Bryn Mawr to the governorship of New Jersey, he had been marked by those who knew him as a man of exceptional intellect who had a special ability to set out a vision of future growth and development and to inspire others to seek to achieve it with him. But even those who loved and admired him were compelled also to recognize less attractive aspects of his personality—egotism, inability to accept criticism, stubbornness—that had already led him into catastrophic battles while he was president of Princeton and that might be fatal flaws in a democratic leader. In quality of mind and knowledge of the functions and possibilities of government, Wilson was as well qualified for the presidency as any man who has ever held the position. Success or failure in the White House also depend, however, on personal qualities that go beyond intellect. Only time would reveal whether Wilson could meet the tests to which he would be subjected.

By the time the president-elect and his family moved to Washington in March 1913 he had traveled even farther intellectually than physically from the South of his childhood. Although he paid lip service to regional loyalty and respected Democratic traditions of states' rights, his goal had become a united nation under a strong national government. Only such a government, he believed, could bring to all Americans alike the benefits of modern industrial society, and only a strong president could manage and direct the government so as to win the loyalty and confidence of the American people. His legacy would be to make Americans think of the White House as the center of government more than they ever had before and to make the American presidency the focus of world hopes and fears as well. In seeking to infuse the governmental system with energy to make it "serviceable," as he was fond of saying, he and other progressive leaders so raised public expectations of what government could do that disappointments were inevitable. Yet Washington would become the heart of the nation and a world capital as it had never been before.

2

1912

"In the year 1920," began a utopian novel published anonymously in 1912, "the student and the statesman saw many indications that the social, financial and industrial troubles that had vexed the United States of America for so long were about to culminate in civil war."[1] The author of that apocalyptic prediction, Edward M. House, had recently been introduced to Woodrow Wilson, in whom House discerned a commitment to reform that might avert catastrophe; but House's novel stood, nevertheless, as a warning of what he feared might happen if reform were thwarted.[2]

Other than House and Theodore Dreiser, whose novelistic attack on business, *The Financier*, was published in 1912, American writers did not seem especially pessimistic that year. Nineteen twelve's most popular novel was Zane Grey's *Riders of the Purple Sage*; the next year's would be Eleanor Hodgman Porter's *Pollyanna*. The muckraking books of a few years earlier seemed to be giving way to more optimistic tales; even Jack London would publish in 1913 *The Valley of the Moon*, in which economic problems are solved by a return to the land.

By 1912 times were good for most Americans, and the stridency that had characterized reformism a few years earlier was subsiding. Farmers were enjoying their most prosperous period in living memory; and if urban workers were feeling a pinch from gradually rising prices (the cost of living rose 35 percent between 1897 and 1913), unemployment at 4.6 per cent was lower than it had been for several years. Moreover, working conditions were improving. The six-day, ten-hour-a-day work week was gradually being shortened to an eight-hour, six-day week. By the beginning of the Wilson administration, some federal agencies even had a seven-hour, six-day week. Close behind were state governments, the railroads (where safety considerations made shortened hours desirable), and strongly unionized manufacturing industries. With more than 2.5 million members in 1912, unions were beginning to be a significant economic and political force, but union members still made up no more than 10 percent of the total work force.

The average American worker earned about six hundred dollars a year in 1912, although manual laborers might receive as little as a dollar a day and white-collar workers might have salaries of twelve to fifteen hundred dollars a year. Despite the fact that flour cost about four cents a pound, steak twenty cents a pound, eggs thirty-four cents a dozen, milk (delivered) eight cents a quart, and potatoes twenty-two cents for ten pounds, most workers could expect to spend more than half their annual incomes to feed their families. In the decade before 1912 worker productivity had grown by more than 50 percent, but wages had not kept pace with that increase. Although the gross national product was so large that measured on a per capita basis American incomes were the highest in the world, well ahead of Britain, the nation's nearest rival, prosperity was not widely shared. What was needed, reformers thought, was a system to make the distribution of the national income a little fairer.

Working conditions also seemed to need some improvement. Unemployment rose and fell unpredictably, and workers could do little about it. Despite the generally high levels of employment in the period, in 1908, 1914, and 1915 unemployment rose to over 12 percent. Accidents and injuries also took an appalling toll on workers. In 1913, for example, twenty-five thousand people died in industrial accidents, and thousands more were injured or crippled. Because nearly four million women and children (under the age of fifteen) were employed in manufacturing, many of those killed and injured were women or children. In one famous 1911 case, a fire at the Triangle Shirtwaist Company of New York, 146 workers, mostly women and young girls, were killed in a single disaster.[3]

Frequently, middle-class women were going to work along with their poorer sisters, although not usually in jobs that were as dangerous. In 1910 about 24 percent of women worked outside the home, and desirable clerical and technical jobs created by the invention of the telephone, typewriter, and telegraph went often to women who had been able to take advantage of new opportunities for education.[4] Between 1880 and 1900 the number of women in college had doubled, and from this new generation of educated women came not only clerical workers and teachers but also a large number of social workers and activists in various fields, particularly in the movements for women's suffrage, Prohibition, conservation, and child-labor legislation.[5] Such women became the consciences of reform, never tiring of pointing out the injustices and inequities of modern progress.

For the nation as a whole, however, the industrial boom brought a new level of national prosperity. In the decade between 1890 and 1900 national wealth doubled, and the United States became the world's largest producer of food, raw materials, iron, steel, and coal. By 1913, when Woodrow Wilson was inaugurated, American industries were also pioneering in the production of a new flood of consumer goods, including automobiles, telephones, and movies.[6]

In the late nineteenth century rising industrial production coupled with relatively fixed wages had begun to create what appeared to be a crisis of overproduction in the United States. The diagnosis was simplistic, but it became one of the forces along with the ideas of Social Darwinism, the development of a modern navy, evangelical Christianity, traditional expansionism, and the international climate of imperialism that led the United States to seize a new Caribbean and Pacific colonial empire after the Spanish-American War in 1898.[7] "I think no one now would question that the Spanish war marked the entrance of the United States into world affairs to a degree which had never obtained before," said Senator Henry Cabot Lodge in 1919.[8]

Even more strikingly, the United States became a world economic power. Annual exports leaped from $1,394 million in 1900 to $2,466 million in 1913, and in the same period manufactured goods went from 35.37 percent of exports to 48.84 percent. By 1913 only cotton led iron and steel products in value as an export, and some thirty-seven companies had built or purchased factories in other countries. American overseas investments, concentrated in the Western Hemisphere, were over four billion dollars.[9]

Whether or not Americans approved of overt imperialism—and many did not—the economic and military power of the United States put American leaders of the early twentieth century in a position to exercise regional authority and even world power for the first time. They disagreed sharply about how to employ that power, but by the time Woodrow Wilson was elected president in 1912 the Platt amendment, Roosevelt's corollary to the Monroe Doctrine, intervention in Panama, and Dollar Diplomacy had illustrated America's determination to control its own region, and the Open Door policy had revealed a desire to influence events in Asia.[10] During Wilson's presidency the United States would have an opportunity to exercise a similar influence in Europe and throughout the world, and gradually Americans would begin to realize that such power carried a heavy price, not only in military danger but also in terms of changes necessitated at home—especially as more power and authority accrued to the federal government and less autonomy remained for the individual. Individual liberty, notes historian William Graebner, "evoked a spirit of individualism and atomism that was inappropriate to a land of giant corporations, big unions, interest-group lobbies and a nation girding for war."[11]

For most Americans at the turn of the century, however, world power was a distant abstraction and the maldistribution of wealth an immediate concern to be addressed through domestic rather than foreign policy. Many individuals and corporations regarded profit as the rightful reward only of capitalists, but others had begun to make an effort to use at least a part of their good fortune for the benefit of society. Andrew Carnegie was perhaps the most famous individual philanthropist, but his personal charities were soon to be overshadowed by the far larger activities undertaken by the Rockefeller Foundation, created in 1913, and the Rockefeller-funded General Education Board (founded in 1902), which in 1913 provided $133,000 to teach southern farmers better methods. A few large corporations, such as the National Biscuit Company, Firestone Tire and Rubber, the E. I. du Pont de Nemours Company, and International Harvester, permitted employees to share in profits by buying stock; and in 1914 the Ford Motor Company went even further by introducing not only a profit-sharing plan for workers but also a five-dollar-a-day wage. Ford's action scandalized his fellow manufacturers and caused a riot among job-seekers outside his factory. Yet all of these activities, commendable and responsible as they were, did not redistribute wealth in any meaningful way or provide the basis for the United States to become a modern consumer economy. The real foundation for that change would be laid by the Wilson administration when it began to collect an income tax as authorized by the Sixteenth Amendment to the Constitution, approved by the states in February 1913.

For the most part, American business in the early twentieth century was concerned neither with the claims of its workers nor with charity. The principal reason for that attitude was that the economy was dominated by a handful of near-monopolies, commonly referred to as "trusts," although most of them did not meet that definition technically. Between 1887 and 1903 the number of industrial combinations rose from 12 to 305, 2,600 smaller companies were absorbed into larger corporations, and only 1 percent of companies came to control over 40 percent of manufacturing output.[12] In such crucial areas as banking, steel, and petroleum a handful of powerful men dominated decision making. The United States Steel Corporation, organized in 1901, controlled 80 percent of production; six railroad companies controlled 95 percent of all railroad trackage after 1899; the banker J. Pierpont Morgan alone controlled U.S. Steel and more than half the nation's railroad trackage and with various associates held more than $22 billion in banking capital.[13]

Like Woodrow Wilson, most Americans were "for big business, and . . . against the trusts," making a distinction between "good" and "bad" corporations.[14] In general, they thought that large corporations produced economic efficiency, which was good, but that they might also gouge the public and exploit their workers, which would be bad. They hoped that the government would somehow find ways to alleviate the evils of bigness while maintaining its benefits, but in practice neither the man in the street nor the politicians found it easy to define what was good or bad, or to specify remedies for abuses and still maintain efficiency. Fearful of doing irremediable damage, lawmakers had proceeded toward corporate regulation during the last decade of the nineteenth century and the first decade of the twentieth with more caution than vigor. Antitrust laws existed, to be sure, but they had been drafted vaguely by confused legislators and interpreted by the courts in ways that seemed to inhibit large corporations very little. Some people have suspected, as Thurman Arnold wrote in the 1930s, that antitrust laws were mainly "a great moral gesture" intended to create the illusion "that in a nation of organizations individuals really are supreme; or, if not, they are going to become so very soon through the intervention of the Federal Government."[15] The contradiction inherent in the notion that a strengthened federal government was to enhance individual liberty was something that most people preferred not to think about, just as they tried to evade the similar implications of a more active foreign policy.

Organized labor provided only a limited counterbalance to the power of business, at least in part because a large number of immigrants provided industry with a plentiful, generally docile, and nonunion labor supply. About a million people a year continued to pour into the United States, and according to the census of 1910 more than thirteen million of ninety-two million Americans, about one of every seven people, were foreign born. In the great cities where they tended to congregate, the "new immigrants" from Italy and Poland and Russia and other eastern and southern European countries often outnumbered native-born Americans. By playing off one ethnic group against another, factory managers could keep workers unorganized and labor costs down.

In a history of the United States published in 1902 Wilson revealed the common prejudice of native-born Americans against the "new immigrants" when he wrote that the "sturdy stocks of the north of Europe" had been replaced recently by inferior immigrants who had "neither skill nor energy nor any initiative of quick intelligence."[16] Although a decade later he had changed his mind on this subject and become an opponent of immigration restriction, his earlier statements were used against him by Republicans in 1912 with some effect among ethnic voters.

Wilson's prejudice against immigrants, like that of many Americans, was not deep-seated. After all, the stream of immigrants was a profound compliment to America, a constant reminder of how much the world envied American political liberty and economic opportunity. Yet Americans were uneasy about the immigrants because they were confused and uncertain about the economic transformation of American society in which the immigrants seemed to be playing a central part. Since in the minds of many Americans immigrants were linked to the political-boss system that, with the aid of corporate money, seemed to be corrupting American politics in the early twentieth century, it was easy to blame immigrants for the nation's problems. Moreover, making the immigrant a scapegoat resolved ambivalent feelings about the corporations that on the one hand seemed to be sources of corruption yet on the other were regarded by most people as natural and desirable.[17]

Immigrants congregating in the cities were convenient targets for the concerns of native-born Americans about urban growth. In 1860 only about five million Americans lived in cities; by 1910 there were forty-five million such urbanites, and in New York, Chicago, and Detroit more than 80 percent of the residents were foreign-born or first-generation American.[18] Pollution, crowding, rising crime rates, health problems, and corruption were all centered in the cities; and although Americans flocked to urban centers, they worried about the physical and moral problems that seemed to fester there.

Adding to these concerns was the beginning of a great migration of black Americans from the rural South to the urban North. Between 1890 and 1910 about a quarter-million African-Americans moved from the South to such cities as New York, Chicago, Philadelphia, and Washington, D.C., in search of jobs and political and social opportunities. Although more than 90 percent of blacks still lived in the South, the relatively small northern urban population took the lead in challenging segregation and discrimination through such organizations as the Niagara Movement (1905) and the National Association for the Advancement of Colored People (1909). Rising racial tensions led to the tightening of state and federal segregation and to an increase in lynchings, but the pressure of the civil rights organizations was not the main source of growing racism. The truth was that most progressives did not oppose and often supported segregationist policies, especially in the South, where segregation was part of a "post–Populist reconciliation among . . . whites, without which the struggles to reform and improve life among white people would not have gone forward."[19] Outside of the South many middle-class progressives saw African-Americans as dangerous for the same reasons that immigrants were: because they threatened a breakdown of social control and seemed to impede reform. Blacks and immigrants blended together in the minds of reformers as the supporters of corrupt political machines that enabled the trusts to control and to exploit the political system for their own profits.

Until the 1890s Americans had showed little concern about governmental corruption. Then, however, a disastrous depression demonstrated that something was seriously wrong with the nation and made people willing to believe the revelations of investigative journalists dubbed "muckrakers" by Theodore Roosevelt. Writers such as Lincoln Steffens and Ray Stannard Baker wrote not only about corruption but a *pattern* of corruption that was national, not merely local. They produced, writes historian Richard McCormick, "the first systematic accounts of how modern American society operated," and Americans did not much like what they saw.[20]

At the heart of the progressive reform movement, which arose partly in response to these revelations, was the hope of the victims of industrialization to mitigate its human costs, the desire of middle-class reformers to preserve the benefits of corporate business but to end political corruption, and the hope of business leaders for the "stabilization, rationalization, and continued expansion of the existing political economy."[21] Merely stating the problems did not suggest solutions, however, since increasing governmental power to deal with various concerns might worsen the situation rather than correct it, and the proposals of the various reform groups were often in conflict with each other. Reformers proclaimed that their goal was to distance government from business through regulating lobbying, limiting campaign contributions, establishing regulatory commissions, and altering tax structures; but of course the substance of reforms was subject to negotiation and compromise among concerned interests. Major economic interests often favored regulation, which they saw as a rationalizing process in the market, but they wanted to be partners in the process, not merely the subjects of rules written by others.[22]

The effect of reform, one might expect, would be to increase the confidence of Americans in their governments, and to some extent that was true. In the late 1890s, and especially the early 1900s Americans asked more of government than ever before, expecting it not only to "ameliorate and improve the conditions of industrial life" but also to provide both "social justice and social control"—that is, to cure the causes of poverty, crime, and disease while preventing those suffering from these ills from disrupting society.[23] Progressives turned to experts such as social scientists and engineers to diagnose and prescribe solutions to society's ills, and they used governmental power vigorously both to change unhealthful, unsafe, and wasteful conditions and to regulate the behavior of individuals and organizations whose actions seemed injurious to the general welfare.[24] The variety of progressive concerns—business abuses, slums, crime, disease, waste of natural resources, education, urban planning, drugs and alcohol, prostitution, racism, immigration, and labor relations, among others—should not obscure the underlying theme that united them all: a deep conviction that society needed both justice and order. More than any previous group of American reformers, the progressives expected and demanded that government exercise a constant role in the daily life of groups and individuals.

Yet, paradoxically, as government became more active and important in daily life, participation by citizens in the political process declined. Beginning about 1900 the percentage of eligible voters who actually cast ballots fell steadily, with women, minorities, and younger voters especially inactive. In the 1904 presidential election voter turnout was below 70 percent, the lowest since 1836; and in 1912, despite vigorous campaigns by Theodore Roosevelt and Wilson, fewer than 60 percent of eligible voters cast ballots. Historians and political scientists who have examined this peculiar trend suggest that it resulted from three factors. First, the nineteenth-century situation in which the two parties were very closely balanced and every vote could make a difference had been replaced in the mid-1890s by a new political system in which the Republicans normally had a clear majority, so voters had less incentive to go to the polls. Second, some progressive reforms, although intended mainly to clean up politics, effectively disfranchised many people by imposing stringent registration requirements and making access to the ballot more difficult. And third, a greater degree of governmental activism in turn stimulated the organization of private-interest groups for which voting and the electoral process were less important than the ability to influence legislation and to protect their interests by lobbying and otherwise applying direct pressure on political leaders. The more effective government became, the less individuals were able to affect its decisions and the more they were compelled to act in groups.[25]

To progressive leaders like Woodrow Wilson and Theodore Roosevelt, who believed that only the electoral process could represent the interests of all the people, the rise of pressure groups was distressing. One of their fundamental goals was to recall Americans to the pursuit of a common national interest that would transcend limited, selfish purposes. Whether in dealing with business, labor, racial groups, or other special interests, they constantly insisted that all put the general welfare ahead of their particular interests. Both did their best to reform the political system so that it would make the pursuit of that general welfare its major function.

Wilson and most reform leaders of the period served political apprenticeships at local and state levels before moving to the national government. Beginning with a farm revolt in the 1880s and 1890s and often led by long-standing groups of religious reformers, Americans joined battle with corruption and attempted to compel businesses to become socially responsible. A typical example of these new reformers was Robert La Follette, who, as governor of Wisconsin from 1901 to 1905, built a political machine devoted to reform and used it to make state government more efficient and responsive to public needs. By the time he moved on to the U.S. Senate, Wisconsin had become a national model for civil-service reform, improvement of public education, laws to regulate children's and women's labor, health and pure-food rules, regulation of the railroads and other public utilities, and the adoption of state income and inheritance taxes.[26] Much of Wilson's reform program when he became governor of New Jersey in 1910 was modeled on policies pioneered by La Follette in Wisconsin.

American cities were also laboratories of reform in this era. Cities as different as Galveston, Toledo, New York, and San Francisco experimented with innovations such as the city-manager form of government in an effort to break the power of political machines. Some cities began to provide their own gas and water and to run their own public transportation systems in order to free themselves from the corruption that too often attended the provision of those services by private companies. Urban reformers also campaigned for new city charters to give the cities power to deal with rapid growth and its attendant social problems. New city agencies were created to provide police, fire protection, garbage collection, sewage treatment, parks, and other social services. Among the prominent national reform leaders to get their starts in these urban reform movements was Theodore Roosevelt, who served as a police commissioner of New York City from 1895 to 1897.[27]

The first leader of the new reform movement to run for president was William Jennings Bryan, who burst out of the western farm-protest movement in 1896 to capture the Democratic presidential nomination. Bryan spoke for the thinly populated and economically undeveloped West and for a South still struggling to recover from the destruction of civil war a generation earlier. He voiced the resentment of those regions at being dominated economically and culturally by the East and the Midwest as well as their hope that the federal government would help them to share in the new prosperity. His 1896 proposal to create inflation through the unlimited coinage of silver sought to achieve both those ends but was unattractive to urban voters whose wages and salaries were fixed. He was never able to escape his regional identification to win broad national support, but as presidential candidate in 1900 and 1908 and as party leader he began the transformation of the Democrats "from a party hostile to the exercise of government to a party committed to use government 'to make the masses prosperous,'" as he put it.[28] In tireless campaigns for the income tax, the direct election of senators, women's suffrage, tariff reduction, reform of banking laws, and regulation of railroads and the trusts, he popularized reform proposals that won support from both national parties. The White House was never to be his, but his influence was felt powerfully there.

During the Bryan era most urban reformers felt far more comfortable with Theodore Roosevelt than with Bryan. Roosevelt was in many ways a typical leader of the Progressive Era: a colorful man who for many years produced more sound and symbolism than real reform but who ultimately committed himself to a program of substantial reforms that became a basis for future changes. Beginning in the 1880s as a reform member of the New York Assembly and a sometime Dakota cattle rancher, Roosevelt became even more a celebrity in the 1890s by colorful service as a New York police commissioner and as a volunteer colonel in the Spanish-American War. In these early years, he later admitted, he had "no strong governmental convictions beyond the very strong and vital conviction that we were a nation and must act nationally." Believing further that "no man can render the highest service unless he can act in combination with his fellows, which means a certain amount of give-and-take between him and them," he parlayed his war fame into the governorship of New York and then in 1900, into a nomination for the vice-presidency with the conservative incumbent, William McKinley.[29] Although McKinley's death in September 1901 elevated Roosevelt suddenly to the presidency, he was always aware of the power of the conservatives in his Republican party and continued during his seven and a half years in office to mediate between the Old Guard and the rising progressive or insurgent wing of the party. He was enormously important in popularizing such progressive reforms as conservation and sermonized incessantly about the misbehavior of the trusts, but he was actually responsible for few substantive reforms and carefully avoided proposing changes in some issues important to the conservatives, such as the tariff.[30]

When he retired from the presidency and departed on a hunting trip to Africa, Roosevelt left behind a hand-picked successor, William Howard Taft. Taft proved to be a terrible disappointment. An inept politician and an instinctive conservative, Taft tried but failed to sustain Roosevelt's delicate balancing act between the Old Guard and the insurgents. By the time of the 1910 congressional elections, Taft was siding with and campaigning for overt conservatives against reformers. Moreover, Taft lacked Roosevelt's vision. He did not share Roosevelt's burning conviction that the nation must seek a "public good . . . higher than and separable from individual, private ends."[31]

While Taft was moving to the Right, Roosevelt seemed to swing to the Left. In summer 1910 he attacked the courts for overprotecting property rights and proposed strengthening the power of the federal government to regulate corporations and to protect individuals from the power of irresponsible wealth.[32] "The man who wrongly holds that every human right is secondary to his profit must now give way," he declared, "to the advocate of human welfare, who rightly maintains that every man holds his property subject to the general right of the community to regulate its use to whatever degree the public welfare may require it." Included among those regulations, he argued, should be "comprehensive workmen's compensation acts . . . , laws to regulate child labor and work for women . . . , better sanitary conditions and . . . [the requirement of] safety appliances for our workers." Through a "New Nationalism," he promised, "the executive power" would become "the steward of the public welfare."[33]

Other than the phrase "new nationalism," which he borrowed from Herbert Croly's popular book, *The Promise of American Life* (1909), Roosevelt's 1910 speeches offered elaborations of ideas he had long held. He called for subordination of selfish, material interests to the national welfare, but he also stressed that protection of the weak and poor must not involve the expropriation of honestly acquired wealth. "If I could ask but one thing of my fellow countrymen," he said, "my request would be that, whenever they go in for reform, they remember the two sides, and that they always exact justice from one side as much as from the other."[34] Class legislation, he warned, was not reform but a prelude to revolution, and he argued that responsible leadership should "meet the nationalization of the big business by nationalized government control."[35]

Everyone knew that when Roosevelt spoke of leadership, he thought first of himself. In 1912 he challenged Taft for the Republican nomination, but the president, using patronage ruthlessly, dominated the Republican convention and assured his renomination. Furious at being thwarted by the man he had put in the White House, Roosevelt retaliated by summoning Republican insurgents to join him at the convention of a new party, the Progressives, in Chicago in August. There his social welfare proposals were embodied in the party's platform, which he declared was "a contract with the people."[36] Accepting the Progressive nomination for the presidency, he promised to carry out that contract.

A Democratic landslide in the congressional and gubernatorial elections of 1910 had already heartened party leaders who had not held national power since 1897, and the split in the Republican party encouraged them even more. Indeed, the Democratic party, under Bryan's vigorous leadership, had been building its strength as the "party of reform" for several years. In Congress, southern progressives formed the backbone of the party, and even urban machines were undergoing a cleansing that recommitted them to the interests of the public.[37] With a unified party and a divided opposition, a vigorous competition took place for the 1912 Democratic presidential nomination.

On the strength of his record as a reformer in New Jersey, Woodrow Wilson jumped out to the early lead for the nomination in 1911, but his advantage faded in 1912. Southern party leaders, distrustful of his long residence outside the region and suspicious of his lack of ties to the party organization, rallied the South behind House Majority Leader Oscar W. Underwood of Alabama. Outside the South, many party regulars, equally dubious about Wilson, preferred Speaker of the House Champ Clark of Missouri. In primaries and conventions during spring 1912 Clark and Underwood piled up delegates and seemed to deny Wilson hope of the nomination.[38]

At the convention in Baltimore in July, however, events played into Wilson's hands. Clark led the early balloting and secured a majority (but not the two-thirds vote needed to win) on the tenth ballot when New York's Tammany Hall machine gave him the state's ninety votes. Wilson was prepared to concede defeat, but a convention manager, William Gibbs McAdoo, persuaded him to fight on. With nothing to lose, Wilson joined William Jennings Bryan in denouncing Clark for accepting the support of Tammany and Wall Street and thus emerged as the champion of progressivism among the candidates. The delegates did not know that behind the scenes his managers were negotiating frantically with other machines in Illinois and Indiana for support. On 2 July, after four days of voting, the Underwood forces threw their support to Wilson on the forty-sixth ballot and gave him the victory. Ironically, he had won as a progressive by making deals with the machines and by exploiting the antiquated two-thirds rule of the convention.[39]

The election campaign that followed pitted Wilson against Roosevelt, with Taft a distant and often forgotten third. There were differences between the two men on a traditional issue, the tariff, with Wilson favoring reduction and Roosevelt supporting continued protectionism, and relatively minor disagreements between them about how to achieve a common goal, banking and currency reform. But the topic that came to dominate the campaign, however, was the trusts and what to do about them.

Roosevelt opened the issue. Stressing that the nation needed big business, he nevertheless admitted that its behavior had sometimes been greedy and exploitive, and he offered a comprehensive program to ameliorate its abuses and direct its energies to the public's benefit. He urged strict enforcement of safety rules, child-labor laws, minimum-wage and maximum-hour regulations, workmen's-compensation laws making employers responsible for on-the-job injuries, and government-supported pension and insurance programs. Above all, he emphasized that the way to deal with big business was to regulate its "conduct," not its "size," and he argued that trust-busting alone would promote "not . . . progress, but . . . Toryism and reaction."[40] He proposed to make the corporations behave responsibly by creating "a national industrial commission" with "complete power to regulate and control all the great industrial concerns engaged in interstate business" just as the Interstate Commerce Commission was supposed to regulate the railroads.[41]

In contrast to Roosevelt, Wilson had no comprehensive trust program in mind when the campaign began. He had been saying for several years that businessmen should be held personally responsible for the misdeeds of their companies, but that was more a slogan than a program. Only after accepting the Democratic nomination did he actually sit down with advisers, most notably the Massachusetts reform lawyer Louis Brandeis, to shape serious proposals.

Wilson did not believe that Roosevelt's regulatory commission would work because the monopolies would quickly find a way to control the regulatory body. "When once the government regulates the monopoly," he said, "then monopoly will have to see to it that it regulates the government."[42] The only lasting solution to the problem was to ban unfair practices that enabled monopolies to drive competitors out of business.

The assumption behind Wilson's analysis was that monopoly was unnatural. Like many of the professional economists of his day, he reasoned that the great profits enjoyed by monopolies would naturally attract competitors but that the trusts used unfair methods to block competition.[43] By having the government regulate competitive practices, the natural competitiveness of the marketplace would be restored, making it unnecessary to have government constantly looking over the shoulders of businessmen. Believing that most businessmen were patriotic and honorable, Wilson assumed that they would cooperate voluntarily with the government once behavioral rules were clarified. Moreover, the reopening of competition would benefit the whole nation by reviving creativity and economic mobility. It would, he argued, serve "the men who are on the make rather than the men who are already made."[44]

Wilson's call for a "New Freedom" was appealing to middle-class Americans but unspecific. When he asked Brandeis to list unfair competitive practices to be outlawed, he discovered the difficulty of specifying everything that businessmen might do to obstruct competition. By the end of the campaign he had fallen back on assuring audiences that the Democrats would "take care of the little businessman and see that any unfair interference with the growth of his business shall be a criminal offense."[45] The difference between that and Roosevelt's alleged paternalism was difficult to discern. Both candidates had made it clear that they believed the federal government must act to control business abuses, but they were both talking in terms of working cooperatively with businessmen to draft specific reforms. Thus differences between them were less sharp than they had seemed at the beginning of the campaign and less definite than they are often depicted in textbooks.[46] They both sought a restoration of individual freedom and opportunity in a world of big business and big government. The concepts seemed mutually incompatible, the prospects for success not very bright.

Although both candidates campaigned hard before large and friendly audiences, general public interest in the election was tepid. In mid-October a lunatic's pistol wounded Roosevelt slightly during a campaign speech in Milwaukee, and he and Wilson both halted campaigning briefly while Roosevelt recuperated; but even that event did not seem to stir the public much. The voter turnout in the 5 November election was only about 150,000 higher than four years earlier, and much of the increase was attributable to the fact that Eugene Debs, the Socialist candidate, more than doubled his vote, from 420,890 to 962,573. Wilson won the election with 435 electoral votes from forty states; Roosevelt had 88 from six states, and Taft 8 from two states, but Wilson's 6,293,019 popular votes were actually 100,000 fewer than Bryan had won in 1908. Had Roosevelt's 4,119,507 votes been added to Taft's 3,484,956, the Republicans could have won, but even so their combined total was 70,000 votes below Taft's 1908 total.[47]

In addition to the general causes for low voter turnout in 1912, Republican leaders made no great effort to get out the vote that year. Confident in the majority they had enjoyed since the mid-1890s, they believed that although the split between Roosevelt and Taft made a presidential victory impossible that year, the party would soon come back. Republican candidates continued to be strong in areas they had controlled for several years, and Progressive candidates other than Roosevelt were no threat, so party regulars simply did not work very hard in 1912. They preferred to wait for the progressive storm to blow itself out. The rapidity with which the Progressive party eroded as its members returned to the Republicans after 1912 showed that their confidence was justified.[48]

Rejoicing Democrats had reason to be optimistic about the long-term implications of Wilson's victory. Not only did the party win the presidency and control of both houses of Congress, but it was reasonable to assume that in a straight, two-way struggle with the Republicans the party would have done even better. "The fight for the 1912 Republican nomination was a fight for the soul of the party," concludes David Sarasohn, and the walkout of progressives when Taft was nominated would have been paralleled by a walkout of conservatives had Roosevelt been chosen, with progressives left with no choice but to support Wilson. Even had Roosevelt won the regular party nomination, Sarasohn asserts, "conservative leaders in power would have been forced to choose between losing the presidency to Wilson or losing control of the party," and he has no doubt that they would have preferred to keep their own power than to hold the White House.[49] With a united party and an attractive candidate, the Democrats could thus look to the future confidently.

Nevertheless, 1912 was not a "realigning election."[50] It did not turn the Democrats into a majority party. Wilson promised to build the party by attracting reformers from both major parties, but as James MacGregor Burns has pointed out, such party restructuring is difficult for a president, requiring him to alienate some members of his coalition before he can be sure of attracting new groups to take their places. As president, Wilson would gamble that he could achieve his end by skillfully using the existing party to pass a reform program that would attract other reformers, but in so doing he always risked losing control of the process if conservatives and urban regulars dug in to oppose him. Whether he would have been successful in this effort had the war not intervened, as Sarasohn contends, or whether the war saved him from a rebellion by conservatives in his own party, as Burns argues, cannot be settled definitively at this point.[51]

At the crest of his 1912 success Wilson dreamed that he would be able to unite and build the Democrats as Bryan and other party leaders of the past decade had been unable to do. The Republican split encouraged progressive and conservative Democrats to forget their differences for the time being; and Wilson's reform proposals, stressing the restoration of active competition and individual opportunity, had a broad appeal to all factions of the party. His ideas were both conservative in their emphasis upon individualism and reformist in stressing that the government should intervene constantly and actively to "open the market to fresh entrants."[52] Only when the time came to translate general principles into actual programs would it begin to appear that seeking individual opportunity through federal action was as difficult as squaring the circle.

Perhaps in the end many voters in 1912 stayed away from the polls because they sensed that the candidates offered them not clear programs but an insoluble dilemma: how to mitigate the costs of industrialization without losing individual liberty. Both candidates promised to do that, but neither offered a convincing program for achieving it. There were differences between them, to be sure, but they were differences of emphasis more than basic disagreements. Real decisions would be made only when Congress and the administration began to hammer out specific legislation.

3

MAJOR DOMESTIC ISSUES, 1913–1916

During a speech in Richmond on 1 February 1912 Wilson set out the theme of his administration's domestic policy. "Our laws are still meant for business done by *individuals*," he said; "they have not been satisfactorily adjusted to business done by great *combinations*, and we have got to adjust them." The candidate thus stated his determination to accept big business as inevitable but to control its abuses and to maintain an open door of opportunity for "the genius which springs up from the ranks of unknown men."[1]

Recognizing frankly that it would be "futile and ridiculous" to attempt to restore some mythical era of absolutely free competition, Wilson nevertheless insisted that "the Congress of the United States and the Legislature of every State [are] called upon in every session to intervene in the regulation of business." The reason for that demand, he explained, was that though some combinations "grew just as naturally as an oak grows; some of them grew just as naturally as a weed grows." The task of government was not to attempt to repeal the "irresistible forces" that had led to business consolidation nor even to declare such forces "immoral" but to make accountable the men who "may have made deeply immoral uses of them."[2]

Wilson also believed that it was essential to control corporate behavior to prevent corporations from stifling opportunity for creative and ambitious people. He declared that "the nations are renewed from the bottom, not from the top; that the genius which springs up from the ranks of unknown men is the genius which renews the youth and energy of the people."[3] Setting the benefits of size against the desirability of opening opportunities for creativity and energy and accepting the reality that business consolidation was inevitable and might be beneficial, yet insisting that great corporations behave in the public interest: These were the delicate balances Wilson sought to achieve and maintain.

To convey to the business community the message that he would support honest and honorable business, Wilson appointed to sensitive positions in his cabinet men who were experienced in business but not of the inner circles of large corporations. William Gibbs McAdoo as Treasury secretary, James C. McReynolds as attorney general, and Secretary of Commerce William C. Redfield were all men associated with the business community who were unlikely to arouse alarm.

Central to the selection of the cabinet members, as he would be to virtually every issue from 1913 to 1919, was Edward M. House. House was a wealthy Texan who longed for political power to achieve his progressive ideals but who was prevented from seeking office himself by delicate health. Introduced to Wilson shortly before the 1912 campaign, he later wrote that he "was like a disembodied spirit seeking a corporeal form. I found my opportunity in Woodrow Wilson."[4] The two men agreed so completely on issues that they seldom needed to discuss them in detail, and if they disagreed, House was the master of the discreet silence. Unlike Wilson, who was a political newcomer, House knew everyone of importance in the national Democratic party; but his greatest value to the president was that, accepting no office, he could be a seemingly disinterested friend and adviser on every subject, a confidant above ambition. Although he played little role in the campaign, when it was over he had a major part in helping Wilson to define issues and, most immediately, in selecting his cabinet.

House and Wilson found it easy to settle on William Gibbs McAdoo for the Treasury. He was a Georgia-born lawyer turned successful businessman, and his company had built the first tunnel into New York City under the Hudson River in 1904. At the 1912 convention McAdoo was instrumental in persuading Wilson not to pull out of the race when the nomination seemed unobtainable, and he was the principal organizer and fund-raiser of the campaign. Although some progressives had reservations about McAdoo because of his New York business connections, any doubts were overwhelmed by his reputation for integrity and executive ability, and the president's sense of obligation for his campaign work. Pragmatic and ambitious, McAdoo proved a strong secretary but never became close to the president, although he married Wilson's daughter, Eleanor, in May 1914.[5]

Wilson chose James McReynolds for attorney general for strictly practical reasons. "I simply could not appoint a radical," he told a friend, adding that he felt compelled to reassure the business community of his moderation.[6] A Kentuckian, McReynolds had served the Roosevelt and Taft administrations as an antitrust prosecutor and had the reputation of being hostile to monopoly but otherwise conservative, which appealed to Wilson, who knew of him only through House. As it turned out, no one in the cabinet liked McReynolds personally, and although he effectively shaped the administration's vigorous antitrust policy, everyone was relieved when Wilson appointed him to the Supreme Court in August 1914.

William C. Redfield, the first secretary of the newly created Commerce Department, was the most obvious businessman and probably the wealthiest man in the new cabinet. He had made a fortune in iron and steel and was "a prominent member of the corporate community, enjoying the respect and confidence of corporate leaders."[7] Although he had never been associated with any business that might have been called a "trust," he had been president of the American Manufacturers Export Association, organized in 1910 by some of the largest corporations. Wilson appointed him to the Commerce Department, however, not primarily for his business connections but because, while serving as a member of Congress between 1910 and 1912 Redfield had made a speech advocating reduction of the tariff that, reprinted and distributed in more than a million copies by the Democrats, had greatly impressed Wilson. "I primed myself on Mr. Redfield's speeches," he told a New York audience.[8] As secretary, Redfield took as his principal mission the expansion of governmental services to business at home and abroad, building up his new department's statistical programs and sponsoring conferences for business groups.

Redfield in the Commerce Department was to some extent balanced by the appointment of William B. Wilson, a former secretary-treasurer of the United Mine Workers, as the first secretary of labor. Although Secretary Wilson was a union man, he was no more associated with the most militant wing of the labor movement than Redfield was with the trusts.[9]

Other members of the cabinet were also chosen to appeal to as broad a spectrum of Democrats as possible and to convey the president's determination to follow a moderate reform program. Wilson knew, for example, that Secretary of State William Jennings Bryan, although still regarded as a dangerous radical by some conservatives, held views very close to his own on both domestic reform and foreign policy, and even more important, that Bryan still had a tremendous following among southern and western Democrats. So did Secretary of the

Navy Josephus Daniels, a North Carolina newspaperman whose credentials as a southern progressive were much stronger than his qualifications to run the navy. Californian Franklin K. Lane was an equally logical choice for the Interior Department, where the new administration wanted to distinguish itself from its Republican predecessors' antagonistic relationships with westerners over conservation issues; and the appointment of David F. Houston, an academic economist, as secretary of agriculture sent a message of restrained reformism to farmers. Indeed, of all Wilson's original cabinet members, only Secretary of War Lindley M. Garrison, a New Jersey judge chosen at the last moment on a suggestion by Wilson's private secretary, Joseph Tumulty, was not picked primarily to appeal to the moderate reformers among some particular group.

Perhaps equally indicative of Wilson's intentions was an appointment he did *not* make. The Boston reform lawyer, Louis Brandeis, had been important in the development of Wilson's antitrust policy during the campaign, and Wilson wanted to name him attorney general or secretary of commerce. Bryan, speaking for southern and western Democrats, was enthusiastic about Brandeis, but businessmen and conservative Democrats from the Northeast persuaded House and Wilson that "a large number of reputable people" did not trust the lawyer. Unwilling to engage in a major fight over the issue, Wilson passed over Brandeis, thus leaving out of the cabinet one of the most brilliant critics of business consolidation in the country.[10]

The decision to pass over Brandeis did not shield the president from criticism about appointees entirely. Aside from predictable conservative attacks on Bryan and Daniels, most of the cabinet were too little known to attract controversy, but Wilson's decision to appoint Joseph Tumulty as his private secretary caused a major storm. Tumulty had been Wilson's secretary since 1911 and was absolutely loyal to the "Governor," as he always called him, but Wilson hesitated to bring him to Washington because he thought Tumulty was too provincial and because he had become the target of a vicious anti-Catholic campaign. However, Wilson, encouraged by House, finally overcame his doubts and made the appointment. It was a wise decision. Tumulty's political skills served the president well, soothing feelings his chief sometimes ruffled, building political alliances, dealing effectively with the press, interpreting public opinion to Wilson, and often providing thoughtful and practical advice about policy.[11]

While he was president-elect Wilson attempted to reassure businessmen that although he intended that "the business of the United States" should be "set absolutely free of every feature of monopoly," he meant to "restore, not destroy" and would act "in the spirit of those who question their own wisdom and seek counsel and knowledge."[12] Late in February he sent Colonel House to New York to promise financial leaders that "there would be no measure enacted into law, over his signature, which was in the least degree demagogic."[13]

As he began to think about the specifics of his program during late 1912 and early 1913, Wilson adopted an approach toward Congress that proved remarkably effective. "It is the actual temper and disposition of the two diverse chambers with which he deals that the President must study if he is to bring his party, as well as the opinion of the nation, to any program or measure of his own," Wilson had written in 1908, and he acted on that observation five years later.[14] Wisely, he outlined the main objects he wanted to achieve and left the legislators to draft specific bills. To prevent conflict and diffusion of energy, he set strict priorities and did not launch a second proposal before the first was well on its way to passage. Above all, he made unprecedented use of public opinion to influence the legislative process by going personally to the Capitol to address Congress and by making other public speeches. No president had addressed the legislators in person since John Adams, and no president had ever appealed so openly to public opinion to put pressure on a sitting Congress as Wilson did.[15] A series of dramatic successes resulted that have become "the classic example of presidential marshaling of support behind a predetermined program" and a model of one way a president can lead the country effectively.[16]

Tariff reduction was Wilson's first concern. One of his earliest public political statements had been a traditional southern argument against protectionism before the tariff commission in Atlanta in September 1882. Moreover, tariff reduction was the one issue upon which there was broad agreement within the Democratic party. He made tariff reform the centerpiece of his acceptance speech on 7 August 1912; and although the issue did not catch the attention of voters in the campaign and Wilson later emphasized other issues, he continued to believe, as he said in the acceptance speech, that protective tariffs had been "a method of fostering special privilege" and had made it possible "to establish monopoly in our domestic markets." To restore "untrammeled energy in manufacture" it was essential to confront American trusts with foreign competition that would stimulate domestic competition. "Big business is not dangerous because it is big," he said, "but because its bigness is an unwholesome inflation caused by privileges and exemptions which it ought not to enjoy."[17]

Despite his own election and the election of Democratic majorities in both houses of Congress, Wilson expected tariff reform to be a tough fight. The Republicans, who had split on almost everything else in 1912, were agreed on continued protection, and he believed that big business would fight any real reform as it had done in 1909. Moreover, Democratic majorities might erode if the president tried to reduce or abolish tariffs on such products of Democratic states as sugar, shoes, or woolens. Wilson's old friend, Walter Hines Page, urged him to dramatize the issue by calling a special session of Congress to deal with it and to impress his leadership on the legislature by addressing them personally about it. Ten days after the election Wilson announced that he would summon a special session of Congress to meet in April 1913.[18]

Before the session began Wilson met extensively with Congressman Underwood to work out the details of a bill lowering or abolishing most tariffs, and he also met several times with Louisiana congressmen and senators in an effort to satisfy them that sugar tariffs would be phased out gradually so as not to destroy their state's economy. On 8 April the president, always a fastidious dresser, put on his most formal clothes to speak personally to a joint session of Congress about tariff reform. Keenly aware of the drama of the moment, he began by remarking that he wanted to assure the legislators "that the President of the United States is a person, not a mere department of the Government hailing Congress from some isolated island of jealous power." He then called upon Congress to reform the tariff to adjust to "the radical alterations in the conditions of our economic life which the country has witnessed within the last generation. . . . The sooner that is done the sooner we shall escape from suffering from the facts and the sooner our men of business will be free to thrive by the law of nature (the nature of free business) instead of by the law of legislation and artificial arrangement."[19]

There was never any doubt that the House, with its large Democratic majority, would approve the Underwood bill. With Underwood and Speaker Champ Clark backing the administration strongly, the bill passed on 8 May 1913 by 281 to 139. Only five Democrats, four of them from Louisiana, opposed it, and they were offset by two Republicans, two Progressives, and an independent who voted with the majority.

In contrast, in the Senate, traditionally a bastion of wealth and protectionism, the Democrats had a majority of only six, and several western and southern senators were under pressure to reinstate protection on wool and sugar. Progressives and progressive Republicans had favored tariff reform previously; but in 1912 Roosevelt and Taft had both endorsed protection, and the partisan nature of the issue made it difficult for them to break ranks.

Recognizing the problems that faced him, Wilson broke another precedent on 9 April (this one dating from Grant's administration) by going to the Capitol to meet with Democratic members of the Senate Finance Committee. Afterward he told reporters that there would be no "difficulty in standing together on any sort of party programme," which of course was more wishful thinking than reality, but he was obviously pleased that he had focused public attention on the issue.[20] At a press conference two days later a reporter immediately asked him if he planned to break any more precedents.[21] He denied that he did, but he plainly relished the stir his actions had caused. Unlike his predecessors, he believed that the public ought to have a direct and constant influence on the legislative process, and he saw his activities as giving them that influence.

His efforts seemed to bear little fruit, however. After the House's quick action the tariff bill bogged down in the Senate, and Wilson became more and more frustrated. On 26 May he again captured the headlines by charging that Washington was "swarming with lobbyists" who were presenting "a systematic misrepresentation of the facts" and spending "money without limit" in order "to overcome the interests of the public for their private profit."[22] It seemed improbable that Wilson had any evidence to back these charges, and of course conservatives and legitimate lobbyists were infuriated. By the same token, the more extreme enemies of big business were delighted. Apparently Wilson had blundered into exactly the sort of wholesale attack on business that he had said so often he wanted to avoid.

Republican Senator Albert B. Cummins of Iowa, certain that the president was bluffing in his charges about lobbyists, introduced a resolution calling for an investigation. Wilson was not the least discomfited, however, and replied that he thought the resolution was an excellent idea and that he would provide the names of lobbyists, whereupon senate Democrats made Cummins's proposal their own, putting the investigation into the hands of the Senate Judiciary Committee. On 2 June a subcommittee of the Judiciary Committee chaired by Lee S. Overman of North Carolina opened hearings.[23]

The Overman Committee's hearings confirmed what most people already knew in a general way, that many senators had large personal holdings in businesses that were protected by the tariff and that a few industries, most notably the beet-sugar industry, were spending large sums on lobbying. These disclosures were sufficiently sensational to force Democratic dissidents back into line, and on 25 June the Senate Democratic caucus voted thirty-nine to six in favor of putting wool on the free list and forty-seven to two to put sugar on the free list after three years of gradually diminishing duties. On 7 July the caucus voted forty-seven to two to endorse the whole bill.

No one seemed to notice that the Overman Committee had turned up no evidence of large-scale industrial opposition to the bill. In fact, big business seemed to favor it. "I approve of the Underwood bill," said a former president of United States Steel; and Republican Senator George T. Oliver of Pennsylvania, a large stockholder in United States Steel, declared that "as far as the iron and steel schedule of the tariff is concerned, the United States Steel Corporation is very much less subject to menace than would small manufacturers be to a change in rates." Ogden Armour, president of the so-called meat trust, endorsed the new tariff as did the Eastman Kodak Company, manufacturers of seven-eighths of all cameras made in the United States, and the Singer Company, America's largest maker of sewing machines. Secretary of Commerce Redfield, the member of the administration most closely associated with big business, had spoken for tariff cuts since 1911. In contrast, a parade of representatives of small- and medium-sized interests testified before House and Senate committees that cutting tariffs on their products would "wipe us out," as one said. Far from being "the mother of trusts," concludes historian Frank Burdick, the protective tariff had become by 1913 "the mother of competition."[24]

The Wilson administration's policy in regard to tariff reform presents one of the strongest arguments for the theory that reformers sought not to control big business or to restore competition but to institute a "corporate liberalism" under which the corporations, in partnership with government, would run America efficiently, humanely, and profitably.[25] Wilson himself, after all, frequently spoke of the necessity to adjust laws to economic realities, and it may thus be that he intended tariff reduction not to benefit small producers and to enhance competition but to confirm corporate dominance. It is difficult to see how anyone could have imagined that reducing the tariff would do anything but force corporate giants to become more efficient and thus *less* vulnerable to domestic competition than they had been previously.

If that is the case, however, historians must ignore or regard as hypocritical all of Wilson's even more frequently stated promises that tariff reform would destroy "the system of favoritism which has benefitted the rich and influential manufacturers of the country at the expense of the people."[26] Although issues involving human motives can never be resolved with absolute certainty, it is possible that in this instance Wilson, with his relatively unsophisticated economic understanding, may have been wrong. Indeed, to say this is hardly to criticize his intelligence or knowledge, since professional economists and such experts as Brandeis were also predicting that tariff reduction would enhance competition. There is certainly evidence that Wilson's tariff policy had the effect of advancing corporate liberalism, but if it did the result was unintended and substantially contrary to what he actually wanted and expected.

The Underwood Tariff reduced rates from about 37 to 40 percent ad valorem to an average of 26 percent and greatly expanded the free list. It brought the country nowhere near free trade, but it was a real reduction. Before its supporters and opponents could evaluate its long-term effects, however, World War I disrupted world trade and accelerated corporate dominance of the American economy, and a return to protectionism in the 1920s ended the experiments with tariff reduction for many years to come. In the end, the most important part of the Underwood bill had nothing to do with trade at all but lay in its income tax provision, enacted under the recently passed Sixteenth Amendment to replace the revenue to be lost when duties were reduced.

Debate over the income tax provided the tensest moments during the Senate's consideration of the Underwood bill in summer 1913. The problems were raised, however, not by opponents of the tax but by its overardent supporters. After two months of boringly technical debate about tariff schedules, on 27 August, while Wilson was vacationing in New Hampshire, Republican progressives led by Albert Cummins, William E. Borah of Idaho, Joseph H. Bristow of Kansas, and Robert La Follette of Wisconsin introduced an amendment raising the maximum income tax rate from 3 to 10 percent on incomes over one hundred thousand dollars a year. Although the proposed rate was hardly burdensome by modern standards, it alarmed conservatives in both parties and threatened to disrupt Democratic unity so badly that the whole bill was endangered. On 28 August the Democrats united to vote down the proposed amendment, but that evening several southern and western progressives demanded a special meeting of the Democratic caucus to consider tax rates.[27]

Believing that a 10 percent maximum rate might infuriate conservatives and doom the bill, Wilson hastily agreed to a compromise proposed by Democratic leaders in the Senate. They suggested raising the top rate from 3 to 7 percent and holding southern and western dissenters in line by having Bryan issue a special appeal to them.[28] The deal succeeded, and on 5 September the caucus agreed to support the bill with the 7 percent maximum rate. Other proposed amendments to reduce some duties even more or to add a heavy inheritance tax to the measure were beaten back, and on 9 September the Senate passed the bill by forty-four to thirty-seven. "We have set the business of this country free from those conditions which have made monopoly not only possible but in a sense easy and natural," said Wilson as he signed the bill into law on 3 October.[29]

The significance of the Underwood Act is debatable, but the ingenuity, skill, and flexibility Wilson had showed in steering it through Congress are not. Although frequently distracted by the decisions and appointments required to start up a new administration and faced with a series of foreign conflicts with Mexico, China, and Japan, the president had maintained his equilibrium and worked with congressional leaders on an almost daily basis to keep the bill moving forward. It was appropriate that when he signed it nearly fifty cabinet members, senators, congressmen, staff members, and other political leaders should have been invited to the ceremony, for the achievement was truly a cooperative one.[30]

The evolution of a banking and currency bill was equally an example of cooperation. Wilson came into office with a strong conviction that "the credit of this country must be opened upon equal terms . . . to everybody" and with a determination to break up what he regarded as a New York "money monopoly," but he had no specific plan in mind.[31] According to House, neither did Chairman Carter Glass of the House Banking Committee, but others definitely did.[32] Southern and western Democrats strongly favored a banking system under tight governmental control; bankers generally preferred a system entirely in private hands. Wilson needed to educate himself quickly on the issues and to use all his leadership skills to work out an acceptable and workable compromise.

Nearly everyone agreed on the urgent need to reform the banking and currency system, which was essentially unchanged since the Civil War and inadequate to the needs of an urban, industrialized nation. The country's seven thousand individual banks operated without central control or coordination by any national agency, and in times of crisis there was no way to mobilize reserves. During a panic, soundly managed banks were as likely to become victims of public hysteria as those whose practices had created the crisis in the first place. Also, the currency, which consisted of about $3.8 billion in gold, silver, gold and silver certificates, and national bank notes backed by government bonds was adequate in normal times but could not be expanded or contracted to compensate for economic fluctuations or even for seasonal needs. As a result, bankers often had either too much or too little money on hand, and no one had the authority or ability to moderate economic cycles by raising or lowering interest rates.[33] Wilson and other Democrats tended to believe that the main problem in the system was caused by the centralization of power in the hands of a few New York banking firms, but in fact the undoubted power of such companies resulted less from a conspiracy than from the weakness and lack of central authority elsewhere in the system.

Following a panic in 1907, Congress appointed a National Monetary Commission headed by Senator Nelson W. Aldrich of Rhode Island to make recommendations for reform. In 1911 the Aldrich Commission proposed the establishment of a privately owned national bank, with fifteen branches around the country. The National Reserve Association, as Aldrich suggested calling the system, would deal only with banks, not with the general public. It would hold a portion of each member bank's reserves, would loan money to members as needed, and would issue currency called national reserve notes based upon its reserves and upon its holdings of commercial paper (the promissory notes signed by businesses when they borrow). Member banks could also use commercial paper as security when they borrowed from the Reserve Association. The national reserve notes would in effect be a sort of private currency, being obligations of the banking system, not of the federal government.

Businessmen and large bankers generally liked the Aldrich plan because it left control of the banking system in private hands. Smaller bankers who were less likely to share in the benefits of the system and who feared it would strengthen the big companies were less enthusiastic, and many progressives demanded full governmental control of the system. Wilson initially preferred a decentralized version of the Aldrich plan that would have created privately owned regional banks but no central bank, but he admitted frankly that he did not know much about the whole issue.[34]

Various proposals were drafted during spring 1913 while the tariff bill was in the spotlight, but it was not until May that Wilson finally settled on a proposal similar to the Aldrich plan except that it provided for more governmental supervision of the reserve system. When he circulated the proposal to his advisers for comment, Bryan insisted adamantly that the government must control the system completely and issue the currency. Any bill which did not include those features, he said, "would be sure to arouse great opposition in the Democratic party and might jeopardize the passage of the tariff bill through the Senate." Personally, he added, if he gave in on this issue, he "would forfeit the confidence of those who trusted me—this confidence being my only political asset, the loss of which would deprive me of any power to assist" the administration. Wilson was angered by this polite blackmail, but he had to recognize Bryan's ability to block the bill.[35]

Bryan's objections to the bill were the most forcibly stated but by no means the only ones. Secretary of the Treasury McAdoo said much the same thing, and so did Louis Brandeis when Wilson talked to him on 11 June 1913. Business, said Brandeis, must have confidence that "the

Government will control the currency . . . and that whatever money is available, will be available for business generally, and not be subject to the control of a favored few."[36] Convinced by these objections, Wilson altered the draft bill to include governmental control of the system and told a joint session of Congress on 23 June that "the control of the system of banking and of issue which our new laws are to set up must be public, not private, must be vested in the Government itself, so that the banks may be the instruments, not the masters, of business and of individual enterprise and initiative."[37]

If Wilson believed that these concessions to progressives would assure an easy passage for the bill, he was soon disillusioned. During July and August House Democrats from the South and West demanded that the bill do more to abolish the "money trust," which they believed was drawing capital from productive enterprises all over the country into the speculative securities markets of New York. They also demanded that a reform bill include provisions for short-term agricultural credit. During August Wilson tried to satisfy some of their demands. He promised that forthcoming antitrust legislation would ban interlocking bank directorates and accepted an amendment to the Federal Reserve bill making bills of exchange based on warehouse receipts for stored agricultural products eligible for rediscount by the Federal Reserve along with commercial paper. The concessions did not go as far as farmers wanted, but when Bryan urged all Democrats to "stand by the President," party discipline prevailed.[38] On 18 September the House passed the bill 287–85, with three southern Democrats opposing and thirty-three Republicans and Progressives voting for it.

Conservative opposition to the bill centered in the Senate. In October the American Bankers' Association and the United States Chamber of Commerce declared their opposition to it amid a rising chorus of criticism from corporate interests. Taking advantage of the fact that three of the seven Democrats on the Senate Committee on Banking and Currency were at odds with the administration over various issues, Frank W. Vanderlip, president of the National City Bank of New York, proposed a substitute bill that would have restored complete private control of the system but maintained strict federal regulation. Wilson and Glass were sure the Vanderlip proposal was only a "red herring" intended to sabotage the passage of any bill, but the idea quickly won the endorsement of banking interests and even appealed to some progressives who were seduced by its provisions for federal regulation.[39] The president wooed and cajoled the wavering Democrats on the committee with some success, but when the committee voted on 7 November 1913, it was tied—five Republicans and one Democrat against six Democrats.

Two weeks later, unable to break the tie, the committee reported both bills to the floor of the Senate.

Once the bills were out of committee, the going became a little easier for the administration. After a vigorous debate, during which conservatives denounced "Bryanism" and predicted the Federal Reserve would ruin the country, the Senate voted on 19 December to reject the Vanderlip proposal (44–41) and to adopt the Federal Reserve Act (54–34). In the end, all Democrats voted for the bill, as did six Republicans. On 23 December 1913, after differences between the House and Senate versions were reconciled, the president signed the act into law. In a brief statement he applauded it and especially praised the Republicans who had supported it and the committee chairmen who had navigated it through to passage. It showed, he said, evidence of teamwork and commitment to the public welfare on all sides.[40]

Even more than the tariff bill, the evolution and passage of the Federal Reserve Act typified the efforts of the Wilson administration to maintain a balance between the interests of corporate capitalism and the need of ordinary Americans to have their opportunities protected. The act as finally passed was by no means a capitulation to the interests of corporate America; many opposed it. Although the bill originally proposed by Wilson in May would have been much more satisfactory to big business, that had not been his reason for favoring it. Indeed, his original plan was actually more radical in that it accepted as its starting point the southern and western agrarian reformers' contention that a New York money monopoly was preventing development elsewhere in the country by engrossing capital. Throughout the process of developing the final legislation he had showed his willingness to listen to reformers who distrusted business. The result was a surprisingly balanced compromise measure, under which all six of the members of the central Federal Reserve Board and three of the nine members of each regional board were to be presidential appointees (but with the proviso that several of them had to have banking experience). Yet despite this element of federal control, solid majorities of all boards as well as ownership of the regional branches remained private. The currency issued by the system would be backed in part by private commercial paper, but it would be a federal obligation. And by authorizing federal-reserve-member banks to establish foreign branches, it freed the American banking system from a limitation on the expansion of business and profits. At the same time, the federal oversight built into the system gave some assurance that the new powers would be exercised responsibly. The law was good evidence that the sort of "adjustment" of law to economic reality Wilson had intended was neither uncritical acceptance of corporate aims nor a fanatical anticorporatism. Insofar as possible, he wanted corporate capitalism and "a broadly based small-enterprise capitalism" to coexist.[41]

Wilson's effort to shape the Federal Reserve Act into a measure that would serve the interests of the whole nation rather than those of a particular interest group illustrates a major focus of his administration, yet he also favored some measures that might be considered special-interest legislation. In most cases he justified these departures from principle by arguing that they were necessary to correct an existing injustice, but frequently political expediency was involved as well.

His desire to correct an injustice seems to have been virtually the only motive in his support of the 1915 La Follette Seamen's bill, which endeavored to assure decent living and working conditions for an exploited group of workers. He signed the bill, he explained, "because it seemed the only chance to get something like justice done to a class of workmen who have been too much neglected by our laws."[42] On the other hand, when he used the same argument in 1916 to explain his decision to sign a law creating special banks for farmers, which he had opposed six months earlier as class legislation, his conversion seemed more attributable to the impending presidential election than to any change of conviction.[43] Equally suspect was his sudden decision to support a federal child-labor law. In 1914 he said that "no child labor law yet proposed has seemed to me constitutional," but in the election year 1916 he urged Congress to pass the Keating-Owen Child Labor bill, announcing that he supported it "with all my heart."[44] Likewise, his willingness in summer 1916 to avert a threatened railroad strike by accepting the Adamson Act providing for shorter hours and higher pay for railroad workers and a rate increase for railroad users seems to have resulted from the fear of political damage that might be done by a railroad strike as much as from concern about the sufferings of railway workers.[45]

To acknowledge the political motives behind Wilson's support of these measures is not necessarily to say that his shifts were cynical, hypocritical, or deceitful, however. In 1889 Wilson had written in *The State* that governments could legitimately promote the general welfare "by forbidding child labor, by supervising the sanitary conditions of factories, by limiting the employment of women in occupations hurtful to their health, by instituting official tests of the purity or the quality of goods sold, by limiting the hours of labor in certain trades, [and] by a hundred and one limitations of the power of unscrupulous or heartless men to out-do the scrupulous and merciful in trade or industry."[46] And in the 1912 campaign he supported the right of workers to organize into unions and endorsed "the betterment of men in this occupation and the other, the protection of women, the shielding of children, the bringing about of social justice."[47] Although he may have intended some of these powers to be exercised only at the state and not at the federal level, in fact Wilson's conservatism had never been of the rigid sort that insists government must confine itself only to "the protection of life, liberty, and property." Limitations on the powers of government, he wrote in *The State*, were merely matters of custom, principle, or prejudice and could be changed at the will of the people. The fundamental point was, as it always had been, that "*government does now whatever experience permits or the times demand.*"[48] As a responsible political leader it was therefore his duty to change his positions in response to changing public demands. To change with the times was to be *consistent* with principle, not to abandon it.

On some issues, however, Wilson found it very difficult to believe that the public wanted change. Like everyone else, he had prejudices, and these yielded only slowly to pressure of any sort. Given his background, it is not surprising that one such issue was race.

Raised in a genteel southern family, where the attitude toward blacks was condescending and paternalistic, Wilson had none of the crude, vicious racism of James K. Vardaman or Benjamin R. Tillman, but he was insensitive to African-American feelings and aspirations. He made a limited appeal to black voters in the 1912 election but declined to promise them anything specific. Soon after his inauguration, Oswald Garrison Villard, on behalf of the National Association for the Advancement of Colored People, urged him to appoint a privately funded National Race Commission to investigate and report on racial conditions in the United States. Wilson seemed sympathetic at first, but in August 1913 he changed his mind and told Villard that he would not act because of the "extremely delicate" situation in the Senate, where important legislation was pending.[49] The point was clear: Wilson was unwilling to take even this small step toward changing racial relations if it might jeopardize other reforms, all of which had a higher priority. That remained his attitude for the remainder of his time in office. Moreover, he permitted subordinates such as William Gibbs McAdoo and Albert S. Burleson to segregate, discharge, or downgrade black employees, often in cruel ways. In the Post Office Department, for example, all but one of the black workers were transferred to the dead-letter office, and the only one who remained worked at a desk surrounded by screens to save white workers from having to look at him. When the NAACP and others protested this segregation, Wilson insisted the policy was "in the interest of the colored people, as exempting them from friction and criticism in the departments."[50] As a result of the president's attitude racism was licensed in the federal bureaucracy more than it had been before, but practices were not uniform throughout the administration. Some departments, like the Treasury and Post Office, instituted strict segregation; others made few changes or even resisted the practice. Overall, the percentage of black civil servants dropped from about six to five, but the total number of African-Americans holding federal jobs actually increased because of the growth of the size of the government during the war.[51]

Paralleling the administration's insensitivity toward blacks was its relationship with native Americans. Under the Dawes Act of 1887, the Curtis Act of 1898, and the Burke Act of 1906, federal policy was to dissolve tribal governments, divide up tribal property, and allot tribal lands to individual natives, all with the supposedly benign goal of integrating them into white society. Because the distribution of tribal lands in small parcels opened up large areas of former reservations to white farmers and cattlemen, the process was vigorously supported by western politicians, although honest officials such as the military officer in charge of the Pine Ridge Agency in the Dakotas pointed out bluntly that allotment would "result in the degradation of this people and their speedy extinction."[52] Yet Wilson's secretary of the interior, Franklin K. Lane, a Californian, accepted the convenient fiction that allotment would "save a great people," and his commissioner of Indian affairs, Cato Sells, claiming that the program was "the main chance of perhaps 70 per cent of the Indians to become self-supporting," pressed it vigorously. Whereas 9,894 land patents had been issued to Indians between 1906 and 1917, between 1917 and 1920 10,956 patents were issued.[53] Ignoring protests from a small number of citizens appalled by this policy of reducing native Americans to beggary in the name of progress, the Wilson administration played a significant role in the reduction of Indian lands from 138 million acres in 1887 to 47 million in 1934.[54]

If a few progressives were saddened or angered by the administration's attitude toward blacks and Indians, many were mystified by its twists and turns on antitrust policy. In the 1912 campaign Wilson's ideas had seemed relatively clear. He had argued that competition should be promoted and large corporations prevented from using unfair competitive practices. He had denounced Theodore Roosevelt's proposal for establishing a new federal commission to regulate business as "a consummation of the partnership between monopoly and government" because, he said, business would be sure to capture control of any such commission.[55] As president, however, he seemed to abandon his own ideas and to take up Roosevelt's instead.

By the time Wilson was inaugurated in 1913 the consensus among American leaders was that industrial monopolies were undesirable and that at least some measure of competition must be preserved, but there was sharp disagreement about what new steps, if any, should be taken in that direction. Under the Sherman Antitrust Act, adopted in 1890, every "contract, combination . . . , or conspiracy, in restraint of trade" was "declared to be illegal," but until the Roosevelt and Taft administrations, the law was rarely used.[56] Scarcely had reformers begun to believe that the law could be an effective tool for maintaining competition, however, when the Supreme Court ruled in the 1911 Standard Oil case that the Sherman Act applied only to unreasonable or excessive restraints of trade, not to all mergers, consolidations, or monopolies. This "Rule of Reason" delighted conservatives but alarmed progressives, who nevertheless did not agree on what should be done. Theodore Roosevelt and his followers believed that large corporations were natural and efficient and should only be kept under strict governmental supervision. Wilson, backed by Brandeis and many agrarian reformers, had argued in the 1912 campaign that the Sherman Act needed to be amended to prohibit or restrict very large corporations and to make illegal all practices that tended to restrict competition.

Antitrust legislation was the third major priority of Wilson's first administration, the subject to which his attention turned after tariff reform and the banking and currency bill were well under way. In his annual message to Congress on 2 December 1913 he asked for a new antitrust law to spell out unfair competitive practices. "I think . . . we should let the Sherman antitrust law stand, unaltered, as it is, with its debatable ground about it," he said, "but that we should as much as possible reduce the areas of that debatable ground by further and more explicit legislation."[57]

That vague statement was in line with what Wilson had been saying during the campaign, but when he addressed the subject again in a special speech to a joint session of Congress on 20 January 1914, he seemed to shift his ground. Although he called again for "a further and more explicit legislative definition of the policy and meaning of the existing antitrust law" that would among other things ban interlocking directorates and holding companies, he also proposed the creation of an "interstate trade commission," which sounded somewhat like Roosevelt's suggestion. Wilson stressed, however, that it was intended not to regulate monopoly but to promote competition and to facilitate the breakup of trusts. It would be, he suggested, a "clearinghouse" for information for business and the public and also a body "capable of directing and shaping . . . corrective processes" such as the dissolution of trusts into smaller competing units "not only in aid of the courts but also by independent suggestion, if necessary."[58]

Wilson's change resulted from his realization that it was impossible to specify in legislation all the unfair competitive practices that might in the future occur to businessmen. The enormity of the problem was obvious when Congressman Henry D. Clayton of Alabama, chairman of the House Judiciary Committee, introduced a bill intended to plug the loopholes of the Sherman Act. The bill prohibited sellers from offering goods at different prices to different buyers (discriminatory pricing), from requiring a buyer who purchased one item to buy others as well (tie-in selling), and from requiring that buyers purchase exclusively from one company (exclusive dealing). It also banned interlocking directorates among banks, railroads, and large corporations so that, as Wilson said, "those who borrow and those who lend" would no longer be "practically one and the same." And it empowered individuals to sue under antitrust laws, limited antitrust prosecution of unions, set conditions under which companies could buy their competitors' stock, and clarified the criminal responsibility of executives for corporate violations of the Sherman Act.[59]

Clayton's proposals immediately came under attack from different directions. One group of congressmen argued that the list of prohibited practices should be longer and more specific; another insisted that no list could be complete and that general language should be inserted, which the courts and the regulatory commission would interpret and apply to specific cases. In addition, organized labor demanded a complete exemption from the antitrust laws rather than the statement Wilson wanted, which was simply that labor unions were legal and not, per se, combinations in restraint of trade. As labor leaders pointed out, the courts had already ruled unions legal, so the new statement really gave them nothing they did not already have. Finally, the bill also came under attack from small businessmen, terrified that business decisions might send them to jail, and from still others who foresaw a return to the competitive jungles of the late nineteenth century.

Like the storied committee that set out to design a horse and ended up creating a camel, Congress's attempts to satisfy the critics of the Clayton bill produced a piece of legislation that pleased no one. It prohibited discriminatory pricing, tie-in selling, exclusive dealing, and interlocking directorates and limited the right of one company to buy the stock of another, but businessmen found little difficulty in circumventing these restrictions. Union leaders tried to put the best possible face on the bill's labor clause by describing it as their "Magna Charta," but a spokesman for one of the country's leading anti-union organizations was closer to the mark when he said that it made "few changes in existing laws relating to labor unions."[60] Others criticized different features of the act. Senator James A. Reed said sarcastically that the bill should be entitled "an apology to unlawful restraints and monopolies," and the president himself admitted when he signed it on 15 October 1914 that it was "so weak you cannot tell it from water."[61] A more recent expert concludes that the act's crucial language was "about as general as . . . that . . . of the Sherman Act" and that it "has not done much . . . to help judges interpret the law uniformly or to help businessmen understand its provisions exactly."[62]

The Clayton Act was unsatisfactory in part because well before Congress passed it Wilson had given up on the effort to list unfair competitive practices and had decided that a strong regulatory agency would be a better approach to the problem. His original Interstate Trade Commission bill, which passed the House on 5 June 1914, had envisioned a commission with little regulatory power that would have served mainly to advise businesses on how to conform to the law and to court rulings. Wilson had then believed that such a commission would be effective because he thought that most businessmen were honorable and would try to live up to the spirit of the law if given a chance, but some of his influential friends did not agree. Like Louis Brandeis, they argued that the "alleged consciences" of businessmen had not in the past offered much protection to the public.[63]

While the ITC bill was working its way through the House during spring 1914, Brandeis was absorbed by other matters and gave the issue only cursory attention. In his place, his friend and associate, New York lawyer George Rublee, worked with Congressman Raymond B. Stevens of New Hampshire to draft a substitute bill that created an ITC with wide discretionary powers to interpret and apply antitrust laws. Brandeis had earlier opposed a commission of that sort, believing that sheer corporate size was the real problem and that laws could be written to ban monopoly and to restore competition; but at a White House meeting on 10 June, Wilson, Brandeis, Stevens, and Senator Henry Hollis all agreed that a strong ITC was necessary.[64] Why they changed their opinions is not clear, although with criticisms of the Clayton bill mounting on all sides some other approach to the antitrust problem was obviously necessary.

The 10 June meeting resulted in a new trade commission (now renamed the Federal Trade Commission) bill that was introduced by Senator Hollis. It created a nonpartisan, five-member commission with broad investigative authority and the power to order companies to stop unfair practices, enforcing its orders through the courts if necessary. The bill easily won approval by the Senate Committee on Interstate and Foreign Commerce, but on the floor of the Senate it was attacked by conservatives as "socialist" and by some progressives as simply creating a body that would be dominated by business. Wilson of course had warned of just such a danger when Roosevelt proposed a regulatory commission during the 1912 campaign, but the president defended the bill. It was virtually impossible, he argued, to arrive at "any definition whatever of unfair competition," and the only way to handle the problem was to build up precedents from "individual decisions with regard to particular cases and situations." What was "most to be desired," he concluded, was "elasticity without real indefiniteness, so that we may adjust our regulation to actual conditions,. local as well as national."[65] Thus supported, on 5 August a bipartisan coalition of Republican and Democratic progressives passed the bill in the Senate, fifty-three to sixteen. When a conference committee met to reconcile the drastically different Senate and House versions of the bill, Wilson's intervention was again decisive; the House accepted the Senate version, although it attached one weakening amendment expanding the power of the courts to set aside FTC rulings. On 26 September 1914 Wilson signed the bill into law.

Wilson's support of the Federal Trade Commission bill marked an important shift in his thought but one not as dramatic as might be imagined. He had never sought to abolish large corporations and to establish absolutely free competition; he had never believed in a passive government that would keep its hands off the economy. His essential difference with Roosevelt had been over methods rather than ends. Had it proved possible to draft a law that would have spelled out business practices in sufficient detail to maintain economic opportunity for everyone, Wilson would have preferred that course but, like Brandeis and his other advisers, he eventually concluded that it was impossible. At that point a trade commission with broad discretionary powers became logical.

Nevertheless, he did not ever come to accept Roosevelt's approach fully. Wherever he could, he tried to strengthen law and to minimize executive discretion. Thus the Clayton Act, maligned though it was even by the president, was an important and integral part of his antitrust program. It is also why the FTC Act did not give the commission a power Roosevelt had suggested for it in 1908, namely, the power to determine in advance whether a proposed action by a corporation would constitute a restraint of trade. The FTC would "have no power," Rublee wrote, "to authorize the use of a method of competition or to give immunity from the Sherman Act." Moreover, its first priority was not to license giant corporations but to "protect small business men, to keep an open field for new enterprise, and prevent the development of trusts."[66] Those were objectives Wilson had always sought, and he was now satisfied that an FTC balancing some administrative discretion with clarified law could advance them and that it would be substantively different from what Roosevelt had proposed.

It is essential in assessing the administration's antitrust policy to realize that at the same time it was working on new laws, it was also pursuing a vigorous antitrust policy in the courts. Its legislative program aimed mainly at banning unfair competitive practices by which so-called "bad trusts" achieved restraint of trade. Its policy in the courts went beyond that to argue that even "good trusts" that dominated an industry but avoided the use of unfair methods of competition should be broken up if they prevented effective competition. Although Wilson sometimes made a doubtful distinction between giant corporations that were supposed to have grown naturally by internal development and those that were put together artificially from separate components, with the former being acceptable and the latter not, in practice his Justice Department paid no attention to this distinction. Put in the simplest possible terms, the essence of its policy was that any company that controlled more than 50 percent of raw materials, transportation, distribution, or production in a given industry was probably a "combination in restraint of trade" within the meaning of the Sherman Act and ought to be broken up. Preferred targets were the "good trusts" that had previously escaped prosecution.[67]

Under Attorney General James McReynolds and his successor, Thomas W. Gregory (appointed 29 August 1914), the Justice Department sought dissolution of United States Steel, International Harvester, Quaker Oats, National Cash Register, and American Can Company, all generally accounted "good trusts," and seventy-four other companies. Of these cases, at least 70 percent were eventually won, either through court judgments or out-of-court agreements. In addition, the Federal Trade Commission brought 224 restraint-of-trade cases between 1915 and 1920.[68] President Wilson endorsed this policy repeatedly and expressed his determination to see "real competition" restored in the American economy. He declined to transfer Solicitor General John W. Davis, who proved to be exceptionally able in pressing the government's cases, to the State Department in 1915 when Secretary of State Robert Lansing requested it, and he held off on nominating Judge John H. Clarke of Ohio for a vacancy on the Supreme Court in 1916 until he was sure of Clarke's position on antitrust issues. His most notable appointment to the Supreme Court was of course that of Louis Brandeis in January 1916. Brandeis was not only a main architect of Wilson's legislative antitrust program, but he was also the most prominent exponent of the theory that all great size in business was probably dangerous.[69]

When the United States entered World War I, corporate leaders and some bureaucrats argued that antitrust suits should be suspended in the interest of national defense. Wilson and Attorney General Gregory agreed in October 1917 to proceed with pending suits, however, including one against United States Steel.[70] This policy was altered only when the Treasury Department protested that if companies were ordered dissolved, the process would precipitate heavy private borrowing that would compete with the government's own war loans. During 1918, therefore, the administration postponed some pending antitrust suits that were near resolution but nevertheless began ten new ones. There were obvious practical reasons for not pressing the antitrust policy too aggressively during the war, but the administration did not intend to retreat from its earlier stand. When the war ended, Attorney General A. Mitchell Palmer renewed the U.S. Steel suit as a test case. The Supreme Court's decision against the government in 1920 was a severe blow to the administration's policy and paved the way for the relaxed antitrust attitudes of the Republican 1920s.[71]

Overall, the Wilson administration's relationship to corporate capitalism was complex. Wilson recognized and welcomed the efficiency and power of the modern, large-scale corporation. He also believed, however, that many of those corporations were the result of an unnatural growth and that they had the effect of curtailing rather than of promoting progress. His goal, therefore, was to use the government to maintain an economic system that permitted the large corporations to operate provided they acted morally but that also allowed opportunities for smaller entrepreneurs to compete. The major legislation of his first administration—tariff reform, the banking and currency law, and the antitrust laws—were all intended to promote these dual goals. Whether the laws would have achieved their purpose is open to debate, but in any event the war created a situation entirely unanticipated by Wilson that made it substantially impossible to maintain the delicate balance for which he had struggled.

4

THE DEPARTMENT
OF AGRICULTURE

"There are no more hours in the President's day than in another man's," wrote Wilson in 1908. "If he is indeed the executive, he must act almost entirely by delegation, and is in the hands of his colleagues."[1] Wilson followed his own advice, and for the most part, wrote Secretary of Agriculture David F. Houston, the president depended on the "heads of departments to take the initiative in matters under their jurisdiction," expecting them to "assume full responsibility and bother him only when in their judgment it is essential."[2]

The obvious question raised by such a style of leadership is whether Wilson knew what was happening in his own administration and was actually in control of it. An examination of his Agriculture Department reveals, however, that even in an area of governmental activity in which he seemed to have little interest and certainly exercised no day-to-day leadership Wilson knew when important decisions were to be made, grasped the essentials of issues, and shaped policy as he wanted it.

Secretary of Agriculture David Franklin Houston was invited into the cabinet by a process that was typical of the seemingly casual way Wilson chose the officials upon whom he leaned so heavily. Born in 1866 in Monroe, North Carolina, but raised and educated in South Carolina, and with a master's degree from Harvard in political science and economics, Houston had taught at the University of Texas and been its president from 1905 to 1908. When selected for the cabinet, he had been chancellor of Washington University in St. Louis since 1908.[3] Although he and Wilson were both academics, they had not known each other professionally, having met fleetingly only three times before December 1911, according to Houston's later recollection. While he was at the University of Texas, however, Houston had become a friend of Colonel Edward M. House, and in December 1911 House brought Wilson and Houston together at his New York apartment, where they discussed tariff and currency reform.[4] On the basis of earnest recommendations from House and from Wilson's old friend, Walter Hines Page, Wilson decided in February 1913 to appoint Houston secretary of agriculture.[5] Wilson asked House to send Houston to see him, but for some reason the meeting never took place; and when Houston was sworn in at the Department of Agriculture on Thursday, 6 March 1913, he had had "no direct word from the President, oral or written" that he was to be the secretary.[6]

Houston seemed in many ways an odd choice for the cabinet and especially for Agriculture. He had "a national reputation for administrative efficiency and academic integrity," but his academic work had been in political science and economics, not in agriculture, and even his political loyalty was questionable.[7] He was a conservative, anti-Bryan Democrat who according to House had voted for Taft in 1908, and he was suspect among progressive farm reformers of the Midwest for his links to the Rockefellers through the General Education Board.[8] Obviously in this as in other instances, House's influence over the president-elect rather than Wilson's political philosophy accounted for the appointment.

Nevertheless, despite the oddity of his selection and his lack of clear qualifications for the position, Houston proved to be one of Wilson's best cabinet members. Along with Secretary of the Navy Josephus Daniels, Postmaster General Albert K. Burleson, and Secretary of Labor William B. Wilson, he served through all eight years of the administration, although he switched in February 1920 from Agriculture to the Treasury. An outstanding administrator, he modernized and strengthened his department and steadfastly refused to become involved in issues that were the concerns of other departments. Wilson came to trust his discretion and loyalty, often asking him for advice on delicate matters and relying on him to smooth conflicts within the administration.

Moreover, despite the offhandedness of Wilson's appointment of Houston, the president seems to have had quite a clear idea of where he wanted agricultural policy to go. Soon after his election, on 15 November 1912, he was visited by an old friend and major campaign supporter, Walter Hines Page. A North Carolina–born publisher and editor,

Page had been for more than a decade a strong advocate of projects to improve rural life in the South. Since 1901 he had been a member of the Southern Education Board, which coordinated the work of southern educators and northern philanthropists; and in 1902 he was active in forming the General Education Board (of which Houston was also a member), through which over the next seven years John D. Rockefeller channeled $53 million into southern rural education, especially the demonstration-farming work of Dr. Seaman A. Knapp. Page was appointed in 1908 by Theodore Roosevelt to the president's Commission on Country Life, which was supposed to find ways "to make country life more gainful, more attractive, and fuller of opportunities, pleasures and rewards" for farm families. He was also instrumental in the establishment in 1909 of the Rockefeller Commission for the Extermination of the Hookworm Disease, with a $6 million endowment.[9] Why Wilson did not offer Page the Agriculture secretaryship is somewhat unclear, but in their November meeting and in subsequent memorandums Page urged the president-elect to make the reorganization of the Agriculture Department, the upgrading of agricultural education, and the improvement of farm marketing and distribution central aims of his administration. These proposals represented a significant shift in the orientation of the department, which, under "Tama Jim" Wilson (secretary from 1897 to 1913) had concentrated heavily on scientific research rather than on direct service to farmers.[10] Moreover, the appointment of Houston, a southerner and an economist who seems to have hoped to revive competitive opportunities for small farmers just as the president sought to restore competition in business, also indicated emphases on helping small and especially southern farmers, with whom the large commercial farmers of the Midwest would not necessarily be in sympathy.[11]

Houston followed the agenda Page had laid out for the president-elect. He consulted extensively with Page, with other members of the General Education Board, with representatives of the land-grant colleges, and with his newly appointed assistant secretary, Beverly T. Galloway, a scientist with experience in the department since 1887. By autumn 1913 he was ready with a plan to reorganize the department's bureaus into new services (Rural Organization Service, Research Service, States Relations Service, Weather Service, Forest Service, and Regulatory Service) that would emphasize the delivery of scientific information to farmers and would separate the department's regulatory work from its scientific research. "I feel that agriculture is peculiarly the educational and developmental department of the government," the secretary told reporters.[12]

The administration's plan offered a logical way to make information more accessible to farmers, but it invaded the semiautonomous fiefdoms that had been built up by powerful bureau chiefs and increased the power of the secretary. Thus when Congress finally authorized reorganization in 1915, Houston got only part of what he had sought. The old bureaus remained, but they were ordered to separate research and regulatory work, a number of functions were reassigned among the bureaus on a more rational basis, and, in Houston's most important victory, the Office of Experiment Stations became the States Relations Service. Through it, he began to shift the department's focus from research to educating farmers and improving farm conditions. Gradually, he made the office of the secretary the central coordinator for the whole department. Agency chiefs who had previously dealt directly with members of Congress now had to go through an assistant secretary (two more were added in August 1917 to handle wartime duties), who oversaw and coordinated departmental work and a budget that increased by 50 percent between 1914 and 1917.[13]

Wilson, Houston, and Page all believed that farmers needed better systems of credit and distribution to make farming more profitable, that they needed help in raising their productivity, and that rural life must be made "comfortable, healthful, and attractive." Their personal experiences suggested that these challenges were most serious in the South.[14] Reorganization thus tended to reorient the department's activities from programs that benefited successful commercial farmers, especially in the Midwest, to policies aimed at the farmers of the South and Southwest, strengthening the secretary's control over departmental bureaucracy, and whether deliberately or not increasing the administration's ability to serve its southern constituents.

This change of direction aroused some opposition in Congress, but Houston shrewdly enlisted the assistance of the six-term South Carolinian who was chairman of the House Committee on Agriculture, Asbury Francis Lever. First elected to Congress in 1901 at the age of twenty-six, Lever was a charming and energetic man who impressed Houston as "one of the ablest and most satisfactory legislators it has been my fortune to know," which was not surprising, considering their alliance on issues. Perhaps more to the point, Lever had deep ties to the staff of the Agriculture Department and to the faculties of the land-grant colleges and was admired by his congressional colleagues for his skill in handling legislation in committee and on the floor of the House.[15]

Early in January 1913, in his last annual message to the New Jersey legislature, Wilson had urged that the state assist farmers by adopting a demonstration-farming program similar to one that had been successful in Texas.[16] Soon after the inauguration of the new administration Houston convened a series of conferences to draft a new farm bill embodying this same idea. The meetings included Lever, Houston, Galloway, various departmental experts, and academics from the agricultural colleges. From these discussions emerged a bill to be introduced by Lever providing that the federal government would partially subsidize a demonstration-farming program, under which working farmers would try out techniques proposed by experts. Participation by counties and by individual farmers would be entirely voluntary. In its stress on voluntarism and in its emphasis upon giving small entrepreneurs an opportunity to compete successfully in the marketplace, the bill demonstrated characteristic Wilsonian approaches to social and economic reform.

Demonstration farming had begun in 1903 on a single "community demonstration farm" in Terrell, Texas. Pioneered by Dr. Seaman A. Knapp of the department's Office of Experiment Stations to break down barriers between farmers and scientists, the demonstration-farm movement spread rapidly through Texas during the next several years as Knapp showed how farmers could reduce the ravages of the Mexican boll weevil and save cotton, the principal cash crop of the region. In 1904 Congress made a small appropriation to fund the cotton-demonstration work in Texas, but it was not until 1906, when the General Education Board secured Rockefeller money, that demonstration projects dealing with crops other than cotton were made possible throughout the South. By 1914 the largest part of the funding for the enlarged program was being provided by the General Education Board ($113,000 in 1911; $130,000 in 1912; $133,000 in 1913; $863,250 in 1914), with additional support coming from local businessmen, who stood to profit from better farming, and from state and county governments. Nevertheless, even the Rockefellers could not finance a full-scale demonstration program for the entire country. In 1912 Congressman Lever introduced a bill to have the federal government fund and operate a demonstration program, but differences between the House and Senate versions prevented its passage before Congress adjourned.[17] When Governor Wilson proposed a demonstration program to the New Jersey legislature early in 1913, he was picking up an idea with growing support among farm experts.

That American farmers were in need of new help seemed obvious to administration leaders in 1913. Secretary Houston estimated that less than 60 percent of the nation's arable land was under cultivation, and of that "not more than 12 per cent. of it was yielding reasonably full returns."[18] Agriculture Department publications, seldom written in language comprehensible to farmers, went unread; farmers rarely attended lectures by experts; and above all, a growing system of farm tenancy encouraged reckless mining of the land rather than prudent husbandry. According to Roosevelt's Country Life Commission there were few obvious solutions to these problems, but the demonstration program in the South offered one promising approach.[19]

Yet despite these considerations and the near passage of Lever's 1912 bill, significant opposition to a federal demonstration program existed. Some land-grant college faculty opposed it because they feared it would undermine their influence; some Agriculture Department scientists believed that their function should be pure research, leaving dissemination of knowledge to local governments; and many farmers opposed having the government send experts to tell them what to do. Even Secretary Houston, who as a member of the General Board had been a supporter of the privately funded demonstration program, expressed conservative objections to federal interference in local affairs and characterized the 1912 Lever bill as a "vicious policy."[20]

A way around these objections was gradually mapped out during spring and summer 1913 in conferences among Houston, Lever, Senator Hoke Smith of Georgia (the chairman of the Senate Agriculture Committee), and the Executive Committee of the Agricultural Colleges and Experiment Stations.[21] On 6 September Lever and Smith simultaneously introduced a revised bill in both houses. The Smith-Lever bill attempted to disarm local opposition by providing that the federal government would provide part of the funding for the demonstration or the extension agents but that county governments could choose to join or stay out of the programs and must match federal funding if they joined. Also, the agents would be under the direction of the states' agricultural colleges, not of the Agriculture Department. With the strong support of Secretary Houston, the bill quickly passed the House; but in the Senate it encountered opposition, especially from westerners, who saw it as beneficial primarily to the South.[22]

Two objections in particular posed serious threats. First, Senator Albert B. Cummins of Iowa insisted that the bill ought to apportion money to the states on the basis of farm acreage rather than number of farmers (the bill provided for a flat sum to each state, with additional grants to be distributed according to farm population). The second was embodied in amendments sponsored by Senators Wesley L. Jones of Washington, John F. Shafroth of Colorado, and Gilbert M. Hitchcock of Nebraska, who thought that the bill would discriminate against black farmers and ought to guarantee aid to both races. The Cummins amendment attracted only the support of a few western senators and was easily defeated, but the race issue aroused passions and was not so readily settled. When the bill passed the Senate, it contained Shafroth's requirement that the agricultural colleges receiving federal money be designated by the governors and the secretary of agriculture rather than by the state legislatures, but the Jones-Hitchcock proviso that extension work must be conducted "without discrimination as to race" was defeated. During the House-Senate conference to reconcile the two versions of the bill, even the weak Shafroth amendment was dropped, and no ban on discrimination was included in the bill that President Wilson signed into law on 8 May 1914.[23]

The Smith-Lever Act was in many ways a rousing success. By 1924, 2,084 counties (three-quarters of the agricultural counties in the country) were taking part in the program, and agents "conducted almost three million demonstrations, made more than ten million visits, and participated in almost a million meetings. In the South, the yield of lint cotton on the million and one-half acres worked by demonstrators more than doubled that of nondemonstrators. In the nation at large, almost a million and one-half corn growers improved their practices."[24]

Yet the administration's goal of changing small farmers into effective competitors with large producers was not achieved. Figures published by the department on the eve of America's entry into World War I showed that food production was rising but not keeping up with increasing domestic and foreign demand.[25] Isolated rural counties often resisted the introduction of agents, and individual farmers frequently ignored or opposed them; farmers in general were slow to adopt recommended soil conservation measures; southern farmers did not diversify their crops, no matter how hard the agents pushed that message; and western farmers insisted on planting wheat on land better suited to grazing. And in many counties the bill had undemocratic results because it strengthened the power of local elites, who decided whether or not the program would be welcomed in the first place and who then often were made even more powerful because county agents obviously wanted to have the most successful local farmers serve as demonstrators.[26] Although on balance the demonstration system improved American farming practices and contributed to limited progress in soil conservation, it did not reverse a trend toward agricultural consolidation; nor did it much benefit the weakest farmers, the tenants and sharecroppers. Neither did it avert a serious agricultural recession at the end of World War I, which became a depression in the 1920s. The hope that the demonstration program would be a panacea for farm problems was as much an illusion as the attempt to equalize competition between trusts and small businesses.

Another of the department's striking shortcomings was in its failure to meet the needs of black farmers. In August 1914 Booker T. Washington wrote to Secretary Houston, pointing out that existing programs were benefiting whites far more than blacks in Alabama and urging that the new extension act rectify the imbalance. Houston replied vaguely that he would "be glad to give this matter consideration," but there is little evidence that he did so.[27] In 1918 the secretary assured Congressman Tom D. McKeown of Oklahoma that the department was encouraging "the appointment of negro agents in communities where there is a sufficient number of negroes and where the conditions are favorable to the inauguration of the work," but of 2,260 county agents and assistants in 1918, only 115 were black. By 1921 there were 2,137 agents and assistants, of whom 151 were black.[28] Although the power of county governments to invite or reject the demonstration program was a major reason for the small number of black agents, the department certainly did not push very hard to increase their numbers, either during or after the Wilson administration.[29]

On the other hand, given its southern focus, the department was surprisingly free of the vicious segregationist policies that were adopted in the Treasury and Post Office departments. In autumn 1913, when reports of the new administration's segregationist intentions were first circulating, the Chicago branch of the NAACP protested the adoption of any such policy in the department. Assistant Secretary Galloway replied that "no segregation policy" existed in the department, and fragmentary evidence for the remainder of the administration suggests that there was never pressure from the top to adopt one.[30] In the absence of an official policy, practices varied from office to office. The Forest Service, for example, reported that its only black stenographer "occupies a room by herself," but the Office of Public Roads stated that black employees "work right alongside of white employees" and in the Bureau of Plant Husbandry black workers were "not segregated in any way."[31]

During the war the department joined with the Food Administration in encouraging both black and white farmers to increase production and slightly stepped up its recruitment of black agricultural agents, but it did not follow the lead of the Food Administration in establishing a special "Negro division or office."[32] Moreover, when some southerners expressed concern that the wartime migration of blacks from the South to the North would create a serious agricultural labor shortage, the department took the position that this was a problem for the Labor Department.[33] Whatever Agriculture Department officials may have thought privately about racial tensions, their avowed policy was to minimize friction and to avoid public stands either for or against change in racial relations.[34] This neutral stance, of course, resulted in continued segregation; but given the department's heavy dependence upon southern support in Congress and the local veto on extension programs, it is difficult to see how a more liberal policy could have been followed.

In addition to trying to make small farmers more competitive through education, the administration also proposed to put farmers "in quick touch with the markets for foodstuffs," as Wilson said in December 1913. "Better production in all lines awaits better distribution," Houston declared, "and without better distribution, better production is not desirable."[35] The second great mission of his Agriculture Department thus became the provision of new services that would permit farmers to transport, store, and market their products more efficiently and profitably.

Assistant Secretary Galloway made marketing his special area of concern and in March and April 1913 began to formulate plans for new initiatives. At the same time a conference of the Association of Agricultural Papers in Chicago focused on marketing and urged President Wilson to establish a marketing agency in the Department of Agriculture and to provide better credit facilities for farmers. On 16 May 1913, Secretary Houston set up an Office of Markets within the new Rural Organization Service, which was responsible directly to the Office of the Secretary rather than to any of the established bureaus.[36] He intended the Office of Markets to become an independent bureau as soon as Congress would authorize it, which it did in 1917.[37] The importance of the Office of Markets was indicated by its rapidly growing budget, which leaped from $50,000 in 1913 to $1,242,000 in 1916.[38] With these funds the office moved rapidly to study marketing, transportation, and storage of agricultural products; to provide information and market news services to farmers; and to regulate the grading, storage, and marketing of some crops.

When World War I began in summer 1914 the disruption of foreign markets led to a dramatic fall in the price of agricultural products, especially cotton, and forcibly reminded farmers of just how important foreign markets were. Before the war, the secretary reported in 1915, the United States had exported 65 percent of its cotton crop, 40 percent of its tobacco, and 15 percent of its wheat; and in fact in 1913 cotton alone accounted for 55 percent of the value of all agricultural exports.[39] It was obvious that even if the foreign demand for American products recovered quickly, as everyone expected, it would be wise to learn more about foreign markets. Beginning in 1916, therefore, the Bureau of Markets launched an effort to study and to open foreign markets. Special investigators were sent to Europe, Asia, and the South Pacific, and in August 1918 a special Agricultural Commission made up of officials from the department, scientists, and agricultural college professors was sent to

Europe to study conditions in the wake of the war and prospects for the future.[40] "The more I see of conditions over here the more I feel the importance of having our Department represented in all these war activities," reported an assistant secretary serving on the committee, and his conclusion was strongly seconded by other members.[41]

Nor did the concern with foreign sales end with the war. In 1919 and 1920 special representatives were sent to report on markets and to promote American products in Europe and Latin America, and in 1920 Secretary E. T. Meredith welcomed a report from the American Manufacturers Export Association arguing that the 10 percent of U.S. farm products sold abroad before the war could be expanded beyond the wartime level of 14.3 percent to as much as 20 percent.[42] In a period of serious recession such predictions were music to the secretary's ears, although the department did little to follow up on them.

Closely related to the gathering and disseminating of information about markets were the regulatory functions of the Office (or Bureau) of Markets. The main point of the regulations adopted, it must be stressed, was not to protect consumers but, as Secretary Houston said, "to enable the producer to sell his product as nearly as possible for what it was, to get a fair price for each part of it according to its character and quality and to control the exchange transactions in such manner as to eliminate certain abuses which had developed."[43] In short, as was often the case in the Progressive Era, regulatory reforms were supported by producers because they brought order and predictability to the marketplace. At the same time, however, the establishment of governmental standards for cotton and grain also had the indirect and unsought effect of reducing the competition that other programs tried to foster. Predictability thus carried a price for farmers and merchants, as it did for other businessmen.

Three main agricultural regulatory acts were passed during the Wilson era: the Cotton Futures Act of 18 August 1914 (reenacted as part of the Appropriation Act of 11 August 1916 because of a constitutional quibble), the Grain Standards Act of 11 August 1916, and the United States Warehouse Act of 11 August 1916. Other regulations, governing stockyards and the grading of beef, were adopted informally during the war but dropped after it ended.[44]

The Cotton Futures Act may serve here as an example of how these regulatory acts functioned and of how they served the interests of producers. Early in 1914 the Office of Markets drafted a bill to set uniform cotton grades that would be acceptable in international markets, thus helping American growers to sell cotton overseas. Before the bill was introduced, however, Congressman Lever asked the department to report on ways of regulating the cotton futures market—that is, the sale of cotton for future delivery—and in the course of doing so, the Office of Markets realized that in order to regulate the futures trade it would be necessary to standardize grades. Hence grading was included in the cotton futures proposal.[45] Cotton traders were encouraged to support the new system by means of a law that placed a "super tax" on objectionable transactions and a much lower levy on those regarded as fair and proper.[46]

There was considerable resistance among cotton growers and traders to the new law. Whatever its advantages in rationalizing the market, neither group liked its regulatory features. The New York *Economic World* editorialized that the law was "essentially vicious" in the opinion of "the great majority of those whose names stand highest in the cotton trade," and Charles Brand of the Office of Markets admitted that, rightly or wrongly, such opinions were widely held. Passage of the law, Brand reported, had been either a reason or an excuse for a delay in the opening of the New York Cotton Exchange that contributed to the slump in cotton prices in autumn 1914.[47] Only gradually did cotton growers and traders (as well as wheat producers and traders) come to understand that standardized grading helped them sell in foreign markets by assuring purchasers of the quality of their products.

Farmers thus at first resisted the imposition of reform from above signified by the standard grades for agricultural products and were slow to see the benefits of the program to them, yet the idea of a separate rural banking system was very popular with the agricultural community. This concept ran into opposition from Secretary Houston and the president, however. The possibility of setting up a banking system to provide credit for farmers at reasonable interest rates had been under discussion for several years when the Wilson administration came into office, and all three parties had endorsed the creation of some such system in their 1912 platforms. In his inaugural address Wilson had called for the establishment of "facilities of credit" suited to the "practical needs" of farmers, but the question was what sort of a system should be created.[48] Although many farmers wanted the government to provide the capital for a farm-bank system and to run it as well, Wilson and Houston did not want the government directly in the banking business. They made a limited concession to the agrarians by including some agricultural credits among the functions of the Federal Reserve System, but that did not satisfy farmers.

In spring 1914 a joint subcommittee of the House and Senate banking committees drafted a land-bank bill that would have created twelve privately controlled land banks, chartered by the federal government, with power to loan money at low rates to farmers organized in credit co-operatives. If private investors did not buy up the stock of these new banks, the federal government was to do so.[49]

The public-ownership provisions of the draft bill were anathema to the administration. In November 1913 Houston told the annual meeting of the national Grange: "I am not impressed with the wisdom and the justice of proposals that would take the money of all the people . . . and lend it to the farmers or any other class at a rate of interest lower than the economic conditions would normally require."[50] And in May 1914, when the bill was about to come before the House, Wilson hinted strongly that he would veto it. "I have a very deep conviction that it is unwise and unjustifiable to extend the credit of the Government to a single class of the community," he wrote to Congressman Carter Glass in a letter to be read to the Democratic caucus.[51]

By early 1916, however, principle was yielding to expediency. With a presidential election drawing near and with farmers who would be vital to a Democratic victory still demanding federally supported land banks, pressure on the administration grew intense. Frank G. Odell, secretary of the American Rural Credits Association, warned bluntly that "the support of farmers, which would be engaged by rural credit legislation, is necessary to the Democratic Party in the Middle West." After similar warnings from others, Wilson underwent a conversion. At a White House conference with Senator Henry F. Hollis of New Hampshire and Congressman Lever on 28 January 1916, Houston repeated the old objections to federal funding of the rural banks only to have Wilson cut the ground out from under his feet by endorsing the principle of federal underwriting of the system. Special assistance to the farmers was justified, the president explained at a ceremony when the Federal Land Bank Act was signed on 17 July 1916, because agriculture had hitherto been discriminated against.[52]

In the land-bank controversy, although Wilson had seemed uninterested in the doings of the department for months on end, he was paying more attention than appeared to be the case; and he could and would take a decisive role in policy when necessary. Equally striking was his aptitude for pragmatic politics. When it was politically expedient he could not only reverse himself but also take the opposite course with an enthusiasm that assured him the benefits of leading a victorious cause.

If the administration thus seemed to respond to pressure from below in 1916, American participation in World War I revived its tendency to dictate policy paternalistically. Despite the enormous expansion the war forced on the Agriculture Department, Houston and his successor,

E. T. Meredith (appointed 2 February 1920 after Houston became secretary of the treasury), never seemed comfortable with the idea of the department as a broker among established groups. They generally attempted to set wartime policies from the top rather than seeking the advice of farmers or farm organizations. Their goal was to win the war, not to foster farmers' organizations or to move toward governmental regulation of the farm economy. At war's end, they reduced the size, cost, and role of the agricultural establishment as quickly as possible even when that meant cutting successful programs.

The department was growing in size and expenditures even before the war began as a result of Houston's aggressive programs. Its budget for fiscal 1913 was $19,687,316; that for 1916 was $29,936,025. On 1 July 1913 it had 14,478 employees; on 1 July 1916 it had 17,167. The war of course accelerated the process, despite the administration's efforts to avoid permanent governmental expansion. The budget for fiscal 1918 (the year the nation was most involved in the war) was $47,130,513; there were 25,239 employees as of 1 July that year. Thereafter both spending and size were cut back but never to anything like prewar levels. The budget for 1920 was still $42,976,144, and the number of employees on 1 July 1919 was 22,967.[53]

Ever since his appointment in 1913 Houston had been concerned about what he saw as lagging agricultural production in the United States, and the nation's entry into the war in April 1917 added greatly to his worries.[54] Cereal-grain production in 1916 was not only below the record level of 1915 but below the 1910–14 annual average as well, and the 1916 wheat crop was especially poor. The production of meat, poultry, and dairy products was up in 1916, but so was demand. Beginning in January 1917, therefore, the department began to issue appeals to farmers to raise production to meet growing domestic and foreign demand. Early in February, at Houston's suggestion, the president instructed the Federal Trade Commission to investigate and report whether there were possible antitrust violations among large meat packers that were artificially limiting meat supplies.[55]

By the beginning of April 1917 the department was preparing for war even though it had not yet been declared. On 3 April the Office of Information began distributing a series of press releases and stories to newspapers and magazines, offering tips to housewives on saving food and proposing such measures to increase production as backyard gardening. The next day Houston summoned a conference of state commissioners of agriculture, land-grant college agricultural experts, and officers of agricultural organizations to meet in St. Louis on 9 and 10 April. At that meeting, and at another for similar experts from the West

Coast held at Berkeley, California, on 13 April, Houston and his deputies presented proposals to increase production and to improve distribution and won endorsement of them. On 15 April the president issued an urgent appeal to farmers to increase production. Three days later the administration asked Congress for an emergency appropriation for the department of $25 million and for the concentration of extensive powers in the hands of the secretary to promote production, encourage food conservation, coordinate policy with local governments and private bodies, and regulate the transportation of agricultural products. Subsequently, Wilson and Houston met with members of the House and Senate Agriculture committees to urge speedy passage of the legislation.[56]

Despite the administration's aggressive steps to increase agricultural production, some people believed that the challenge required planning and regulation beyond anything envisioned by the department. In late 1916 and early 1917 increasing European demand and short crops led to dramatic increases in food prices and to consumer anger that erupted in February 1917 in food riots in New York and other eastern cities.[57] At the same time, the food situation was becoming desperate among the Allied and neutral nations, and as soon as the United States declared war, the British government sent over a large delegation headed by Arthur J. Balfour to step up Allied purchases. These large foreign demands of course presaged even more domestic shortages and price rises and forced the administration to take urgent steps. Because increasing production would necessarily take time, the emphasis now shifted to making efficient use of existing production and to improving transportation to prevent bottlenecks and disruptions, but at the back of everyone's mind was the disagreeable possibility of price controls if other measures failed.[58]

Among those alarmed by the dangers posed in this situation were the members of the Council of National Defense, created by the president in August 1916 to coordinate defense production. On 5 April 1917 the Council cabled Herbert Hoover, who had been coordinating the Belgian relief program, to return to the United States to advise on food production and distribution at home and in Europe. In the view of the president (who first suggested his name to the Council) and the members of the Council, Hoover was the only man with real experience in handling the sort of problems that now confronted the United States.[59]

The invitation to Hoover aroused alarm in the Agriculture Department. Houston was out of town conferring with agricultural leaders when the decision was made, but his subordinates complained that setting up new "organizations, boards or commissions" would "lead to endless confusion to no good purpose." At the same time, however, the department's own internal documents showed that its leaders had not yet fully grasped the dimensions of the problems they were facing. Concerning themselves primarily with increasing production, they had little concept of the problems of distribution ahead and were reluctant even to talk about price controls, or worse yet, of rationing.[60] Their concern had always been with improving services for independent producers, and they were extremely uncomfortable with the idea of centralized planning and regulation.

Hoover's European experience was of course more with the distribution than with the production of food, and when he arrived in the United States in May he recommended the appointment of an independent food administrator to promote food conservation and to coordinate distribution.[61] By that time, as the real scope of the problems ahead began to be clear, opposition to such a course was dwindling in the Agriculture Department. As one of Houston's assistants pointed out, food shortages and restrictions on the uses of agricultural products were bound to be unpopular; it was better, he argued, if resentments about such things were focused on some temporary agency rather than on the department so that the department could maintain its traditional role as friend and ally of the farmer.[62]

With the opposition of the department thus reduced, Wilson announced on 20 May that he would appoint Hoover as food administrator as soon as requisite legislation passed Congress. But that proved difficult. Although Hoover planned to staff the Food Administration with volunteers and to depend heavily on patriotic appeals to encourage conservation, he was also asking for near-dictatorial powers "to control exports and imports, to enter contracts . . . with our Allies, to stop hoarding and speculation, to compel distribution, requisition and operation of establishments, to fix or guarantee prices, and to purchase or finance purchases, to secure all information as to stocks, methods, costs and ownership of foodstuffs."[63] Despite the rhetoric of patriotic voluntarism in which these proposals were clothed, it was impossible to conceal that what Hoover was asking for was actually "revolutionary in the extent of control of private business." Not until 10 August did Congress finally pass the Food Production Act and the Food Control Act, which authorized the creation of a Food Administration and appropriated $11,346,000 for stimulation of production. By that time Hoover had already begun to organize the Food Administration informally, as the president had asked him to do on 12 June.[64]

Houston's acceptance of the Food Administration did not eliminate friction between the two organizations. Wilson's 20 May announcement sought to divide responsibility between them, with the Agriculture Department in charge of production, marketing, and conservation and the Food Administration controlling distribution, consumption, exports, imports, prices, the purchase and requisition of commodities, and storage.[65] However, these broad divisions left considerable overlap between the agencies (how did one separate marketing and distribution, for example?), and a basic difference still remained over whether the government should regulate or merely assist private producers. Not until the eve of the passage of the new legislation did Houston and Hoover manage to hammer out a division of authority that both could live with, but even so, for the remainder of the war diplomatic relations between the two agencies were sometimes strained.[66]

Although the Food Administration was breaking new ground in the centralized control of the agricultural economy, it did its best to create the impression that it was relying on voluntary cooperation rather than on regimentation. "To most Americans," writes historian David Burner, "the Food Administration was an agency of exhortation." Its campaigns for meatless and wheatless days, its incessant propaganda for food conservation, and its sustained efforts to stimulate production led to the introduction of a new verb, "to Hooverize," meaning to economize with a good purpose. "Working with Hoover," wrote one of his many admirers, "gave me an understanding of the tremendous power of voluntary cooperation that exceeds the power of law or threats of punishments."[67]

That was precisely the theme that Hoover sought to convey to the public at the time and that dominates official histories of the Food Administration. Although it is true that voluntary efforts increased production, in reality the Food Administration and other similar wartime agencies were pioneering a radically new form of federal regulation that depended not upon legal sanctions but upon cooperation between government officials and large producers. If most Americans thought of voluntarism in terms of housewives finding substitutes for items in their families' diets or of farmers bringing unused lands into production or of the herd of sheep the president pastured on the White House lawn, its more important (and more controversial) manifestation was in the activities of large businesses and trade organizations. Here voluntarism meant that corporations voluntarily assumed the functions of apportioning production among supposedly competing companies and voluntarily set profit levels for the goods they produced and that many of their executives ran wartime agencies in Washington as volunteer "dollar-a-year men." With the antitrust laws largely suspended for the duration of the war, "the distinction between the public and private sectors became increasingly blurred." "The whole theory of controlling and supervising industry by means of penal statute, whatever its previous justification, is no longer tenable," wrote two advocates of the new order; "there must be a spirit of mutual confidence and cooperation between government and industry."[68] With such thinking determining wartime relations between business and government, it is not surprising to find that some corporations and businessmen seized the opportunity to put profits ahead of patriotism and that many commercial farmers learned the lesson that they too could benefit from the new opportunities if they organized.

Hoover, who was often an enthusiastic booster of the cooperative order, was compelled to recognize that it was vulnerable to serious abuses. Disillusioned by the lack of patriotism of some businessmen, he advocated an excess-profits tax and sought increased price-fixing powers although he much preferred to control prices indirectly. Using their influence with the Allied governments and with large private purchasers of agricultural products, executives of the Food Administration aimed at a stable and guaranteed market for American products at prices that would be high enough to stimulate production but would keep the cost of living under control.[69] By means of constant behind-the-scenes manipulations, intimidation, and concessions, Hoover and his assistants were able to secure both goals, but the achievement was not simply the result of a voluntary patriotic commitment, as Hoover's promoters would subsequently claim. Businesses could afford to be patriotic because they were guaranteed high profits from subsidies in the form of American loans to the Allies, which enabled them to buy American products at inflated prices.

And even these methods did not solve all the problems. In the case of wheat, for example, by May 1917 foreign demand was approximately twice that of the prewar period. Since the 1916 crop had been very small, the deficiency was made up only by selling a large part of the country's stored surplus. Even so, the price of Number Two Red winter wheat rose from $1.15 a bushel in July 1916 to $3.24 in May 1917.[70] Bread prices doubled, and some Americans urged an embargo on sales of wheat abroad. Wilson dodged the issue during the presidential election of 1916, but when the nation entered the war in spring 1917 he could no longer avoid it. When the Food Administration was approved in August 1917, it immediately set a "guaranteed" wheat price of $2.20 a bushel, which in fact, because of the agency's control over foreign and domestic purchasing, became essentially the maximum price, to the distress of wheat producers.[71]

The administration bowed to consumer pressure to control wheat prices because food was so vital and because the need to placate the public outweighed the disadvantage of angering unorganized farmers.

In the case of cotton, however, the same arguments did not hold, and the price was allowed to rise with the demand. Already before the war the United States had been exporting about 65 percent of its cotton crop, so the war did not cause the same domestic shortages as in wheat. Moreover, cotton, though economically important, was not a food product and so did not carry the same emotional weight. Nor was it irrelevant that the South was a traditionally Democratic region and the midwestern wheat region was Republican. For all these reasons, the administration consistently opposed cotton price controls. "The price of cotton or any other commodity," it announced in November 1916, "must inevitably be controlled by the laws of supply and demand."[72] This pious affirmation of the laws of the marketplace helped to hold the support of the South in 1916, but it was revealed as hypocritical when wheat prices were set in 1917. In September 1918 the cabinet debated instituting cotton price controls but came to no conclusion, and two months later the administration paid the price. In congressional elections, the Democrats lost twenty-three seats to the Republicans in midwestern wheat-producing districts that had been Democratic in 1916.[73] The result was evidence that the administration's effort to defuse the price-control issue by putting it in the hands of the temporary Food Administration did not shield the Democrats from a serious political backlash. Yet in truth, no policy would have satisfied everyone: controlling wheat prices but leaving cotton uncontrolled antagonized wheat farmers; controlling both would have alienated both groups; controlling neither would have outraged consumers.

Since price manipulation was the method chosen to promote agricultural production, the role of the Agriculture Department during the war was less visible and central to agricultural policy than that of the Food Administration and of course less controversial. The department stepped up its scientific and technical work and expanded its efforts to get information to farmers. More than sixteen hundred emergency demonstration agents were employed in 1917, and the Extension Service expanded to nearly two thousand counties. Under a special appropriation provided by the Food Production and Control Acts of 1917, seeds were purchased and sold to farmers at cost, and fertilizer was distributed as well. By 1918 farmers had increased their crop acreage by 11 percent and actual production by 5 percent. The department began inspecting agricultural products at central markets in 1917, and a program of licensing warehouses, stockyards, farm equipment companies, and fertilizer producers was begun also. In 1918, when drought hit western grain-producing states, Wilson authorized the use of $5 million from his special national defense funds for seed loans to farmers in the affected areas, and the program was continued the following year although the war was then over.[74]

The Food Administration's wartime activities were generally more showy than those of the Agriculture Department, but that should not obscure the long-term importance of what was happening in the department. After all, though some Food Administration policies would become precedent-setting, the agency itself expired at the end of the war. On the other hand, the expanded activity and visibility of the federal government at the local level through the county-agent system, the greater stress on technical and scientific expertise within the government bureaucracy, the increasing role of the government in inspecting and regulating agriculture and related industries, and even a modest welfare role for the government in mitigating the impact of drought on farmers were all indicative of substantial and enduring changes in the way the government functioned and in the relationship between the government and the American people. The Agriculture Department would neither give up all its new functions after the war nor cut its personnel back to prewar levels. And whether administration leaders were willing to recognize it or not, the Food Administration's policies had demonstrated to many farmers the value of organizing to demand new services from the department that would regulate and make the farm economy more predictable.

5

★ ★ ★ ★ ★

INDUSTRIAL DEMOCRACY

The Wilson administration brought about an important change in the relationship between labor and capital in the United States but never achieved the fundamental transformation at which it aimed. Its attitude was revealed by the appointment of a "responsible" unionist, William B. Wilson, as the first secretary of labor and by his effort to promote "industrial democracy," in which labor unions and corporations were to work together to create a prosperous, productive economy. In the end, however, he succeeded only partially, strengthening the union movement but failing to supplant labor-management conflict with a re-unified society.

Woodrow Wilson had not always been sympathetic even to conservative unionism. Raised in southern and academic circles, he had little experience with organized labor until he ran for governor of New Jersey in 1910. His religion stressed the individual's obligation to battle evil, work hard, and practice self-denial in return for God's promises of support and salvation, and his education in nineteenth-century liberalism at Princeton reinforced those ideas. Like most Americans of his background and class, he regarded unionism as contrary to basic American values.[1]

Some of those prejudices were challenged by Professor Richard T. Ely when Wilson studied under him at Johns Hopkins University in the 1880s. Ely taught that unrestrained self-interest benefited only the rich and that the state must intervene in an economy dominated by great corporations to maintain equality and freedom. These ideas appeared in

73

a nascent form in Wilson's *Congressional Government* in 1885 and more clearly in *The State* in 1888. Wilson's concern about the dangers posed by large corporations did not, however, lead him to favor unions. On the contrary, he feared that powerful unions threatened violence and conflict and could be just as dangerous to individual liberty and freedom of opportunity as irresponsible corporations. Moreover, by the early 1900s he had begun to distinguish between "good" trusts, which brought benefits of size and efficiency, and "bad" ones, which acted selfishly and monopolistically. He made no such distinctions among unions. All unions, he warned, tended to lower production to the level of the laziest or least efficient worker and held back talented individuals from rising. The best way to improve working conditions, he argued, was not through unions but by appealing to the consciences of enlightened businessmen.

Judging all businessmen by his Princeton friends who chose that profession, Wilson concluded that most businessmen wanted to act morally and that the few who misbehaved could be punished individually. Because he lacked firsthand experience with industrial conditions, he did not yet grasp that corporate managers were less often immoral than amoral, that they were guided more by iron laws of profit and loss than by their individual consciences. From the worker's standpoint, the issue was less the behavior of individual businessmen than the impossibility of a single laborer negotiating successfully with an impersonal organization.

During his 1910 gubernatorial campaign Wilson met labor leaders face to face for the first time and received a lesson in the political power of organized labor. When his opponents used his earlier antiunion statements against him, he reversed his position. Stressing again as he had in the 1880s the threat posed by malevolent trusts, he now expressed wholehearted support of unions to counterbalance big business.

That was expedient but not entirely honest. The evidence suggests that Wilson's contact with union leaders in 1910 genuinely convinced him that working conditions needed to be improved but did not persuade him that unions were the best way to achieve that goal. Just as in the late 1880s, he still saw the problem as essentially a humanitarian issue that the state should address through new laws. "How can society justly protect those who cannot protect themselves?" he asked a campaign audience in November 1910. His answer was that "the splendid body of American workmen should be protected as much as it is fair for law to protect them," not that workers should be empowered to defend their own interests through unions.[2] While governor, he secured a state workmen's-compensation law and a dozen other measures to protect workers but did little to strengthen unions. In 1912 American Federation of Labor president Samuel Gompers preferred Champ Clark to Wilson for the Democratic nomination and eventually endorsed the party's pro-union platform but not the candidate.

Ironically, Wilson's position that workers should be protected by law rather than through unions was reflected more in the 1912 Progressive party platform than in that of the Democrats. When he met with Louis Brandeis in August 1912, however, Wilson clarified his antitrust ideas and also received some forceful advice about labor issues. "There can be no progress for the workingman under an absolutism," Brandeis told the candidate. Workers must be enabled to defend their own interests.[3]

Brandeis's suggestion that protective legislation was like the "corrupt paternalism" of Roosevelt's trust policy pushed Wilson to think in terms of encouraging workers to guard their own interests and advance themselves rather than in terms of protecting them through law. Yet he was still not comfortable with the paradox that individual rights would be defended through collective action. His campaign stressed renewed individual opportunities and denied the permanence of class divisions and interests while promising workers justice, and his administration's industrial policy stressed individual opportunity at the same time that it recognized the necessity of collective action.

The times seemed to demand that the government develop a more active labor policy. A rising tide of labor conflict and violence, culminating in the bombing of the *Los Angeles Times* building on 10 October 1910, alarmed conservatives and reformers alike. "What are we going to do," asked muckraker Lincoln Steffens, "about conditions which are bringing . . . a growing group of labor [to believe] that the only recourse they have for improving the conditions of the wage earner is to use dynamite against property and life?"[4]

In August 1912 Congress created a Commission on Industrial Relations (CIR), proposed by President Taft, who appointed a group of conservative business and labor leaders to it. The Democratically controlled Senate refused to confirm any of them, however, and Samuel Gompers visited Wilson to urge a more labor-oriented membership, emerging from the meeting "very much relieved" by the candidate's assurances.[5] When Wilson made his nominations to the commission in spring 1913 he kept many of Taft's conservative appointees but added a number of prominent reformers and named as chairman a flamboyant Missouri lawyer-reformer, Frank P. Walsh.[6]

For two years Walsh drove the commission to expose the dreadful conditions of the poor in America and the greed of some employers.

Having thus become the *bête noire* of conservative businessmen, he also split even the liberal members of the commission by insisting that unions should be freed of all legal constraints, that labor should take an active part in politics, and that government should set rules and then stand aside while labor and management struggled for power. In August 1915 the CIR dissolved in a flurry of conflicting reports and bitter recriminations; but it turned Walsh into a hero of the Left, and its findings made it much more difficult for the administration and the nation to deny the reality of class conflict in America.[7]

Neither Wilson nor his major labor advisers were eager to hear that message. Like the labor and business leaders represented in the National Civic Federation (NCF), from which the president had appointed most members of the CIR, Wilson believed that class conflict was manageable because he was confident that constantly expanding production would guarantee larger and larger profits to be divided between labor and capital.[8] Seeing no limit to growth, he had no reason to believe in a permanent, bitter class struggle. His goals, therefore, were to protect workers, to enlarge individual opportunities, and to oversee business behavior, all with as little governmental interference in the economy as possible.

To implement that policy Wilson chose as the first secretary of labor a man with similar opinions. Born in 1862 in Blantyre, Scotland, William B. Wilson came to America with his parents and six brothers and sisters in 1870. The next year, when he was nine, he followed his father into the coal mines of central Pennsylvania. When he was eleven he joined a miners' union, and by the time he was fourteen he was already a successful union organizer. In 1890 he was instrumental in organizing the United Mine Workers and in 1900 became its secretary-treasurer, a position that he held for the next eight years.

By 1906 William Wilson was a marked man in an industry bitterly hostile to unions, while in general the union movement seemed to be threatened by falling memberships, increasingly militant employers' organizations, unfriendly courts and governments, and competition from the Left from more radical unions and from the Socialist party. Like Samuel Gompers, Wilson decided it was time for conservative unionists to take a more active role in politics, and in 1906 he ran for and was elected to Congress from a normally Republican district. The key to his success was not only the strong support of labor but also his endorsement by some businessmen who were wise enough to see that with his conciliatory approach to labor-capital conflicts he had, as one executive said, "done more to keep conditions peaceful in these counties than any other man in the district."[9] In 1912 a Socialist challenger split Wilson's union support and allowed the Republicans to regain his seat, but Samuel Gompers immediately recommended him to be the first secretary of the new Labor Department for which he had drafted the enabling legislation.[10] He was the only candidate ever considered for the post.

The ambiguous mission of the new department was revealed in the secretary's first annual report in December 1913. There, in language personally approved by the president, he explained that the purpose of the department was to "foster, promote, and develop the welfare of the wage earners of the United States" whether they were union members or not, and he promised to promote the harmonious solution of all labor-capital conflicts. At the same time, however, he pointed out that as a practical matter, the department would be forced to consult labor organizations to find out what workers wanted because it was impossible to canvass the opinions of all workers (even though only about 13 percent of workers then belonged to unions). He also made clear his own belief that "unless wage earners . . . act collectively through their own agents," they would be at a hopeless disadvantage with "collective financial interests" and big business.[11] Insofar as these somewhat contradictory messages can be harmonized, the secretary seemed to be saying that a changing economy had made some adjustment necessary in the mechanisms of industrial relations but that these changes did not imply irreconcilable cleavages.

Finding a method of settling disputes fairly was central to the establishment of an industrial order such as the new administration envisioned. Accordingly, the secretary wrote that "first among the duties of the Secretary of Labor are those with reference to the new Federal function of mediation in labor disputes," but that expressed more of a wish than a fact.[12] Although Congress had authorized federal mediation in railroad labor conflicts as early as 1888, there was no general mediation program until the passage of the Labor Department Act on 4 March 1913, which authorized the secretary of the new department "to act as mediator and to appoint commissioners of conciliation in labor disputes whenever in his judgment the interests of industrial peace may require it."[13] Even then, however, there is little evidence that most members of Congress thought that mediation would be an important function of the new department. The legislators did not create a mediation agency in the Labor Department, and Secretary Wilson had to borrow men from other services to undertake mediations. Nor was any money appropriated to support mediation until October 1913, when Congress reluctantly provided five thousand dollars to pay mediators' expenses but refused to pay their salaries. Thereafter, appropriations gradually increased, reaching seventy-five thousand dollars in 1916, when a Division of Conciliation was approved just in time to confirm its usefulness during the war, finding solutions to more than a thousand conflicts in 1919 alone.[14]

Nevertheless, the service did not command the universal support for which Secretary Wilson hoped. Many businessmen assumed that the department would always favor labor in a dispute and thus rejected the service. During its first two years in operation, the mediation service received only seventy-five requests for assistance, and most of those were in minor disputes. With no power to enforce findings, Secretary Wilson authorized mediation only when it was requested by at least one side, but even that was no guarantee of success.

The matter was complicated because businessmen who perceived the Labor Department as prounion were at least partly correct. In a November 1913 speech in Seattle Secretary Wilson addressed delegates at an AFL meeting as "Fellow Unionists" and outraged conservatives by declaring that capital would be useless without labor and that society's interests antedated and were superior to those of property.[15] Despite complaints from conservatives, the secretary refused to modify or retract his remarks. He believed that "when wage earners are unorganized . . . , it is evident that they can neither bargain nor be bargained with," but when "both sides to a controversy have attained such a form of organization that they can send responsible delegates to confer with each other, there has always been not only a possibility but almost a certainty of agreement."[16] A worker alone, said the secretary, was "as impotent and negligible as a medieval peasant kneeling before the council of a king."[17]

Such language offended conservatives, who either did not want to admit that the nature of industrial relations had changed or who missed the fundamental conservatism of Secretary Wilson's argument. Not only did he believe that the organization of big business required a balancing organization of labor, but he was convinced that recognition of responsible unions would block the development of labor radicalism and class conflict. "The result of refusal on the part of the employing interest to recognize the right of labor to organize," he said, "is to force the development of labor organizations of a revolutionary or even of a lawless type."[18] His goal, like that of the president, was not to insist upon radical change but to reinstate an old and friendly relationship between worker and employer by adjusting the laws and the accepted mechanisms of labor negotiation to the new reality of great corporations.[19]

Some business leaders such as those in the National Civic Federation had long agreed with the secretary's contention that responsible unions could have a stabilizing effect, but others, such as the members of the virulently antiunion National Association of Manufacturers (NAM) and the Rockefeller interests, rejected any such idea. As the Colorado coal strike of 1913–14 made clear, there was no consensus on this aspect of corporate liberalism in the business community.

The Colorado strike began in September 1913 when some six thousand United Mine Workers walked out in search of higher pay, better working and living conditions, and recognition of their union. Because Colorado produced only a small amount of the nation's coal, the strike probably would have attracted little attention except for two things: The largest producer in the area, the Colorado Fuel and Iron Company, was controlled by the Rockefeller family; and the strike produced unusual violence in which more than fifty people were killed.[20]

At the request of the union the Labor Department attempted to mediate the conflict, but the operators, dominated by Colorado Fuel and Iron, refused even to talk, insisting that all the workers were prosperous and happy. They denounced the administration's proposal for mediation as "a conspiracy with organized labor" and "a first indication of a nationwide assault on the right of businessmen to manage their own affairs."[21]

During late winter and early spring 1914 a congressional investigation requested by the president publicized the miners' plight but failed to budge the operators. On 20 April a Colorado militia unit made up largely of company guards and hired thugs opened fire with a machine gun on a miners' camp at Ludlow, and the attack and ensuing burning of the camp killed five miners, two women, and twelve children. When the strikers retaliated in kind, arming themselves and roaming the region attacking mine guards, burning company property, and driving off superintendents, Governor E. M. Ammons of Colorado asked the president to send federal troops to restore order. Believing that maintenance of order was a state responsibility, Wilson was reluctant to act; but on 28 April 1914 he did so, and federal troops remained until 10 January 1915. Unlike most previous federal interventions in strikes, however, these troops were under strict orders to be impartial, disarming all sides, maintaining order, and preventing the companies from bringing in strikebreakers.[22]

With order restored, President Wilson asked the Labor Department to attempt mediation again. By this time the union was running out of money, so it was willing to drop its demand for recognition. Thus the mediators were able to propose a plan that provided for the rehiring of strikers and a mechanism to arbitrate future disputes. The union accepted the plan in mid-September, but the operators remained intransigent. On 10 December 1914 the union, more than a million dollars in debt as a result of the strike, called it off.[23]

Although the miners clearly lost the strike, several important changes emerged from it. Most significant for the miners, the publicity about their working and living conditions led to much tighter state enforcement of health and safety regulations and to closer public scrutiny of conditions. In addition, the companies proved more generous in victory than might have been expected, moving to establish paternalistic programs to resolve differences with the miners in hopes of weakening the union and preventing future strikes.[24]

From a more general point of view, the Colorado strike challenged the administration's assumption that labor and capital could be brought to see that their interests were the same, moving it reluctantly to recognize that it must give open support to the right of unionization and collective bargaining and that it might sometimes be forced to intervene in conflicts. For its willingness to confront such unpleasant realities in Colorado it won the trust and lasting gratitude of organized labor. But there is little evidence that the president had accepted class conflict as inevitable or that he had been converted to the concept of a "broker state," in which government mediates between conflicting private interests. He read Samuel Gompers's long and frequent letters sympathetically and often met with the labor leader, yet he still believed that a common national interest transcended and incorporated the interests of private groups.[25]

Moreover, President Wilson still retained some of his old belief that government should look out for workers through the passage of protective legislation rather than through support of unionization. When, for example, the AFL leadership learned in 1914 that the administration proposed to amend the antitrust laws, they urged that the changes include an exclusion of trade unions from the provisions of the Sherman Act, under which the federal courts had sometimes held that unions were conspiracies in restraint of trade. The administration's Clayton bill, however, merely affirmed the legality of trade unions and did not ban antitrust suits against them. By active lobbying the union was able to secure a compromise declaring that unions and their members were not to "be held or construed to be illegal combinations or conspiracies in restraint of trade under the antitrust laws," but later court decisions showed that this language offered far less protection for unions than a flat exemption from antitrust prosecutions. Despite its good will toward labor, the administration would not liberate the unions from governmental supervision through the courts as most unionists wanted.[26]

On the other hand, much that the administration did pleased not only more radical labor leaders but other leftists as well. The president's appointment in June 1916 of Louis Brandeis and, a month later, of John Hessin Clarke to the Supreme Court thrilled the Left and infuriated conservatives. The administration's Revenue Act of 1916 financed a military preparedness program, which most liberals feared, with an income surtax, an estate tax, a corporate tax, and a stiff tax on munitions profits, all of which delighted them. And the president's support of the La Follette Seamen's Act of 1915, the Keating-Owen Child Labor Act of 1916, the Kern-McGillicuddy Federal Workmen's Compensation Act of 1916, and the Adamson Act of 1916, which averted a threatened railroad strike by imposing an eight-hour day on the companies, all won the applause not only of the AFL, but of labor leftists, social reformers, former Progressives, and several prominent Socialists.[27] In the 1916 campaign some Socialists endorsed Wilson, praising him for the "social justice already gained" and arguing that his reelection would assure "much immediate progress."[28]

Although it is certainly true, as a number of historians have pointed out, that Wilson's 1916 move to the Left was politically expedient, it also appears that the administration's actions in that period fitted the ambiguous pattern that had characterized the president's thought for several years.[29] He rejected Roosevelt's welfare-statism as more likely to benefit the rich and powerful than the poor and weak, but he nevertheless favored the passage of similar programs himself. He had come to support unions but trusted only conservative unionists and would not free even them from governmental supervision. The logic in these apparent contradictions lay in his intention to modernize the law so that it would deal effectively with contemporary industrial practice, restoring a balance between owners and workers and maintaining individual opportunity. In such a situation, he believed, there would be little need of constant governmental intervention.[30]

A modern audience may doubt that Wilson's concept was workable, but in fact it never had a chance. By 1916 pressures engendered by deteriorating neutrality in the face of world war were already undermining the stability the president sought, and the nation's entrance into the war in April 1917 weakened it further. To maintain restraints on business when the nation needed production and to keep labor from exploiting wartime manpower shortages to demand raises and improvements in other benefits proved to be equally difficult. Between these two large millstones of self-interest the administration's hopes for harmonious advancement of the public interest were ground away.

The first attack on the administration's delicate balance came from labor, but capital quickly retaliated. When the United States entered the war, the draft and the cessation of immigration created an apparent labor shortage. Labor exploited this situation aggressively, with the number of strikes rising dramatically from 979 in 1914 to 4,233 in 1917. Capital fought back with lockouts, strikebreakers, blacklists, appeals to patriotism, and every other device they could imagine.[31]

The Labor Department could do little about the situation. Although American entrance into the war almost doubled requests for mediation (521 between 6 April and 25 October 1917 and 1,217 in the fiscal year ending on 30 June 1918), Congress was still reluctant to authorize establishment of a Conciliation Service or to provide money to support the department's informal program.[32] The best that Secretary Wilson could do was to run a skeleton program with employees borrowed from other duties.

The department also attempted to alleviate labor conflict by correcting a maldistribution of workers. Because three-fourths of defense contracts were awarded to firms in seven eastern and midwestern states, those regions had labor shortages while others had surpluses.[33] Aside from solving problems in transportation and housing, the department wanted to bring workers and jobs together, but here also congressional fears of strengthening organized labor blocked Secretary Wilson's efforts to create an Employment Service within the department. As with mediation, the secretary had to patch together an organization by using employees of the Division of Information and the Immigration Service and by scrounging money wherever he could get it.[34] Hampered by a relatively weak staff, the opposition of antiunion businessmen, obstructionism from business and civic leaders in labor surplus areas who did not want labor costs to rise, and the continuing hostility of Congress, the Employment Service nevertheless found work for more than three million people, including more than half a million women, between 1 July 1917 and 1 January 1919.[35]

The problems of the Labor Department at the beginning of the war were partly those of a new agency that had not yet established a solid relationship with allies in Congress or won the trust of the constituencies with which it had to deal; but even more, its difficulties were those of a government utterly unprepared for the task that now faced it. In August 1916 Congress had created a Council of National Defense made up of the secretaries of war, navy, interior, agriculture, commerce, and labor to promote "the coordination of industries and resources for the national security and welfare," but the council and its seven-member Advisory Commission of experts did little before the United States entered the war.[36] This lack of planning resulted in chaos. An army could be raised quickly through the draft, but it could not be housed, clothed, moved, or equipped. Newsreel films showed uniformless new soldiers practicing attacks with wooden guns against trucks carrying signs identifying them as tanks.

In the absence of central coordination, businesses competed

fiercely with each other and with military procurement officers for civilian manpower, resources, credit, and transportation. The practice of awarding cost-plus contracts to defense industries under which the government guaranteed to pay all costs plus a fixed percentage of profit encouraged companies to outbid each other for supplies and men, secure in the knowledge that they did not have to absorb inflated costs. Railroad inefficiency compounded a shortage of freight cars, and no one knew where the ships were to be obtained to send men and supplies to France. Secretary of War Newton D. Baker tried to solve the problems by assuming power personally over the military, industry, and labor, but by the end of 1917 drastic reforms obviously had to be adopted if the war effort was not to fail completely.[37]

Particularly dramatizing the crisis in summer 1917 was the outbreak of strikes in the copper mines of Arizona. Spurned by the AFL because they were unskilled, copper miners had turned to the radical Industrial Workers of the World in hopes of securing living wages and decent conditions. Beginning in June the union led a series of strikes, and the operators retaliated with vigilante violence against anyone suspected of IWW membership or sympathies. Because copper was crucial to defense production, appeals poured in on the administration from all over the country to find a way to end the crisis, and on 19 September 1917 Wilson appointed a President's Mediation Commission (PMC) to investigate the situation and seek solutions.

After traveling through the strike region, the commission concluded that the general problems were low wages, long hours, discrimination against union members, and lack of collective bargaining machinery. It proposed to settle disputes through wage increases, promises of nondiscrimination against union members, and the creation of a permanent system for negotiating. In return for these corporate concessions, the commission asked workers for no-strike pledges. Lacking sympathy with the IWW, it made no effort to win union recognition, and its arrangements left large loopholes that allowed the companies to fire "radicals." Although the administration claimed that the PMC was a success, continuing strikes nationwide and the growth of a general antiunionism showed that labor problems were not over.[38]

Late in 1917 the Council of National Defense asked a special interdepartmental committee to investigate labor problems, and in December, in a report written by Assistant Secretary of the Navy Franklin D. Roosevelt, the committee recommended creating a new war-labor agency.[39] A month later Felix Frankfurter, the former secretary of the PMC, proposed to Secretary of War Baker the appointment of a single industrial coordinator, someone equivalent to Herbert Hoover in the

Food Administration. Urged to the same course by House, Brandeis, McAdoo, and others, in March 1918 President Wilson reorganized the War Industries Board (WIB), but he gave it little authority over labor.[40]

Although the Labor Department did not have the political muscle to secure the adoption of Assistant Labor Secretary Louis Post's argument that the department alone should have authority over labor issues, Secretary Wilson was able to win the president's approval of a compromise that kept substantial power in his hands rather than turning it over to the WIB.[41] Proposing as a model a series of special boards made up of representatives of industry, labor, and the public, which were already dealing with labor issues in several defense industries and which had been endorsed by the National Industrial Conference Board, an association of major manufacturers, the secretary recommended the creation of a similar board on a national scale. On 4 January 1918 the president named Secretary Wilson as war-labor administrator to set up this agency, which would draft wartime labor policies and oversee their enforcement.[42]

After conferring with the moderate business leaders of the National Industrial Conference Board and the conservative labor leaders of the AFL, on 29 March and 8 April Secretary Wilson approved a labor code and established a National War Labor Board (NWLB) to enforce it. The code pleased the AFL by recognizing the right of unionization and making rather vague promises of fair wages and hours, and it allowed industry to hope that no-strike pledges would enable them to freeze the status quo during the war. The same effort to please everyone was evident in the NWLB, which included "responsible" members from labor and capital and was co-chaired by former president William Howard Taft and the former chairman of the Commission on Industrial Relations, Frank P. Walsh. The board's power to apply its nebulous code was limited to cases where no other mechanisms for settlement were in effect, and even then it could not force either side to accept its findings.[43]

Although Secretary Wilson claimed that the NWLB would succeed because its principles of voluntarism "are in a peculiar sense the principles of the United States Government," others were less optimistic.[44] Felix Frankfurter, who had been one of the strongest advocates of the appointment of a single labor czar, predicted that the new board would not resolve the chaos resulting from competing and conflicting adjustment boards; in the coming months he was proved right. Private contractors competed with governmental agencies for workers, and there were no agreed-upon standards for wages or hours among the various adjustment boards. Frankfurter urged the president to appoint Brandeis as labor administrator, but Wilson had more confidence in the existing system than Frankfurter; and in any case he was unwilling to lose Brandeis from the Supreme Court, to which he had recently been confirmed by the Senate after a bitter fight. On 7 May 1918, however, the president did name Frankfurter chairman of a new War Labor Policies Board (WLPB) made up of representatives from all the governmental agencies concerned with war production. The board was given the impressive sounding assignment of coordinating all federal labor policies, but notably its chairman, far from being independent, was named "Assistant to the Secretary of Labor." Despite his mild appearance, Secretary Wilson was proving adept at defeating challenges to his authority, and the WLPB never did much.[45]

The National War Labor Board ended up resolving few cases in comparison to the department's regular mediation services because it was slow to organize. From its creation until the armistice in November 1918 the board received 847 cases but managed to resolve only 72.[46] In most of these cases both sides accepted the board's findings, but in its two most important cases it had to go beyond voluntarism. In the Western Union strike, the president secured congressional authority to have the Post Office Department take over the company when it rejected an NWLB ruling; and in a bitter conflict at the Smith & Wesson arms factory, the War Department seized the company when it spurned an NWLB finding. Moreover, the president forced Smith & Wesson's recalcitrant employees back to work by threatening to blacklist them from defense jobs for a year and by warning them that they could lose their draft exemptions.[47] The message thus delivered to both labor and management was unmistakable: Disputants would be wise to accept the NWLB's findings "voluntarily."

With the signing of the armistice the president lost the authority to enforce the board's findings through seizures and other extraordinary methods, and the board was forced to fall back on genuine voluntarism. The result, reports historian Valerie Conner, was that "employers evaded its edicts, employees became skeptical about its ability to function, and the NWLB members dropped all pretense of harmony."[48] Soon after the armistice the board decided not to take up any new cases unless the president asked them to do so or unless both sides agreed in advance to abide by a ruling. By June 1919, however, even those conditions had failed to make the mediation system work, and the board voted to end its operations. On 12 August it went out of existence.[49]

In general, conservative labor leaders and even prowar Socialists were pleased with the administration's wartime attitude toward labor. Labor leaders liked being consulted and included at the highest levels of policymaking. Although profits skyrocketed for many corporations during the war and in some industries workers would have received "much higher wages" without the special boards, labor leaders patriotically suppressed any doubts they may have felt for the duration of the conflict.[50]

When the war ended, however, the collapse of the NWLB revealed that regardless of wartime rhetoric the administration had not succeeded in persuading both sides that their common interests transcended selfish concerns. The NWLB did not produce a new era of employer-employee cooperation, but it did achieve a modest improvement in the status of organized labor, a reasonable increase in the wages paid to unskilled workers, a much wider acceptance of the eight-hour day, and a set of precedents that gave unions greater respectability and thus began to establish a balance between labor and capital.[51] Although worthwhile, these achievements did not reveal the way to escape class conflict that the administration had always sought. Rather, they demonstrated the necessity of continued governmental involvement in the process of negotiating settlements.

The most important limitation of the NWLB, aside from its role in the voluntarist myth, was that like the rest of the administration's mobilization efforts it substituted administrative consultation among a small group of corporate and labor leaders for an open political process involving everyone concerned with the issues. By narrowing the range of people consulted and excluding intractable issues, the NWLB was able to create the illusion of cooperation. At the end of the war, neither workers nor businessmen who had been excluded from the process were willing to prolong it, and even its participants began to see defects previously overlooked, so it broke down into confrontation and violence. Nevertheless, the image of cooperation was seductive, not only to those who had benefited from it but even to many who had been excluded from the charmed circle. A desire to perpetuate and extend the system lay behind the associational movement of the 1920s and much of the New Deal's early recovery programs.

Among those who were especially entranced by the possibility of replacing competition and conflict with cooperation were a group of men whom Robert Cuff characterizes as "business ideologues and dreamers."[52] In the eyes of men such as Bernard Baruch (Wall Street speculator and chairman of the War Industries Board), Walter Gifford (AT&T executive and director of the Council of National Defense), Howard Coffin (vice-president of the Hudson Motor Company and chairman of the Aircraft Production Board), Edward Hurley (machine-tool manufacturer and president of the United States Shipping Board), and many other businessmen who became administrators during the war, the conflict presented a golden opportunity to bring together not only labor and capital but also competing businesses. The first goal of such cooperation was to win the war, but other important aims were to strengthen the American economy in preparation for what most felt would be a cut-throat competition for international markets after the war, to promote wiser uses of resources and improved products, and to lower prices. At the same time, however, such business leaders did not want to seek these goals under heavy governmental oversight and bureaucratic direction. Ideally, they preferred free cooperation among businesses. The problem was how to achieve it without encouraging the conspiracies that the antitrust laws were designed to prevent and, equally important, without arousing a public backlash.[53] In the histories of the War Industries Board and the NWLB may be traced the ambiguities and contradictions to which these conflicting aspirations necessarily led.

Wilson created the WIB in July 1917 ostensibly to define defense needs and to coordinate industry's production, assign priorities, and if necessary, fix prices, but in fact his real goal was to circumvent section three of the pending Lever Food and Fuel bill, which prohibited governmental agents from signing a contract with any companies in which they had interests. That provision threatened to force most of the business volunteers upon whom the administration was counting for the management of mobilization to resign. But the creation of the WIB did not succeed in heading off the passage of section three, and as the president feared, the dollar-a-year men began to leave the government in large numbers because they could not buy from the industries from which they had been recruited.

By autumn 1917 the administration found itself caught in an intolerable situation. Either it must accept a hopelessly inefficient purchasing system in which business and government were separated by an impassable legal wall or it must create an all-powerful federal purchasing board that would violate all principles of voluntary cooperation between business and government. The WIB thus was "largely a cosmetic creation, even a political ploy, intended as much to stymie the administration's critics and hold the line against radical institutional reordering as to render mobilization more efficient."[54]

Predictably, the WIB failed to achieve order, and during autumn and winter 1917 it was plagued by resignations and a general sense of futility.[55] By winter 1917–18 fuel shortages were so serious that local officials were stopping coal trains as they passed through, police had to be called out to protect coal piles from raids by desperate homeowners, the shipbuilding, aircraft, and armaments programs were paralyzed, and in

January 1918 Fuel Administrator Harry Garfield had to order that all factories east of the Mississippi be closed for four days in order to secure coal for ships carrying desperately needed supplies to France. Across the country there was a howl of outrage and condemnation of the administration's handling of mobilization, which was amplified by the president's seeming complacency. "The President and Secretary [of War Newton] Baker seem to be the only ones who think the organization is as it should be," observed Colonel House.[56]

The winter crisis aroused criticism of the administration even among Democrats. Oregon Senator George Chamberlain introduced a bill calling for the creation of a civilian war cabinet to take over control of mobilization from the president. Wilson sent Baker to testify against the bill before the Military Affairs Committee and was able to sidetrack it, but obviously something had to be done. In a shrewd counterattack the president had Senator Lee Overman of North Carolina introduce legislation giving the executive wide authority to reorganize agencies without specific congressional approval. Although the Overman Act, which became law on 20 May 1918, further reduced congressional control of mobilization, critics in Congress had to support it because they were caught in a trap of their own making. All along they had insisted that their aim was not to curtail the president's power but to make the administration of the war effort more vigorous and efficient. Passage of the act thus deflected congressional criticism for the time being.[57]

At the same time, the president also reinvigorated the War Industries Board. For that difficult task he turned to Bernard Baruch, who had worked to win business support for the administration in 1915–16 and who had been a generous campaign contributor in 1916. Like Herbert Hoover, Baruch was something of an outsider in the business world, a man of independent wealth who was associated with no particular company and was willing, even eager, to put his talents at the disposal of the administration. Also, like Hoover, he was an articulate and enthusiastic proponent of the idea that an efficient mobilization could be achieved through voluntary cooperation—provided the process had the right leader. Many of Wilson's advisers, including House, were prejudiced against Baruch (as they had been against Brandeis) because he was Jewish, but Wilson ignored their insinuations. Pleased by Baruch's courtly southern manners and impressed by his knowledge of details (Wilson referred to him as "Dr. Facts"), the president appointed Baruch as head of a reorganized WIB in March 1918.[58]

"The experience of the War Industries Board," wrote Baruch after the war, "points to the desirability of investing some Government agency . . . with . . . powers . . . to encourage, under strict Government supervision, such cooperation and coordination in industry as should tend to increase production, eliminate waste, conserve natural resources, improve the quality of products, promote efficiency in operation, and thus reduce costs to the ultimate consumer."[59] That was, at least by implication, a large claim for the importance of the WIB, but in reality the organization was less revolutionary than Baruch later believed.

Rather than reshaping business-labor-government relations, the WIB actually blurred even more the already fuzzy lines between public and private. Its dollar-a-year bureaucrats were organized into "commodity sections," from which they negotiated contracts and purchase specifications with private businessmen organized in "war service committees" under the auspices of the United States Chamber of Commerce. Men and interests flowing back and forth across this line largely vitiated the attempt to avoid conflicts of interest embodied in section three of the Lever Act, and so much intercorporate cooperation was necessary to make the system work that eventually the administration, against its own wishes, had to suspend the antitrust laws for the duration of the war.[60]

That was fine with Baruch, but Wilson did not fully share his vision of a corporate millennium. When the president appointed Baruch as head of the reorganized WIB in March 1918, he left control of military purchasing in the hands of the War and Navy Departments, authority over transportation under the Railroad Administration, and price-fixing power in a separate committee headed by Robert S. Brookings. Having almost no legal powers, Baruch succeeded by negotiating, cajoling, intimidating, and otherwise manipulating companies and agencies into doing what he wanted. The whole extralegal system disappeared almost instantly upon the signing of the armistice, and as a model for the future organization of the national economy, it was a joke.[61]

The example of steel prices suggests some of the complexities inherent in the administration's industrial policies. When the United States entered the war in April 1917, the demand for steel increased tremendously, and with it prices, which doubled and tripled on many products within weeks although costs did not increase for most producers. Liberals, including the president and former Secretary of State William Jennings Bryan, were appalled that supplying the necessities of war could be so lucrative; military purchasers demanded lower prices to keep their costs manageable; the public insisted that something be done to keep the cost of living down; and Secretary of the Treasury McAdoo struggled to hold down government spending. On the other hand, steel-company stockholders were delighted by increased dividends;

smaller, less efficient companies insisted that they needed higher prices to spur investment and enable them to maintain production; organized labor hoped to divert a part of increased profits into higher wages; and many leaders, including a large number of executives of big steel companies, argued that high profits could be controlled through excess-profits taxes that would in turn help to finance the war. Moreover, although many steelmen believed that the government should be charged a lower, preferential price, they argued that foreign and private purchasers should pay the market price to keep demand under control. They pointed out, too, that prices were only part of the problem. Determining allocations, setting priorities, and controlling civilian demand were equally vital. Secretary of the Navy Josephus Daniels, who lamented that the whole issue was "complicated and difficult," grossly understated the problem.[62]

Even from within the administration the president received conflicting advice. By summer 1917 Daniels was convinced that the government should fix steel prices for all purchasers, foreign and domestic, public and private. Secretary of War Baker believed, however, that price-fixing was impossibly complex and might disrupt vital production. Caught in the middle, Wilson in July ordered the new Federal Trade Commission to investigate the steel industry in preparation for setting a uniform price. At the same time, Senator Atlee Pomerene, recognizing that existing legislation did not authorize regulation of steel prices, introduced a price-fixing bill.[63]

Despite these pressures, steel producers and the government could not reach a voluntary agreement on prices during summer 1917, and on 21 September the War Industries Board summoned representatives of sixty-four steelmakers to a conference in Washington on the subject. The meeting, reported Baruch, "was a stormy one with much heated argument and impassioned oratory," but in the end the steelmen were forced to give in when Baruch threatened that the president would take over the mills if they resisted.[64] Three days later they agreed to fix prices near levels that the WIB had proposed.

Relations between Baruch and the steelmen recovered slowly from this confrontation. In February 1918 U.S. Steel's Henry Clay Frick accused Baruch of being "a leader of the socialistic movement," and Baruch remained suspicious of every claim made by the companies.[65] Nevertheless, price-fixing proved a boon to the large companies and to those smaller mills that could arrange to pool contracts, largely because it guaranteed them a stable market. When the initial agreement expired at the end of December 1917, the industry and the WIB easily agreed to extend it; and at the end of the war U.S. Steel proposed to Baruch that it be continued into the postwar period, which could not be done because there was no legal authority for it.[66]

Obviously the history of the steel price-fixing arrangement does not sustain the myth that the economy was managed during the war entirely through voluntary means, although it is also clear that by the end of the war steel executives had discovered benefits in "voluntarily" fixed prices. The benefits to the government and to the public were less clear. Robert Brookings's Price Fixing Committee had nothing but praise for the steel companies under its supposed authority, but the president and Attorney General J. Mitchell Palmer demonstrated considerable doubt about the new relationship when they renewed an antitrust suit against United States Steel that had been suspended during the war.[67] The whole episode shows that neither voluntarism nor a corporatist vision dominated the administration's policy during the war. There were elements of business-government cooperation, to be sure, but there was also an underlying distrust between the two, and much of what was later touted as voluntary cooperation was in fact coerced.

6

DEVELOPING
A FOREIGN POLICY

Two great forces united to give the Wilson administration's foreign policy a distinctive direction even before World War I thrust American diplomacy to the forefront of the world stage. One was the traditional national commitment to liberty and democracy, the conviction that America was "a city upon a hill," destined to show the rest of the nations better ways of governing themselves. The other was a newfound sense of economic and military maturity that justified claiming a place among the great powers. Few people imagined that there could be a conflict between idealism and self-interest; the United States would do well by doing good.[1]

On the eve of his inauguration Wilson allegedly said to a friend, "It would be the irony of fate if my administration had to deal chiefly with foreign affairs," but in fact he had been thinking for many years like a foreign policy activist.[2] At the time of the Spanish-American War he had said that the "impulse of expansion" was "the natural and wholesome impulse which comes with a consciousness of matured strength."[3] The war had "pushed us out into the political field of the world" just as the nation's economic growth had "pushed us out into the trade of the world."[4] But power and profit could be reconciled with traditional American values. "Our greatness is built upon our freedom—is moral, not material," he said. "Principles lie back of our action. America would be inconceivable without them. These principles are not incompatible with great material prosperity. On the contrary, unless we are deeply mistaken, they are indispensable to it."[5] Having become a great power, the United States must remember that "the service of humanity is the best business of mankind" and "shape our course of action by the maxims of justice and liberality and good will" and "think of the progress of mankind rather than of the progress of this or that investment."[6] The American political and economic systems had produced happiness and prosperity within the nation; they could do the same for the rest of the world. The country was now strong enough to begin exporting its values along with other products.

The elements of idealism and self-interest were symbolized to a certain extent in the bureaucratic structure of the administration. Idealism seemed to dominate William Jennings Bryan's State Department, and self-interest was a major concern of William Redfield's Department of Commerce, although in neither case was policy determined by only a single point of view.

Although appointed secretary of state because of his influence over Democratic legislators gained during three unsuccessful presidential campaigns and not because of his opinions about foreign issues, Bryan nevertheless brought to the State Department strong convictions about the proper direction of policy. A deeply committed Christian, he neither smoked nor drank, and he refused to serve alcohol at official functions, thus arousing much ridicule but showing the importance that religious principles would have in his policy. Quite simply, Bryan believed that nations ought to treat each other according to the same standards that governed Christian individuals. He proposed a series of bilateral "cooling-off" treaties that he hoped would make war impossible; he negotiated a treaty apologizing to Colombia for American participation in the Panamanian Revolution of 1903; he developed a scheme to free Latin American nations from dependence on foreign bankers by having the United States government make direct loans to them; and after he successfully weathered a crisis with Japan, he had some old army swords beaten into miniature plowshare paper weights for distribution to visiting diplomats. Eventually, in 1915, he resigned from the State Department because he believed Wilson's policies were leading the United States toward an unnecessary war with Germany.[7] Thus although Bryan symbolized an idealistic strand in the administration's foreign policy, obviously his ideas did not always prevail.

On the other hand, William C. Redfield, the first secretary of the recently created Department of Commerce, had been a very successful businessman and president of the American Manufacturers Export Association and was aggressively committed to advancing American economic interests abroad. Although Wilson appointed him more for his support of tariff reduction than for his economic expansionism, the president's own speeches during the campaign indicated that he also believed that the United States needed to follow a more aggressive commerical policy. As secretary, Redfield secured increased funding for the department's Bureau of Foreign and Domestic Commerce, won Congress's approval to send commercial attachés to countries with which the United States had large trade, greatly increased the department's activities in providing information on business opportunities abroad, encouraged the organization of a National Foreign Trade Council made up of fifty of the nation's leading businessmen and worked closely with it, and pushed effectively for the adoption of legislation that permitted American banks to establish foreign branches and that loosened antitrust restrictions on exporters. Yet despite these achievements, Redfield resigned from the cabinet in 1919, frustrated by what he saw as the administration's antibusiness posture and its refusal to give him a free hand to promote American economic interests.[8]

Nor was the tension in the administration's policy simply between material and idealistic interests. Administration leaders saw no problem in expanding business interests under high standards. One had but to require, as Bryan said, that every American businessman abroad give "a dollar's worth of service for every dollar that he asks in recompense" and to guarantee, as Wilson promised, that Americans would never seek exploitive "concessions" in other countries but would "make investments."[9] The idea that even honorable business dealings might give the United States a sort of economic domination over other nations was beyond the imagination of these leaders, just as they did not envision the military and political interference to which their efforts to encourage the growth of democracy would lead.

In a famous speech in Mobile in October 1913 Wilson promised that the United States would "never again seek one additional foot of territory by conquest."[10] He did not realize that there was an implication of dominance just as offensive to Latin Americans in his earlier promise that the United States would "lend [its] influence of every kind" to the support of "just government based upon law, not upon arbitrary or irregular force" and that it would "prefer those who act in the interest of peace and honor, who protect private rights and respect the restraints of constitutional provision."[11] Such an insistence upon particular forms of government seemed to Latin Americans very like overt imperialism, whether it was based upon economic self-interest or on a commitment to idealistic principles.[12]

The nature of the difficulty was exemplified by the administration's experience with a proposed Pan-American nonaggression treaty. In November 1913 Bryan forwarded to the president a proposal for such a treaty that had been made by Congressman James Luther Slayden of Texas. Wilson liked the idea, but distracted by a crisis with Mexico put it aside until reminded of it by Colonel House in December 1914 after the beginning of World War I. Delighted by House's suggestion that such a pact could "serve as a model for the European Nations when peace is at last brought about," the president took a pencil and drafted two main clauses for the proposed treaty: first, a "mutual guarantee of political independence under republican forms of government and mutual guarantees of territorial integrity," and second, an agreement that signatories would "acquire control" of the "manufacture and sale of munitions of war."[13] House then took the proposal to the ambassadors of Argentina, Brazil, and Chile. Chile quickly rejected it, fearing it might jeopardize a border claim against Peru. Chilean leaders, concerned about the growth of American investments in their country from $5 million in 1900 to $171.4 million by 1914, also believed that Wilson aimed "at United States domination in Latin America" and feared that the treaty's requirement for "republican forms of government" would "tend to erect a United States tutelage over Latin America."[14] By 1916, Argentina, which had initially applauded the treaty proposal, also rejected it, largely because of fears aroused by American intervention in Mexico.[15] The proposed treaty thus died, a victim of a belief by Latin America that although Wilson had renounced overt imperialism, his interventionism, the growth of American economic influence, and his insistence on political conformity all added up to a sort of informal imperialism that was just as objectionable as the cruder colonialism of an earlier day.[16]

In May 1914 Wilson told a group of Princeton alumni that "service is not merely getting out and talking and being busy and butting into other people's affairs. Service also and chiefly consists in comprehension . . . . If I want to serve the lowest of human beings I have got at least to put myself, imaginatively, in his place and see the world as he sees it."[17] Ironically, the president's inability to see the world through others' eyes was a principal cause of the failure of his Pan-American proposal and a major reason for failures he was experiencing in dealing with other nations of Asia and Latin America, including Mexico.

Mexican problems were waiting on Wilson's desk when he entered the White House. In 1911 Mexican liberals led by Francisco Madero had overthrown a forty-year dictatorship and established a constitutional democracy, only to be ousted themselves by a military coup led by Victoriano Huerta early in 1913. Although Wilson was advised by State Department experts that traditional American practice had been to recognize whatever government actually held power in a country, regardless of how it acquired that power, the president was shocked by Huerta's murder of Madero and declared, "I will not recognize a government of butchers."[18] More important, the president had heard rumors that "those seeking to foment revolution" elsewhere in Latin America were taking the election of the Democrats, who had been critical of Republican policies of promoting stability and encouraging foreign investments, "as an encouragement." Fearing a wave of revolutions in the area, Wilson wanted to make his opposition clear to "those who seek to seize the power of government to advance their own *personal* interests or ambition."[19]

One of the greatest obstacles to formulating an effective Mexican policy was the absence of accurate information about what was happening there. Taft's ambassador to Mexico City, Henry Lane Wilson, had been involved in the plotting of Huerta's coup and could not be relied upon, nor could the ambassador be replaced without extending recognition to the new government. In April, therefore, President Wilson asked a journalist, William Bayard Hale, who had recently written a laudatory biography of him, to travel to Mexico and report on the situation. Hale knew no Spanish and little of Mexico, but he shared the president's values. Beginning in mid-June his reports stressed that Huerta had launched "an assault on constitutional government" and concluded that if the United States had "any moral work to do, it is to discourage violence and uphold law."[20] This confirmed Wilson's belief that the problem in Mexico was essentially a political one and that if Huerta could be held to his promise to conduct free elections, all would be well.

To convey that message to Huerta, Bryan and Wilson chose another special agent, John Lind of Minnesota. A man of integrity and devotion to democratic principles, Lind was a longtime friend of Bryan's but was otherwise even less suited for his delicate mission than Hale. He knew no Spanish, had no experience in Latin America, and despised Catholics. In Arthur Link's apt words, the reason for his appointment "remains as much a mystery today as it was to Lind at the time."[21] Given his own lack of qualifications and his message demanding that Huerta call immediate elections in which he was not to be a candidate, it was no wonder that Lind's mission was a failure. In mid-October Huerta confirmed the administration's worst fears by dissolving the Mexican legislature, arresting most of its opposition members, and proceeding to rule dictatorially.

Huerta's defiance was baffling to Wilson and Bryan. They attributed it to the support of his regime by the British, who allegedly hoped for economic concessions, especially oil, from Mexico.[22] It cost the British a great deal of effort to convince Washington that their policy was neither anti-American nor imperialistic and that it was intended only to protect existing British interests in Mexico. The British regarded American policy in Mexico as quixotic but realized that they had no choice other than to follow the American lead.

With his attempt to restore constitutional government in Mexico at a dead-end by late 1913, Wilson seized upon a suggestion from William Bayard Hale to send someone to interview leaders of an armed opposition to Huerta in northern Mexico.[23] Hale's suggestion offered a new approach to the problem, and in November Wilson sent him to talk to the Constitutionalists, as the rebels called themselves.

In a series of reports in mid-November Hale gave the president important and disturbing new information. On the whole Hale was impressed by the rebel leaders, but he reported that they would not accept any form of American intervention and that their demands went well beyond the restoration of constitutional democracy. They were determined, he wrote, on "the total destruction of the old regime" and would not agree to hold elections until they had enacted by decree "social and political reforms which they agree upon as fundamental."[24]

Wilson quickly grasped a part of what the Constitutionalists were saying. In February he told the British ambassador that "the real cause of the trouble in Mexico was not political but economic," that it was in fact "the land question," and that until the power of the landowners was shattered "in a fight to the finish," there could be no lasting political stability. Accordingly, he had lifted an American embargo on the sale of arms to the rebels, but he would avoid intervention, which "would unite against the invading party all the patriotism and all the energies of which the Mexicans were capable."[25]

The president's definition of the term "intervention" was, however, substantially different from that of the Constitutionalists. They equated intervention with interference of any kind; Wilson seemed to define it only as full-scale invasion with the goal of imposing "a government upheld by a foreign power as a consequence of successful intervention."[26] In short, he defined intervention only as conquest and believed that all other forms of pressure or interference were acceptable. Given that limited and eccentric definition, the ground was prepared for conflict.

One of the mistakes into which Wilson's faulty definition could lead him appeared in April 1914. On 9 April a small boat carrying American sailors mistakenly landed in a prohibited zone of the port of Tampico, and the sailors were arrested by Huertistan authorities. Mexican officials immediately released the sailors with apologies, but the American naval commander, Admiral Henry T. Mayo, took it upon himself to demand a formal apology and a twenty-one gun salute to the

American flag. The president seized upon this situation as what he later referred to as "a psychological moment" when there was at least a pretext for action; on 21 April he sent a thousand marines and sailors ashore to take the nearby port of Veracruz, which was the main entry point for arms shipments to Huerta.[27]

Secretary of State Bryan and Secretary of the Navy Josephus Daniels had said publicly that they believed a peaceful solution to the crisis could be found, but Wilson overruled them. It now became clear their advice had been wise. In a gallant but futile effort, Mexican naval cadets resisted the American landings, killing 19 and wounding 71 but losing 126 dead and 195 wounded themselves. The Americans took the city, but a flashfire of nationalism raced across Mexico. The Constitutionalists and Huertistas closed ranks; thousands of Mexicans volunteered to defend their country; and mobs stormed American consulates. Stunned by the Mexican reaction, exactly the opposite of what he had expected, Wilson sent orders to the American commander at Veracruz that "under no circumstances" was he to expand the area held by American forces and that he was to avoid doing anything that "might tend to increase the tension of the situation or embarrass" the American government.[28] Plans to blockade the Mexican coast and to expand military operations were abandoned, and the president hastily accepted a mediation offer by Argentina, Brazil, and Chile.[29]

Wilson realized that the intended show of force to persuade Huerta that he must resign had failed, but he did not abandon his object. Any settlement of the crisis, he told the ABC ambassadors, must include "the entire elimination of General Huerta."[30] His intransigent stand on that point during the mediation conference that took place at Niagara Falls, Ontario, during May and June 1914 led to the conference's failure but at last persuaded Huerta that his situation was hopeless. In mid-July the dictator, his army crumbling before Constitutionalist attacks, fled to Spain. Four months later Wilson at last withdrew American forces from Veracruz.

Soon after Huerta's flight Wilson wrote jubilantly to a friend that although the situation was "still a little blind," the administration's policy had "cleared the stage and made a beginning" and that now "it should be possible to hold things steady until the process is finally complete."[31] His words and the continued presence of American troops in Veracruz suggested that he did not yet understand that the Mexican definition of intervention was a great deal broader than his own.

Nevertheless, Wilson was cautious about taking any further action, perhaps because he hoped that the most overtly pro-American of the Constitutionalist leaders, Pancho Villa, whom he regarded as "a sort of

Robin Hood," might soon take over as the new leader of Mexico.[32] That naive hope disappeared in the anarchy that instead gripped Mexico, and in June 1915 Wilson threatened simply to pick out one of the factions to recognize as the government of Mexico. Fortunately, he was saved from having to try that form of intervention when a faction dominated by Venustiano Carranza routed Villa and secured substantial control of the country. Assured by Carranza that he favored constitutionalism, separation of church and state, public education, and land reform by legal means and that he would respect foreigners' lives and property, Wilson joined with several Latin American states on 19 October 1915 to grant de facto recognition to Carranza's government.[33] Once again the president flattered himself that his policy had pushed Mexico toward a desirable settlement of its internal conflict.

Pancho Villa responded to American recognition with hysterical charges that Carranza had sold out to the gringos in return for an American loan. Gathering the remnants of his army, on 9 March 1916 Villa attacked the town of Columbus, New Mexico, killing eighteen Americans and wounding eight others before being driven off by American cavalry.[34] Realizing that failure to respond quickly to the Columbus raid would invite political attack and might encourage Villa to try again, Wilson convened the cabinet on 10 March to discuss the matter. Everyone agreed that Villa must be pursued into Mexico, although there was disagreement about whether Carranza's permission should be sought before an expedition was sent. Finally, cabinet members decided that because Carranza might refuse if permission were asked before the expedition marched, the only logical course "was to send the expedition and convey a broad intimation to Carranza that the American government would be grateful if he would kindly close his eyes to the requirements of diplomatic etiquette."[35] A short statement issued to the press after the meeting announced the expedition in pursuit of Villa and assured the Mexicans that the United States did not mean to affront Mexican sovereignty.[36]

Carranza's response to this announcement was immediate. There was, he declared, "no justification for any invasion of Mexican territory by an armed force of the United States, not even under the pretext of pursuing and capturing Villa to turn him over to the Mexican authorities." The clear implication of this message seemed to be that the Mexicans would resist any American expedition, but Wilson and Secretary of State Robert Lansing decided that it had been issued only for political reasons and could be ignored. On 15 March 4,000 soldiers, led by General John J. Pershing, entered Mexico in pursuit of Villa.[37] In subsequent months the expeditionary force was increased to almost 10,000.

The Pershing expedition, yet another form of intervention, was no more successful than others Wilson had tried. The American forces failed to find Villa, and Carranza's troops converged on the American column. On 21 June a clash occurred at Carrizal in which nine Americans and thirty Mexicans were killed, twelve Americans and forty-three Mexicans wounded, and twenty-five Americans captured. The next day Wilson confessed to House that he might have made "an error of judgment" in not withdrawing the American forces as soon as it was obvious that Villa had escaped.[38] Nothing indicated that he believed the sending of the expedition had been a mistake in the first place, and indeed in the days after the Carrizal incident the president seemed to be moving toward full-scale war with Mexico, mobilizing almost 130,000 National Guardsmen and dispatching 30,000 regulars to the border area in the largest concentration of American forces since the Civil War.[39]

Certainly sending Pershing had been politically expedient, for the administration's Mexican policy had been under attack by Republicans as weak, and the situation in Congress was so volatile that inaction might have sparked an uprising.[40] Even more important, Wilson genuinely believed that the Pershing expedition did not constitute intervention, and he was confident of his ability to prevent it from turning "into intervention of any kind in the internal affairs" of Mexico. "On the contrary," he insisted, the expedition was "deliberately intended to preclude the possibility of intervention."[41] Obviously he had not learned that his definition of intervention as conquest was unacceptably narrow to Latin Americans, nor had he grasped the more important point that interference of any kind whether called intervention or not would be met with fierce opposition. Behind his dedication to putting himself and the nation at the service of others was a strong belief in the superiority of America. To serve "the lowest of human beings," it was necessary to go down to his level and "give him a boost."[42]

Nevertheless, the Carrizal incident shocked Wilson just as the Mexican resistance at Veracruz had done, and he looked for a face-saving way out of the mess. When Carranza released the American prisoners, Wilson took the opportunity to forward to Mexico Secretary Lansing's suggestion for the creation of a joint commission to resolve the immediate crisis and to draft agreements on the future status of the border regions. Carranza regarded even this proposal as interference in Mexico's affairs but agreed reluctantly to reduce the risk of war. The joint commission met from September to mid-February of 1917 without tangible results, and when Pershing's troops were called home in early February because of growing tensions with Germany, the commission quietly expired. It had, however, fulfilled its main purpose.

At the end of February 1917 a minicrisis flared up briefly when the British turned over to the American government an intercepted cable from German Foreign Secretary Arthur Zimmermann to the Mexican government proposing a German-Mexican-Japanese alliance in the event of war between the United States and Germany. Zimmermann suggested that Mexico might thereby win back the territories lost to the United States in 1848; but the Mexican government rejected any part in the fantasy, and no one in the United States took the matter seriously except as evidence of Germany's hostility to the United States.[43] By this time the European crisis had made Mexico a secondary concern to most Americans.

But not to everyone. For American businessmen with interests in Mexico, especially oil interests, in 1917 Mexico became an even more urgent problem because of the adoption in February of a new constitution that permitted compensated expropriation of surface lands and reserved subsurface minerals for Mexican nationals or for those foreign companies that renounced the protection of their home governments. American oilmen demanded that their government shield them from the operation of these provisions. Secretary of State Lansing was sympathetic to their desires, but Wilson was not. He had never been willing to act in Mexico for purely commercial reasons, and when Carranza suggested that companies already exploiting oil claims in Mexico might be allowed to continue unimpeded, Wilson extended full de jure recognition to Carranza's government instead of intervening. Efforts by oilmen the following summer to promote a military expedition to seize the Mexican oilfields were likened by the president to the German invasion of neutral Belgium. "If we could not get the oil in a peaceful manner from Mexico," he instructed a State Department officer, "we would simply have to do without."[44]

The most that Wilson would do for the oilmen was to instruct the American ambassador to warn Carranza against arbitrary confiscation, but he specifically admitted the right of compensated expropriation "for sound reasons of public welfare." As for Mexico's internal affairs, he told a group of Mexican editors, they were "none of our business."[45] The oilmen had succeeded in doing what two failed military expeditions had not—in convincing the president to refrain from further meddling in Mexico's affairs. Whether they had convinced him of the unwisdom of such policies in general remained to be seen.

In autumn 1919 Republican Senator Albert Fall of New Mexico confirmed Wilson's determination not to interfere further in Mexico by attempting to pressure him into intervention. A partisan Republican and ally of oil interests, Fall attempted in a series of hearings to show that

Carranza's government was tainted by "bolshevism" and linked to such "left wing organizations" in the United States as the American Federation of Labor.[46] In a hysterical atmosphere engendered by a postwar "Red Scare" in the United States such ridiculous charges frightened some people, including Secretary of State Robert Lansing, but Wilson, despite a paralytic stroke suffered on 2 October 1919, was firm. Summoning Fall to his sickroom on 5 November, he made it clear that he would not be pushed into intervention, and early in 1920 he fired Lansing, partly because of the secretary's sympathy with intervention. For the rest of his time in office Wilson, despite new outbreaks of violence in Mexico, remained steadfastly opposed to any form of intervention.

In retrospect the complaints of oilmen from 1919 to 1920 were clearly disingenuous. Between 1914 and 1920, regardless of all the problems of doing business in Mexico, American oil investments increased from $85 million to $200 million. Yet even if their alleged disasters had been real, it is unlikely that Wilson would have been sympathetic. As Mark Gilderhus has pointed out, Wilson acted most dramatically in Mexico "when convinced that he shared common goals with the Constitutionalists."[47] By 1920 he could no longer believe that American intervention would benefit the cause of progress in Mexico instead of the selfish interests of businessmen; hence, ironically, he could no longer justify intervention to himself. He gave up the policy not because he had decided it was mistaken or ineffective but because its support by greedy men had corrupted it and made it unacceptable.

Wilson's Mexican policy did not become an unmitigated disaster because he prudently refrained from committing large forces to a militarily unpromising situation and because, despite his sometimes insensitive approach, his aims and those of the Constitutionalists were fundamentally similar. In Haiti and the Dominican Republic, however, he found the temptation to intervene equally strong and the restraints fewer.

American involvement in Haiti had been minimal before 1909 because the island's French-speaking black population had stronger ties to France than to the United States. Fearing that an excellent harbor on the island's north coast, the Môle St. Nicholas, might become a French or a German naval base as payment of part of Haiti's large foreign debt, President Taft had urged American businessmen to invest in the island, but they were reluctant to do so because of political instability.

Wilson and Bryan were even more concerned about the Môle St. Nicholas because the Panama Canal was to open in 1914, and France and Germany were now saying that they wanted to share in a foreign customs-control arrangement in Haiti similar to that run by the United

States in the Dominican Republic since 1905. The new administration failed to secure a pledge from the Haitians not to sell the harbor; and despite the beginning of war between France and Germany in Europe, Wilson continued to regard rumors of "sympathetic cooperation" between them in Haiti as plausible and "sinister."[48]

Why the American leaders should have given credence to such nonsense is a mystery. Perhaps they were naive, or perhaps their belief simply allowed them to find a reason to try to do what they wanted to do anyway: set Haiti on the road to democracy and constitutionalism. People are most likely to feel a moral obligation to relieve the sufferings of others, writes Thomas Haskell, when they not only have the means to intervene but also when "the relevant techniques are so familiar that not to use them would stand out as an abnormality, a suspension of expected levels of carefulness."[49] By 1914 the United States, with its easy victory over Spain in 1898 and its growing economic strength, was becoming habituated to exercising the dominance over the Western Hemisphere that it had long claimed. In Haiti as in Mexico the temptation to use that power for the curing of evils and the promotion of assumed universally applicable reforms was irresistible. Indeed the failure to act would have seemed to this generation "an abnormality." Few Americans doubted that the United States could remake the hemisphere in its image or questioned the wisdom of doing so.

Haiti, torn by incessant revolutions and chronically impoverished, drew Wilson's and Bryan's concern like a magnet. During 1914 and 1915 they urged a series of Haitian governments to accept an American customs-control arrangement and were baffled when their offers were rejected. When Bryan reported new rumors of Franco-German intervention in early 1915, the president lost patience. Ordering the navy to plan for a landing by the marines, he told Bryan, "I think . . . that it is evident we shall have to take a very decided stand with the government of Haiti."[50]

Delayed for a few months by renewed negotiations, the final crisis came in July 1915 when Haitian president Vilbrun Guillaume Sam massacred nearly two hundred political prisoners and was then himself torn to pieces by a mob that pursued him into the French embassy. "I suppose there is nothing for it," said a horrified Wilson, "but to take the bull by the horns and restore order."[51] Four hundred American sailors and marines under the command of Rear Admiral William B. Caperton quickly occupied Port-au-Prince and controlled the rest of the country. A puppet government, functioning under the authority of a Haitian-American treaty signed in September 1915 and a new constitution imposed in 1918, governed Haiti for the next decade. It brought honest government, fiscal order, and the construction of new roads, schools, and sewers; Haitians' standard of living was higher than it had ever been before. Yet the Americans could not force the Haitians to be democratic, and the racism of the occupying forces poisoned their good works. Intervention did indeed bring order but not the democratization that had been Wilson's more basic goal.[52]

As in Haiti, so in the Dominican Republic. The United States had overseen the Dominican customs service since 1905 and assumed that fiscal stability would assure political order, but the 1911 assassination of the Dominican president brought the orderly period to an end. The country was under a provisional government when Wilson took office. Rashly, Secretary Bryan agreed to send observers to supervise congressional elections in 1913, believing once again that the maintenance of constitutional forms would solve all problems.[53] Instead the congressional elections worsened the situation because they produced a congressional majority opposed to the provisional president, who refused to give up his office. Frustrated, his opponents prepared for rebellion, and the provisional president asked the American customs service to divert money from the payment of foreign debts to allow him to build up his forces and keep order.

American policy now began to sink into a bottomless swamp. The American receiver general of customs reported that with the provisional government blockading its own ports to prevent supplies from reaching the rebels, customs revenues were plummeting; meanwhile the venal American minister encouraged the provisional president in hopes of securing banking concessions for friends in the United States. The receiver's report, said Wilson with considerable understatement, revealed "a distressing state of affairs."[54] When the provisional president ignored Bryan's call for a cease-fire and conducted a rigged election that confirmed his power, the situation worsened.

Within the State Department experts searched for some policy that might clear the tangle. Eventually they recommended that the United States send to the Dominican Republic a special delegation whose task it would be to arrange a cease-fire and to set up machinery for American-supervised elections. Once those elections took place, Wilson wrote in his instructions to the peace commissioners, "the Government of the United States would feel at liberty thereafter to insist that revolutionary movements cease and that all subsequent changes in the government of the republic be effected by . . . peaceful processes."[55]

Under the guns of American warships sent by the president to supervise the peacemaking process, the "Wilson Plan" was put into effect in autumn 1914; and a new president, Juan Isidro Jiménez, was elected in December, just as the *New York World* was embarrassing the administration with a series of articles alleging corruption on the part of the American minister to the Dominican Republic.[56] Bryan now proclaimed that "the election having been held and a Government by the people having been established, no more revolutions will be permitted."[57]

The assumption behind that arrogant declaration, that the Dominican Republic would pose no more problems for the United States, proved wrong during 1915 and 1916. The State Department pressed the Dominicans to accept American supervision over their internal finances as well as over the customs service, but the Dominican congress threatened to impeach President Jiménez if he agreed to any such program. In failing health and unable to satisfy either his congress or the Americans, Jiménez resigned in May 1916. Secretary Lansing seized the excuse to land 600 marines and sailors and to begin a full-scale military occupation of the country. In November, Wilson, "with deepest reluctance," approved the State Department's plan to impose a military government on the Dominican Republic. It was, the president concluded, "the least of the evils in sight in this very perplexing situation."[58]

Although Wilson played a relatively small personal role in shaping American policy in either Haiti or the Dominican Republic, actions there bore the stamp of his ideas. Benevolent motives, backed by seemingly unlimited force, tempted the Americans to intervene where they were not wanted and where they did not understand the situation. Moreover, they sought to force peoples to become democratic, a task that proved beyond the ability of even the strongest military expedition. Security concerns and economic interests played only small parts in determining this policy; indeed, its main motive was genuine, albeit patronizing, benevolence. Its result was a dangerous, destructive, and ultimately unsuccessful moral imperialism. "If the U.S. were measured by its intentions in Latin America," concludes one historian, "there would be statues of Woodrow Wilson in virtually every capital"; but of course it is deeds, not intentions, for which men are remembered, and Wilson, like his compatriots, had not yet learned the bitter lesson that some intentions cannot be realized.[59]

The Wilson administration's dream of spreading constitutional democracy and economic progress was not confined only to Latin America. Similar motives guided its policy in Asia, but distance forced it to be more restrained.

One place where it could and did act, however, was in the Philippines. Secretary of State Bryan had opposed imperialism since 1898 and welcomed an opportunity to redeem his old promise to liberate the Filipinos. Wilson, on the other hand, had supported imperialism at the time of the Spanish-American War and still had no fundamental objections to a system that he believed might be used to the benefit of subject peoples. Yet his ultimate goal was always freedom and self-government for every people, and when a special agent sent to the Philippines reported that the islands were ready for much more self-government, Wilson made the report the basis of his policy. On 6 October 1913 the new American governor of the Philippines arrived in Manila and read aloud a message from the president of the United States promising that "every step we take will be taken with a view to the ultimate independence of the Islands."[60] Three years later in August 1916 the Jones Act turned that promise into law. As the president wanted, American policy was to prepare the Filipinos for independence over a long period, but the direction was irreversible.

Accomplishing similar purposes in China proved to be more difficult. Wilson and Bryan were heavily influenced in their Chinese policy by American missionaries, who believed against all reason that China was on the verge of becoming Christian and democratic.[61] Bryan strongly urged the president-elect to "seek men of *pronounced Christian character* [as ministers to] China and Japan." Wilson, agreeing, initially hoped to appoint the head of the YMCA as minister to China but eventually settled on Paul S. Reinsch, a University of Wisconsin professor who believed that the United States had a moral obligation to assist China.[62] To that end, Wilson announced on 18 March 1913 that the United States would withdraw from an international consortium of bankers that had been formed in 1911 to provide loans for Chinese development. The consortium, said the president, infringed on China's "administrative independence" because it obligated the Chinese to maintain antiquated taxes and used foreign agents to collect them. He promised that the United States would act independently to assist China in developing its resources.[63] Soon afterward, he announced that the United States would recognize the shaky Chinese republican government even though other nations were withholding recognition. He suspected that "certain great powers" preferred that China not secure a stable government, thus enabling them to extort more concessions.[64]

State Department experts and most foreigners were shocked by Wilson's unilateral changes in policy. The Japanese in particular believed that the Americans were professing concern for China only in order to expand their economic and political influence. Since the Japanese hoped to dominate China themselves, the American announcement worried and irritated them.

Further complicating the situation was the protracted dispute between Japan and the United States over land ownership by Oriental aliens in California. Prejudice against Orientals was long-standing on the

West Coast; and when Japanese farmers began to compete successfully with Americans, tension boiled over into a demand for state legislation to prohibit land ownership by Oriental aliens. Theodore Roosevelt had tried to relieve the situation by negotiating a so-called "Gentlemen's Agreement" under which the Japanese voluntarily limited immigration to the United States; but in 1913 California's Progressive governor, Hiram Johnson, saw an opportunity to build his popularity while taking a slap at the national Democratic administration at the same time. He announced his support for a bill in the California legislature declaring that aliens "ineligible to citizenship" (i.e., Orientals) would be forbidden to own land.[65]

The administration could do little about the California situation, despite angry protests and rumors that Japan was preparing for war. The federal government had no veto over state legislation and almost no political influence over the Johnson administration. Wilson sent Secretary of State Bryan to Sacramento with the "thankless task" of trying to persuade the California legislature to stop or to soften its pending legislation, but the trip accomplished nothing except to show concern to the Japanese.[66]

Upon his return from California, Bryan put off Japanese protests with soft words while the president blocked a recommendation by the Joint Board of the Army and Navy to move three gunboats from China to the Philippines. Subsequently, the administration signified its willingness to continue discussing the issue at infinite length with the Japanese and even agreed to negotiate a treaty that would have banned similar discrimination in other states. That was a remarkable offer, considering the sensitivities of southern senators about any treaty touching on racial policy, and in the end Wilson got cold feet about it. Early in 1914 he asked the Japanese for permission to delay submitting the treaty to the Senate until pending domestic legislation passed. They agreed, and shortly thereafter the Japanese government fell; by the time another renewed the request for the treaty, World War I had begun and Wilson, having become suspicious of Japanese intentions in China, had lost interest in placating them.[67]

He had good reason for his suspicions. When the war began, the Japanese invoked a 1902 treaty with Great Britain to declare war on Germany in order to seize German concessions in China. "When there is a fire in a jeweller's shop," explained a Japanese diplomat, "the neighbours cannot be expected to refrain from helping themselves."[68] With the British admitting that they could not prevent their allies from doing as they wished, it became obvious that only the United States could interpose between Japan and China.

For all their talk about acting to help China, however, American leaders had no stomach for a confrontation with Japan over this issue. The State Department informed Minister Reinsch that "it would be quixotic in the extreme to allow the question of China's territorial integrity to entangle the United States in international difficulties."[69] Several months later, as rumors began to reach Washington that Japan had delivered to China a harsh set of twenty-one demands for new concessions that would have turned large parts of China into virtual Japanese colonies, Bryan protested mildly but undermined his own protest with the admission that "territorial contiguity creates special relations between Japan and these districts."[70]

Up to this point in March 1915 American policy had been set by Bryan with the tacit consent of the president. When the Japanese replied on 21 March to Bryan's note, however, arguing that their "demands" were really only "requests" and exploiting Bryan's unfortunate "territorial contiguity" phrase to justify everything they were asking, Wilson decided to take a tougher line. Whatever the difficulties in Sino-Japanese relations, he told the secretary, the proposed requests "go too far" and "constitute a serious limitation upon China's independence of action, and a very definite preference of Japan before other nations, to whom the door was to be kept open."[71] In mid-April, after learning further details of the Japanese demands, he ordered the secretary to tell the Japanese ambassador informally that the United States regarded the demands as "incompatible with the administrative independence and autonomy of the Chinese Empire and with the maintenance of an open door to the world."[72]

Wilson's sharp change in the direction of American policy culminated on 5 May when the secretary of state handed to the Japanese ambassador a strong protest, drafted by the president, against virtually every concession then demanded by the Japanese and even against concessions that had been specifically accepted in Bryan's March note.[73] The president could not have known as he thus boldly challenged Japan that on 4 May the Japanese had decided to soften their demands as a result of an internal power struggle within the Japanese government and as a result of British protests. On 7 May these new demands were forwarded to the Chinese, and on 9 May the Chinese accepted them.

Despite this resolution of the issue, Wilson was still not satisfied. "It will not do," he wrote to Bryan, "to leave any of our rights indefinite or to seem to acquiesce in any part of the Japanese plan which violates the solemn undertakings of the nations with regard to China." Accordingly, he ordered the secretary to send to Tokyo on 11 May a strong protest drafted by Counselor Robert Lansing declaring that the United

States would not recognize any Sino-Japanese agreement that violated "the treaty rights of the United States and its citizens in China, the political or territorial integrity of the Republic of China, or the international policy relative to China commonly known as the open door policy."[74]

The American notes of May 1915 showed that Wilson had changed his mind about acquiescing in Japanese imperialism in China and was determined to speak up for the Open Door policy; but they gave no indication of what, if anything, he was willing to *do*, and they were equally vague about what he expected the Japanese to do. Understandably, the Japanese were angered by the notes but uncertain of their meaning. Since the Americans apparently did not intend to act forcefully in Asia, the Japanese assumed that the harsh language of the notes was a bluff that could be called at the appropriate moment.

Not until 1916 did the administration begin to take steps to implement a more active role in Asia. That year the State Department reversed another early policy by proposing American membership in a new international loan consortium for China. Delayed by the war until 1918 and touted by Wilson as significantly more in China's interest than the original one from which the United States had withdrawn, the 1918 consortium was in fact a tacit admission that the United States could not act alone in China in opposition to Japan.[75] The consortium was a failure both in getting the Japanese to open their concessions to other nations and in helping China, but it nevertheless represented a belated yet realistic recognition by Wilson and his advisers that there were practical limits to American power in the world.

A similar pragmatism was also evident in American-Japanese negotiations in 1917. The Japanese had been promised title to German islands in the North Pacific and to German concessions in Shantung Province of China by a secret treaty with Great Britain, and they hoped to use American entrance into the war in April 1917 as a lever to pry some recognition of these concessions out of Washington. In June, therefore, they suggested that the United States reaffirm its acceptance of Japanese influence in China, which had been endorsed by Bryan in his March 1915 note but rejected by Wilson in May of that same year. Lansing, however, denied any contradiction between the two notes. The United States, he wrote, realized that "special relations" existed between Japan and certain districts of China, but it "might . . . in the future be justified in expressing its views" about "even these districts."[76]

Obviously that answer was unsatisfactory to the Japanese, and, taking advantage of American naval weakness in the Pacific as a result of the Atlantic war, they decided to push the matter. In September 1917 they sent to the United States a special delegation headed by former foreign minister Viscount Kikujiro Ishii. He was instructed to secure an American guarantee that the United States would not attempt to influence China against Japan and that it would recognize Japan's sphere of influence in South Manchuria and Inner East Mongolia; he was also to seek a treaty guaranteeing Japanese aliens resident in the United States the same rights as other foreign nationals. On the American side, Wilson ordered Lansing to demand that Japan give up special concessions in China and reaffirm its commitment to the Open Door policy.[77]

Although it was immediately clear that the Japanese and the American positions were far apart, neither side wanted an open break. In a series of meetings during September, October, and November 1917 Lansing and Ishii struggled to find language that would conceal disagreement under an appearance of harmony. Eventually they signed a memorandum of agreement on 2 November that reiterated both governments' support for the Open Door but declared that "territorial propinquity creates special relations between countries." It also stated that the United States recognized Japan's "special interests in China, particularly in that part to which her possessions are contiguous."[78]

Of course all of that was self-contradictory and left each side free to make of the agreement whatever it wished. Wilson claimed that "there has not only been no change of policy, but there has been a distinct gain for China," and the Japanese justified tightening their grip on Shantung in 1917 and demanding further concessions from China in 1918 on the basis of the Lansing-Ishii agreement.[79] Offensive though these actions might be to Americans, they had little choice but to accept them in early 1918 because the Bolshevik Revolution had taken Russia out of the war against Germany and opened all of Siberia to the possibility of the same sort of Japanese imperialism that was at work in China. The only hope of restraining the Japanese seemed to be to maintain friendly relations with them.

With Russia out of the war and dissolving into civil conflict early in 1918, Wilson faced yet another crisis in Asia. The British and French hated bolshevism and urged the president to support Japanese intervention in Russia, which might somehow get the Russians back into the war. Lansing, also anti-Bolshevik, endorsed their recommendation, but Wilson objected to the whole idea. Perhaps having learned from his Mexican experience, he warned that attempting "to stop a revolutionary movement with ordinary armies is like using a broom to sweep back a great sea. . . . The sole means of acting against Bolshevism is to make its causes disappear." Fair treatment of Russia would be the "acid test" of Allied commitment to principle rather than to self-interest in the war, he had argued in his Fourteen Points address in January 1918.[80] Those were sound insights, yet they meant less than they seemed to. Despite his problems in Latin America, Wilson still defined intervention only as conquest and had never clarified in his own mind what could or could not be accomplished through the use of armed force in others' internal affairs.[81] When the British and the French insisted that specific war aims could be advanced by intervention and that Japanese aggression might be thwarted by it, his opposition faded.

Ultimately, his resistance was broken by the argument that the Allies desperately needed the support on the Western Front of some 70,000 Czech soldiers who had been interned in eastern Russia before the Russians left the war but who now wanted to cross Russia on the Trans-Siberian Railroad and sail from Vladivostok around the world to France. In July Wilson agreed to send 7,000 American soldiers as part of an Allied intervention force. He insisted, however, that the Americans should stay out of Russian internal affairs and confine themselves to keeping the railroad line open. He still believed that the Japanese "had more in mind than merely assisting the Czechs," and he suspected the British and the French of wanting to turn limited intervention "into an anti-Soviet movement and an interference with the right of Russians to choose their own form of government."[82]

As Wilson feared, the intervention was a nightmare. The British and the French urged the Czechs to move west instead of east in order to try to recreate an Eastern Front, and the Japanese built up their forces to 70,000 for purposes that were vague but suspect. Perhaps fortunately for all concerned, the end of the war and the victory of the Bolsheviks in the civil war removed any justification for further intervention and cooled the enthusiasm of the Allies. Nevertheless, the Europeans did not pull out until 1919, and the Americans stayed until April 1920 to keep an eye on the Japanese. Not until October 1922 did the last Japanese troops finally leave Siberia.[83]

The Wilson administration's experiences in Asia and Latin America revealed some important features about the administration and about America. Although it is certainly true that the administration had a distinctive tone of Christian service in its policy, there is no reason to believe that this aspect of its policy was fundamentally different from what most Americans wanted. Contemporary criticisms of the administration's policy most often were that it was not active enough rather than that it was trying to do the wrong things or seeking unobtainable goals. There was, in short, a substantial consensus among Americans that Wilson's purposes in the world were desirable.

Because of that consensus Americans did not analyze their goals very deeply. Like the president, they simply assumed that other peoples would be happier and better off if they had political and economic systems like those of the United States. It did not occur to them to think that their motives might be self-interested, and they would certainly have been insulted if someone had suggested that their motive was *only* self-interest. Nevertheless, a world of capitalist democracies would have been generally safer and more congenial to the United States than a world dominated by militarism, dictatorships, and bolshevism. Experience since 1945 does not prove that a world dominated by capitalist democracies would be free of competition and conflict; but on the other hand, it does not disprove Wilson's belief that people living in such countries are generally more satisfied with their lots than those living under the other systems thus far devised by men. While Wilsonian policy thus may be faulted for a measure of selfishness, the amount was not greater than in the foreign policies of other nations, and the claim of benefit to others was sustainable.

The real weakness in Wilsonian policy, as it was exemplified in Asia and Latin America, lay in its methods. Although Wilson had written many times that democracy had to evolve gradually over generations, he was seduced by the possession of great power into thinking that the process could not only be shortened but bypassed altogether and democratic constitutionalism imposed from outside on peoples who did not want it or who in any case did not want to be told what to do by the United States. Few if any of Wilson's predecessors had had at their fingertips so much military and industrial power; neither he nor anyone else had any real understanding of what could and could not be done with it. To be sure, he foreswore intervention because he understood that it was anathema to most people around the world; but because he was also confident of the rectitude of American motives, he excluded from his definition of intervention everything except outright conquest. Ironically, his experience suggested that his original analysis of the evolutionary nature of democracy, before he experienced the temptations of power, was more accurate than his later opinions; the scholar was wiser than the statesman.

7

NEUTRALITY
AND WAR, 1914–1917

The booming of the great guns, smashing half a century of European peace in late summer 1914, could easily be heard in Paris, less than fifty miles from the lines, and sometimes, when conditions were right, the thunder was audible even in London. The weapons were those of the twentieth century, but the imaginations of the commanders were still caught in the nineteenth. As a result, the long lines of men attempting to advance and engage each other in the open were mowed down by machine guns or blown to bits by high explosives. Desperate to escape the slaughter, the soldiers burrowed into the ground, and by mid-September the moving armies had come to a halt, trapped in a web of trenches. But the killing continued. In the first month of the war, more than half a million men died. Soon, miles before they reached the lines, arriving reinforcements could smell the stench of rotting flesh that hung over the trenches.[1]

Three thousand miles to the west, across the Atlantic, the rumble of guns was inaudible, the smell of death did not hang in the air. Although the news from Europe dominated the front pages of the newspapers, to most Americans the issues that were throwing peoples and armies of England, France, and Russia into battle against Germany and Austria-Hungary seemed puzzling and irrelevant. Americans were concerned about a threatened railroad strike and worried by a slump in wheat and cotton prices as a result of the war. South of the border Mexico's incessant civil war was worrisome, too, but the opening of the Panama Canal scheduled for 15 August seemed to prove America's power to do whatever it wished in the Caribbean area. The social season was in full swing at coastal resorts. On the waters off Connecticut trials were taking place to select a yacht to defend the America's Cup against another British challenge (a contest quickly canceled by the war). And in tennis the Americans were being defeated by a talented Australian team in the Davis Cup. In short, despite the headlines, summer 1914 did not seem to Americans to mark any grand turning point in the history of the world.

The administration, of course, could not ignore the events in Europe. Decisions had to be made about the implementation of the policy of neutrality upon which everyone agreed. If there was any hope of bringing the war to an early end, it seemed essential to propose mediation quickly. Yet the president, prostrated by his wife's fatal illness and death on 6 August, was scarcely able to attend to the daily routine of his office.

Ellen Axson Wilson had been indispensable to Wilson since their marriage in 1885. Amid the pressures of academic and political life their deep love for one another had sustained him, and the realization in late spring 1914 that she was dying of Bright's disease was crushing. Day and night he sat at her side, holding her hand and willing her to live, and when she died on 6 August he was near collapse. "Whenever I tried to speak to those bound to me by affection and intimate sympathy," he told a friend, "it seemed as if a single word would open the floodgates and I would be lost to all self control."[2] In his despair, he blamed his own ambition for her death. For the next two weeks, during and after her funeral, he was hardly able to deal with routine business and in no condition to think about large and complex issues of American policy or the war.

Had Wilson been able to act quickly and decisively in the first days of the war, tantalizing hints came from Europe that American mediation might have been possible; but whatever the opportunity, he did not grasp it.[3] Perhaps, in addition to his personal crisis, he hesitated because at first he believed that the Allies were right, that they were defending values shared by Americans, and that an Allied victory would be desirable. Yet if that was his initial reaction, further study of the causes of the war convinced him that all virtue was not on one side. The military stalemate following the first Battle of the Marne in early September made it apparent that neither side could win quickly and decisively and that the only course for the United States was neutrality. He urged Americans to be "neutral in fact as well as in name . . . , impartial in thought as well as in action," so that being free of the passions of war, they could at the right moment assist the belligerents in achieving a fair peace.[4]

Wilson's advisers and the great majority of the American people all agreed that scrupulous neutrality was the only course for the United States. Aside from the self-interested reasons for neutrality—the remoteness of the war's issues from the United States, the nation's ethnic divisions, and the economic benefits of trade with both sides—Wilson believed that sooner or later the belligerents would turn to the United States for aid. They would admit, he predicted, "'You were right, and we were wrong. . . . Now, in your self-possession, in your coolness, in your strength, may we not turn to you for counsel and for assistance?' "[5] In preparation for that day, YMCA leader John R. Mott advised the president that the United States should "keep [our] moral powder dry."[6]

Of Wilson's main foreign policy advisers, Secretary of State William Jennings Bryan was probably the most genuinely neutral. He recommended that the government not only live up to all its obligations under international law but go beyond them to enforce the true spirit of neutrality. Where the law was ambiguous, as in cases involving the operation of German-owned wireless stations on American soil or the sale of submarine parts to the Allies, Bryan successfully urged the president to adopt policies that would avoid any possibility of helping one belligerent at the expense of the other. Bryan also proposed that the administration modify normal practice to discourage private loans to the nations at war. "Money," he wrote, "is the worst of all contrabands because it commands everything else," and the refusal of the United States "to loan to any belligerent would naturally tend to hasten a conclusion of the war." A ban on loans would also discourage Americans from taking sides in the conflict, he argued. Wilson agreed, and on 15 August Bryan issued a statement saying that private loans to belligerents would be "inconsistent with the true spirit of neutrality."[7]

The subsequent fate of the loan ban illustrates the perplexities and defects of American neutrality. The ban worked, and that proved to be its undoing. On the one hand it forced the warring nations—especially the Allies, who needed American goods more than the Central Powers—to pay cash for what they bought and quickly depleted their liquid assets. It soon became clear that the ban, rather than enhancing American neutrality, was actually non-neutral in that it hurt the Allies much more than the Central Powers and might, if continued, cause the Allies to lose the war. On the other hand, by restricting foreign purchases, the ban also curtailed trade and injured American farmers and manufacturers who needed to sell abroad in order to pull the economy out of a recession. Although these effects of the ban were not obvious in August even to the belligerents, within two months the administration faced a crisis as the Allies, finding their need of American goods much greater than they had initially expected, began to exhaust their liquid reserves. In October Wilson and State Department Counselor Robert Lansing agreed to modify the ban to permit American companies to extend "credits" to foreign purchasers as "a means of facilitating trade." Direct loans, which might entangle the emotions of the lenders with the fortunes of the borrowers, would continue to be discouraged.[8]

Between October 1914 and March 1915 over $80 million of such credits were extended to Allied buyers, but in spite of—or perhaps because of—the liberalization, pressure grew to drop the ban. In October 1915 Lansing, now secretary of state, argued strongly that continuing the ban would produce a catastrophic depression in the United States. The president concurred and the ban was dropped, but American bankers had apparently decided that lending to belligerents was dangerous. When the British and the French tried to float a $500 million loan in the United States in late 1915, it was a disastrous failure, with two-fifths of the bonds unsold.[9]

Lansing's role in terminating the loan ban revealed that an important change had taken place in the administration with the resignation of Bryan in June 1915. Unlike Bryan, who was fervently neutral, Lansing was increasingly pro-Allied, and perhaps even more important, he believed that the United States must maintain all its traditional international rights, regardless of changing circumstances that might make old rules impractical. A lawyer with long experience in international law and the son-in-law of former secretary of state John Foster, Lansing was well qualified to be counselor of the department, where he served from March 1914 to June 1915. Yet Wilson had little confidence in his judgment on questions of basic policy and appointed him secretary mainly because the president meant to control foreign relations himself and wanted an adviser only to take care of the details. The reversal of the loan ban showed that Lansing might nevertheless have an important impact on policy; moreover, when Wilson substituted Lansing for Bryan, the president lost the only member of his administration who had the personal stature and breadth of vision to force him to look at issues from a different perspective than his own.

The loan ban originated in the assumptions that the war did not affect American interests and that the United States could shorten it by starving it financially. As soon as these assumptions were seen to be erroneous, the policy was reversed, returning the nation to normal international practice. In the case of the British blockade of the Central Powers, however, the United States never staked out an advanced position. Thus when domestic economic and political pressures forced a retreat from initial objections to the British policy, an unneutral accommodation resulted that was pro-Allied in effect.

The issue first arose on 6 August when Secretary Bryan sent a note to the belligerent capitals proposing that for the duration of the war they agree to abide by the terms of the Declaration of London of 1909.[10] The declaration had been drafted during a conference of major powers in London in 1908–09 but never ratified by either Britain or the United States. From the American point of view it was desirable because it declared that a wartime blockade was illegal unless it actually prevented ships from entering or leaving blockaded ports and because it limited the list of contraband items that could be seized by belligerents, specifically guaranteeing that such American exports as raw materials and cotton were not to be designated as contraband.[11] Recognizing that if accepted the declaration would punch a large hole in a British blockade, the Central Powers quickly endorsed it, but the British replied that they could not adopt it without extensive modifications permitting them to confiscate on the high seas almost any goods destined for the enemy.[12]

Beginning with an Order in Council of 20 August 1914, the British had set out to use their naval superiority against the Central Powers by cutting off their access to foreign products. Keeping a keen eye on American public opinion—for they realized their own dependence on American products—the British government gradually added copper, oil, food, cotton, and other raw materials to the list of goods that could be seized by the Royal Navy when found to be destined for their opponents, even through neutral ports. Their goal was to strangle Germany economically, provided they could do so without driving the United States to retaliate.[13]

Although the United States had traditionally asserted its right as a neutral to trade freely with nations at war and although it seemingly possessed great bargaining power because the Allies desperately needed American goods, the administration found itself under immense domestic pressure to reach an accommodation with the British. Panic in financial circles was so great that the New York Stock Exchange had to be closed from 31 July to 12 December; banks faced catastrophic runs as European creditors called in loans in the United States; cotton prices fell by almost half and southern farmers demanded that the government guarantee prices; the Treasury faced a massive deficit because of declining customs revenues; and congressional elections were coming up in November.[14] The administration dealt with each of these problems on an ad hoc basis, but it was obvious that all of them would be ameliorated by an agreement with the British to restore trade.

For a month after receiving the British reply regarding the Declaration of London, State Department experts reviewed the situation and planned an American reply, drafted by Lansing in the form of a note to Britain on 27 September. "I cannot but feel," Lansing wrote in his covering letter, "that the action of the British Government calls for unqualified refusal of this Government to acquiesce in its legality." The British policy, he noted, was alarmingly similar to that which they had adopted just before the War of 1812.[15]

Colonel House, who was with Wilson when Lansing's draft note arrived at the White House, thought it was "exceedingly undiplomatic." He secured the president's agreement to defer sending it while he talked informally to British Ambassador Sir Cecil Spring-Rice.[16] At their meeting the following day, House stressed the administration's desire to avoid a confrontation with Great Britain and suggested that the whole matter might be adjusted in informal talks between Ambassador Page in London and British Foreign Secretary Sir Edward Grey. In addition, Wilson sent Lansing to Spring-Rice to tell him that if the British would accept the Declaration of London, the United States would assent to the addition of petroleum, wire fencing, and motors to the contraband list and would moreover look the other way if food shipments were cut off from the Central Powers, not by seizure at sea but by an embargo enforced by Holland, through which most of them passed.[17]

If Lansing accurately conveyed the president's position to Spring-Rice, it was, as John Coogan has pointed out, an astonishing concession of American neutral rights in the hope of avoiding conflict between the two nations. Whether one explains this, as Coogan does, as the result of Wilson's pro-Allied sentiments or sees it as a political decision intended to allay domestic discontent, the president seems to have made an extraordinary and unwarranted concession to the British on an issue of vital importance to the United States. At the very least, such an accommodation to the British blockade invited retaliation by the Central Powers, who were bound to view American policy as unneutral.[18]

It is entirely possible, however, that Lansing misunderstood the president and offered concessions that had not been authorized, which would seem to be the conclusion to be drawn from instructions sent to Ambassador Page on the evening of 28 September, after Lansing's conversation with Spring-Rice. In these instructions, as specifically modified by Wilson, Page was told to take the issue up informally with Grey but to stress "that the terms of the Declaration of London represent the limit to which this Gov't could go with the approbation and support of its people." In adding these words, Arthur Link observes with considerable understatement, "Wilson took a more advanced position than Lansing had done."[19]

Be that as it may, Lansing had done substantial damage to the American position, whether or not his words reflected the president's opinion. On 29 September Spring-Rice wrote to Grey, stressing the American desire to avoid conflict and stating that the Dutch minister had told him unofficially that the Netherlands would embargo the export of food.[20] Another month of confusing negotiations followed before the issue was resolved, but during the talks the British had a crucial advantage; they understood that the Americans wanted agreement badly. Wilson was haunted by the apparent parallels between his situation and that of James Madison in 1812 and deeply afraid that unless he could find some compromise, public opinion might force him into war as it had his Princeton predecessor.[21] With their backs to the wall, the British were determined to press this advantage as far as they possibly could, seeking, as Grey later wrote in a much-quoted passage, "the maximum of blockade that could be enforced without a rupture with the United States."[22]

Lansing's conversation with Spring-Rice became the basis for negotiations between Page and Grey during October. Grey took a hard line, arguing that as Parliament had never ratified the Declaration, the government could not put it into operation, even with secret modifications. On 21 October 1914 Wilson and Lansing bowed to this decision, withdrawing the demand for acceptance of the declaration and announcing that henceforth the United States would rely on existing international law for protection of its rights.[23]

From the British point of view this resolution of the dispute was an immense relief since traditional international law placed far fewer restrictions on the use of their navy than the declaration would have done. On the American side, however, the decision is less easy to understand. Lansing believed "that in view of the rigid attitude of the British Government further attempts to obtain an agreement on the Declaration of London would be useless," but in fact the administration had made no real effort to put pressure on London.[24] As Grey admitted later, the British had been bluffing, knowing that "it was better . . . to carry on the war without blockade, if need be, than to incur a break with the United States about contraband and thereby deprive the Allies of the resources necessary to carry on the war at all or with any chance of success."[25]

Ultimately, three considerations seem to have determined American policy. First, as Lansing explained, the British stand on blockade and contraband was solidly based on precedents of the American Civil War and could not be contested legally. Second, it would be unneutral of the United States to demand that the British give up their most effective weapon, and it was unrealistic to expect them to do so.[26] Third, as Wilson hinted to House, the issue was "of the greatest difficulty," in part because it was "under the influence of [public] opinion," which was clamoring for the opening of trade and was little concerned with what seemed to most people, as it did even to Ambassador Page, "academic and of the smallest practical consequence compared with the grave danger we incur of shutting ourselves off" from trade and "from a position to be of some service to civilization and to the peace of the world." As Page pointed out, the United States had "practically no direct commerce with Germany" and only limited trade with neutral nations bordering on Germany, but there was an extensive and rapidly growing trade with the Allies.[27] It did indeed seem pointlessly academic to press these issues to the point of a rupture of that trade when nothing practical could be gained by so doing. No one at the time could have foreseen that the Germans would be able to retaliate effectively against the United States for what they regarded as unneutral assistance to their enemies.

Following the American concession on the Declaration of London, the British government tightened its restrictions even more. There was no justification for these steps under international law, as even the British government's own legal advisers admitted, but the Americans made no general protest against the restrictions for almost two months. In the meantime, Ambassador Page dealt with cases on an individual basis and seemed almost apologetic that he needed to protest at all. Despite a clamor about the situation in Congress and complaints from shippers to the State Department, the administration did not send a general protest until 26 December 1914, and even then it vitiated its own case by admitting that "imperative necessity" might justify a belligerent's actions that would otherwise be illegal under international law. British leaders, regarding the note as no more than a "nuisance" intended for the "consumption of Congress," seized upon the "imperative necessity" phrase to justify actions that otherwise were flagrantly illegal. Far from modifying their policy, the British demonstrated their contempt for the United States by having Spring-Rice deliver to Bryan on 21 January 1915 a note accusing the American government of being dominated by pro-Germans.[28] The Wilson administration, argues John W. Coogan, thus "permitted, and in some cases encouraged, systematic British violation of American neutral rights on a scale unprecedented at the height of the Napoleonic Wars." Its policy was "simple unneutrality."[29]

In addition to the considerations already examined, the administration's negligent attitude toward neutral rights resulted from two broad, interrelated concerns. First was the conviction, widely shared by administration leaders, that although the causes of the war were complex, in general the Allies were fighting for values that were more like America's than the Germans. To permit the nation to be drawn into a conflict with Britain over merely economic issues would be an even greater mistake than Madison had committed in allowing himself to be forced into war over neutral rights in 1812. Second, Wilson and House believed that the United States must avoid involvement with the immediate issues of the war, thus enabling America to serve as a peacemaker. Just as in Mexico Wilson had been willing to sacrifice the interests of American business-men to the greater cause of justice for the Mexican people, so he was willing to endure injustices on the high seas to preserve America's sta-tus above the conflict.

Indeed, the dream of America as peacemaker to Europe antedated the war. As early as April 1913 House had begun making overtures to German and British leaders, and in May 1914 he made a special trip to Europe to promote disarmament and a general accommodation. "It is perfectly delightful," wrote Wilson on 9 July, "to read your letters and to realize what you are accomplishing," but of course the trip was ulti-mately a failure.[30] Nevertheless, neither House nor Wilson relinquished the hope of peacemaking; and on 4 August, as Europe was mobilizing, Wilson sent a message to the heads of the European governments offer-ing American assistance in the pursuit of peace.

House saw little chance of success in the first days of the war when each side was filled with patriotic optimism, but by mid-September as the war bogged down in the trenches he began to be more hopeful. Throughout the remainder of the autumn he searched diligently, work-ing through the belligerents' ambassadors in Washington, for some hint that the warring nations would consider a negotiated settlement. By January 1915, having been unable to make progress in Washington, he decided to return to Europe, partly to see at first hand what the atti-tudes of the various governments were and partly to establish what Wilson called "a channel of confidential communication" through which the belligerents could exchange messages if they chose to do so.[31] On 30 January House sailed for London aboard the *Lusitania*.

While the colonel was in Europe he lost in a competition in which he did not know he was entered. The contest was for Wilson's intimacy and trust, and the victor was a woman, Edith Bolling Galt, whom Wilson had not even met when House set sail. Wilson met Mrs. Galt, a charming widow, in March 1915 and on 4 May proposed to her; she protested that it was too soon after Ellen's death and that she did not know if she loved him. Always passionate and ever dependent upon the love of the right woman, he would not be denied. On 6 October their engagement was announced, and on 18 December they were married. House's relationship with Wilson was an early casualty of this new romance, although neither man was aware of it when House returned to the United States on 13 June. Wilson's marriage to Ellen long antedated the presidency and thus was not threatened by House's political interests; but Edith and Woodrow met while he was in the White House, and his ability to share political secrets and decisions with her became a flattering part of his courtship. Although she had never been especially interested in politics before this, she could not help but regard House as a competitor in this most important area of Woodrow's life. House, she suggested to Woodrow, was "not a very *strong* character . . . , a weak vessel," and the two men thus began to drift imperceptibly apart.[32]

While Edith and Woodrow were shaping their relationship in America, House was meeting with frustration in Europe. There had been little hope for his mission when he set out on it, and now events removed even that small hope. On the Allied side, a series of secret treaties (of which House was then unaware) were signed that extended Allied war aims to include the transfer of the Dardanelles to Russia, the Tyrol and the Adriatic coast to Italy, parts of Turkey's Middle Eastern empire to Britain and France, and German concessions in China to Britain's Asian ally, Japan.[33] Given these Allied aims, House's prospects of being able to secure agreement from the Central Powers to a negotiated settlement essentially disappeared. Moreover, the Germans contributed markedly to a deterioration of the diplomatic situation themselves by announcing on 4 February 1915 that effective 15 February German submarines would sink without warning enemy merchant vessels in a war zone around the British Isles and by suggesting that neutral vessels could avoid accidents by staying out of the zone. Although the Germans then had only twenty-two submarines with which to enforce this threat, the announcement created a crisis with the United States that overshadowed Anglo-American problems and confirmed American beliefs that the Germans were militarists with whom any compromise would be extremely difficult. From the British point of view, nothing but an outright German surrender could have been more satisfactory.

Wilson and Lansing drafted a note to Germany describing the new order as "unprecedented" and declared that the United States would "hold the Imperial German Government to a strict accountability" for damages to Americans that might result from the new policy.[34] They were correct; the policy was "unprecedented" in its implication that merchant vessels might be sunk without warning rather than stopped, searched, and seized as had been the practice with surface warships. The submarine blockade was as much outside normal international law as the British blockade of food shipments to Germany, which the American government had accepted with only minimal protest. There was, however, an important practical difference. The food blockade affected Americans very little, and other British violations of neutral rights caused only economic losses. Submarine warfare threatened American lives.

There is no evidence that anyone in the administration had considered how the threat of "strict accountability" was to be enforced. On 28 March 1915 when an American passenger, Leon C. Thrasher, was killed in the torpedo sinking of the British liner *Falaba*, the problem was raised unavoidably. Secretary Bryan suggested that any American who sailed on a belligerent-owned ship in the war zone was guilty of "contributory negligence" and joined Lansing in pointing out that any protest in the case must assert that submarine warfare was in itself illegal since submarines could not follow the rules established for surface vessels.[35] Wilson took the secretary's argument seriously, but it seemed to him that the central issue was not Thrasher's action but the principle that his death was the result "of acts on the part of German naval officers which were in unquestionable violation of the just rules of international law."[36]

Because the facts in the Thrasher case were not clear, no note was sent either then or when an American ship, the *Cushing*, was slightly damaged by a German bomb on 29 April 1915 (there were no injuries). On 1 May, however, three Americans were killed when the American tanker, *Gulflight*, was torpedoed. "I can not see how this Government can avoid making a vigorous protest," declared Lansing, but to Bryan the issue was less important than the possible result of a protest. "It is the *possibility* of *war* from which I shrink," he wrote, "& I think we have a good excuse for asking that the disputes be settled when reason reigns" after the war.[37]

Although it seems likely that Wilson would have resolved this dispute in Lansing's favor, the matter was taken out of his hands when on 7 May 1915 a German submarine torpedoed the British liner *Lusitania*, causing the deaths of 1,201 passengers and crewmembers, including 128 Americans. Horrified, Wilson evaded his Secret Service guards to spend an hour walking the streets of rainy Washington alone and then retired into virtual seclusion in the White House for the next three days while Americans speculated on what he would do. "If I could but have you at my side to pour my thoughts out to about [the crisis with Germany]," he wrote to Edith Galt, "I would thank God and take courage." To an audience of newly naturalized citizens he revealed something of his perplexity when he said, "the example of America must be the example, not merely of peace because it will not fight, but of peace because peace is the healing and elevating influence of the world, and strife is not."[38] It was not that he believed war would be a catastrophe in itself, as Bryan plainly did. He feared that by becoming a belligerent the United States would lose its moral standing and its power to contribute to a just peace.

On 11 May Wilson read a draft of a protest to Germany to the cabinet. The draft went straight to the heart of the issue, pointing out "the practical impossibility of employing submarines in the destruction of commerce in conformity with . . . the imperative rules of fairness, reason, justice, and humanity" and demanding that the German government "take immediate steps to prevent the recurrence of anything so obviously subversive of the principles of warfare."[39] Realistically or not, the president had concluded that Germany must give up submarine warfare, and he would not be deflected from that conviction by arguments from some cabinet members that the issues should be postponed until after the war or that Americans should be warned off belligerent vessels.[40] He did not say—perhaps did not fully realize—that he was putting the decision for war or peace firmly into the hands of the German government or indeed into the hands of some German captain peering through the lens of his periscope.

Bryan found that situation impossible to accept. For almost a month he urged Wilson to consider banning war zone travel or to agree to discuss the issues further with Germany or even to balance the German note with a protest to the British about their violations of international law, but the president rejected all his suggestions. On 8 June 1915 Bryan resigned in protest against a policy he believed was leading inevitably to war. Realizing that he would be vilified for quitting at a crucial moment, he told Secretary McAdoo, "I think this will destroy me; but whether it does or not, I must do my duty according to my conscience, and if I am destroyed, it is, after all, merely the sacrifice that one must not hesitate to make to serve his God and his country."[41] He had proved a better Christian than a statesman, but his departure was regretted by nearly everyone in the administration. They had come to love him for his character if not his judgment, although that was sometimes more sensible than his rivals would admit. For those whose main goal was the preservation of American neutrality, his resignation meant the loss of their one high-placed advocate. Henceforth the president, who appointed the pedestrian Lansing as Bryan's successor, plainly intended to conduct foreign affairs personally, and that meant more stress on American rights and less on maintaining noninvolvement. Bryan was right; war was increasingly likely, although a hope still remained that the United States might serve as a midwife to peace.

This search for a policy to deal with the submarine threat was revealing of the way in which Wilson reached decisions. Despite his frequently expressed enthusiasm for "common counsel," he did not arrive at conclusions through discussion. He was impatient in meetings where speakers repeated themselves, talked too long, were argumentative, or missed what he thought were the central issues. He welcomed information from knowledgeable people while he was in the process of studying an issue, but in general he preferred to receive submissions in writing rather than orally, and he disliked anyone who tried to tell him how to act. Aside from House, the president had no informal contacts with men or women who were as intelligent as he, as well informed, and who dared to challenge his ideas or even to discuss them. Like a judge in court, he listened to the testimony, heard the arguments of the lawyers, and retired to ponder his decision. Once the decision had been rendered, he tried as hard as possible to avoid hearing rearguments of the case, although he was generally very flexible regarding the details of how a policy was to be implemented. The core of his approach was that a few clear principles were at the heart of every issue, and once he had identified them, dealing with the issue required ingenuity but not additional close analysis. If he was mistaken or if he deceived himself, there was no way anyone could tell him.[42]

Bryan resigned because he realized that in the submarine case Wilson had identified as the central principle the defense of American neutral rights on the seas rather than the avoidance of war. Colonel House, who returned to the United States soon afterward, never seemed to grasp the important shift that had taken place in Wilson's thought, perhaps because it fitted in with his own growing conviction that the Allied cause was just. House believed that German militarism had to be destroyed; Wilson would have held onto neutrality if the Germans gave up submarine warfare. In the end, however, the difference between them did not matter. The future course of the United States was now up to the policymakers in Berlin.

Throughout most of summer 1915 the German chancellor, Theobald von Bethmann Hollweg, who believed that the value of submarine warfare did not outweigh the disadvantages of antagonizing the United States, was able to impose unannounced restrictions on submarines. Wilson and House, who guessed at the situation in Berlin, did not demand that the German policy be avowed publicly; but when on 19 August a German submarine torpedoed and sank the British liner *Arabic* with a loss of forty-four lives, including two Americans, the president's hand was forced. He chose, however, to work quietly through the German ambassador in the United States, Johann von Bernstorff, and the American ambassador in Germany, James Gerard. In this case he was rewarded on 28 August when the Germans announced that they would in future avoid unwarned attacks on passenger vessels and suggested their willingness to arbitrate the *Arabic* and *Lusitania* cases.[43]

The victory was brief. It soon became clear that the Germans had no intention of admitting any fault in the *Arabic* case, and an embarrassing incident revealed possible German espionage in the United States. In November and December 1915 two more British vessels, the *Ancona* and *Persia*, were torpedoed with losses of American lives, although in questionable circumstances both times. Bernstorff attempted to reduce the tension by stating on his own that Germany would pay reparations for the *Arabic* deaths. His government reluctantly accepted the promise, but the basic issue was unresolved.[44]

The strain in German-American relations created by the *Lusitania* and subsequent sinkings changed the president's attitude toward building up the army and navy. When the war began in 1914 the United States Army numbered only 100,000, by far the smallest among nations with any claim to be called great powers; even if the 112,000 reserves of the National Guard were added in, the army was only roughly the size of those of Mexico or Belgium.[45] Military and civilian leaders alike argued that this was dangerously inadequate, but until May 1915 Wilson believed that a military buildup was more likely to create than to avert trouble. A few days after the Germans announced the beginning of submarine warfare in February, however, he began to look into ways of strengthening national defenses. Two weeks after the sinking of the *Lusitania* he authorized a slow buildup of the navy; and in late July, on the same day he sent a third *Lusitania* note to Germany, he asked the army and navy to begin preparing plans for expansion. Although Wilson committed himself publicly in autumn 1915 to what was being called "preparedness" partly in order to make sure that the movement remained under his prudent control rather than in the hands of jingoes, a larger army—as opposed to a navy, which might be purely defensive—implied the possibility of intervention in Europe. To those like William Jennings Bryan, who believed that involvement in the war would be catastrophic, the president's conversion to preparedness was profoundly ominous. "The nation does not need burglars' tools unless it intends to make burglary its business," exclaimed the former secretary of state.[46]

In the meantime, the anger of American shippers over British delays and seizures of American cargoes had been building during 1915 and culminated that summer when it appeared the British might make cotton absolute contraband, thus justifying their seizing it. Up to this time the British had placated American shippers by seizing few cargoes outright, preferring to buy those they might have seized and to coerce European neutrals into refusing to transship goods to Germany rather than overtly confiscating American goods, and above all by not antagonizing the most powerful American interests. The threat of making cotton contraband, however, for the first time affected a major American export and an interest group with powerful political connections. Between October 1914 and March 1915 Americans shipped 1.75 million bales of cotton directly to Germany, and the loss of this market would cause a crash in cotton prices in the South that the Democrats could not permit. Under the circumstances the cotton issue clearly would have forced the administration, already on the verge of protesting other harassments of neutral trade, to have sent a strong note to London if the crisis with Germany had not taken priority.[47]

Recognizing the danger in the situation, the British anxiously sought a way to deprive the Central Powers of cotton without further angering the Americans. In August, after delicate negotiations to assure themselves that the American government would accept the arrangement, they announced that cotton and cotton products would become absolute contraband; but they also arranged to have British agents purchase enough cotton in Liverpool and in the United States to keep cotton prices from falling. American leaders, reassured that this economically and politically important sector of the country would not be ruined, were willing to overlook the expansion of the contraband list and to ignore the further constriction of trade with the Central Powers.[48] Indeed, by finally lifting the remnants of the ban on private loans to the belligerents in October, the administration permitted the economic ties that were linking the United States to the Allies to be strengthened.

The Anglo-American economic rapprochement also had a political side. In December 1914 Sir Edward Grey had hinted to House that Britain might be interested in a negotiated settlement of the war if the peace could be guaranteed by some sort of international organization in which the United States would take part.[49] Pressed by Grey about the issue during his European trip in early 1915, House was evasive but reported to Wilson that given the security of an international organization, the British might be willing to make major concessions on such matters as neutral rights. He and Grey continued to correspond about the idea during summer 1915, and on 22 September Grey asked directly whether the United States would join an international organization that would bind members to "side against" an aggressor or even against a nation that refused to settle a dispute peacefully.[50]

House seems to have been jolted by this question into developing a radical plan. When the president visited him in New York on 8 October he argued that although German concessions in the *Arabic* case had eliminated the opportunity for an outright break in relations for the moment, it seemed likely to him that the Germans would win the war and that when they did, "our turn would come next." He recommended, therefore, that the United States unofficially propose a negotiated settlement to the Allies on the basis of the elimination of "militarism" (i.e., land armaments) and "navalism" (naval arms), with an accompanying secret understanding that if the Germans refused to attend a peace conference on this basis, the United States would "then push our insistence to a point where diplomatic relations would first be broken off, and later the whole force of our Government, and perhaps the forst [force] of every neutral, might be brought against them." The president, House recorded, was "startled" by the suggestion but "seemed to acquiesce by silence." The whole monologue had taken twenty minutes.[51]

Although Wilson subsequently gave qualified approval to this strange scheme, it appears that he, House, and Grey were pursuing three different purposes. House had become overtly pro-Allied and wanted the United States in the war against the Central Powers. Grey seems to have been less concerned with that than with securing binding promises that the Americans would cooperate in maintaining the peace in the future. Wilson was principally interested in mediation and saw House's scheme as one possible device to promote that end.[52] As was often the case with House's grandiose but vague projects, those who "seemed" to him to consent, either by silence or by general affirmation, did not always see things as he did.

Armed with his proposal, House set out for London on 28 December to win the assent of the Allies to the first phase, and on 22 February 1916 he and Grey initialed a memorandum stating that the United States would call a peace conference. If the Germans refused to attend, the United States would "probably" (Wilson's addition to the proposal) declare war on them. If the conference failed, the United States would "probably" (another Wilson amendment) enter the war on the Allied side.[53]

Notwithstanding the strangeness of the idea that an unofficial representative of the president of the United States should be promising that the United States might go to war, the House-Grey Memorandum contained both less and more than met the eye. It meant less than it seemed because Wilson did not have the power to declare war without the approval of Congress (as of course he knew) and because although the Allies were pleased that the Americans seemed to be coming around to their side, they did not want a negotiated peace that would inevitably fall far short of securing their secret war aims.[54] On the other hand, the memorandum was more important than it seemed because it was the first official declaration by President Wilson that he believed the United States should abandon its political isolationism and take an on-going part in the settlement of worldwide issues.[55] Rather than being a declaration of support for the Allies, as House intended, in practice the memorandum was an announcement that the United States would try to promote a negotiated settlement on compromise terms that could assure a lasting and stable peace. That was important, to be sure, but it was less than the Allies hoped to secure; thus it is no wonder that they never invoked the terms of the memorandum.

Even if they had, Wilson was hardly in a position to intervene in any way in the European conflict in spring 1916. Lansing believed that Senator William J. Stone, chairman of the Foreign Relations Committee, had pro-German sympathies; and in the House, Democratic leaders were instrumental in introducing the McLemore Resolution, calling upon the State Department to warn Americans against traveling on any armed ship. Only by the most strenuous efforts was the administration able to secure the defeat of the McLemore Resolution and an even more restrictive one introduced by Thomas P. Gore in the Senate, which called for the denial of passports to Americans traveling on belligerent-owned vessels.[56] If the president was thinking of abandoning isolationism, obviously many Americans, especially in his own party, were not.

From the German point of view, the defeat of the Gore-McLemore resolutions was no disaster. The issue showed, as Bernstorff reported, that "the American people have expressed themselves through their chosen representatives against a war with Germany." The attack by Pancho Villa on Columbus, New Mexico, on 9 March 1916 further distracted Americans and improved the German situation.[57] Nevertheless, Germany very nearly threw away all of these advantages when on 24 March a German submarine torpedoed the channel steamer *Sussex*, killing eighty passengers and injuring four Americans. In the face of overwhelming evidence, the Germans denied their responsibility for the sinking, and Wilson and Lansing finally informed them on 18 April that unless Germany immediately gave up submarine warfare, the United States would break off diplomatic relations.[58]

Receipt of the American ultimatum in Berlin sharpened a long-standing conflict between civilians and the military for control of policy. Military leaders argued that submarine warfare was the only way to defeat Britain. Without it, they insisted, they would be faced with a war of exhaustion, cut off from supplies of food and raw materials, forced to fight defensively, and doomed to defeat. The civilians replied that continuation of the submarine attacks would certainly bring America into the war and that even if that had no military importance, full commitment of American resources would enable the Allies to prolong the war indefinitely and assure German defeat. Neither course seemed to promise victory, but in the end the Kaiser decided that immediate war with America was more dangerous than a restriction of submarine warfare. On 3 May the German government handed to American Ambassador Gerard a note declaring that henceforth German submarines would be instructed to follow international law regarding visit and search (that is, no submerged attacks on merchant vessels would take place) and that the German government also expected the United States to insist that the British adhere to international law in their maritime policy.[59]

Wilson and Lansing were delighted by the "*Sussex* pledge" but outraged that the Germans should try to tie their concession to a demand that the Americans put pressure on the British. "Responsibility in such matters is single, not joint or conditional, absolute, not relative," declared the president.[60] Despite the abrupt and almost hostile tone of his reply, however, the German government accepted it, and German-American relations improved during summer 1916 to a degree of warmth they had not had since the initiation of submarine warfare in early 1915.

At the same time, Anglo-American relations worsened. Even before the *Sussex* pledge American public opinion had been outraged at the brutal suppression of an Irish rebellion during spring 1916, and Wilson believed that the Allies were unreasonably delaying the peace conference promised in the House-Grey Memorandum. More serious still was the meeting of an Allied Economic Conference in Paris in June 1916, ostensibly to coordinate measures of economic warfare against the Central Powers. Lansing warned the president, however, that the meeting was also planning postwar discrimination against the trade of both the Germans and the present neutrals, including the United States.[61] When in July the British added to these long-range plans a "blacklist" of eighty-seven American firms that they believed were trading with the Central Powers and ordered British subjects not to deal with them, Wilson declared it was the "last straw" and considered "asking Congress to authorize [him] to prohibit loans and restrict exportations to the Allies."[62]

In fact matters did not go that far, but the administration's drift toward the Allied side was checked. The president said publicly in a speech to the League to Enforce Peace on 27 May 1916 what he had long thought, that as long as the war continued, "our . . . rights as a nation, the liberties, the privileges, and the property of our people" would be "profoundly affected." It was essential, he believed, that the war should be "brought to an end" and that the United States, as "participants,

whether we would or not, in the life of the world" should become partners "in any feasible association of nations formed in order to realize
these objects and make them secure against violation."[63]

In the minds of some of Wilson's advisers the president's leadership in seeking a solution to the European conflict was mainly important for the coming presidential election, but its actual significance was
far broader.[64] He was both warning Americans that they could no longer
count on the oceans to give them security from foreign crises and beginning to take a much more aggressive role in peacemaking. Although in
his speech to the League to Enforce Peace he carefully refrained from
commenting on the causes of the war and did not suggest specific terms
upon which it might be ended, he had nevertheless made evident his
belief that it was having a serious effect on the United States and suggested that Americans had a right to insist upon its speedy termination.
He hoped that by stressing America's concern, he told House, he would
make it "very hard for the Allies to reject [American mediation], as well
as for Germany."[65]

If he hoped that his speech would draw an invitation to mediate
from either side, he was disappointed. With a large part of the American army either fruitlessly pursuing Pancho Villa in northern Mexico or
guarding the southern border against other possible raids, the belligerents paid little attention to the president's veiled suggestions about intervention. To the frustration of Wilson and House, the Allies rejected
American mediation. The Germans, for their part, were no more enthusiastic, but they were able to delay their reply until it was evident that
the Allies had spurned the offer, whereupon they hinted that they
might be receptive, thus shifting the blame for rejecting the initiative to
their enemies.[66]

The *Sussex* pledge seemed to show that Wilson's policy of firm but
patient negotiation had been successful and enabled him to claim during the forthcoming 1916 presidential campaign that his diplomacy had
reduced the risk of war. Facing no challengers within his own party and
with a strong record of domestic reform that had attracted the support
of many of Roosevelt's old Progressives as well as others even farther to
the Left, the president seemed to be in an extremely strong position. Yet
Wilson was fully aware of how delicate was the arrangement he had
reached with Germany, how explosive were relations with Mexico, and
how tense was the situation with Britain. To a large extent his political
future depended upon nations and events over which he had little or no
control. The confident campaign slogan "he kept us out of war" might
all too easily prove a mockery.[67]

On the other side, the Republicans, who had seemed in a fratricidal mood early in 1916, had closed their ranks by June, rejected Theodore Roosevelt's bid to return to party leadership, and chosen their strongest possible candidate, Charles Evans Hughes. Hughes, like Wilson, was a man of impeccable integrity who had built an attractive record as reform governor of New York and as leader of the liberal wing of the Supreme Court, upon which he had served as associate justice since 1910. Under pressure by midwesterners who knew the isolationist mood of the heartland, the Republican convention adopted a platform that called for a strengthened military but declared its support of "strict and honest neutrality." Given the volatility of the international situation and Hughes's potential to attract progressive Republicans away from Wilson, the outcome of the election might well turn on chance events or on the ability of the Republicans to bring out their superior numbers.[68]

Hughes, however, had trouble defining his campaign. As a progressive, he admired much of what Wilson had done domestically but could not say so without raising questions about why he was running and antagonizing conservatives who were contributing generously to his finances. Nor could he call for a more militant foreign policy without alienating German-Americans who were vital to Republican hopes in the Midwest. And in California, where Republicans were bitterly divided between conservatives and progressives, he allowed himself to be captured by the conservatives, thus infuriating Governor Hiram Johnson and the progressives. "I . . . have a sort of sympathy with the man," Wilson admitted. "He dare not have opinions: he would be sure to offend some important section of his following."[69]

In the campaign Wilson not only defended his domestic record but promised to go further toward reforms that would enhance opportunities for all Americans, and he urged members of the Progressive party to enlist under his banner. He defied and denounced German-American extremists as disloyal and promised that by standing resolutely against violations of American rights he would preserve the peace. Pointing at Theodore Roosevelt, whose bellicose pronouncements had alarmed many people, he warned that the Republicans would abandon neutrality and drag the nation into war. In the end, Wilson, the "peace" candidate, defeated Hughes, the "war" candidate, by 277 electoral votes to 254, but it was two days after the election before that result was certain. The Democratic appeal for peace, added to the administration's popular domestic record, had won strong support especially in the South and West and had overcome Republican advantages in numbers of registered voters and campaign finances.[70]

Yet while Americans were congratulating themselves for their success in staying out of war, economic forces were daily entangling the nation more deeply in the Allied war effort. By late 1916 nearly sixteen hundred British agents were purchasing goods in the United States at the rate of $83 million a week. "Fully 40 percent of British war expenditures," concludes one historian, "was devoted to North American supplies."[71]

For the administration, Allied economic dependence on the United States was both threat and opportunity. In summer 1916 Wilson worked out legislation with congressional leaders that restricted or prohibited British imports into the United States in retaliation for the British blacklist, that made it possible to stop the clearance from American ports of any ship discriminating against American firms in accepting cargo, and that provided for a substantial expansion of the navy to a size just a little smaller than the British navy.[72] That autumn, once he was sure of reelection, he began to move to urge the belligerents to attend a peace conference and to use American economic power to put pressure on the Allies to that end.

About 25 November 1916 Wilson completed a draft of a note that he intended to send to the belligerents. It pointed out the great damage the war had done to the neutrals, argued that the public peace terms thus far announced by leaders on both sides were very much alike, and called upon both sides to state their specific aims as a prelude to a general peace conference.[73] Anticipating that the Allies would continue to resist this call, he also arranged to have the Federal Reserve Board issue a strong statement urging member banks not to purchase Allied securities, but he also added a carrot to the stick by sending a message to Grey through House "that he could be sure that the United States would go any length in promoting and lending her full might to a League for Peace."[74]

While he was still working on the note the German government announced on 12 December that it was willing to discuss peace terms. Lansing suspected that the German move was a trick intended to put the blame for rejecting a peace conference on the Allies, but House urged Wilson to go ahead with his proposal, regardless of the reasons behind the German move.[75] The danger, Wilson realized, was that unless he acted quickly, the Allies might reject not only the German proposal but any conference.[76] On 18 December 1916, therefore, he sent off his note.

House had not seen the note before it was sent. When he had examined the first version of it he had warned Wilson against saying that he did not understand Allied war aims. That statement, he thought, would infuriate the British, who believed they were fighting against German militarism. Wilson had seemed to agree, but in the final note the idea reappeared in the statement that the aims of the two sides were "practically the same." Now that it was too late House characteristically said nothing about the mistake, but in his diary he lamented, "that one sentence will enrage [the Allies]."[77]

He was right. It would have been much wiser to have stressed the battlefield stalemate as the reason for proposing a peace conference. The British in particular were outraged that Wilson seemed so insensitive to their high ideals, and there was a storm of condemnation in their press. The French reaction was more restrained but nevertheless angry. Neither government was willing to reply to the American proposal until they could confer officially later that month.

Lansing, like House, had anticipated a negative Allied response to Wilson's note. He was convinced by now that the United States must enter the war on the Allied side and at the very least that it must not antagonize the British and the French. Accordingly, the secretary took it upon himself to issue a statement to the press on 21 December 1916 saying that the president's message was not a "peace note" but an effort to seek clarification of their goals from the belligerents because the United States was "drawing nearer the verge of war."[78]

The statement set off a war scare on Wall Street and severely damaged any chance that the Germans would take the note seriously. Wilson was furious and considered demanding the secretary's resignation; however, he contented himself with ordering Lansing to issue another statement explaining that he had not intended to undermine American neutrality. The secretary did as he was told, but in private he assured the British and the French ambassadors that the United States would never side with German militarism and that they were therefore free to state their most extreme peace terms without fear of American opposition. The president was never told about these extraordinary conversations, nor was he informed that Colonel House in New York was saying similar things to his British friends.[79]

It is thus clear in retrospect that Lansing and House were following one policy, Wilson another. The president really hoped for a peace conference over which he might preside. His advisers had concluded that only an Allied victory, achieved with American support, could secure the sort of peace the president wanted. Although there was never much hope that Wilson's initiative would succeed, Lansing and House doomed it utterly and by encouraging the Allies to state extreme peace terms that could be imposed only through victory essentially forced the Germans toward unrestricted submarine warfare.

That so serious a difference should have existed on this vital issue between Wilson and his advisers was partly the president's own fault.

His characteristic reluctance to discuss the evolution of his policies or to explain in detail the objectives of his actions left House and Lansing free to interpret his purposes as best they could. Moreover, the subtle and gradual exclusion of House from Wilson's innermost circle, which began about this time and may have partly resulted from disagreements over how to handle the peace initiative, had long-lasting and important implications. If House were shunted aside, only Wilson's wife, Edith, his secretary, Joseph Tumulty, and his doctor, Cary T. Grayson, had access to the president on a daily basis. None of them had the breadth, knowledge, and political sophistication of House. Wilson, already too isolated, became even more so.[80]

The chilly reception given the president's December note led him logically to the next step of suggesting reasonable peace terms himself. His idea, as he outlined it to House on 3 January 1917, was to propose "what, in his opinion, the general terms of settlement should be, making the keystone of the settlement arch the future security of the world against wars, and letting territorial adjustments be subordinate to the main purpose."[81] Without further consultation with anyone, he then sat down and wrote out a draft of a statement to be delivered to the Senate, completing it on 11 January 1917. The next day he read it to Lansing and Senator William J. Stone, chairman of the Foreign Relations Committee. On 22 January he delivered to the Senate his address calling for "a peace without victory" based upon the "equality of nations," acceptance of "the principle that governments derive all their just powers from the consent of the governed," recognition that rights of security, religion, and "of industrial and social development" must be "guaranteed to all peoples who have lived hitherto under the power of governments devoted to a faith and purpose hostile to their own," adoption of rights of access to the sea for all peoples and of freedom of the seas, and the limitation of armaments. Such a peace, he declared, would draw the approval of the American people, and he was confident the United States would "join the other civilized nations of the world in guaranteeing the permanence of peace upon such terms." The drama of the address lay not only in its apparent renunciation of traditional American isolationism but in its bold assertion that the horrors of modern war gave neutrals as well as belligerents moral justification to demand its end.[82]

On the eve of Wilson's address Ambassador Walter Hines Page had cabled from London, warning that seeming to equate the aims of the Allies and the Central Powers would infuriate the British and suggesting that "peace without conquest" would mean the same as "peace without victory" but would avoid this danger.[83] Wilson ignored his advice, and as Page predicted, the speech was much criticized in England and in France, but ultimately that did not matter. On 6 January 1917, at an imperial conference, the Kaiser had approved unrestricted submarine warfare in a zone around the British Isles. Believing that the Americans could not become important militarily before England was starved into submission, the Germans decided to risk war with the United States. On 31 January Ambassador Bernstorff delivered to the State Department a note announcing the new policy. No ships, warned the note, including those of neutrals, would be spared.

To Wilson, the German announcement came as an "astounding surprise." Even after the German government had reached its decision, its foreign minister had assured the American ambassador that such a thing was impossible; and the president could not imagine that the Germans would so spurn his peace proposal. Nevertheless, he tried to keep his balance. Although he announced to Congress on 3 February the breaking off of diplomatic relations with Germany, he told cabinet members that "he didn't wish to see either side win,—for both had been equally indifferent to the rights of neutrals—though Germany had been brutal in taking life and England only in taking property."[84] He also reiterated his belief that "probably greater justice would be done if the conflict ended in a draw," which Lansing dismissed as intended merely to "draw out arguments" from cabinet members. But in fact Wilson still believed, as he told House, that "it would be a crime for this Government to involve itself in the war to such an extent as to make it impossible to save Europe afterward."[85] After breaking off relations with Germany, the president moved very reluctantly toward war, proposing instead to protect American interests through a possible league of neutral nations or by the arming of American merchant vessels for self-defense.

For the British, the renewed submarine war proved devastating, with nearly a quarter of all ships that left port between January and April 1917 being sunk, and 545,000 tons lost in April alone. By then some British officials were for the first time admitting the possibility of defeat.[86] Yet for Americans the conflict was still surprisingly distant. No American ships were sunk during February and the first two weeks of March, and although many shippers refused to risk vessels in the war zone, Congress remained divided over what to do. Even Wilson's release to the press on 28 February 1917 of an intercepted telegram from German Foreign Secretary Arthur Zimmermann to the Mexican government proposing an alliance in the event of war failed to break a filibuster in the Senate against the administration's proposal to arm merchant vessels.

Bitter though he was at the defeat of the armed-ship bill, Wilson rejected House's suggestion that he demand its passage in his second inaugural address on 5 March 1917. Rather, he chose to recognize the differences that still divided Americans. "We are," he said, "of the blood of all the nations that are at war," yet "we [are] not part of it." Although the United States had been "deeply wronged upon the seas," it must not react short-sightedly to those offenses. Americans must realize that they had opportunities for service that made divisions unimportant and concentrate "upon an interest that transcend[s] the immediate issues of the war itself." That interest, he argued, was to secure a peace that would be fair and just to all concerned, a peace based upon the principles he had laid down in his "peace without victory" address in January.[87]

On 12 March, a week after the inauguration, one of the bases of Wilson's proposed peace, the acceptance of the principle that "governments derive all their just powers from the consent of the governed," was reinforced by a democratic revolution in Russia. Some members of the administration had worried earlier that Russian autocrats might find it in their interest to abandon the Allies and throw in their lot with the Germans, but this conversion of Russia to democracy reassured everyone.[88] Even this event, however, was not enough in Wilson's opinion to justify a declaration of war. It was one thing to *fight* for an extension of democracy, another to ask the country to *go* to war, even for that.[89]

The president's hesitation continued even after news was received on 18 March 1917 that the Germans had sunk three American ships in the war zone with the loss of fifteen lives. Lansing argued that the sinkings proved that "the German Government intends to carry out its announced policy without regard to consequences." Sooner or later the United States would have to recognize "that a state of war exists," but still Wilson hesitated. The sticking point, of course, was the president's conviction that a lasting, impartial peace could be secured only through the services of a neutral America, uncommitted to the national goals of either side. Shrewdly, Lansing now suggested almost as an afterthought "that the longer we delay in declaring against the military absolutism which menaces the rule of liberty and justice in the world, so much the less will be our influence in the days when Germany will need a merciful and unselfish foe."[90] The idea, although hardly original with Lansing, struck Wilson at the perfect moment. Perhaps, after all, it might be possible to defend American interests and at the same time to advance the broader ideals that he had been seeking all along.

On 20 March 1917 Wilson placed the situation before the cabinet and asked each member individually for his recommendation. With varying degrees of sorrow and distress, yet with conviction, they agreed that the time had come for a declaration of war.[91] The next day the president issued a proclamation calling Congress into special session on 2 April. Then, closing himself in his office and conferring with no one, he gradually drafted the message he would read to the legislators. Into the White House poured streams of letters advocating various policies, and delegations of concerned citizens, both pro- and antiwar, converged on Washington in hopes of influencing policy, but Wilson ignored them all. Not even Colonel House or the members of the cabinet knew what he would say.

All day on 2 April the House, almost evenly divided between Republicans and Democrats, wrangled over organizing itself, and it was not until late afternoon that its leaders could send word to the White House that they were ready to hear the president. Wilson replied that he would arrive at 8:30, and after an early supper, he set out through the misty rain falling on the crowds lining the capital's streets. In the House chamber where he would speak, every seat was filled. When the clerk of the House announced, "the President of the United States," there was a roar, followed quickly by an intense, expectant silence.

Into that silence Wilson began to speak, quietly, seemingly without emotion. The "recent course of the Imperial German Government," he said, was "in fact nothing less than war against the government and people of the United States." He recommended that the Congress "accept the status of belligerent which has thus been thrust upon" the nation. An army must be raised through conscription; taxes must be levied to pay for the war rather than passing its costs on to future generations through borrowing; money must be made available generously to the Allied governments; everything possible must be done to increase American agricultural and industrial production to support the war. Above all, the nation must commit itself wholeheartedly to the destruction of "Prussian autocracy." It must be willing, if necessary, to "spend the whole force of the nation to check its pretensions and its power. . . . The world must be made safe for democracy."[92]

The address was a stirring call, a recitation both of immediate injuries inflicted by German submarines and a declaration of a great crusade to reshape the world so that such things could never happen again. Yet, strangely, the president said also that the nation's purpose should still be the achievement of the "peace without victory" for which he had called back in January. After the emotions of the moment subsided, some people began to wonder if a serious contradiction lay in the summons to a crusade against autocracy and the vision of a peace fair to all. Wilson's attempt to yoke the two ideas was, wrote Theodore Roosevelt, "nauseous hypocrisy."[93]

Roosevelt, of course, was right in a sense. It was improbable that an impartial peace would result from complete victory by one side. More than that, it was unreasonable to urge Americans to make the world safe for democracy and to expect them to settle for a compromise peace. Yet just as in his war message Wilson linked American national interests in the freedom of the seas with an idealistic call to remake the international political order, so he did not find any inconsistency in seeking a better world through an Allied victory. The two ideas were compatible, he believed, because modern war so affected the interests of all peoples that neutrality was no longer possible. "We have seen the last of neutrality in such circumstances," he said, arguing that only when "the principles of peace" had been vindicated, meaning that "autocratic governments backed by organized force" had been destroyed and replaced by "free peoples" holding "their purpose and their honour steady to a common end" and preferring "the interests of mankind to any narrow interest of their own," could lasting peace be expected.[94] As he had throughout his career, Wilson called upon his countrymen to live up to his own high standard of duty, to give up personal, selfish interests for the common welfare. Expecting to use the leverage provided by American military and economic power to achieve victory and then to shape the peace, Wilson called upon Americans to undertake the sacrifices and to pay the price to secure "a universal dominion of right by such a concert of free peoples as shall itself bring peace and safety to all nations and make the world itself at last free."[95] It was a noble but rash challenge.

8

THE WAR, 1917–1918

When the United States entered the war in April 1917, it had already become the foremost industrial power with more than half of all world manufacturing, and it was well on its way to becoming the world's greatest financial power, its bankers having lent some $2 billion to the British and the French between 1914 and 1917. Over the next year and a half, the American government would extend nearly $7.5 billion worth of credits to the Allies.[1] Such figures made it obvious that the most important contribution of the United States to the war effort might well be to supply "the nations already at war with Germany with the materials which they can obtain only from us or by our assistance," as Wilson said in his war message.[2]

Yet the president had no intention of confining the American contribution merely to goods and money; he also declared his plan to add at least half a million men to the armed forces "upon the principle of universal liability to service." On 7 April the administration revealed the details of its scheme for accomplishing that goal. Secretary of War Newton D. Baker proposed to recruit volunteers to increase the regular army to 298,000 and to federalize a National Guard enlarged to 440,000, but his main recommendation was to create a "National Army" by drafting half a million men at once, with the likelihood of adding another half million later.[3] Junior officers for the National Army were to come initially from men trained privately between 1914 and 1917 by the Military Training Camps Association, a corporate-funded organization that had been organized partly at the urging of leaders like Theodore

Roosevelt, who thought Wilson hopelessly weak in dealing with Germany. The association was also intended to lay the foundations of an enlarged army capable of defending worldwide American interests after the war. When war was declared, the War Department also established sixteen officer training camps at army posts around the country to produce the nearly 200,000 officers needed for the immediate emergency.[4]

The vanguard of this new army, the second battalion of the Sixteenth Infantry, marched triumphantly through the streets of Paris on 4 July 1917 while a million people cheered, but officers and men alike knew that most of the marching soldiers were virtually untrained. Nevertheless, their presence was important. They were a symbol, a first response to the plea of French Marshal Joseph Joffre, who visited the United States in late April and declared bluntly, "we want men, men, men."[5]

To many Americans, the idea that American soldiers would be fighting in France was as shocking as the concept of a draft, and that was saying a good deal. A year earlier Wilson's opposition to a draft had led to the resignation of his first secretary of war, Lindley M. Garrison, but had been strongly approved by southern and western Democrats, many of whom still felt the same way in April 1917. House Speaker Champ Clark, for example, declared that his constituents saw "precious little difference between a conscript and a convict."[6] The idea that the conscript army would be expected to serve overseas was even more stunning. "Good Lord!" exploded Virginia Senator Thomas S. Martin when first informed of the plan, "you're not going to send soldiers over there, are you?"[7]

Opponents of the draft plan denounced it as the imposition of a Prussian, authoritarian system, but its supporters lauded it as a thoroughly democratic measure that would Americanize immigrants and level class distinctions. Wilson himself had shifted between these contradictory opinions, but practical and political considerations finally won him over to the draft. It was an important element in a national mobilization policy that administration leaders hoped would avoid the labor shortages in critical industries and the heavy losses of educated and talented men experienced by the British during the first two years of the war when they had depended solely on a volunteer army. A draft would also avoid the political embarrassment caused by the efforts of "the country's most visibly eligible volunteer," Theodore Roosevelt, who had proposed to raise a volunteer division made up of Ivy League students, descendants of Civil War generals, German-Americans, and blacks (with white officers) to win the war with a few dramatic gestures.[8]

In Congress and especially in the House debate over the administration's draft bill tended to divide along sectional lines, with rural areas preferring a volunteer system and urban areas favoring the draft. By the time both houses voted on 28 April, however, many proponents of the volunteer system had been persuaded that in a volunteer army the "slackers" would stay at home while the best became soldiers. "We shall have to keep an army at home to protect the country against the men left alone when the best men go to war," declared Congressman William C. Adamson of Georgia.[9] In both houses, the votes in favor of the administration's plan were overwhelming, although quibbling over details delayed final passage of the measure until 16 May. As he signed the measure into law two days later, the president explained that its central principle was that "each man shall be classified for service in the place to which it shall best serve the general good to call him."[10]

That was true, but it was not the whole truth. In reality, the draft law, like almost all of the administration's mobilization policy, was an illogical mixture of the voluntary and the compulsory, a compromise between those who welcomed the implications of intervention and those who hoped the nation would remain as it had always been. Supported largely by sophisticated, urban people who favored a strengthened national government and an active world role for the United States, the draft was made palatable to people with more traditional and rural values only by giving it a veneer of local control and voluntarism. Thus the measure was referred to as "selective service," and the president declared that it was not "a conscription of the unwilling" but "selection from a nation which has volunteered in mass." Local draft boards rather than federal bureaucrats were to decide who was drafted or deferred, yet the basic argument for the system was that the government rather than the individual must decide where each man could best serve, whether on the job or in the lines. Like it or not, Americans were finding that modern, industrialized war required sacrifices of traditional individual rights and freedoms. To those who used it so frequently in this era, the term "service" connoted both individual autonomy and the meshing of the individual into a more powerful collective unit.[11]

Recalling the sometimes violent opposition to the draft during the Civil War, federal officials awaited the 5 June national registration day with apprehension, but it went off well; nearly 10 million men registered without incident. By the end of the war the 4,648 local boards had registered 24 million men and actually drafted 2,758,542 into the armed forces.[12]

The system was not without its flaws, however. Nearly 340,000 men who were registered for the draft failed to report for duty when called;

political influence sometimes affected appointments to local boards and their decisions; almost one of every five draftees was foreign-born and frequently could not speak or understand English; blacks, at first excluded by the draft system because no one knew what to do with them, lacked the skills to justify exemptions and ended up providing 13 percent of draftees although they made up only 10 percent of the population; some pacifists, Socialists, and German-Americans resisted the draft outright.[13] Yet despite its defects and strains the system worked far better than the Civil War draft, at least for the short time the United States was in the war, thus reinforcing the confidence of those who believed it possible to fight the war without overtly coercive measures at home.

Once the draft was under way, the War Department turned next to the problem of housing the recruits. In May Secretary Baker created a Cantonment Division to construct sixteen camps provided with wooden barracks for the new National Army and an equal number of tent camps for the National Guard. In a stupendous effort, the division located thirty-two sites, rounded up 200,000 workers, and provided 30,000 tons of construction material each day so that by 1 September the new cantonments were two-thirds finished and ready to receive 400,000 men. Eventually, the government spent nearly $200 million building what amounted to thirty-two new cities of 40,000 inhabitants each. Shortly after the armistice Secretary Baker reported with justifiable pride that "in spite of the stupendous difficulties involved, the entire housing enterprise was completed practically on schedule, constituting one of the most remarkable accomplishments of the war."[14]

If housing the draftees was an enormous undertaking, supplying them was an even more awe-inspiring problem. When the war began, the army had five semi-independent supply services that competed with each other to purchase from civilian suppliers, to secure raw materials, and to find storage and transportation for their purchases. They also competed with civilian manufacturers and with the purchasing missions of the Allies. To make matters worse, the army's scanty reserves of many items had been exhausted by the American punitive expedition into Mexico in 1916. Supply officers estimated that it would take from six to eighteen months to equip a million-man army for overseas service.[15]

Since the war obviously would not await such leisurely preparations, Secretary Baker cut corners. Soon after the declaration of war he discarded the practice of advertising for bids and announced that purchases would be made on the open market with the advice of a civilian board. Baker also relied heavily on various civilian wartime agencies for help, including the Food Administration and the Railroad Administration, after the railroads were nationalized in December 1917. Above all, the army cut through red tape to obtain whatever weapons and vehicles they could find rather than insisting upon standardized equipment. The result of this improvisation was a hodgepodge of equipment that was a nightmare to maintain, and even then the American Expeditionary Force in France had to depend heavily on British and French weapons and ammunition. Charles G. Dawes, a Chicago banker who entered the military when war was declared, served as General Purchasing Agent in France and undertook to buy as many supplies as possible on the spot in order to save valuable cargo space on the trans-Atlantic crossing. Eventually, Dawes secured ten million tons of supplies in Europe despite the competition of the Allies. By these means, against all odds, the army managed somehow to feed, clothe, and supply its men and after a year of enormous delays and frustrations land them in France to fight.[16]

The navy, which was supposed to protect soldiers on their way to France and to battle aggressive German U-boats, had only about 65,000 men when the United States entered the war and was little prepared for the conflict. In February 1916 the president had called upon Congress to build "incomparably the greatest navy in the world," not as a preliminary to entering the war but because he recognized that "the peace of . . . America depends upon the aroused passion of other nations, and not upon the motives of the nation itself."[17] But building up the navy would inevitably take considerable time, and neither he nor most naval officers fully grasped the task before them.

As with the army, the first problem was men. When war began, the navy had about 60,000 enlisted men and about 4,400 commissioned and warrant officers serving on 300 ships and 130 shore stations. The draft could supply ordinary sailors, but training 26,000 new officers required the creation of training programs for enlisted men and recruits, recruitment of some merchant marine officers, and provision of special courses and an abbreviated program at the Naval Academy to train reservists and new officers. The marines, facing a parallel problem of sextupling its size in a short time, adopted equally novel and drastic expedients.[18]

Every bit as important as providing new men and officers was revolutionizing the thinking of senior officers. Secretary of the Navy Josephus Daniels had reformed the promotion system to base it on selection rather than on seniority, but the service was top-heavy with aging and rigidly conventional officers. Like other naval experts throughout the Western world, they were enchanted by the giant battleships known as "dreadnoughts" and oblivious to the revolution created by the introduction of submarines. As Admiral George Dewey put their views in November 1915, "the submarine is not an instrument fitted to dominate naval warfare. . . . The battleship is still the principal reliance of navies, as it has been in the past."[19]

When the United States entered the war in April 1917 its naval construction program was just getting under way in the wrong direction. What was needed was not a few more battleships but many smaller antisubmarine vessels. The recognition of that reality resulted largely from the efforts of the lowest ranking rear admiral in March 1917, William S. Sims. A brilliant and aggressively outspoken man, Sims, then president of the Naval War College, was chosen by Daniels in late March to go to England to confer with the British about naval coordination if the United States entered the war. Welcomed in London as a long-standing Anglophile, Sims was let in on a closely guarded secret: British shipping losses to German submarines were horrifyingly worse than had been admitted publicly. In February and March the British had lost a million tons of ships and expected that total to double by the end of April. "It is impossible for us to go on with the war if losses like this continue," senior British officers admitted frankly.[20]

Appalled, Sims recommended to Daniels that the United States immediately send as many antisubmarine vessels to Britain as possible and urged the British to maximize the effect of such vessels by adopting a convoy system, which would force the submarines to come to the destroyers rather than making the destroyers search large areas of empty ocean in hopes of finding a submarine. Senior British officers doubted that merchant vessels could maintain the tight formations and carry off the difficult maneuvers demanded by convoy sailing, but continued heavy losses forced them to try the system in May; it was an instant success. By November sinkings were down to about one-third of the April total, and construction of new ships now kept ahead of losses. During the last six months of the war the convoy system reduced losses to 1 percent of sailings. In combination with American contributions, including 120 subchasers, a substantial commitment to minelaying, and nearly 20,000 navy pilots and mechanics who operated spotting planes and bombers, the British navy gradually nullified the submarine menace.[21]

Defeating the submarine was essential to winning the war; getting American troops and supplies to Europe was equally critical. The problem was not only that submarines sank merchant vessels but even more that there were nowhere near enough such vessels. As a presidential candidate in 1912 Wilson had argued that expansion of the American merchant marine was as vital to promoting economic growth as the reduction of the tariff (American ships then carried less than 10 percent of the world's commerce), but he had little success in persuading Congress of that even after the war began.[22] Gradually, however, the administration began to win over businessmen and trade groups. The opening of the Panama Canal in August 1914 drew attention to opportunities in Latin America that American businessmen did not have the shipping to exploit and the war engrossed more and more Allied merchant ships that had previously carried American goods. In June 1916, moreover, an Allied economic conference in Paris considered plans for a postwar economic union that might exclude American products from many lucrative markets. Goaded by the administration, Congress responded to the new challenge by passing a Shipping Act that created a United States Shipping Board to own and operate a merchant fleet during the war and for five years thereafter. The point of the new legislation was not only to prepare for possible involvement in the war but also to lay a foundation for an aggressive expansion of American commerce after the war.[23]

Like many other preparedness programs, the Shipping Board was slow to start. Only after Wilson named industrialist Edward N. Hurley as its head in July 1917 did it begin to act effectively, and by then it was almost too late. Small and antiquated American shipyards, already deluged with orders from the Allies, could not build ships fast enough to have a significant impact on the war. Not until the last four months of the war did new shipyards, staffed by 300,000 people, begin to turn out really large numbers of ships—over three million tons, which by war's end made the American merchant marine 40 percent the size of Britain's. The board's inadequate wartime fleet was not American-built but was secured by seizing 700,000 tons of German ships interned in American ports when the United States declared war and by requisitioning 163 ships being built in American yards for the British.[24]

The shortage of ships meant that even as the new American army was drafted and trained, there was no way to get the men to France. By the end of 1917 only 175,000 troops had reached Europe, and draft calls had to be cut back sharply because of the backup.[25] Then early in 1918 draft calls rose again, and by the summer 10,000 men a day were on their way to Europe. The explanation for this dramatic change lay not in what the Americans were doing but in an Allied determination to provide ships at any cost in order to bring American soldiers to the front. In October 1917 a German-Austrian offensive had shattered the Italian front and captured 275,000 prisoners; in November a British offensive in Flanders cost 300,000 casualties and gained barely two miles before bogging down; and the Bolshevik Revolution in Russia led to negotiations for a separate peace and freed hundreds of thousands of German troops to take part in a huge offensive in the West in March 1918 against the British and the French.[26] Facing imminent defeat, Allied statesmen and generals implored the Americans to send "men, men, men," as Joffre had put it; and even at the cost of cutting back still more on vitally needed supplies, they made ships available to transport the Americans.

The desperate military situation also led the British and the French to propose that American units be integrated into existing Allied forces. In that way the raw troops could be trained in the field by experienced soldiers, removing the need to create a complex separate supply system for the Americans. On the other hand, Wilson believed that "England and France *have not the same views with regard to peace that we have*" and that merging American forces with those of the Allies would weaken America's influence over the peace settlement. "Nothing except sudden and manifest emergency," he ordered Secretary Baker in February, should "be suffered to interfere with the building up of a great distinct American force at the front, acting under its own flag and its own officers."[27]

The commander in chief of the American Expeditionary Force, General John J. Pershing, agreed absolutely with Wilson. Slim, erect, and imposing, Pershing looked every inch the general; moreover, he was the only American commander with recent experience under difficult conditions—in Mexico during the 1916 pursuit of Pancho Villa. In Pershing's opinion, amalgamation of his troops into Allied units would be unpopular with the American people and with the troops themselves. Most important, it would undermine the only strategy that he believed would win the war: to hold back American forces until they were massed in sufficient numbers to mount an overwhelming frontal attack on the Germans, overrunning the trenches and shattering the enemy lines. No pressure the Allies could bring to bear on him could shake him from this course.[28]

With his contempt for British and French acceptance of the trench stalemate, Pershing failed to realize that his strategy was exactly the same as the Allies had been following through three and a half years of war. They, too, had massed great armies in attempts to break through the enemy's defenses, only to be beaten back time after time by the entrenched Germans armed with machine guns, artillery, and gas. The only difference was that by the time Pershing was at last ready to attack at the end of August 1918 with a million-man army, the European belligerents were all so exhausted that the Americans stood a real chance of success. Despite monumental transportation foul-ups and heavy casualties, the first major American offensive in the Aisne-Marne sector of the front was a success. By the beginning of November, with two million

American soldiers now under his command, Pershing was confidently poised for a major part in the invasion of Germany when the German government sued for peace. At a cost of 53,000 killed and 204,000 wounded (with another 63,000 soldiers and sailors dying from noncombat causes, largely during the influenza epidemic of 1918), the Americans had made a significant contribution to the Allied victory and purchased a place at the peace conference. Yet compared to the immense sacrifices made by the Allies, the American losses were small. President Wilson would find that the British and the French did not believe he had any right to dictate peace terms to them.

American wartime experience reiterated and underscored some of the dilemmas at the heart of the progressive movement. Just as the draft with its rhetoric about voluntary service was an effort "to create an American substitute for the expanded, modern, bureaucratic State," so mobilization attempted to create voluntarily the same sort of universal commitment of resources and efficiency that European governments had achieved only through centralized control and compulsion.[29] Many conservatives and even some progressives believed the attempt would fail and that much greater federal authority was necessary and desirable. Old debates about how to achieve order and justice were thus revived. Conservatives stressed order, but progressives, emphasizing justice, were divided among those who, like the president, focused on individual liberty and opportunity, those who, like Walter Lippmann, argued that the war offered an opportunity to institute national planning and an excuse to have the federal government act on social problems, and those who, like Lincoln Colcord and Colonel House, were hardly interested in domestic reform and focused on the opportunity that the war offered for instituting a new international order.[30] Amid these various currents the administration steered a sometimes erratic course.

Adding to the complexities of shaping wartime policies was the southern dominance of the administration and the Democratic party in Congress. Although only a minority of Wilson's cabinet actually lived in the South, six of the ten cabinet members and the president himself were all southern-born, and the leadership of the party in Congress was overwhelmingly southern. The implications of this situation were significant, not only in the administration's predictable sympathy for agriculture and in some coolness toward business but also in a general suspicion of federal authority and a respect for traditions of states' rights, although not necessarily for the individual rights of blacks, recent immigrants, and political radicals. To urban critics of the administration, its southernism and especially the anti-militarism and social progressivism of the president, Secretary of the Navy Daniels, and Secretary of War Baker meant that the administration was incapable of leading the nation successfully in a war that would require discipline, toughness, and expansion of federal power.

To fight the war with a minimum of domestic coercion required the administration first of all to create and maintain a high degree of public enthusiasm for the American cause. Its principal channel was the Committee on Public Information (CPI), established by presidential order in April 1917 under the leadership of the journalist George Creel. The committee's twin goals were to censor the news, not by crude suppression but by publicizing positive information and withholding as little news as possible, and to "arouse ardor and enthusiasm" among the American people by popularizing the rectitude of the Allied cause.[31] No one seemed concerned that entrusting news management to a propaganda organization might create a conflict of interest.

From the beginning the CPI envisioned its main function as publicizing "the absolute justice of America's cause, the absolute selflessness of America's aims."[32] A majority of its staff members were dedicated reformers who believed that the war had called forth a new spirit of cooperation, service, and self-sacrifice and who were eager to enlist that spirit to the fullest in the war effort. To that end they recruited writers, filmmakers, artists, cartoonists, and above all speakers to spread their message. Millions of pamphlets poured off the committee's presses; seventy-five thousand volunteer speakers, known as "Four Minute Men" delivered patriotic harangues to more than 314 million people; news releases rained down on the country's newspapers; posters, cartoons, and films conveyed patriotic images.

The CPI certainly succeeded in its main goal: to convince Americans that they should set aside individual interests and submerge themselves in the common cause. Yet such unity came at a price. The Allies were portrayed as wholly pure, the Germans as absolute villains. The unrealistic hope that the war would make the world "safe for democracy" became widely accepted, and Americans were encouraged "to associate Americanism with loyalty to the nation, rather than with loyalty to democratic individualism."[33] In seeking to avoid the overtly coercive measures that were deplorable aspects of European war efforts, the administration found an effective alternative in the CPI, but its manipulation of public opinion was just as dangerous as the methods it sought to avoid.

The dark side of the CPI's emphasis on Americanism was that in evoking national unity it licensed persecution of dissenters and nonconformists. German-Americans, Socialists, pacifists, labor radicals, or anyone who did not accept common values became targets of vilification, abuse, and legal prosecution. Administration leaders, struggling to wage a difficult war, were as likely to yield to the temptation to silence critics as were conservatives who exploited public conformity to attack any individual, group, or organization they chose to define as "radical." In this way the Wilson administration contributed to the rise of a conservative reaction and weakened the prospects that further reforms would be adopted in the near future.

Protection of civil rights in any nation at war is of course a difficult problem. Although American patriotic excesses were never as great as in the European nations, the administration often trampled on the rights it claimed to be defending. Its main justification for the restrictive laws it supported lay in heading off extremists like Theodore Roosevelt, who would have liked to adopt martial law and firing squads to suppress dissent, but the laws passed proved harsh enough. The Espionage Act, passed in May 1917, provided heavy fines and jail terms for spying, sabotage, refusing military service, or obstructing recruitment and authorized the postmaster general to withhold mailing privileges from newspapers or magazines he considered seditious. In October Wilson signed into law the Trading with the Enemy Act, which forbade trade with the Central Powers and forced all foreign-language publications to submit to the Post Office Department, prior to publication, English translations of all articles dealing with the government or with the war. Under the Alien Act of 1918 foreign residents of the United States suspected of disloyalty or even accused of membership in an organization that advocated violent overthrow of the government could be deported without trial. The Sedition Act, passed in May 1918, permitted the jailing of citizens who uttered anything "disloyal, profane, scurrilous, or abusive" about the government or the armed forces.[34]

The first and perhaps most enthusiastic enforcer of these laws was Postmaster General Albert S. Burleson, a former Texas congressman who had spent his career battling for farmers and small businessmen and who feared and distrusted anyone who did not fall into one of those categories. Pompous and bigoted, Burleson relished the opportunity to deny mailing privileges to any publication he regarded as disloyal, which included Socialist materials as well as those sympathetic to the enemy. In a long appeal to Wilson to restrain Burleson's excesses, author Upton Sinclair wrote that the postmaster general was "a person of such pitiful and childish ignorance concerning modern movements that it is simply a calamity that [in] this crisis he should be the person to decide what may or may not be uttered by our radical press."[35] Socialist Norman Thomas, a former student of Wilson's at Princeton, remarked acidly that Burleson "didn't know socialism from rheumatism," but such criticisms had no effect on Burleson and little on Wilson.[36]

Among the more bizarre of Burleson's rulings were decisions to ban from the mails a publication that proposed financing the war by raising taxes rather than by borrowing and Thorstein Veblen's *Imperial Germany and the Industrial Revolution*, which George Creel's Committee on Public Information was recommending to American readers as an indictment of the structure of German society.[37] When the clamor against such excesses grew embarrassingly loud, Wilson gently urged the postmaster general to "act with the utmost caution and liberality in all our censorship," but the president did not pursue the matter further when Burleson assured him that he was acting "with moderation and caution but with firmness and dispatch."[38] Only once—in September 1918—did Wilson overrule Burleson, when in an excess of zeal he banned the liberal *Nation* from the mails, apparently because it had criticized Samuel Gompers.[39]

Equally enthusiastic in his pursuit of radicals and subversives was Burleson's fellow Texan, Attorney General Thomas W. Gregory. Appointed in August 1914 after James McReynolds was named to the Supreme Court, Gregory had a distinguished record as an antitrust lawyer but no sensitivity to civil rights issues. Like many other attorneys of his time, he placed more stress on the law's obligation to punish criminals than on the protection of individual rights. If there was a choice between social justice and social control, without doubt he would always choose the latter. Yet Gregory thought of himself not as an extremist but as a reasonable and moderate defender of the nation's interests. He argued that the Sedition Act, which he pushed through Congress, was the only alternative to lynching when the public was outraged by "individual casual or impulsive disloyal utterances."[40]

Though Gregory certainly did not mean to license lynching, he was obliged by a manpower shortage to rely on private vigilantes for much of the enforcement of the antisubversive laws. At the time the war began, Gregory was engaged in a contest with Treasury Secretary William Gibbs McAdoo for control over federal police. The Justice Department's Bureau of Investigation (later the FBI) was smaller and less well known than the Treasury's Secret Service, and until the war began, Gregory believed that the bureau lacked statutory authority to pursue spies and saboteurs. McAdoo, on the other hand, had no such compunctions, and in 1915 the Secret Service exposed German propaganda projects in the United States and a plan to urge Austro-Hungarian citizens not to work in American munitions plants. Stung by his rival's coups, Gregory welcomed a 1917 offer by the private American Protective League (APL), a reactionary superpatriotic group, to investigate and report to the bureau on "disloyal" activities.[41] President Wilson, when he heard of the APL, described it as "very dangerous," but he did not insist that Gregory break off relations with it any more than he reined in Burleson's excesses of censorship.[42]

By November 1918 the APL had some 250,000 members and was organized in every state and city and in most towns and rural areas. APL agents, glorying in their quasi-official status, infiltrated suspect organizations, spied on individuals, bugged telephones and opened mail, and provoked groups they disliked to commit illegal acts. Among the organizations they most attacked was the radical union, the Industrial Workers of the World (IWW). In cooperation with federal officials, APL agents arrested and jailed nearly two hundred IWW members on various charges; and in Bisbee, Arizona, in summer 1917 APL agents joined the local sheriff in rounding up 1,186 IWW members, loading them on boxcars, and shipping them out into the desert for two days with little food or water. For conservative labor leaders of the AFL as well as for reactionary businessmen, the APL's zeal offered an opportunity to purge every area of American economic and political life of radicalism.[43]

Among the approximately three thousand Americans prosecuted under the Espionage and Sedition acts was Eugene V. Debs, frequent Socialist candidate for president, who was sentenced to ten years in prison for saying that the United States was not a democratic nation. Federal courts, caught up in the passions of the moment, provided no protection for those arrested under the wartime laws. State and lower federal courts seemed to compete with each other in persecuting alleged offenders, and although the Supreme Court did not rule on any Espionage Act case until after the armistice, not even then did it question what had been done. Indeed, in *Schenck v. United States* in March 1919 Justice Oliver Wendell Holmes's majority opinion laid down two standards for freedom of speech—one for peace and a more restrictive one for wartime. Just as a citizen must not shout "Fire!" in a crowded theater, Holmes argued, so he must exercise special restraint in times of national peril. Although in subsequent years the justice rethought this opinion and reversed his position in a series of notable dissents, the damage had largely been done. The organization of the National Civil Liberties Union (later the ACLU) in 1917 signified that the issues opened in the war would not soon be laid to rest.[44]

Not all the war's coercive measures were regarded by progressives as undesirable, however. The Creel Committee's stress upon Americanism offered to many progressives who had worried about a perceived threat to American values in the influx of immigrants a justification for demanding that foreigners living in America give up all loyalties to their former countries, learn English, and merge as quickly and as completely as possible into American society. Likewise, reformers concerned about the moral evils of prostitution and alcohol found in the war an opportunity to force virtue on all Americans. Around each of the new military training camps a zone was established where no liquor was to be sold, and local governments were urged to suppress local red-light districts. And lest "the emotions of war playing upon the emotions of sex" should lead virtuous young women into trouble, women's groups undertook to patrol the vicinities of the camps with the result that "soon young couples all over the country were being accosted and protected from their own emotions."[45] Moreover, professional social workers, who for many years had insisted that studies did not support the contention that Prohibition would raise living standards for the poor, now embraced the cause of the Prohibitionists. Backed by these professionals as well as by others who argued that a ban on brewing and distilling would save grain needed for the war effort, a temporary ban sailed through Congress in summer 1917. In January 1919 the Eighteenth Amendment permanently prohibited the manufacture and sale of all alcoholic beverages. President Wilson, who doubted the feasibility of Prohibition, in October 1919 vetoed the Volstead Act that was to enforce it, but Congress repassed the measure over his veto and alcoholic beverages were banned nationally on 15 January 1920.[46] For the moral reformers, the war had permitted the achievement of goals about which they had only dreamed in the prewar era. They found no irony in Walter Lippmann's 1917 exclamation that "we stand at the threshold of a collectivism which is greater than any as yet planned by a socialist party."[47]

Perhaps the greatest opportunity for progressives who saw in the war a chance to achieve reform through governmental power was in taxation. Secretary of War Newton D. Baker spoke for many reformers when he declared in April 1917 that progressive writers must "stand firmly against profiteering in this war, to arouse sentiment that will prevent large business enterprises from making extravagant profits." A month later Amos Pinchot proclaimed, "I feel that any rich man who stands out against a practically confiscatory tax is playing the Kaiser's game."[48] Wilson, in his war message, had seemed to be saying much the same thing when he recommended that the war should be "sustained as far as may be equitable by taxation," which according to Secretary of the Treasury McAdoo meant that "fifty per cent of the cost of the War should be financed" by taxes.[49]

Congressman Claude Kitchin and Senator Robert La Follette did their best to achieve this goal by sharply increasing income taxes on the wealthy and corporate taxes on war profits and in fact succeeded in establishing these taxes as the replacements of the regressive tariff and excise taxes, which had been the main source of government income. Yet the administration did not fully support their efforts to "soak the rich" to cover expenditures, primarily because the cost of the war was much greater than anyone had imagined. The entire federal budget for fiscal year 1916 was $1 billion; that for 1917 was $2 billion; for 1918 it was $14 billion; and for 1919, $19 billion. No one had predicted such leaps. Secretary McAdoo first estimated the 1919 budget at $6.5 billion, then at $15 billion, and later at $18.4 billion; and even that proved low. Despite tax increases, which ultimately covered about one-third of the cost of the war, the national debt climbed from $1 billion in 1915 to $24 billion by 1920.[50] Even without counting $11 billion in loans to the Allies, per day costs of the war were twelve times as great as during the Civil War.[51]

A second major obstacle in the way of covering costs with taxation was political. Businesses and private citizens strongly opposed major tax hikes, and Wilson did not back his own tax program very energetically. His declaration in May 1918 that "politics is adjourned" and that voters would reward those who favored high taxes was spectacularly unrealistic. The members of Congress who delayed a vote on the tax bill until after the fall elections were more attuned to reality. As a result of political opposition, tax increases did not even keep pace with the growth of the gross national product so that federal revenues, as a percentage of the GNP, actually fell during the war years.[52]

Finally, the administration was seduced from its tax policy by the lure of borrowing. Knowing that heavy borrowing was inevitable, McAdoo determined early in the conflict that interest rates would be kept down—3½ to 4½ percent—so that interest costs would be low over the life of the bonds. To make the bonds attractive to investors at these rates, which were below those of any other belligerent, the administration made interest on them tax exempt. The strategy succeeded so well that wealthy individuals and institutions sometimes found it advantageous to borrow money in order to buy bonds, and under the Federal Reserve Act their notes could then serve as a basis for the issuance of additional Federal Reserve Notes. As a result, the amount of money in circulation almost doubled between 1916 and 1920, and a strong inflationary pressure was put on the economy, which was already inflated because of shortages of civilian goods and rising wages. To hard-pressed Treasury officials, this situation meant that borrowing became more attractive because debts would be paid in the future in devalued dollars, thus adding more turns to the upward spiral.[53]

Borrowing also had another advantage. Four "Liberty Loans" and a 1919 "Victory Loan" not only raised money but involved sixty million citizens in a direct, individual way in the war effort. In contrast to the compulsory contributions exacted through taxes, the loan campaigns, with their enormous ballyhoo, reliance upon sophisticated advertising, and patriotic fervor were the epitome of the voluntarism that the administration wanted to believe would win the war. Like the draft, the loans suggested an American alternative to European approaches to war.

Administration leaders did not seem to realize that their allegedly voluntary program carried an enormous price tag in ways that went even beyond the rising national debt and inflation. Daily war expenditures for the United States during fiscal 1918 and 1919 averaged $42.8 million, $10 million a day more than any other belligerent during this period.[54] The basic reason for this was the voluntary system, under which the cooperation of business and farmers was purchased through high profits and that of labor through rapidly rising wages. The dollar-a-year men might flock to run the machinery of economic mobilization, workers might perform miracles of production, and farmers might provide brimming harvests, but they did so as much for profit as for patriotism.[55]

World War I brought a striking example of just how much governmental spending could stimulate the economy and how much its activities could benefit average people. Because the administration chose not to impose rationing or to order suspension of consumer production, business boomed as it supplied both the civilian and the military markets. Farmers, benefiting from increased domestic and foreign sales, enjoyed their most prosperous period ever. Labor shortages drove up wages, especially for less skilled workers. The AFL, patriotically promising not to strike during the conflict, grew from three million members in 1917 to five million in 1920. Although they grumbled about the high cost of living, to most Americans the war was not even an inconvenience; and they came out of it, both individually and as a nation, stronger and better off than when it began.[56]

Among the obvious gainers during the war were American women. As a result of curtailed immigration and expanding industry, more jobs, and a greater variety of them, opened to women. A million and a half women found jobs in war industries, many in manufacturing, which had previously been largely closed to them; by 1920 there had been a marked shift among working women from domestic service to clerical and manufacturing jobs. President Wilson responded to this new situation by instructing the National War Labor Board, established in April 1918, to look into working women's problems, especially in regard to pay, which in 1918 averaged one-half to two-thirds of men's pay in comparable jobs. The board struggled with the problem and did not succeed completely, although by 1920 women's pay had risen to about three-fourths as much as their male counterparts, and in addition they had secured shorter work days and the right to unionize.[57] Women who benefited from these changes rejoiced, sometimes prematurely. One female trade unionist proclaimed, for example, that "at last, after centuries of disabilities and discrimination, women are coming into the labor and festival of life on equal terms with men." In fact the rapid gains of the war years did not continue in the 1920s, when women continued to work in large numbers but mostly in low-paying, low-status jobs.[58]

The most obvious and lasting wartime gain for women was the right to vote, resulting from the passage of the Nineteenth Amendment to the Constitution in 1920. Wilson, raised in a traditional southern household, had always taken a rather patronizing approach to women, whose company he sought eagerly but whose opinions he did not usually respect. As a professor at Bryn Mawr in the 1880s he made disparaging remarks about the women students; he frequently referred to his first wife, Ellen, as his "little wife," although she was not especially small; and his pet name for his second wife, Edith, was "Little girl," which could hardly have been less appropriate. On the other hand, Ellen Wilson had done much to arouse her husband's social conscience, and his three daughters were all notably independent and strong-minded women, whose own support for suffrage may well have affected their father. As president, Wilson faced an increasingly militant national suffrage movement that in 1917 added twenty-four-hour-a-day picketing and hunger strikes outside the White House to more conventional political pressures on the president to live up to the 1916 Democratic platform's endorsement of women's suffrage. In January 1918, rationalizing his stand as a reward for "the marvelous heroism and splendid loyalty of our women" during the war, Wilson urged Democrats in the House to support a suffrage amendment, which passed with just one vote over the necessary two-thirds.[59] The more conservative Senate did not act until June 1919 when, again with Wilson's support, it too passed the amendment, which after approval by the states went into effect on 26 August 1920.[60]

Black Americans also gained during the war, although their progress was less clear than that of women. About 400,000 blacks served in the armed services and about half a million more moved from the South to northern cities in pursuit of war jobs. Both groups faced segregation and discrimination. The administration, which had extended segregation in the government bureaucracy before the war, had no desire to fight the system in the military or in defense industries, and it was sympathetic to southerners who complained that northern jobs were luring away their cheap labor.

Though many blacks shared in the general prosperity of the times, their hold on their gains was tenuous. By the end of the war racial violence, already endemic in the South, was rapidly spreading northward, beginning with a race riot in East St. Louis, Illinois, in July 1917. Black leaders pled frantically for federal intervention to restore order and to protect civil rights, but Wilson did nothing. An even worse riot tore Chicago apart for thirteen days in 1919 and left fifteen whites and twenty-three blacks dead. Lynching, too, was on the rise in the war period, with an estimated thirty-eight in 1917, fifty-eight in 1918, and more than seventy in 1919. By summer 1918 members of the administration were becoming seriously alarmed, although not apparently at the violence being done to blacks as much as at the possibility that black unrest might disrupt the war effort. On 26 July 1918 Wilson at last issued a proclamation condemning lynching and mob violence as undemocratic but saying nothing about the discrimination that lay at the root of the problem.[61]

The president who "swapped negro stories" with a friend while aboard ship on his way to make the world safe for democracy at the peace conference in 1919 was not especially sensitive on racial matters.[62] Unlike such southerners as Senators James K. Vardaman or Benjamin R. Tillman or even Secretaries McAdoo and Burleson in his own administration, Wilson was not a radical racist, but neither was he an advocate of racial equality. Throughout his administration, his attitude was always that there were more important issues to be pursued than racial justice.

Wilson's leadership did not include encouraging debate over such basic issues as these, particularly during the war; rather, he sought to avoid such discussions as much as possible. Even in his cabinet meetings there was rarely much discussion, and as his May 1918 "politics is adjourned" statement indicates, he hoped also to avoid partisan controversy over war measures.[63] That did not mean, however, that he meant to follow a genuinely bipartisan policy. It was inconceivable to Wilson to work with such Republican leaders as Theodore Roosevelt or Senator Henry Cabot Lodge. Angered by their pre-1917 criticisms of his neutrality policy as cowardly, after the declaration of war the president interpreted all disagreement with his leadership as personal and partisan. He rebuffed even Democrats who questioned his policies, refused to debate his basic goals, and excluded Congress from a major share in planning war policy. In the short term this approach gave him great freedom, but whether it was equally wise in the long term was another matter. Democrats as well as Republicans believed that the legislature should have a larger part in the control of war policy, and sooner or later that belief was bound to alter relations between legislature and executive.

The 1918 Congressional elections revealed the logical outcome of the president's determination to exercise sole leadership over the war effort. The Republicans, having lost two presidential elections and not having controlled Congress since 1910, were in a nasty mood, and Wilson played into their hands. During summer 1918 he spurned overtures for cooperation from such moderate Republicans as William Howard Taft and Elihu Root and worked to purge Bryanite senators and congressmen who had voted against the war resolution from the Democratic party. Then in October he yielded to requests from various Democrats to support their candidacies and despite his earlier "politics is adjourned" statement, urged the voters to elect Democrats to Congress, "not for my own sake or for the sake of a political party, but for the sake of the nation itself."[64]

The direct effect of the president's appeal is open to debate. Even Wilson's friends later declared that his intervention had been a mistake because Democratic majorities of eleven in the Senate and six in the House became Republican majorities of two and fifty. But such erosion is normal in midterm elections, especially in a president's second term, and in this case there were some specific local reasons for losses, particularly in farm states where the price of wheat was a major issue. Of course the Republicans interpreted the outcome as a repudiation of Wilson's leadership, but that was not necessarily the correct reading of the situation. Nevertheless, whether the Republicans were right or wrong about the voters' message, Wilson had revived partisanship. Republican majorities on Capitol Hill guaranteed that he was in for some rough battles in the future, particularly in the Senate, where Lodge now became both majority leader and chairman of the Foreign Relations Committee. With the war coming to an end and a peace treaty that would have to be approved by the Senate about to be negotiated, Wilson had picked an unfortunate moment to indulge his partisan instincts and an equally bad one to show his scorn for the legislature.

The president's reluctance to engage in real political debate with his opponents may have heightened a dilemma facing the nation during the war years, but it was not the central issue. The basic problem, evident before 1917 but intensified by the war, was how to reconcile an urban, industrialized, world power's need for planning, unity, and centralized control with a tradition of individual decisions and private freedom. Wartime experiences offered no new or magical solutions to the problem. Tensions between voluntarism and coercion, between order and justice, between public responsibilities and private interests remained. Wilson had imagined that the New Freedom would provide middle ways in these dichotomies, but that had not been the case in peacetime and it proved to be even less true in war. Nevertheless, the nation—rich, powerful, and distant from obvious dangers—managed to muddle through, and in the end that satisfied most Americans. They would in future read the meaning of the war years in different ways and thus draw from the period conflicting lessons that would perpetuate old struggles.

9

THE PEACEMAKER

On 4 December 1918 President Wilson, his wife, and a large delegation of American experts set sail from New York aboard the *George Washington* for France. The war was over; now the president was going to Europe, as no incumbent president had ever done, to negotiate a peace that might prevent such a catastrophe from taking place again. The drifts of confetti in Manhattan's streets, the shrieks of boat horns in the harbor, and the roar of naval airplanes overhead proclaimed the American people's confidence and hope that this slender, ascetic-looking man could indeed accomplish the miracle—bring an end to war.

As he had done so many times before while president, Wilson was shattering precedent, but his decision to go to Europe was not frivolously reached. He believed that if old rivalries were to be set aside, if old relations based on fear and intimidation were to be replaced by new ones based on trust and justice, only he, with the full prestige of his office and the strength of the United States behind him, could hope to make the breakthrough. Nothing and no one less could expect to break the pattern of the past.

Even before the United States entered the war Wilson had begun to try to impose his ideas on the shape of the postwar world. "Is the present war a struggle for a just and secure peace," he asked the Senate in an address on 22 January 1917, "or only for a new balance of power?" He went on to state his own conclusion that "there must be, not a balance of power, but a community of power; not organized rivalries, but an organized common peace." The only way to avoid a renewal of the

163

conflict in the future, he declared, was to negotiate "a peace without victory . . . the very principle of which is equality and a common participation in a common benefit." The treaty must settle territorial and ethnic issues; it must be negotiated by governments that "derive all their just powers from the consent of the governed"; it must assure "freedom of the seas"; and it must provide significant arms reduction.[1]

A year later, on 8 January 1918, nine months after the United States entered the war, the president reiterated and expanded this peace plan in the Fourteen Points address to a joint session of Congress. The purpose of the speech was partly to encourage dissension within Germany and the Austro-Hungarian Empire and partly to seize control of the peace process from Russian Bolsheviks who were negotiating with the Germans at Brest-Litovsk and urging the other belligerents to join in. But its main goal was to outline once more the only sort of peace that Wilson believed could be lasting.[2] As in the 1917 speech the president recommended self-determination for national groups, including colonial peoples, freedom of the seas, arms reduction, and a concert of power, now referred to as an "association of nations." The 1918 address went beyond that of 1917 in its specificity about which territories should receive self-determination and in demanding the evacuation of occupied Belgian, French, and Russian territories, in recommending the removal of economic barriers among nations, and in denouncing secret treaties; but the president's basic goal in 1918 was the same.[3] Essentially, he was still proposing a "peace without victory."

The president did not delude himself that achieving such a peace would be easy. The leaders of France, Britain, and Italy were determined, he told his personal physician on the way to Europe, "to get everything out of Germany that they can." It would be his first and most difficult task to make them see that the treaty "must not be a peace of loot or spoliation" and to make them understand that if they insisted on such a peace, Wilson would "withdraw personally and with [his] commissioners return home and in due course take up the details of a separate peace."[4]

The main reason for Wilson's decision to go to Europe stemmed from his belief that only his prestige as president of the nation that had at last made victory possible could force the British and the French to accept the peace he sought. Yet there were also, of course, less noble motives. The president did not fully trust either his secretary of state, Robert Lansing, or his friend and frequent emissary to Europe, Colonel Edward M. House. Even less did he trust prominent Republicans such as William Howard Taft, Elihu Root, Charles Evans Hughes, or Henry Cabot Lodge, who might have been on the peace delegation. Especially after the congressional elections, all Republicans were anathema. And Wilson's vanity was involved, too. In autumn 1918 he was the most popular man in the world, and he would have been more than human had he not wanted to add to his reputation as a warmaker that of peacemaker as well.[5]

Most immediately behind Wilson's 18 November announcement was the experience of negotiating the armistice that had ended the war on 11 November. In those talks the president had been able to see just how difficult it would be to get the Allies to accept the sort of peace he had in mind, and he had also confirmed that even House might not be up to the challenge.

At an imperial conference on 29 September 1918 German leaders had agreed that their military situation was hopeless and that they must seek an immediate armistice. The most influential German leader, General Erich Ludendorff, recognized that an appeal for an armistice would deprive the country's leaders of legitimacy and would almost certainly be rejected by the enemy unless it was accompanied by an end of autocracy. He recommended to the Kaiser that the military government be replaced at once by a parliamentary regime based upon the majority in the Reichstag. On 3 October the Kaiser appointed Prince Max von Baden chancellor, and three days later the new government appealed to Wilson to negotiate an immediate armistice on the basis of the Fourteen Points and his subsequent pronouncements.[6]

The Americans at first suspected the German offer of being a propaganda trick designed to undermine Allied support for the war. Moreover, Tumulty warned that any impression that the president was conciliating the Germans would anger Americans and might lead to Democratic losses in the coming congressional elections. Lansing, however, urged that the German offer not be rejected out of hand but that a response be sent to leave a "ray of hope" and to encourage the German people to overthrow their autocratic government. At the very least, Lansing thought, such a reply would undermine the morale of the German army and weaken its ability to fight.[7] On 8 October, therefore, the State Department sent Germany a note that asked whether the Germans accepted the Fourteen Points completely; whether they would immediately evacuate all occupied territory; and whether the peace offer came only from Germany's rulers or whether it reflected the wishes of the people.[8]

Wilson sent his 8 October note to Germany without first consulting with the British and the French because he regarded the exchange as merely clarifying the German proposal, but the Allies were understandably fearful that it represented a step toward separate peace negotiations or toward setting peace terms with which they might not agree. They protested that the Associated Nations had never formally adopted the Fourteen Points as the basis for peace and warned that there might be considerable difference of interpretation as to what the Fourteen Points meant. They also insisted that Germany must pay reparations for damages inflicted at sea and recommended that military terms of an armistice be left to the soldiers to make sure that the Germans were not able to use a cease-fire to prepare to resume the war. As a result of this pressure, when Berlin replied on 12 October with apparent affirmatives to all the questions Wilson had asked in his note of 8 October, the president sent them another note on 14 October stressing the Allied concern that a military cease-fire must be set up in such a way as to make resumption of war impossible. He also pushed much harder than before a concern in which the Allies had expressed no interest but that had become politically important in the United States—the democratization of the German government. Although he did not quite say so, the president seemed now to be implying that peace would be impossible until the German people overthrew their government and instituted a new, democratic one.[9]

The president's position was difficult. He shared Allied suspicions about German intentions and was under political pressure at home to make Germany, if not the world, safe for democracy. At the same time he knew that British and French leaders did not share his peace goals and wanted concessions from Germany that he regarded as unreasonable. To try to thread a way between these twin perils, on 16 October he sent Colonel House to Europe to handle armistice negotiations on the spot. Perhaps not sure himself of exactly where he should stand on these complex questions yet confident that House shared his basic goals, he gave the colonel no specific instructions. "I feel that you will know what to do," he told House the evening before the Texan was to sail.[10]

While House was still on his way to Europe, Wilson's confusion was compounded by the arrival of a third German note on 20 October. This note offered new assurances about the democratization of the German government but seemed to anticipate a withdrawal of German armed forces back into Germany rather than a surrender, thus giving substance to Allied fears. The Allies responded to this proposal by demanding that the armistice include occupation of some German territory as a safeguard against resumption of hostilities. At the same time, domestic political pressure was mounting on the president to insist upon the Kaiser's resignation. On 23 October Wilson replied to the third German note, informing Berlin that the details of the armistice would be settled by military officers on terms that would "make a renewal of hostilities on the part of Germany impossible" and warning them that "the nations of the world do not and cannot trust the word of those who have hitherto been the masters of German policy." If such men remained in power, the allies "must demand, not peace negotiations, but surrender."[11] He then forwarded the whole correspondence to the Allied leaders, without recommendation.

Even seventy years later it is by no means certain what Wilson meant by this note, but House, without specific instructions, was certainly justified in drawing two conclusions from it: that the president had yielded to Allied insistence upon an armistice whose terms would be set by the military and that would include the occupation of some German territory; and that Wilson wanted a revolution in Germany that would completely overthrow the old regime.[12] House also knew from talking to British agent Sir William Wiseman, who was traveling with him to Europe and who had met with Wilson on 16 October just before sailing, that the president was still committed to the Fourteen Points, including freedom of the seas.[13] House was also well aware of the president's suspicions of British and French objectives, which he and Wilson had discussed several times. Thus, though the 23 October note certainly could be read as a sign that Wilson had shifted from "peace without victory" to an imposed settlement and the colonel might well be confused about just what the president wanted, the basic message seemed to be that he was to regard both the Germans and the Allies with suspicion and to attempt to find armistice terms that would not give either side all it wanted.

When House arrived in Paris on 26 October, he saw as his major goal winning the agreement of the British and the French to the Fourteen Points and apparently had not anticipated any difficulty about accomplishing that. He seems to have been taken aback to discover that neither the British nor the French were particularly sympathetic to the Fourteen Points in general and that they appeared quite willing to defer discussion of a league of nations to some time after the peace conference. They did not even seem impressed by his threat that the United States might sign a separate peace. Only after several days of difficult discussions did he win general agreement from them on the Fourteen Points, except that the British rejected freedom of the seas and the French demanded reparations for civilian as well as military damage.[14]

Focusing on the Fourteen Points, House largely ignored the military terms of the armistice, agreeing that they should be set by the military and conveyed to the Germans through Marshal Foch rather than through the political leaders. Very likely he thought that was what Wilson had agreed to, and he did not seem to realize that empowering the military to set armistice terms would affect political issues such as borders and the postwar occupation of German territory and thus might shape the peace indirectly. In a triumphant cable to the president on 5 November he proclaimed his "great diplomatic victory" and urged Wilson to come to Europe for the peace conference to consolidate it.[15] He said nothing about having agreed to accept the principle of reparations and the occupation of the German Rhineland nor about various boundary clauses, including the setting of the Austrian-Italian border where the Italians wanted it rather than where it belonged ethnically. Both he and Wilson had seemed aware of the political implications of such issues before House went to Europe, but in the end the colonel allowed himself to be maneuvered into agreement.[16] Studying the full terms of the armistice back in Washington, Wilson must have concluded that House was not the man to negotiate the final peace the president had imagined.

Adding to the urgency of the situation was the president's race with a formidable competitor for control of the European situation. Following the Bolshevik Revolution in Russia in autumn 1917, Western leaders feared that communism, feeding on defeat, destruction, and hunger, would engulf all Europe, but they did not agree on how to meet the danger. Wilson believed that food and a liberal peace were the weapons to combat the red specter, but the French in particular seemed to prefer repression and intervention. As with the other issues that were emerging by autumn 1918, the president dared not leave the red menace to be faced by others who seemed to him to be dealing with it mistakenly.

From the American point of view the problem posed by communism had first arisen in May 1917, even before the Bolshevik Revolution, when the Petrograd Soviet issued a call for an international conference of Socialist parties to meet in Stockholm to seek "peace without annexations or indemnities on the basis of the self-determination of peoples."[17] Wilson's first reaction to the Petrograd proposal was to allow American Socialists to take part in the proposed conference on the theory that they would "make themselves hated or ridiculous," but as he began to see that any defection of European Socialists from supporting the war would be serious, his position toward the conference turned hostile.[18] Although his position distressed liberals in the United States and Europe, he argued mistakenly in a Flag Day speech on 14 June 1917 that the conference of Socialists was only a German device "to deceive all those who throughout the world stand for the rights of peoples and the self-government of nations."[19]

The situation grew much more serious in November 1917 when the Bolshevik uprising brought to power V. I. Lenin, who declared that "war is evil, peace is a blessing" and promised to negotiate an armistice "forthwith" on the basis of "the liberation of all colonies; the liberation of all dependent, oppressed, and non-sovereign peoples."[20] Wilson feared that Lenin's "crude formula" of "'no annexations, no contributions, no punitive indemnities,'" might seduce the nations into a "premature peace . . . before autocracy has been taught its final and convincing lesson." He therefore determined to formulate a declaration of war aims that might appeal to the Russians and recommit them to the defeat of Prussian militarism but even more important that would go beyond Lenin's proposals to define broader objectives and would unite liberals everywhere.[21] That declaration, delivered in January 1918, was of course the Fourteen Points address.

Point number six of the Fourteen Points called for the evacuation of Russian territory and the settlement of all questions concerning Russia in a way that would assure her "an unhampered and unembarrassed opportunity for the independent determination of her own political development and national policy and assure her of a sincere welcome into the society of free nations under institutions of her own choosing." Such a policy, he said, would be the "acid test" of the good will and unselfish sympathy of the nations.[22] Considering that the new Russian government had signed an armistice with Germany on 15 December and was then negotiating a separate peace that would free thousands of German soldiers for service on the Western Front, Russian policy would indeed be an acid test of the good will of the nations fighting Germany.

The most striking failure of Wilson's acid test was of course in Russia itself, but the challenge in Central Europe became hardly less dangerous.[23] During summer and autumn 1918 the collapse of Russian, German, and Austro-Hungarian military power left Central Europe in chaos, "during which the Successor States battled each other in a confused way, like impassioned men in a darkened room, for advantage or survival," and during which communism seemed likely to expand.[24] By autumn the Allied Supreme War Council was considering using troops to reestablish order in the region, but Wilson was opposed. "On principle and for the sake of incalculable difficulties of the future keep hands off the pieces of Austria-Hungary and reduce outside intervention to minimum," he warned.[25] He was, however, sensitive to the danger of a situation in which hungry people wandered in ruined countries without real governments. "Hunger," he told Congress as he asked for the creation of a relief program like that which had fed Belgium during the war, "does not breed reform; it breeds madness and all the ugly distempers that make an ordered life impossible."[26]

The Bolshevik government in Russia, equally aware of the unstable situation in Central Europe, issued an appeal on 3 November 1918 to the people of the new states to "unite in a common struggle against world capital" and in particular against "Anglo-American capital."[27] Hungary, fearful that the Western nations would dismember it, adopted a Soviet government under Bela Kun in March 1919, which lasted five months, and strong Communist movements appeared in Poland and Germany as well. The French proposed to the leaders gathered at the peace conference in Paris a military response to this growing threat, but Wilson and British Prime Minister David Lloyd George argued that what was needed was not repression but a sound, liberal program. Germany would turn to "Bolshevism, or something that would promise them relief" rather than accept an impossible burden of reparations, Wilson warned Clemenceau. Lloyd George agreed, urging instead the adoption of "a peace, which, while just, will be preferable to all sensible men to the alternative of Bolshevism."[28]

To Wilson the issue of bolshevism was but one more aspect of the fundamental question to be decided at the peace conference: whether the peace would be based upon power and the threat of force or whether it would strike out in a new direction and attempt to win acceptance by being just. He was no longer using the phrase, "peace without victory," but that concept still lay at the root of his peace plans. As the originator of that idea and the only one of the victorious leaders still committed to it, his presence at the conference was essential.

Important as Wilson believed his presence to be in Paris, however, he did not delude himself that he could handle the whole task alone. On 2 September 1917 he asked Colonel House to seek out experts who would study the probable issues of the peace conference and recommend "what influences we can use" to achieve American goals.[29] House accepted this commission and put together a group of experts known as the Inquiry.[30] As the Executive Committee of this body House chose Sidney E. Mezes, his brother-in-law and a religious philosopher who was president of the City College of New York, David Hunter Miller, law partner of his son-in-law, Gordon Auchincloss, and Walter Lippmann, whom House described as particularly in touch with "the extreme liberals of the country."[31] The colonel obviously intended to control the Inquiry, at least indirectly, and to see that it shaped a liberal peace.

These careful preparations, however, did not assure the well-prepared and unified American peace delegation for which House and Wilson hoped. The members of the Inquiry feuded with each other and with Lansing, who was jealous of their role and insisted that the delegation also include a large number of State Department people and military officers. In addition, the peace commissioners at the head of the delegation—Wilson, House, Lansing, General Tasker H. Bliss, and the lone Republican, professional diplomat Henry White—each had a substantial personal staff that was not integrated into the general delegation. Although these various groups were capable of giving the president excellent advice, in practice he often heard nothing or received contradictory recommendations; in turn, most members of the delegation did not really know what was going on and thought they had too little influence. Wilson frequently asked the experts for detailed recommendations on specific points and sometimes left technical matters to be negotiated by them, but neither they nor Lansing, Bliss, or White had significant influence on his broad policy. As had always been the case, the president did not reach decisions through consultation. Far too often he and House were largely on their own.[32]

On "the other side of the water," as Wilson was fond of saying, Allied leaders had shaped peace aims that differed radically from Wilson's. The French, having lost two million men killed or wounded, having had a large part of their territory occupied for four years, and having suffered mines flooded, towns destroyed, and factories shattered, believed that Germany would rebuild and attack yet again. They were determined not only to take back the provinces of Alsace and Lorraine but to disarm Germany, to create a buffer state along the Rhine, to compel the Germans to pay the costs of the war, and to negotiate security arrangements that would give them reliable allies in the future.[33] The British, on the other hand, came to the conference with a more ambiguous program. Three days before Wilson's Fourteen Points address, Prime Minister David Lloyd George had delivered a major speech in London before a gathering of trade unionists, in which he mentioned all of the points Wilson would include in his speech except open covenants, freedom of the seas, and the lowering of trade barriers.[34] Yet the British proposals were not quite all they seemed. Although they genuinely wanted a peace that would be accepted as fair by the Germans and that would engage the United States permanently in maintaining order, they had made pledges during the war that limited their freedom. They had promised their dominions and Japan, Italy, and others slices of German, Ottoman, and Austro-Hungarian territories; their navalists demanded that the Royal Navy's predominance not be lost; and their public was calling for Germany to pay war costs and for the punishment of German leaders for war crimes.[35] Innumerable other nations and groups were gathering in Paris in the hope that the conference would satisfy their often conflicting goals. Above the swirling tumult of demands Wilson's long-range aspirations floated like foam on storm waves, beautiful but not quieting or diverting the surges below.

The president arrived in Paris on the morning of 14 December 1918 and was given a tumultuous welcome. Signs greeting him were everywhere, and hundreds of thousands of people lined the boulevards and cheered ecstatically as the president's carriage passed. "The French," reported one American observer, "think that with almost a magic touch he will bring about the day of political and industrial justice," but he added, "Will he? Can he?"[36]

Others were wondering the same thing. Newspaperman Frank Cobb, an old admirer of Wilson's, had rushed home from Paris to try to warn the president not to come to France because he was sure there was an Anglo-French conspiracy against the American peace plan. Yet House, who ought to have known how difficult Wilson's task would be, especially after his own experience during the armistice negotiations, was all optimism.[37] "I gave the President a brief summary of the situation," he recorded in his diary, "particularly the relations between France, England and ourselves, relations which seem to grow steadily better. Our relations with Italy have always been good."[38] Although the great public welcomes the president received when he traveled to Italy and England during the next month seemed to support House's opinion, it is hard to imagine how the colonel could have mistaken public acclaim for Wilson as the symbol of Allied victory for the full agreement of Allied statesmen with Wilson's program.

Whatever the reasons for House's misevaluation of the situation facing Wilson, it almost certainly contributed to one of the president's most serious mistakes at the conference. Without reflecting on the importance that being able to appeal to public opinion might have if he were to be successful in imposing his plans on his reluctant colleagues, he allowed himself to be talked into imposing a news blackout on the sessions. Given his adversarial relationship with the press during most of his presidency and his preference for developing policies away from public scrutiny, the decision was not surprising, but as it turned out it damaged Wilson's cause in several ways. The blackout infuriated reporters and editors, all of whom interpreted it as a repudiation of the "open covenants, openly arrived at" promise of the Fourteen Points; it encouraged reporters to turn to special-interest groups and the representatives of small nations, who provided slanted information to serve their own ends; it permitted major delegations, especially the French, to use leaks to apply pressure on the negotiations; and it led reporters to concentrate on the superficial and trivial outward appearances of the conference, thus minimizing the important and complex issues really on the agenda. All the great powers were losers as a result of the blackout because the world was denied the opportunity to understand the difficulty of the issues and the reasons for compromises; but the Americans, who had sent Wilson off with such unrealistic expectations, lost the most. Unable to observe the pressures of the negotiations, which necessitated compromises, they were profoundly surprised and shocked by the treaty's imperfections.[39]

At the first sessions of the conference in mid-January 1919, this decision on press coverage was paralleled by another, which although less serious also had unfortunate results. It was decided to cut down the working sessions of the conference from the full twenty-seven nations in attendance to a Council of Ten, consisting of Wilson, French premier Georges Clemenceau, British prime minister David Lloyd George, Italian premier Vittorio Orlando, their foreign ministers, and two Japanese delegates, and to a Council of Four, made up of Wilson, Lloyd George, Clemenceau, and Orlando. Necessary as this reduction was if the conference was to make any progress at all, it conveyed the obvious message that whatever Wilson might say, all nations were not equal; and it cast the smaller nations to some extent into the same position as the reporters.

The first sessions of the Council of Ten, beginning on 11 January, showed beyond doubt that the conference would be difficult. The first contentious issue was the future of Germany's colonies, which the Japanese, Italians, and British (backed by Australia, New Zealand, and South Africa) all wanted to annex and which Wilson, in keeping with the Fourteen Points, insisted should become wards of smaller nations under the proposed league of nations. This was not an unexpected issue. Soon after the armistice House and the earl of Derby, British ambassador to France, had discussed the questions of the colonies and freedom of the seas. House had suggested that if the British supported Wilson's plan for a league of nations, the president might adopt a favorable attitude on the other issues. When Wilson arrived in Paris in December, however, Derby's delicate hints about such an arrangement received a cold reception.[40] At the conference everyone quickly agreed that the colonies would not be returned to the Germans and then began wrangling over what to do with them. By the end of the month tempers were becoming very short when, fortunately, South African General Jan Smuts proposed an acceptable compromise: The colonies would indeed go to the great powers and the British Dominions that had demanded them, but they would go as mandates under a league rather than as outright grants. With this fig leaf affixed to the transfers, Wilson was willing to accept them. The principle of the mandate system had been maintained, even if not in the form he had first wanted. [41]

The battle over the colonies demonstrated how wrong House's easy optimism had been and also undermined Wilson's own confidence, which had been based largely upon the belief that American economic dominance in the last days of the war would force the other nations to do as he wished. By the time the war was over, he had predicted confidently in summer 1917, the British and the French would "be financially in our hands," so that we could "force them to our way of thinking." He now found that economic power did not translate readily into diplomatic leverage.[42] In fact, as the Allies began canceling orders from American factories at the end of the war, it began to appear that the American economy was more in the grip of the British and the French than the other way around.

Accepting that he could not dictate a peace based on the Fourteen Points, Wilson focused on securing from his colleagues a commitment to the establishment of a league of nations. He told a plenary session of the conference on 25 January 1919 that although "we may not be able to set up permanent decisions" on the issues before the conference, "we can set up permanent processes" that could continue to solve problems.[43] He was delighted when the session endorsed his proposal and named him chairman of the commission to draft the constitution of the new organization.

Given the isolation of the United States during most of its early history, Americans before the twentieth century had taken little interest in plans for world order, and only with the beginning of the war in 1914 did a significant organization to promote that goal spring up, the League to Enforce Peace. The league's program envisioned a body made up of sovereign states that would collectively enforce international law and could invoke economic or military sanctions by its members against any state that refused to settle a dispute peacefully.[44]

Wilson had been a member of the American Peace Society since 1908 and was much interested in various projects to promote world peace, but he held the League to Enforce Peace at arm's length, although in a speech before it in May 1916 he became the first head of state to call for the creation of an international organization. He also endorsed the idea of American membership in a league but made no specific proposals as to its organization, saying that getting into details at that stage would invite international controversy and might create the appearance of an organization that was only a military alliance against Germany.[45]

In fact Wilson already had the rudiments of a plan in mind, however. It was based upon a Pan-American nonaggression treaty that he and House had been working on since 1914. Like the proposal of the League to Enforce Peace, the Pan-American treaty offered mutual guarantees of sovereignty and territorial integrity, but it lacked any mechanism for enforcement.[46]

While Wilson was publicly silent about his ideas on a league, a lively public debate was going on in Britain about the maintenance of world order. Lord James Bryce, former ambassador to the United States, was an early and effective advocate of an international organization; and by autumn 1914 Foreign Secretary Sir Edward Grey had become a supporter of the idea, which he urged on Colonel House as a key to a negotiated settlement of the war. The private League of Nations Society, organized early in 1915, served much the same publicizing function as the League to Enforce Peace in the United States although it was less specific than the American group on how states were to be compelled to live up to their obligations.[47] At the cabinet level only Robert Cecil, minister for blockade, was a strong supporter of the idea after the resignation of Grey in December 1916 even though the 10 January 1917 Anglo-French reply to Wilson's December peace note declared that "in a general way" the two governments wished to "associate themselves with . . . the project for the creation of a league of nations to insure peace and justice throughout the world."[48]

During 1917 Wilson thought little about the issue of a league, but in Britain leftists vigorously urged the idea on the coalition government headed by David Lloyd George where ironically the chief spokesman for a league remained the Conservative Robert Cecil. At the end of the year, when Russo-German negotiations at Brest-Litovsk released a flood of propaganda for peace, Cecil and others were given the task of drafting a new statement of war aims for the prime minister. On 5 January 1918 Lloyd George delivered a major speech based on their ideas and included Cecil's call for an "international organization" as "an alternative to war [and] a means of settling international disputes."[49] Three days later, President Wilson also proposed an "association of nations" as part of the Fourteen Points.

Vague though both men's words were, the British were actually moving more quickly than the Americans to winnow various proposals and to come up with a practical plan for a league. On 3 January 1918, at Cecil's urging, Lloyd George appointed a committee chaired by Sir Walter G. F. Phillimore to explore the matter. The committee's report, submitted in late spring, recommended the creation of an organization in which all members would agree not to go to war with each other without submitting the dispute to arbitration or to a conference and would promise that if any state broke the agreement, the others would take economic or military measures to enforce order.[50]

Receipt of the Phillimore Report in the United States put new pressure on Wilson and House to define their own ideas. House warned the president that the British or the French might well "hit upon some scheme" around which "public opinion will chrystalize [sic] to such an extent that it will be difficult to change the form at the peace conference." He enclosed a draft of a letter to Cecil suggesting an organization in which nations would promise to submit all disputes to arbitration and promise to punish violators by cutting off "diplomatic, financial and economic relations of every character and, when and where possible, also exert physical force against the offender." The president, without indicating his own opinion, then asked House to turn his letter into a draft of a "constitution" for such an organization.[51]

House's draft, presented to Wilson on 16 July, differed from the Phillimore Report in a number of minor points and in two major ways. In the first place it proposed the establishment of an international court to deal with disputes over the interpretation of a treaty, commercial issues, or any other issues submitted by consent of the parties; no court had been suggested by the British. Second, the Phillimore Report had proposed sanctions on transgressors up to and including war, but House's draft confined sanctions to suspension of diplomatic relations, to economic penalties, and, as a last resort, to blockade.[52] House's draft, in short, emphasized international law more than Phillimore's, but ultimately it relied most of all upon public opinion and international ethics.

On 15 August Wilson visited House at the latter's summer home in Magnolia, Massachusetts, and they talked about revisions Wilson had proposed in House's draft. Aside from reorganizing it to reduce its articles to thirteen, a number Wilson superstitiously regarded as lucky, the only substantive change that House noted was that the president had dropped the international court, which the colonel thought a mistake but hoped the conference would rectify. He did not comment on Wilson's other significant change, which was to add the phrase, "use any force that may be necessary," to the section on sanctions.[53] Why Wilson dropped the provision for a court is unclear, but his addition of the phrase about the use of force suggests that he was closer to the views of the League to Enforce Peace than he had been willing to admit publicly.[54]

At that point, with uncertainty even in House's mind as to what the president wanted and everyone else almost completely in the dark, the planning ceased until the conference began. Although it was true, as Wilson said, that broad public discussion of the details of an international organization would have invited conflict within and between nations, that approach was short-sighted. The discussion would come, either before or after the treaty was negotiated. By avoiding it beforehand Wilson deprived himself of the benefit of having an American consensus behind him in Paris and put the Senate in the position of having to take or leave an accomplished fact. He assumed that Americans would support the league because he believed he could sense the public's desires, but on this issue, as Felix Frankfurter pointed out, the concept was "too new, too vast to enlist the understanding and the faith of the American people, in view of our traditional isolation."[55]

Nor was there agreement by any means among the nineteen men who made up the peace conference's League of Nations Commission under Wilson's chairmanship. Except for the British, represented by Cecil, and South African Jan Smuts, none of the nations fully endorsed the idea. To complicate matters even more, several different proposals were offered to the commission before it first met. Rather than trying to discuss all of these, the members agreed to ask the British and the American legal advisers, C. J. B. Hurst and David Hunter Miller, to prepare a working draft based on an official proposal of the British government and the second of three revisions of the House-Wilson draft, which the president had made since coming to Paris. At the ten meetings of the commission between 3 and 13 February 1919, the Hurst-Miller draft became the basis of discussion and eventually of the completed covenant of the League of Nations. Wilson chaired and dominated most of the meetings, and the final document reflected his convictions on most important issues, except that on the basis of recommendations made by Smuts and some of his own people he agreed to add a few new sections to the final document. The additions vested the organization's main enforcement powers in a Council made up of large and small nations and added new sections on mandates, labor, and minority rights. Suggestions from Miller and others of the American delegation resulted in the addition of new clauses on freedom of the seas, religious equality, disarmament, publication of treaties, and equality in trade.[56]

Specifically, the League Covenant provided that the organization would be made up of "fully self-governing State[s], Dominion[s] or Colon[ies]" all of which would be represented in an Assembly. The great powers, plus four other powers to be elected periodically from among Assembly members, would serve on a Council. Although unanimity was required in votes in both the Assembly and the Council, major peacekeeping functions of the organization were given to the Council. The Council was instructed to "formulate plans" for arms reduction and to take the principal role in maintaining peace. "All Members of the League," however, promised in Article 10 "to respect and preserve as against external aggression the political integrity and existing political independence of all Members of the League." In Articles 12–17 they undertook to settle such disputes through investigation, arbitration, a Permanent Court of International Justice, or ultimately, through use of economic coercion or military force, which could be recommended by the Council to individual members. Article 22 formally established the mandate system; other articles provided that all treaties and international agreements would be registered with the organization's secretariat and published, that regional understandings such as the Monroe Doctrine remained in effect, and that the organization would work to promote such humane goals as improvement of labor conditions, reduction of the drug trade, and the prevention of disease.[57]

On 14 February 1919 Wilson presented the covenant to a plenary session of the conference. Its essence, he declared, was that it depended "primarily and chiefly upon one great force, and that is the moral force of the public opinion of the world . . . so that those things that are destroyed by the light may be properly destroyed by the overwhelming light of the universal expression of the condemnation of the world." Behind this moral force, he noted, was the threat of "armed force," but he stressed that "it *is* in the background . . . because this is intended as a constitution of peace, not as a league of war."[58]

In the president's opinion, the covenant was the most important achievement of the conference, and his success in getting what he wanted gave him confidence that no matter what else might happen a structure had been created through which wrongs could be righted and justice advanced. On that optimistic note he returned to the United States briefly to deal with urgent domestic business at the end of the congressional session. There he discovered that not everyone shared his vision of the emerging world order. At a White House dinner for the House and Senate members of the Foreign Affairs Committees on 26 February the president attempted to explain the covenant and to win the support of those present, but questions about the effect of the agreement on the Monroe Doctrine, about the right of withdrawal, and about possible curtailment of American sovereignty showed their concerns. After the meeting ended few were as open as Senator Frank Brandegee, who said, "I am against it, as I was before"; but others, unwilling to be quoted directly, indicated that they "did not expect that the League project would go through without change."[59] A few days later, on 3 March 1919, Senator Henry Cabot Lodge sent Wilson a round-robin letter signed by more than one-third of the senators and senators-elect saying that they would not approve the treaty without changes. Furious, Wilson defied his critics, telling them that "when the treaty comes back gentlemen on this side will find the Covenant not only in it, but so many threads of the treaty tied to the Covenant that you cannot dissect the Covenant from the treaty without destroying the whole vital structure."[60] It was a rash challenge.

Word of Wilson's troubles with the Senate of course preceded him across the Atlantic and weakened the American position at the conference, which had been continuing in his absence with House in his place. Indeed the pace of negotiations had been hectic in the month of the president's absence, even though the other heads of government had also been absent for various reasons. Everyone hoped that upon Wilson's return it would be possible to complete the conference's work quickly. As a result, all the negotiators were under considerable pressure to reach agreement even on the most difficult issues.

House was not at his best in this sort of situation. His strength was in his ability to win the trust of the people he met, and his methods for doing that were flattery and acquiescence. He was not good at defending a fixed position in tough negotiations. Wilson, for his part, did not help the situation by telling the members of the Peace Commission just before he left that he had no specific instructions to give them on the issues that would come up because no decisions would actually be made in that period.[61] He intended to keep final control in his own hands and did not seem to realize that in leaving House without detailed orders he was allowing the colonel to make preliminary decisions that would later limit his own choices severely.

In Wilson's absence an important split was apparent in the American delegation between House, who took a relatively punitive attitude toward Germany and favored compromising with a similar but even more strongly held view among the British and the French, and Lansing, Bliss, and White, who held firmly to Wilson's original goal of a peace that would reintegrate Germany into Europe and so opposed compromise with the Allies.[62] The effects of this division were immediate and practical. House was willing to compromise with French demands that they occupy the Rhineland and the Saar Valley coal mines; the others were opposed, as was Wilson. House was willing to compromise with the Allies on reparations, moving toward acceptance of their demand that Germany be required to pay most of the cost of the war; the others were opposed to that too, as was Wilson.[63]

How well House and Wilson understood the disagreement over basic policy that now began to open between them is difficult to discern. A new code implemented just as Wilson was leaving Europe proved to be difficult to use and susceptible to garbling. Messages in both directions were often difficult to interpret. And at the same time, the French came up with new proposals that House believed were acceptable within the vague guidelines Wilson had laid down. That sort of freedom of interpretation was after all a logical inference from the president's failure to issue specific orders, and of course House's vanity urged him on to complete terms of an agreement before the president returned to France.[64]

When Wilson arrived, he found that without informing him House had agreed to support a French proposal for the creation of an independent German republic under inter-Allied supervision on the west (left) bank of the Rhine River. Although slightly less obnoxious than the original French demand to annex the territory outright, this was still a serious violation of self-determination and in conflict with the goal of reintegrating Germany into Europe.[65] House also had reacted to the news of opposition to the League in America by hinting to the Allies that it might be possible to modify the League into something weaker and vaguer, which might evolve later into the sort of organization Wilson wanted. In his opinion, the peace settlement was more important than the details of the League, and he seems even to have been willing to separate the League Covenant from the peace treaty—a very serious misunderstanding of Wilson's viewpoint.[66] And finally, on the difficult question of reparations, House had been willing to consider setting the bill at a very high level to relieve political pressure on the British government—provided that it was agreed tacitly that the whole amount would not be paid. Agreement on this startling departure from Wilson's position was avoided only because of the enormous difference between the amounts calculated as justifiable by the American and Allied experts.[67] Thus Wilson, weakened at home by senatorial criticisms, found himself facing in Paris a set of proposals made by his chief lieutenant that substantially subverted his whole program. His relationship with House never recovered.[68]

So confident had House been that Wilson would applaud what he had done that he had talked with British and French leaders about inviting the Germans to Paris to receive a completed treaty as early as 20 March, just a week after Wilson was to land at Brest. Those plans were abruptly shelved when Wilson learned what had been happening. Although it is impossible to know with certainty what Wilson said to House, there was no mistaking the president's determination to change course. On 15 March 1919 he released a statement that he would not approve the separation of the League of Nations from the peace treaty, and he made it absolutely clear to the Allied leaders that he would not consent to a treaty on House's terms.[69]

Nevertheless, Wilson realized that his position was weak. Not only did he have to repudiate much of what House had done, but he understood that to secure agreement to the treaty in the United States it would be essential to ask for amendments to the Covenant of the League that would satisfy American fears about the Monroe Doctrine, possible League interference in internal affairs, a right of withdrawal, and other issues. It may have been for this reason that even as he reasserted his earlier position in public, he also agreed in private to join with Britain and France in a separate treaty obligating the English and the Americans to come to France's aid if Germany attacked.[70] He apparently regarded this extraordinary departure from American tradition as a price that had to be paid to keep the conference going.

March 1919 turned out to be perhaps the most difficult month of the conference for Wilson, with the French in particular determined to impose a punitive peace on Germany and the president's position weaker than it had ever been before. Bitter disputes over the west bank of the Rhine, over the Saar Basin, and over reparations made relations extremely tense. Wilson frankly admitted his "great irritation" with the French, who would seem to yield on a point only to bring it up all over again a little later. It was, he said, "like pressing your finger into an indiarubber [sic] ball. You tried to make an impression but as soon as you moved your finger the ball was as round as ever." Clemenceau, for his part, was equally annoyed. Wilson, he told a member of the British delegation, "thought himself another Jesus Christ come upon the earth to reform men."[71]

By the end of the month Wilson was in despair, but in fact the deadlock was beginning to break. The French were still demanding annexation of the Saar Basin, which had not been French since 1814; but the British proposed a temporary French occupation of the region under a League mandate instead, with a plebiscite to determine its ultimate fate. Wilson did not like the plan, but he admitted that the French were entitled to compensation for German destruction of French coal mines during the war.[72] On the issue of reparations, the central problem had become whether pensions could be included in the total bill. Wilson had steadfastly opposed any such inclusion, which would greatly increase reparations claims, but a memorandum by Jan Smuts seems to have convinced him, despite the advice of his own experts, to accept the inclusion of pensions because otherwise "England would not get what she was entitled to in proportion to the other countries."[73] Even on the issue of the Rhineland the willingness of the Americans and the British to consider an alliance with France had suggested a way out of the dilemma, although the French were not yet prepared to give in.

To deal with these and other matters, Wilson spent hours in meetings of the Council of Ten and the Council of Four, in meetings of the reconvened League of Nations Commission, in private meetings with other leaders and with his own delegation, in reading and drafting memorandums, and in reading and answering queries and statements from the United States about domestic issues. Probably he worked longer hours and carried a greater burden of responsibility in this period than ever before in his life—certainly longer and heavier than he had at any time while president. By the end of the month he was exhausted, and not surprisingly he came down with a viral infection. The effect of this illness on Wilson has been the subject of some debate among historians, but Dr. Bert Park has suggested plausibly that the illness, superimposed upon Wilson's "diffuse cerebrovascular disease" made him unusually susceptible to delirium and may account for a series of disturbing acts and odd behavior.[74]

Aside from some relatively minor incidents noted by observers, such as Wilson's sudden conviction that all his French servants were spies, his abrupt order that members of the delegation were not to use official cars for recreation, and a suspicion that someone was stealing the furniture from the house in which he was staying, the president also made abrupt changes of his position on a number of important issues.[75] Before his illness, for example, he had opposed a British proposal to try the Kaiser for war crimes, but after it he suddenly reversed himself. Indeed, his whole attitude toward the Germans, which had previously been sympathetic, became hostile, and he accepted a clause for the treaty drafted by John Foster Dulles that placed the whole guilt for the war on Germany. Even more important, at just this point he abruptly overruled his own experts and accepted the Anglo-French position on reparations; he agreed to the French demand for a fifteen-year occupation of the Rhineland, despite continued British opposition to the plan; and he accepted French control of the Saar coal mines under a fifteen-year League administration.[76] And in all these cases he asserted that he had won victories, claiming that it had been his threat, delivered on 6 April in the midst of his illness, to leave the conference and return to the United States that had forced the other leaders to give in.[77]

The evidence is thus substantial that Wilson's illness of late March and early April, on top of previous vascular disease, had a serious effect on his mind and on American policy. Because he had insisted on going to France himself and because he had monopolized control of the negotiations, his breakdown had a serious effect on the American position. Several of the compromises with the Fourteen Points that later alienated liberal supporters of the president took place in this period, and as a result the possibility that the peace treaty would actually bring into effect a new system of international relations was significantly reduced.

Nor was the compromising at an end. While the conference had been concentrating on Franco-German issues, the Italians had been quietly biding their time. Italy had entered the war in 1915 on the Allied side because the Treaty of London promised them Austrian territory in the Alps and along the Dalmatian coast. Now they advanced a specific claim to the Brenner Pass region of the Tyrol and to Fiume on the Dalmation coast. Since the Tyrolians were Austrian and the people of Fiume's hinterland Slavic, both claims violated the principle of self-determination. Nevertheless, the Italian position was strong, not only because of the Treaty of London but also because in the prearmistice negotiations, the Americans had promised Italy a defensible border in the north.[78]

When Prime Minister Orlando raised these issues at the conference, Wilson tried to argue that the Treaty of London had been intended only to protect Italy from the Austro-Hungarian Empire. With the empire gone, the treaty should be superseded by the principle of self-determination.[79] The Italians, of course, were unmoved by that argument, and after Orlando walked out of the conference, Wilson decided to appeal directly to the Italian people. On 23 April he issued a statement urging Italians to sacrifice immediate self-interest to "the right of the world to peace and to such settlements of interest as shall make peace secure."[80]

It may be that Wilson's rash attempt to appeal to the Italian people over the heads of their leaders was another example of the irrationality that seems to have been triggered by his illness, but of course it was also in keeping with his long-standing belief that his mission was to articulate the inchoate wishes of the people. In this case it was a failure. Orlando informed Clemenceau and Lloyd George that he could not remain at the conference and issued a statement that despite its temperate language made clear the offense given to Italy. When the Italians eventually returned to the table, however, Wilson was unmoved, meeting their renewed demands for Fiume with steely resistance, and the issue was never resolved during the conference. Not until 1920 did the Italian-Yugoslav Treaty of Rapallo settle the issue by giving the Italians less territory in Dalmatia than they had been promised by the Treaty of London but including Fiume in an independent free state that was annexed by Italy in 1924.[81]

Wilson displayed an inflexible insistence upon the principle of self-determination in dealing with Italian claims to the Dalmatian coast that he did not evince elsewhere and that was particularly in contrast to his handling of a Japanese crisis in the same period. The Japanese had come to the conference concerned especially with two matters: the recognition of their territorial, economic, and political control of parts of China, and a specific recognition of racial equality. The other nations did not like either of these ideas, but the proposal for racial equality set off alarm bells especially for the Americans and the British.

On 11 April in a meeting of the reconvened League of Nations Commission, the Japanese delegate, Baron Nabuoki Makino, introduced a variation of his racial equality proposal in which he suggested that the preamble of the covenant should endorse "the principle of the equality of Nations and the just treatment of their nationals."[82] A number of delegates, pointing out that this statement sought only recognition of the equality of nations and fair treatment of all peoples, promptly endorsed it, but Viscount Cecil argued that the clause "opened the door to serious controversy and to interference in the domestic affairs of States." Wilson, presiding over the session, said that "the greatest difficulty lay in controversies which would be bound to take place outside the Commission over the Japanese proposal" (in the Senate, for example) and therefore opposed the amendment, although he stressed that the "fundamental principle" of the League was "the equality of nations." Despite an eleven-to-six vote for the amendment, the president ruled that it had failed because the commission's rules required unanimity, even though he admitted that he had not always enforced that requirement when dissenters did not raise "serious objections," as was the case in this instance.[83]

Wilson's evident embarrassment at having to oppose the racial-equality clause strengthened the Japanese in their pursuit of their other goal—concessions in China. In fact, their position on this issue was already very strong. When the war began Japan had invoked a treaty of alliance with Great Britain and declared war on Germany, seizing German concessions in Shantung Province. Subsequently, their claims had been validated by the signing of secret treaties with Britain (16 February 1917) and France (1 March 1917) and to a lesser degree by the Lansing-Ishii talks with the United States.[84] Moreover, the Japanese promised that sovereignty over the territories in question would be returned to China eventually. Although the Japanese claims represented a major violation of the principle of self-determination, it was difficult for the Western nations to oppose them.

Secretary Lansing pointed out that under the Sino-Japanese arrangement reached in May 1915 the Chinese would have only a paper title to the territories; the arrangement "would leave the kernel to Japan and restore the shell to China."[85] The Chinese and their friends in the State Department also underlined this concern. Nevertheless, Wilson found it difficult to protest. In a meeting of the Council of Four he could only appeal to Japanese consciences. The world would never have peace, he said, if nations were always "thinking more of [their] rights than of [their] duties."[86]

The dilemma posed by the Japanese demands was very real to

Wilson, as a conversation Ray Stannard Baker recorded in his diary demonstrates:

> The Japanese question worries him. "They are not bluffers," he said, "& they will go home unless we give them what they should not have."
>
> "The opinion of the world," I said, "supports the Chinese claims."
>
> "I know that," he said.
>
> "Especially American public opinion," I added.
>
> "I know that, too," he replied "but if Italian [Italy] remains away & Japan goes home, what becomes of the League of Nations?"
>
> He is at Gethsemane.[87]

American attempts to find a way out of this quandary were fruitless, but the British, who had promised to stand by their treaty obligations to the Japanese, were eventually more successful. After lengthy negotiations, Foreign Secretary Arthur Balfour produced a formula under which Japan promised to drop its demand for a racial-equality clause and to turn over sovereignty in the disputed territories to China in return for confirmation of its economic interests.[88] Lansing, most of the American delegation, and the Chinese denounced this "iniquitous agreement"; but Wilson, backed by House, reluctantly approved it, convinced that it was "the best that could be accomplished out of a 'dirty past'" and the necessary price for Japanese membership in the League of Nations.[89] Through that organization, he argued in a message to the American people, "all extraordinary foreign rights in China and all spheres of influence" could be "abrogated by the common consent of all the nations concerned."[90]

With agreement on the Chinese provisions, the last major issue of the negotiations was settled, and on 7 May the treaty was handed to the Germans for the first time. Then followed a remarkable two-month period in which the supposedly "dictated" peace was substantially renegotiated and softened, largely because the nearly bankrupt Allies could not see how they would be able to sustain a lengthy occupation of Germany if, as seemed likely, any conceivable German government refused to sign the treaty. On 2 June Lloyd George, under heavy pressure from the Left in Britain, vastly complicated the whole matter by suddenly proposing a reduction in German reparations, a plebiscite in Upper Silesia to determine whether it would become German or Polish rather than being assigned to Poland as provided in the original treaty draft, a redrawing of the Polish-German border in Germany's favor, a substantial reduction of the period of Allied occupation of the Rhineland, the prompt admission of Germany to the League, and the removal of other "pin-pricks" from the treaty.[91]

Lloyd George's demands, backed by a threat of withdrawal from the conference, threw everyone into an uproar. Wilson discussed the whole issue with the other American peace commissioners and with several of the experts from the delegation and declared that he had "no desire to soften the treaty, but [he had] a very sincere desire to alter those portions of it that are shown to be unjust, or which are shown to be contrary to the principles which we ourselves have laid down."[92] Accordingly, in subsequent meetings of the Council of Four, Wilson generally sided with Clemenceau in opposing immediate German admission to the League or any shortening of the period of occupation of the Rhineland, but Lloyd George won significant concessions nevertheless. He got a promise that the costs of the occupation would come only from payments of reparations to the French; he and Wilson won the establishment of a civilian authority to oversee the French occupation of the Rhineland; he secured the changes he wanted in the German-Polish border and the plebiscite for Upper Silesia; and, most important, he at last broke through Wilson's opposition to leaving the amount of reparations indeterminate, to be set later by an international commission rather than fixed at a definite sum in the treaty.[93] In this period Wilson found Lloyd George just as irritating as he had earlier found Clemenceau, but for the opposite reason. He had been exasperated by Clemenceau's obsession with protecting French security by methods he thought would subvert the whole intention of the League of Nations; now he was equally aggravated by Lloyd George's subservience to political pressures and eagerness to soften a treaty whose terms the president thought fair, if harsh. Exhausted by the long strain of the conference, Wilson longed to finish and go home.

One last obstacle remained before he could leave, however. The Germans had to sign the treaty, and in mid-June that looked unlikely. On 13 June the Council of Four discussed what to do in the event of a refusal, and again there was substantial disagreement, with the British and the French proposing a naval blockade for economic reasons and Wilson arguing for an occupation of Germany. A blockade, said the president, would be warfare against women and children and "would only bring about Bolshevism and chaos," yet he agreed to threaten a blockade in hopes it would never be needed.[94] What would have happened if the Germans had actually refused to sign is by no means certain, but fortunately on 22 June came the news that their government had fallen and been replaced by one that would sign. When the news was confirmed and released the following day, pandemonium broke out in Paris, much as it had at the announcement of the armistice. Wilson, who was attempting to go for a ride in the late afternoon, found his car completely blocked by cheering crowds like those who had greeted him in December. From the crowd an old man stepped forward to say, simply, "Mr. President, I want to thank you for peace."[95]

Five days later the sullen German plenipotentiaries were brought to the Hall of Mirrors to sign the final treaty. Huge crowds were on hand, both indoors and outside, to witness the historic moment. Inside all was solemn and dignified, but on the grounds of the palace the fountains were turned on for the first time since the beginning of the war, where they bubbled and splashed in the sunlight, reflecting the champagne mood of the crowd. When Clemenceau, Wilson, Lloyd George, and Orlando appeared outside after the ceremony, there was a happy roar and the crowd rushed forward to surround them. Eventually, French troops had to be called to rescue them from their admirers. In the euphoria of the moment, only a few people wondered whether the treaty so laboriously negotiated would endure and what its effects would be.[96]

In many ways, of course, the optimism of that June day was justified. The treaty was remarkable in that for the first time an honest effort was made not only to accommodate one of the greatest forces of the modern era, nationalism, but also to establish a mechanism within which nationalist ambitions could be satisfied peacefully. Although critics would later charge that the treaty sought to freeze the status quo, Wilson denied that absolutely. His goal, he said over and over, was to accept change but to force it into orderly channels.[97]

In other ways the treaty compromised with perfection but provided for a peace that was fairer than it would have been without Wilson's intervention. The recognition of Poland, Yugoslavia, and Czechoslovakia, as well as other nation-states in Central Europe, satisfied many people even if borders were not always drawn along clear ethnic lines. The occupation of the Rhineland and the Saar Basin outraged Germans, but surely they would have been even more bitter had Germany been partitioned as Marshal Foch had wanted. Even the Shantung settlement, clear though its violations of self-determination were, at least contained a promise that the Japanese would respect Chinese sovereignty in the long run. The mandate system did not fulfill the original promise to settle colonial claims with full regard to the interest of native peoples, but it created a precedent for international scrutiny and supervision of colonies. In all of these areas the treaty was "far from ideal," as Wilson admitted; but he still argued with some justice that it was "tolerably close to the lines laid down at the outset."[98] Having been through the process of negotiation and seen the problems at first hand, the president was justly proud of what he had accomplished.

Others, then and later, were not so sanguine. The fundamental flaw of the treaty, wrote Thomas A. Bailey as World War II neared its end, was that "it was neither a thoroughgoing victor's peace nor a peace of accommodation"; there is still much to be said for that judgment.[99] Wilson had gone to Europe in hopes of establishing a "peace without victory," which by its fairness and by its creation of new peacekeeping machinery would eliminate the causes of war. Once there, he was caught up in the passions and fears of war—passions that he himself shared, it must be noted—and thus participated in writing a peace that tried to punish Germany through machinery that was supposed to eliminate the causes of war. The two goals were incompatible.

In addition, the peace failed to solve some major problems that Wilson had identified before the conference. The most obvious of these were Russia and bolshevism, which were excluded from the conference and unmentioned in the treaty. Equally serious, although less obvious at the time, was the inability of the conference to take more than the most tentative first steps toward the termination of European colonialism, toward disarmament, or toward the removal of economic barriers among nations. On the contrary, as Eric Goldman has pointed out, the dominance of the idea of self-determination "stimulated nationalism" and made it unlikely that nations would agree "to make peace without victory, to reduce armaments, to cut down tariffs, or to consider colonies in the genuine spirit of the mandate system."[100]

In part, then, the flaws of the treaty were inherent in the original Fourteen Points and indeed in all of Wilson's approach to government. From the beginning he had assumed that men could be brought to yield their selfish, individual interests to the common good, if only they could be shown what the common good was. Although that conviction remained unshaken despite reverses during his first seven years in office, it had never been confronted with a more formidable challenge than the president met in Paris, where the other leaders not only questioned his goal of a concert of power but disagreed with his analysis of the problems that needed to be cured. Under the circumstances, it was remarkable that he was able to come as near as he did to bending the world settlement to his own vision, but he could not impose either upon the Allied statesmen or upon his own fellow Americans the consensus that could alone make the peace work.

10

★ ★ ★ ★ ★

PEACE

Wilson returned to the United States on 8 July to face a fight as hard as that he had just fought in Paris. As early as April Joseph Tumulty had begun urging a "tour of the country" to promote the League, but House wisely recommended a lower-key effort to cultivate leading senators before going on the attack. Combatively, Wilson told both House and Lansing that he expected "to make a direct frontal attack" on his opponents, but in the end discretion prevailed.[1]

In his speech presenting the treaty to the Senate on 10 July Wilson took the high road, declaring that "a new role and a new responsibility have come to this great nation that we honour and which we would all wish to lift to yet higher levels of service and achievement." He admitted that the treaty was "not exactly what we would have written," but he avoided discussion of those provisions he knew to be controversial, concentrating instead on positive achievements and stressing that the peace offered the only available opportunity "to make the triumph of freedom and of right a lasting triumph in the assurance of which men might everywhere live without fear." He also offered to meet with the Foreign Relations Committee personally or to send them any information they might want.[2]

The speech did not please everyone. The newspapers reported that Republican senators listened to it stonily and that when the president greeted senators informally in a room next door to the Senate chamber after the speech, only one Republican appeared.[3] Arizona Democrat Henry Fountain Ashurst recorded in his diary his disappointment that the president had avoided such difficult issues as Article 10 and the Shantung question and reported that opponents of the treaty were delighted with the speech; supporters, on the other hand, "wanted raw meat, [and] he fed them cold turnips."[4] Secretary McAdoo, in contrast, thought that the speech would "appeal to the people" but that it was "like casting pearls before swine as far as the Senatorial cabal is concerned."[5]

The chief swine, in McAdoo's opinion, was the majority leader and chairman of the Foreign Relations Committee, Henry Cabot Lodge of Massachusetts. Lodge, an intense partisan and Theodore Roosevelt's close friend, had been critical of Wilsonian foreign policy from the outset of the administration, claiming that its chief characteristics were "feebleness and ignorance."[6] As time passed and Lodge believed that the administration was pusillanimous in dealing with Mexico and Germany, his contempt grew. By 1915 he was telling Roosevelt that he "never expected to hate any one in politics with the hatred I feel towards Wilson."[7]

Behind Lodge's partisan bias and intemperate language lay a substantive difference with Wilson about America's world role. Lodge was no isolationist. "We must do our share to carry out the peace as we have done our share to win the war," he said in December 1918; but he also believed that Americans must assess realistically the obligations the president was proposing. In his opinion, the president's talk about "the moral force of the world" guaranteeing the peace was nonsense; only force or the threat of force could actually assure peace. "If we guarantee any country on earth," he declared, "that guarantee we must maintain at any cost when our word is once given, and we must be in constant possession of fleets and armies capable of enforcing these guarantees at a moment's notice."[8] Convinced that the American people did not want to take on such open-ended obligations, Lodge was as opposed to the basic premise of Wilson's treaty as the most ardent isolationist but for different reasons.

Although the Republicans had a majority of forty-nine to forty-seven when the treaty was submitted to the Senate, Lodge could not be absolutely sure of mustering the thirty-three votes he needed to defeat the treaty or to force major changes in it. He soon learned that he could count on a core of sixteen senators, the so-called "Irreconcilables," who believed either that the treaty had betrayed the idealism of the Fourteen Points or that it was too utopian and who thus opposed it adamantly. But with former president Taft and the influential Elihu Root saying that they would support the treaty with some modifications, Lodge could not expect party unity on the issue, nor could he realistically expect to defeat the treaty outright.[9] His best strategy was to propose amendments or reservations, which virtually all Republicans favored in some form or other, and then to hope he could patch together the thirty-three votes he needed.

On the Democratic side the situation was only slightly less complicated. Two Democrats, James Reed of Missouri and Charles S. Thomas of Colorado, defected to the Irreconcilables. The minority leader, Thomas S. Martin of Virginia, was terminally ill, and the acting minority leader, Gilbert Hitchcock of Nebraska, had disagreements with the administration dating back to 1913. Above all the Democrats had to secure about twenty Republican votes in order to gain the two-thirds majority necessary to approve the treaty. Thus they had to win the support not only of the ten "mild reservationists" who favored the treaty with some minor changes but also of ten more Republicans, who somehow had to be wooed away from Lodge's control.[10]

The simple mathematics of the situation dictated Wilson's initial course. He might want to fight, but he had first to try to court. Accordingly, during the middle of July he invited small groups of senators to the White House, concentrating especially on those who were not publicly committed on the issue. British agent Sir William Wiseman, whose reports on American politics were usually perceptive, believed that these efforts were bearing fruit and that the Republicans doubted if they could do more than delay the treaty's approval.[11]

In reality, however, Wilson's position was weakening because of his absolute refusal to consider anything other than explanatory reservations, a position for which there is no conclusive reason. Certainly the president believed that the people of the United States favored the treaty; he was already planning a late-summer speaking trip across the country to whip up public pressure on the Senate. With his conviction that he could sense the underlying aspirations of the people, he may have believed that compromise was unnecessary. Too, he seems to have had at least for a time a misunderstanding of the ratification process, which was strange for a political scientist who had written extensively on the workings of Congress. On 27 June, for example, he said in a press conference that he thought the Senate could only approve or disapprove the whole treaty, since modifying or amending it was a part of the executive's negotiating prerogative; and on 10 July he told the *New York Times* that he believed any reservations or amendments would have to be passed by a two-thirds vote in the Senate.[12] Had either of those beliefs been correct, the administration's position would have been a great deal stronger than it actually was. Above all the president believed that adoption of the treaty with reservations or amendments would require the approval of the other signatories and would delay the peace interminably as well as opening the treaty to modification by other powers.[13] In this instance he was probably thinking of a situation that had arisen in late June, when the Chinese sought to sign the treaty with a reservation about the Shantung clause. At that point the Council of Four had discussed the issue and the European leaders had all agreed that, as Clemenceau said, "a Treaty which was signed with reservations was not a treaty"; the Chinese had then refused to sign.[14] Whether this position was correct, however, was debatable.

From a broader point of view, Wilson's objections to reservations came from his whole concept of what the treaty was about. As Lloyd Ambrosius has pointed out, Wilson "held firmly to his vision of collective security and refused to accept a more limited, but definite, role for his country" such as would have been necessitated by accepting the specific, nationalistic Senate reservations.[15] The issue, as Wilson saw it, was not merely a matter of details, upon which he had been flexible in dealing with Congress in the past and with the other negotiators at Paris, but rather a question of basic principle, upon which there could be no compromise.

The heart of the matter was Article 10, which said:

> The Members of the League undertake to respect and preserve as against external aggression the territorial integrity and existing political independence of all the Members of the League. In case of any such aggression or in case of any threat or danger of such aggression the Council shall advise upon the means by which this obligation shall be fulfilled.[16]

The significance of that article, in Wilson's opinion, lay in its assumption that all nations have a vital stake in the maintenance of peace and that all must therefore act to prevent disruptions of peace, *"at whatever cost of independent action."*[17] In drafting the article, he had struggled to attain a delicate balance between protecting national sovereignty and submerging the nation in collective security; every proposed reservation to that section sought to tilt the balance decisively toward national independence, thus destroying the whole basis of the covenant.

By 20 July Wilson was eager to take the issue to the country in a speaking trip that he hoped would reveal a national consensus in favor of ratification. Despite his efforts to conciliate moderate Republicans, he now knew that at least thirty-five senators would refuse to approve the treaty unless significant amendments or reservations were attached, and it appeared that his effort to win supporters had failed. Nevertheless, the president's advisers urged him not to make the trip. Not only were they concerned about his health, which had deteriorated visibly, but they pointed out that the Senate was effectively insulated from the pressure of public opinion. Even if Wilson aroused large, enthusiastic crowds, the effect on the Senate would be negligible or even negative.[18]

By the end of July Wilson had decided that further individual meetings with senators were pointless, but he decided to make one last effort to reach agreement with the members of the Foreign Relations Committee as a group at a White House meeting on 19 August. By this time the president had modified his position enough to be willing to accept what he called "interpretive" reservations, provided such reservations were not made part of the actual ratification, which he continued to argue would necessitate renegotiation of the treaty with the other signatories. On 14 August Wilson drafted a letter to Senator Lodge setting out this somewhat softened position but did not send it, despite Tumulty's urging, because of the committee's request to meet. Instead, in an interview with Senator Hitchcock on 15 August, the president declared that "the very thought of reservations" by Senate Democrats was "premature."[19]

It is impossible to know what Wilson may have been thinking as he planned for the meeting with the Foreign Relations Committee on 19 August. His conversation with Hitchcock suggests that he may have thought the opposition was caving in, although that seems hard to believe since Hitchcock and others were warning him explicitly that many Democrats as well as Republicans favored at least some reservations. In the meeting he read his draft of the letter of 14 August as part of his opening statement to the committee, but if he aimed at establishing a spirit of compromise and conciliation, he failed, largely because he then repeated his dubious assertion that if the Senate attached reservations to the treaty, all other signatories would have to consider and approve them. Indeed he even went so far as to say that the Germans, too, would have to approve such reservations, although later in the meeting he admitted that the claim was in error.[20]

The 19 August meeting did more harm than good to Wilson's cause because he absolutely ruled out any substantive amendments or reservations and because he muddied the issue even further by saying that Article 10, which he described as "the very backbone of the whole Covenant," was "binding in conscience only, not in law."[21] That seemed to be double-talk designed to please both those people who believed that a binding obligation was essential to the success of the League and those who wanted to maintain American independence. Instead of laying the issue to rest, it reinforced the argument that a reservation was necessary to clarify American obligations under Article 10.

Moreover, Wilson's offer to accept explanatory reservations in a separate document should not have been made at the 19 August meeting because it had the appearance of an attempt to placate Lodge, who had no interest in such a small concession. In earlier conversations with some mild reservationists Wilson's hints about explanatory reservations had seemed to open a possibility of compromise, but once the matter was put into Lodge's hands that chance vanished.[22] Lodge concluded that the meeting had "not affected a single Senator but has strengthened us in the Senate."[23]

Following the 19 August meeting senatorial Democrats and mild reservationists bargained futilely, with no progress possible because the president would not give his blessing to any specific compromise. Meantime, Lodge urged party discipline and strengthened his program of strong reservations, drawing support from Wilson's intransigence, which cast the president's supporters into despair. More and more minority groups were speaking out against various provisions of the treaty (its failure to provide independence for Ireland, for example), and liberals increasingly were saying that compromises with the original ideals of the Fourteen Points had been fatal to the integrity of the peace. The Shantung settlement, in particular, became a focus of bitter criticism. By the beginning of September Lodge's position had become so much stronger that he no longer thought about delaying or modifying the treaty in minor ways. He now believed that he could amend it significantly or even defeat it.[24]

Wilson knew that too. Having failed to find a way to work with the Senate, he saw that his only remaining chance, slim as it might be, was to arouse such a wave of public support for the treaty that even senators would be carried along. Although he was thin, exhausted, and shaking so visibly that Dr. Grayson feared an extensive speaking trip might kill him, the president overruled all his objections. "I cannot put my personal safety, my health in the balance against my duty—I must go," he said, and on 3 September he set out for the West.[25] Although the heart of isolationism, the West's progressives had given Wilson his narrow victory in 1916. If he were to win his gamble anywhere, it must be there.

Wilson started out in his first speeches arguing mildly that the severity of the treaty was justified by Germany's offenses and claiming that the unity of the nations in the League would intimidate possible aggressors and avoid the necessity of using force, but he soon began to make more exaggerated claims.[26] In speeches at St. Louis, for example, he warned that if the United States did not join the League, it would be "frozen out" of the world's commerce. If it did not join to preserve peace, it would have to maintain "a great standing army" and a "mobilized nation" with a "concentrated, militaristic organization of government." On the other hand, he predicted that if America joined the League, "we will be the senior partner. The financial leadership will be ours. The industrial primacy will be ours. The other countries of the world are looking to us for leadership and direction."[27] The choice, as he presented it, was stark—independence and insecurity or membership and world dominance.

The scare tactics that were a minor theme of the first speeches became increasingly dominant in later ones. "Opposition is the specialty of those who are Bolshevistically inclined," he told an audience in Kansas City; and although he quickly added that he was "not comparing any of my respected colleagues to Bolshevists," no one could miss his message in that autumn of the Red Scare.[28] Nor could anyone miss the message when he began to equate opponents of the treaty with "hyphenated" Americans who were, he declared, "the most un-American thing in the world."[29] Opposition to the treaty, he charged in Portland, Oregon, was "pro-German," and at Pueblo, Colorado, he asserted that "any man who carries a hyphen about with him carries a dagger that he is ready to plunge into the vitals of this Republic."[30] After a year and a half of war's exhortations to unity and conformity, references to "hyphens" and "pro-Germanism" were ugly charges indeed.

Yet if an element of "paranoid style" was in Wilson's attacks on those who criticized the treaty, there was also an effort to shift attention from imperfect details to the promise that the League could "make the rest of the [treaty] work."[31] What was really new about this peace, as he said in Minneapolis, was that the treaty "provides for placing the peace of the world under constant international oversight, in recognition of the principle that the peace of the world is the legitimate and immediate interest of every nation."[32] And especially, he insisted, peace was America's interest because "liberty is suffocated by war. Free institutions cannot survive the strain of prolonged military administration."[33]

For those who were unmoved by the argument that America "was founded to lead the world on the way to liberty," Wilson offered more practical persuasion. "You cannot disentangle the United States from the rest of the world," he argued; "if the rest of the world goes bankrupt, the business of the United States is in a way to be ruined."[34] By the same token, if interdependence could be profitable, it could also mean the spread of infections through the world. The "poison" of bolshevism was "running through the veins of the world," he said, "and we have made the methods of communication throughout the world such that all the veins of the world are open and the poison can circulate."[35] Interdependence had made isolation impossible—and undesirable—in the future.

Wilson also attempted to calm fears about the obligations of Article 10. Over and over he repeated that in the event of a threat to peace, the Council "cannot give . . . advice without a unanimous vote . . . , without the affirmative vote of the United States."[36] Therefore, he insisted, "the Congress of the United States is just as free under that article to refuse to declare war as it is now; and it is very much safer than it is now."[37] He did not explain why, if that were the case, he objected to a reservation saying that explicitly or to reservations that would affirm other points he said were already in the treaty regarding the Monroe Doctrine and the protection of the nation from interference with its internal affairs.

Wilson was asking Americans to accept a delicate structure, in which national independence was combined with a recognition of the reality of interdependence and with some limitations on sovereignty. On the one hand he wanted to reassure Americans that no danger would come from the new order, yet on the other he claimed that immense benefits would result from it. In fact, however, the promise could be only a hope, and the assurance was less than absolute. Wilson frequently said that he believed the treaty offered "a 99 percent insurance against war," but he admitted that it might be only "10 percent"; if that were the case, then the prospective purchasers of the policy were wise to study the fine print closely.[38] When the president himself admitted that "you can [not] get the advantage without assuming the responsibility," his listeners were surely right to ask exactly what responsibilities he was asking them to assume.[39]

If Wilson's speeches thus failed to clarify some of the real questions about the treaty, they had the effect he wanted. By the time he reached the Rockies he was attracting large, enthusiastic crowds, and the opponents of the treaty were sufficiently concerned about his influence to send Senators William E. Borah of Idaho and Hiram Johnson of California after him to give the other side of the argument. His speech at Pueblo, Colorado, on 25 September was the emotional high point of the trip, with a large, spirited audience standing and cheering for ten minutes before Wilson could even begin.

The speech, however, was not very good. The trip had been exhausting, with thirty-seven major speeches in twenty-two days and endless briefer addresses and local functions. Wilson had been suffering throughout most of the trip with headaches so severe that his vision was blurred and with asthma that forced him to sleep much of the time sitting up. When he tried to climb onto the speaker's platform at Pueblo he stumbled, and as he spoke his voice was weak and difficult to hear. Often he paused, seeming to lose the direction of his thought. That evening, as the train continued eastward, Dr. Grayson arranged to have it stop so that the president could take a walk in the country, hoping that might relax him.[40]

During the night Wilson suffered a breakdown. At two in the morning Grayson and Tumulty found him sitting in his drawing room compartment, severely nauseated, drooling from the left side of his mouth, and with his face slightly flattened on the left. The next morning, in tears, he gave Tumulty an odd but accurate description of what had happened: "I don't seem to realize it, but I seem to have gone to pieces. The doctor [Grayson] is right. I am not in condition to go on. I have never been in a condition like this, and I just feel as if I am going to pieces." Grayson immediately recognized the attack for what it was—a clear warning of an impending stroke—and insisted on canceling the rest of the trip. Although the president protested weakly that Lodge would think him "a quitter," he allowed Tumulty, Grayson, and Edith to order the train back to Washington.[41]

In the rushing train, which seemed to Edith "like a funeral cortege," she silently determined that neither the country nor her husband would ever know how terribly ill he was.[42] By the time the train reached Washington on Sunday, 28 September, news of the sudden cancellation of the remaining five speeches of the trip had caused a great crowd to gather at the station. Wilson rallied and managed to walk unaided to the car, although he looked dreadfully gaunt and haggard. Upon returning to the White House, Dr. Grayson immediately made an appointment for Dr. Francis Xavier Dercum, a prominent Philadelphia heart specialist, to examine the president; but on 2 October, the day before Dercum was to visit, Wilson suffered a massive stroke. That morning he awoke complaining of some numbness and weakness on his left side and then fell while dressing. By the time Dr. Dercum saw him at 4:30 he was paralyzed completely on the left side and largely blind in the center and left fields of both eyes. Dercum reported, however, that the attack, which he diagnosed as a "thrombosis of the middle cerebral artery of the right hemisphere," had affected Wilson's face less than his arm and leg, that his mind was lucid, and that he could speak clearly, though he was somewhat somnolent.[43]

For four weeks the president was allowed no visitors at all. He denied his own illness, and Edith insisted on humoring him for fear that forcing him to confront the truth would kill him. At her insistence, Grayson told even the cabinet that Wilson was suffering from "a nervous breakdown, indigestion, and a depleted nervous system," although in private he prepared a reasonably frank statement of the president's condition, which was never released to the press.[44] When Secretary Lansing suggested that the vice-president should take over because of the president's condition, the doctor, probably on Edith's orders, refused to sign a certificate of disability. "I am not thinking of the country now, I am thinking of my husband," she said; and it was all too true.[45]

Dr. Bert E. Park, a neurosurgeon who has examined the recently discovered medical records of Wilson's illness, believes that the president's doctors diagnosed his stroke accurately but were probably misled by his apparent lucidity into thinking that he was more capable of continuing in office than was actually the case. "The psychologic manifestations of strokes were poorly defined in Wilson's day," writes Dr. Park; and the president's physicians failed to realize that despite his "relatively well preserved intellectual function," he was subject to "disorders of emotion, impaired impulse control, and defective judgment." Specifically, the "substrata" of Wilson's personality were "magnified in bold relief" so that traits of "intransigence, stubbornness, insistence upon having his own way, self-righteousness, [and] a tendency to fall back upon principles as a means of finding some basis for policy-making" made it impossible for him to deal realistically with any situation calling for negotiation or compromise.[46] Thus the nation was left with a president who despite his physical illness seemed to be mentally capable of exercising power but was actually psychologically crippled in ways no one around him could diagnose with sufficient certainty to justify removing him from office.

During the first phase of the president's illness, from 2 October to late January 1920, his psychological problems were compounded by extreme physical weakness. He remained paralyzed, with recurrent kidney failure and urinary blockages, and most important, he was simply too weak to understand complex issues or to formulate policy. Although he saw a few political visitors briefly during this period, he did not see Tumulty until mid-November, refused to see Lansing at all, and did not meet with his cabinet. In mid-January Grayson, convinced that Wilson could never recover, urged him to resign, but Edith instantly vetoed the idea.[47]

By the end of January 1920 Wilson seemed to be improving. His strength increased; he resumed dictating to his secretary; and he composed some diplomatic correspondence. With returning vigor came also increased "aggressiveness, irascibility, and pugnacity," all unrecognized manifestations of his illness.[48] In short order he rebuked Tumulty for meddling in policy, fired Lansing for holding cabinet meetings during his illness although in fact he had been told of the meetings months before, claimed erroneously that he had never known about the secret treaties among the Allies that had apportioned some of the loot from the war, rejected any compromise with Italy, France, and England on the still-unresolved Fiume question, and categorically rejected all possibility of compromise with the Senate on the treaty. Such behavior, far from convincing those closest to the president that he was incapable of staying in office, led them to just the opposite conclusion. By late spring 1920 Edith and the sycophantic new secretary of state, Bainbridge Colby, were feeding Wilson's fantasy that he could run for a third term and win a mandate to approve the treaty.

In later years Edith denied that she had ever "made a single decision regarding the disposition of public affairs." She insisted that during what she called her "stewardship," the "only decision that was mine was what was important and what was not, and the *very* important decision of when to present matters to my husband."[49] Even if we take that at face value, her influence was obviously enormous. By providing or withholding information, she was determining what the president knew about the world; if we combine that with her resolve to shield him from anything that might have discouraged or depressed him, it is clear that he knew too little and certainly too little of ugly reality to lead competently.

Yet this does not mean that Edith was actually the "first woman president." As every official who tried to get guidance from the White House during late 1919 and early 1920 has testified, the problem was not that Edith was issuing orders in Wilson's name but that urgent issues were ignored, pleas for direction unheard. Insofar as the government continued to function, it did so on inertia, and anyone who tried to exercise leadership was cut down by the petulant invalid, as was Robert Lansing.[50]

Even before Wilson's massive stroke, Senator Lodge had begun to revise his strategy. He had at first expected to see the treaty ratified after the passage of reservations, but he now believed that it might be possible to defeat it altogether and thus humiliate Wilson and discredit his ideas.[51] To do that, it was critical that he work out with the mild reservationists a set of reservations upon which both they and the more extreme reservationists could agree and even more important that he prevent the president from compromising with the mild reservationists on terms that might save the treaty. In this, of course, Wilson turned out to be his ally, rejecting all reservations to Article 10 in particular even before his stroke. Lodge's proposed reservation to Article 10, which declared that the United States would undertake no obligation to preserve the territorial integrity or independence of any other state unless the Congress specifically approved, was, said Wilson "a rejection of the Covenant. . . . I can say, I believe with confidence, that it is the judgment of the people of the United States that neither the treaty nor the Covenant should be amended."[52] For the mild reservationists, there seemed nowhere to go but into Lodge's camp.[53]

Seizing the moment, on 6 November Lodge introduced fourteen reservations to the treaty. The most important of these stated that the United States would not undertake any obligation to enforce sanctions against aggressors without the explicit consent of Congress in each case; that it would be the sole judge of whether it had satisfied its obligations to the League if it withdrew; that it would accept no mandate without congressional approval; that it would be the sole judge of what was a "domestic" issue; that it would not submit any issue arising under the Monroe Doctrine to the League; that it would not be bound by the Shantung agreement; that no arms-limitation agreement would be binding on the United States unless approved by Congress; and that the covenant must be amended to give the United States as many votes in the Assembly as Great Britain and its dominions.[54]

Alarmed by the deteriorating situation, Senator Hitchcock secured one of the first interviews anyone had had with the president since his collapse to discuss the situation. When Hitchcock asked Wilson what he thought of Lodge's reservations, the president replied that they would be a "nullification of the Treaty and utterly impossible." The reservation to Article 10 "cuts the very heart out of the Treaty," Wilson continued, and adoption of *any* reservations except separate interpretive ones "would humiliate the United States before all of the allied countries" and Germany.[55] At a second interview ten days after the first and two days before the Senate vote on the treaty, Wilson reaffirmed his rejection of all reservations. On 19 November 1919 the Senate, in a series of three votes, defeated the treaty both with and without reservations. On the first two votes, with reservations, the treaty was defeated by thirty-nine yeas to fifty-five nays and by forty-one to fifty-one; on the third vote, with no reservations, the defeat was worse—thirty-eight for and fifty-three against.[56]

The responsibility for the treaty's defeat must be laid squarely at Wilson's door. Although it was true, as some of the president's supporters pointed out, that Lodge had vindictively tried to humiliate the president, Wilson in fact had rejected all efforts to work out a compromise, whether offered by leaders of his own party such as Hitchcock, by Republican mild reservationists in the Senate, or by Republican leaders such as William Howard Taft and Elihu Root. Even Edith Wilson abandoned her previous unquestioning support of her husband on the issue and begged him to consider compromise but with no results. His final order to Hitchcock was "let Lodge compromise."[57]

Before his illness, however, Wilson had admitted the possibility of compromise. In a confidential interview with Sir William Wiseman on 18 July he admitted "that he [might] be obliged, in order to secure a really satisfactory majority, to agree to some reservation defining or interpreting the language of one or more Clauses of the Covenant." He had specified in particular Article 1, dealing with the right of withdrawal, Article 10, and Article 21, regarding the Monroe Doctrine.[58] Before leaving on his western trip he had typed out four interpretive reservations on these topics and given them to Hitchcock with instructions to use them as necessary without revealing their source.[59] Limited as they were, these reservations might have provided a basis for an accommodation with the mild reservationists.

Why then was the president considering compromise in July but rejecting all overtures in November? One answer is that the compromises Wilson was willing to offer in July may have been essentially meaningless—that he was actually never willing to give an inch. In fact one interpretation suggests that a psychological pattern is observable in all the great crises of Wilson's life in which "angry opposition only intensified his anxieties and the more surely dictated a stubborn determination to subjugate his foes."[60] Another historian suggests that Wilson was compelled to reject compromise because any compromise, no matter how small, would endanger his vision of the League "as an instrument of American control over foreign affairs, but without endangering national independence." In this view, Lodge's reservations would have eliminated even the limited concessions of American sovereignty that Wilson had been willing to make to achieve the larger goal of world power and were therefore unacceptable.[61] Thus these historians argue that whether as a result of a psychological compulsion or of a rational calculation of national interest, Wilson was never interested in compromise.

There is of course no way to disprove such theories, and it may be that these forces tended to make the president resistant to suggestions of compromise at the critical moment. Yet there is also some evidence that the possibility of compromise was real in late summer and autumn 1919. A tough initial approach followed by timely concessions had worked to Wilson's advantage in previous struggles with Congress. "The obvious course," argues Thomas A. Bailey, "was for him to seem unyielding, drive as hard a bargain as he could, and then at the last moment, when there was no danger of more reservations being added, make the grand gesture of accepting" Lodge's reservations. That sense of timing and the ability to design a tolerable compromise were lost when he became ill.[62]

Wilson's ability to carry out any plan, whether rational or not, was devastated by his stroke.[63] Its effects made it almost impossible for him to read, impaired his ability to concentrate, and above all compromised his mental capacity so that he lost all sophistication and was forced back upon the bedrock of his character, where all issues were perceived in moral terms as right or wrong. Serious as the physical effects of the stroke were, they were minor compared to the mental damage. For almost four months after 2 October 1919 Woodrow Wilson was physically and mentally incapable of carrying out the duties of president of the United States. Thereafter, although his physical condition improved, his mental impairment remained.

Early in January 1920 he spurned the advice of all his closest advisers to bow to the inevitability of reservations and inserted in his Jackson Day (8 January) message to Democrats a rejection of any compromise with League critics and a call for making the election of 1920 "a great and solemn referendum" on the treaty.[64] He even proposed that all Republican opponents of the treaty in the Senate resign and submit themselves to a special election on the single issue of the League. If enough of them were reelected, he promised to appoint a Republican secretary of state, and then he and the vice-president would resign.[65] Wilson's horrified advisers managed to sidetrack this ludicrous scheme, but it demonstrated that the president's nomination for the Nobel Peace Prize later that same month could only be a cruelly ironic salute to a leader who was now the principal obstacle to the implementation of his own peace plan.

The Jackson Day letter alarmed many Democrats who, like William Jennings Bryan, had hoped that quiet negotiations, which had been going on with some Republicans, would lead to a compromise that would permit ratification of the treaty and American membership in the League. They did not realize that worse was in store. As early as June 1919 Wilson had been considering running for a third term; and in spring 1920, after the Senate on 19 March defeated the treaty again by a vote of forty-nine to thirty-five despite the defection of twenty-one Democrats to support reservations, he revived the idea.[66] Dr. Grayson, who believed that he should resign, and Tumulty, who urged him to announce he would not seek a third term, were overruled, and Edith insisted that the press be given a series of optimistic stories proclaiming his rapid recovery. His son-in-law, William Gibbs McAdoo, who had hoped to be recognized as the heir apparent, was refused even an interview.

That the whole idea was tragically absurd became obvious to the members of the cabinet on 13 April during the first cabinet meeting with the president since his stroke. His face sagged and he could not stand without assistance, but most serious, he could not follow the discussion of issues in the meeting. Although those who had been close to the president throughout his illness were buoyant after the meeting, delighted with how well he had done in contrast to his incapacity of a few months earlier, members of the cabinet seeing him for the first time were appalled, and Grayson realized the farce could not go on.[67]

When Secretary of State Bainbridge Colby loyally tried to secure Wilson's renomination at the Democratic convention in San Francisco, the doctor implored party leaders to "save the life and fame of this great man from the juggling of false friends," and Colby's efforts were quietly blocked.[68] Governor James M. Cox of Ohio was nominated on the forty-fourth ballot to conduct the "great and solemn referendum."[69]

Cox and his running mate, Franklin D. Roosevelt, called at the White House for Wilson's blessing and were welcomed, but the president took no active part in the campaign. He was often depressed and lethargic, failing to answer letters or ignoring pressing business. His left arm remained immobile, he could not rise from a chair without assistance, and he dragged his left leg as he hobbled across the floor, leaning on his cane. At times he could be bright and alert, but at others he had temper tantrums and inexplicable outbursts of crying. Despite mounting evidence that the Democratic ticket would be swamped, he insisted they would win; but when they were defeated, he was unmoved. "I have not lost faith in the American people," he told his brother-in-law. "They have merely been temporarily deceived. They will realize their error in a little while."[70]

11

AFTER THE WAR

In the months after the armistice was signed on 11 November 1918 both liberals and conservatives wanted to believe that the war had inaugurated a new era in the United States as well as in the world, but even if there was any possibility of that being true, the administration lost its opportunity to make any changes permanent.[1] During the first year of peace the president, focused only on the treaty fight, spurned proposals for a planned reconstruction program. Thereafter, desperately ill, he was incapable of leadership on any issue. Despite his optimistic predictions that the transition from war to peace would take care of itself, 1919 brought a recession, strikes, a Red Scare, and a collapse of farm prosperity. Leaderless, the nation drifted into the postwar period at the mercy of uncontrolled political and economic forces.

Initially, Wilson seemed to welcome the idea of planned postwar reconstruction, making permanent the wartime programs that were "translating into action the theory of voluntary cooperation" between business and government, as Grosvenor Clarkson, secretary of the Council of National Defense, recommended in March 1918. "I . . . find myself in substantial accord with you," the president replied to Clarkson's recommendation that the council be turned into a permanent organization.[2] Thus encouraged, Clarkson set up a Reconstruction Research Division of the council in May and put it to work gathering information as the basis for a plan under which wartime's "forced cooperation between strong competitors" could be transformed into a peacetime system of voluntary "cooperation and regulation" and "a more complete understanding between labor and capital."[3]

Soon, however, despite Clarkson's efforts, which were endorsed by secretaries Lane, Wilson, and Houston, and despite support from Samuel Gompers and the National City Bank of New York, among others, the president's enthusiasm for reconstruction programs cooled. It was "a very difficult and exceedingly important matter," he told Gompers in late November; and a few days later in his state of the union message, he rejected all reconstruction plans. "Our people . . . do not want to be coached and led," he declared. "Any leading strings we might seek to put them in would speedily become hopelessly tangled because they would pay no attention to them and go their own way."[4]

By that time deep divisions had appeared within the administration over the issue. Secretary of the Treasury McAdoo was strongly opposed to any program that might force the retention of an expensive wartime bureaucracy or delay the curtailment of war spending.[5] Likewise, suggestions from Secretaries Lane and Wilson for federal programs to settle demobilized soldiers and sailors on federal lands ran into strong opposition from Secretary of Agriculture Houston, who was concerned about overproduction and falling farm prices.[6] Furthermore, although the Council on National Defense was the logical agency to plan reconstruction because its advisory board represented the secretaries of War, Navy, Interior, Agriculture, Commerce, and Labor, other wartime agencies facing a death sentence at the end of the conflict also proclaimed their special expertise for directing reconstruction.[7] Nor was there any shortage of private groups offering reconstruction plans, from the United States Chamber of Commerce to the Socialists.[8] Although it may be that Wilson believed, as Arthur Link has suggested, that "the machinery of mobilization was so powerful that it was unsafe to permit it to exist any longer" because of the danger that "conservative businessmen would gain control" of it, the president did not so much choose to dismantle the machinery of mobilization as to ignore its breakdown (and the appropriation of large parts of it by conservative businessmen) while he concentrated on world reconstruction at Paris.[9]

Yet even if Wilson had been willing to lead an active reconstruction program, doing so would have been difficult because the issue soon became entangled in partisan politics and in the conflict between the White House and Congress. On 27 September 1918 Republican Senator John W. Weeks of Massachusetts introduced a resolution calling for the creation of a joint congressional committee on reconstruction. Wilson, who had fought the creation of a special wartime committee to oversee the conduct of the war, was equally opposed to Weeks's proposal; and on 3 October Senator Lee S. Overman of North Carolina again came to the administration's rescue by introducing a competing proposal for a reconstruction commission to be appointed by the president and confirmed by the Senate. Then came the congressional elections, which gave the Republicans control of both houses, and soon afterward forty Republican senators met to adopt a resolution calling again for congressional control of the process.[10] Faced with this open challenge, Wilson said on 18 November that he doubted that he would "appoint a new and separate Reconstruction Commission" and that he would instead work "through existing instrumentalities."[11] By the time of his annual address, two weeks later, he had obviously decided to avoid any action at all.

After Wilson's rejection of a federal role in reconstruction, Clarkson's Reconstruction Research Division churned out tons of material on what federal and state agencies were doing about various aspects of the problem, but it is doubtful that anyone ever read the material and no organization at any level did any actual planning. In 1923 Clarkson concluded, with deep regret, that "the magnificent war formation of American industry was dissipated in a day; the mobilization that had taken many months was succeeded by an instantaneous demobilization."[12] Whether or not controlled reconversion would have been better for the nation, political tensions made planning impossible.

With the president in Europe, the troops poured back into the United States and were released, helter-skelter, into civilian life. Many had trouble finding jobs, and the unemployment rate rose from 4 percent in 1920 to 11.9 percent in 1921. At the same time, wartime restrictions on prices and allocation of resources were ended, and the cost of living soared. Workers, noting rising business profits, demanded higher wages but were told by employers that it was their patriotic duty to stick to wartime contracts.[13]

Secretary of Labor Wilson, fearing widespread labor conflict, called a conference of governors and mayors in March 1919 to discuss increased public-works projects to make jobs. The conference ended up paying lip service to public works, but the last of its resolutions showed that these officials were content to do very little:

> We face the future firm in the belief that the Almighty intends all things well, and that there remains for us and the generations to come full compensation for the service given and the sacrifice made in the support of the ideals of Democracy.[14]

Congress, apparently agreeing with this benign view of the situation, slashed funding for the Labor Department's United States Employment Service so severely that by March 1920 it had virtually ceased to exist.[15]

Beginning in February 1919 with a general strike in Seattle, Secretary Wilson's worst fears were realized. During that year four million workers went on strike in 3,600 separate conflicts with employers. Only in the crisis year of 1917, with 4,450 strikes, was the situation worse.[16]

With the president in Europe during most of the spring and absorbed in trying to win the Senate's approval of the Treaty of Versailles during the summer, the administration's response to the situation was confused and uncertain. Secretary Wilson supported labor's right to organize and urged the services of the Division of Conciliation upon both sides in disputes; but employers, taking advantage of an increasingly conservative public mood, blamed the high cost of living on excessive wages, depicted unions as socialist, and denounced all strikers as Bolsheviks. Few major conflicts were brought to the Division of Conciliation, and it had little success in dealing with those that were. Moreover, Attorney General A. Mitchell Palmer was under heavy pressure from the public and Congress to go after supposed radicals in the unions, and within the administration his efforts were supported by Secretary of State Lansing, Postmaster General Burleson, and others. Almost inevitably, a major strike would force a general crackdown on the unions.[17]

As it happened, not one but two major strikes were threatened in autumn 1919. The first, beginning on 22 September, was called by the AFL to secure shorter hours, higher wages, and recognition of the union in the steel mills. The other, promised for a month later but blocked by injunctions, was called by the United Mine Workers in support of a demand for a 60 percent wage increase. Together, the two strikes could idle half a million workers and cripple the economy just as winter was coming on. In both cases employers refused to negotiate with the unions, but the unions also rejected appeals from the administration to call off or to delay the strikes. Under the circumstances, even Secretary Wilson found it difficult to support the unions unreservedly. On 6 October the army moved into Gary, Indiana, to keep order in that steel center, and less than three weeks later Attorney General Palmer issued an injunction under the authority of the wartime Lever Act prohibiting the coal strike.[18]

Unionists generally saw the administration's policy as unfriendly in the steel and coal strikes, and in comparison with its previous record there was a basis for the charge. The accusation needs to be kept in perspective, however. There is good reason for believing that the president's stroke kept him from supervising members of his cabinet like

Palmer who were much less sympathetic to labor than the president or the secretary of labor, and he probably never saw injunctions sent out in his name. The coal miners, too, contributed to their own troubles by seeming to spurn the administration's plea for a strike delay and by what seemed to many people to be exorbitant wage demands. When finally forced by injunctions and the jailing of union leaders to settle the strike, they nevertheless received an immediate 14 percent cost-of-living raise and later were awarded an average of 13 percent more by a United States Bituminous Coal Commission appointed by the president as part of a back-to-work agreement.[19]

The steel workers fared much less well. Although the union rejected the president's request in September for a delay of the strike, the companies, especially United States Steel under the chairmanship of Elbert H. Gary, were the real villains. They simply refused to negotiate with the union under any conditions and by January 1920 had broken the strike.

Given the hysterically antiradical mood of the country at the time, the administration's approach to the coal and steel strikes was actually moderate. Indeed, the president later said that he was sorry that injunctions had been sought in the coal strike, and there was never any doubt about the administration's exasperation with the intransigence of the steel companies. Even at the height of the conflict, both Samuel Gompers and the United Mine Workers' John L. Lewis expressed their confidence in the fundamental sympathy of the president for labor.[20] Considering how easily the administration might have used these strikes as an excuse for a wholesale attack on labor, union leaders appreciated its restraint.

If the conservative temper of the times was hostile to workers on strike, it also doomed one of the most radical experiments of the war years: federal operation of the railroads. For many years Populists and advanced progressives had argued that the railroads were so basic to the health of the economy that they ought to be nationalized, and when the nation entered the war, their arguments seemed to be borne out. Inadequate rolling stock on poorly maintained roadbeds would have been severe obstacles to mobilization in themselves, but these problems were compounded by the demands of operators for rate increases and of workers for raises. When the railroad brotherhoods threatened to go on strike early in December 1917, Wilson reacted by announcing on 26 December that the railroads would be operated for the duration of the war by a new Railroad Administration headed by William Gibbs McAdoo.[21]

Operating under the Federal Control Act of 21 March 1918, which authorized control through the war and for a "reasonable time" thereafter, McAdoo and his assistant Walker Hines (McAdoo's successor in 1919) ran the railroads with great efficiency, raising rates to cover badly needed repairs and passing on the costs to taxpayers through generous contracts to producers and shippers of war materiel. Owners, whose profits were guaranteed for the duration, and workers, who received generous pay raises, endured the nationalization without complaint, but when the war ended, consensus evaporated. McAdoo believed that the prewar railroad system had been so inefficient that the government must ask Congress for a five-year extension of federal control to "test the value of unified control" under peacetime conditions.[22] Hines and the president agreed with at least some extension of federal control, but Congress would have nothing to do with a five-year extension.

With federal operation of the railroads scheduled to expire in September 1919 and no agreement on a plan in sight, Wilson called a special session of Congress in May, but preoccupied with the peace conference, he provided no leadership. The result was predictable chaos, from which two competing plans gradually emerged. One, sponsored by Republican Senator Albert Cummins of Iowa, proposed to shift supervision of privately owned railroads from the old Interstate Commerce Commission (ICC), which the companies had come to dominate, to a new Transportation Board, which would have power to consolidate lines, set rates, guarantee minimum profits, require improvements, and arbitrate labor disputes. The other plan, proposed by Glenn Plumb, general counsel for the Organized Railway Employees of America, advocated outright government ownership of the lines and their operation by a board made up of the public, the operators, and labor.[23]

Although Wilson postponed the return of the railways to the operators until the end of the year, it was obvious by mid-autumn that Congress would not pass any radical solution to the railroad dilemma. Instead, early in 1920 a compromise bill gradually emerged, sponsored by Republican Congressman John J. Esch of Wisconsin and Senator Cummins. The Esch-Cummins Act (or the Transportation Act of 1920, as it was called officially) restored the railroads to private ownership under the supervision of the ICC and instructed the commission to set rates in such a way as to guarantee a "fair return" to all lines. In the Senate version the bill also banned strikes, but labor's outraged opposition led to the deletion of this provision from the act and gained the substitution of a Railway Labor Board with power to arbitrate labor disputes but not to impose settlements. Although there were charges that the bill favored management over labor, Wilson signed it into law; and the railroads were returned to private hands on 1 March 1920. One of the labor board's first acts after that date was to order an immediate 12 percent cut in railway shopmen's wages and the repeal of wartime labor protection rules; in 1922 it ordered an additional 12 percent cut.[24] In the absence of effective leadership from the president or anyone else in the administration, the railroad operators clearly had won an enormous victory, having converted even the weak prewar federal regulatory machinery into a system that would encourage rather than prevent consolidation and that was required to guarantee profits for the companies.

At the same time, the nation's political atmosphere became even more highly charged as the wartime persecution of radicals was carried over into the postwar era. The Bolshevik Revolution in November 1917 and the withdrawal of Russia from the war early in 1918 fanned the flames of antiradicalism in the United States just as in Britain and France. Following the armistice, when American Socialists, believing that war's end meant the end of repression, held parades and demonstrations, the American Protective League and its government allies were alarmed anew. In March 1919 Attorney General Gregory resigned and was succeeded by A. Mitchell Palmer, who entered office just in time to confront a series of massive strikes and in April a terrorist campaign in which bombs were sent to prominent citizens. Although most of the bombs were discovered and defused before exploding, one, carried by the bomber, blew in the front windows of Palmer's house just after he had gone to bed. If he had ever been disposed to take the threat lightly, he certainly did not after that.[25]

The attorney general was by no means reluctant to lead an antiradical crusade. An early Wilson supporter who had declined a prewar appointment as secretary of war because of his Quaker faith, Palmer was nevertheless eager to fight the enemy in his own way. Appointed Alien Property Custodian by the president in October 1917, Palmer had stretched his position far beyond overseeing interned enemy property during the war. Under special powers granted by Congress in March 1918 he sold off German enterprises and patents in the United States to Americans eager to get into profitable businesses in chemicals, dyes, and pharmaceuticals. Rumors that many of these sales were to Palmer's friends led Gregory to advise Wilson against appointing Palmer attorney general, but eventually the president made the appointment anyway, largely because of Tumulty's argument that it was politically desirable. Apparently, neither Wilson nor Gregory was concerned that Palmer, as Alien Property Custodian, had followed a policy obviously intended to improve America's postwar international competitive position even though Wilson, then in Europe, was asserting that of the nations at war, only the United States was not seeking economic advantage.[26]

In the postwar atmosphere of crisis it was easy for Palmer to continue to expand his antialien campaign. During November 1919 and January 1920 the Justice Department, armed with a special half-million-dollar congressional appropriation, launched raids against suspected radical organizations that netted about four thousand alleged subversives in thirty-three cities. The raids, which frequently ignored such legal technicalities as search or arrest warrants, concentrated upon aliens rather than on native radicals because under the Alien Act of 1918 foreigners could be deported with only an administrative hearing, but citizens prosecuted under the Espionage or Sedition acts required trials. Although courageous Labor Department officials eventually canceled most of the deportation orders for those arrested, the hysteria engendered during the Red Scare contributed to the growth of a conservative reaction that was cynically manipulated by some employer groups to attack all union activity and by other conservatives to cast suspicion on dissent of any sort. Equally significant was the effect on many progressive reformers, who lost faith in government as a result of the Palmer raids and in labor because of the massive strikes of 1919 and who thus concluded that the classless, democratic society that had been their prewar dream was impossible.[27]

The Labor Department, however, refused to be stampeded by the Red Scare of 1919–20. Under the Immigration Act of February 1917 the secretary was authorized to deport any alien who advocated the destruction of property or the overthrow of the United States government, but Secretary Wilson refused to use the act against foreign-born IWW leaders as western lumbermen demanded. The law, declared the secretary, was aimed not at the IWW but at individual aliens who acted illegally.[28]

Secretary Wilson also courageously defended Assistant Secretary Louis Post when Post canceled arrest warrants for three thousand of the four thousand aliens against whom such warrants had been issued for supposedly radical activities. Post also released four hundred of the aliens already arrested after investigation convinced him that the charges against them were without merit. Outraged at this obstruction of the red hunters, Republican chairman Albert Johnson of the House Immigration and Naturalization Committee demanded that Post be impeached. Impeachment hearings before the House Rules Committee in May 1920, however, gave Post a chance to show the legal basis for his actions and served to rally Americans concerned that persecution of radicals had become more dangerous than the radicals themselves. A report by twelve eminent lawyers of the National Popular Government League concluded, for example, that the attorney general's "ruthless suppressions" had "seriously undermined" the very institutions that they were supposed to protect and had "vastly intensified" the danger of "revolutionary unrest."[29] When Post was cleared, he and Secretary Wilson could take quiet pride in the knowledge that they had played an important part in bringing the hysteria of the Red Scare to an end that summer.

In the polarized state of labor-management relations in the postwar United States it was difficult for the Labor Department to take any action without being accused of partisanship. Its position in the coal and steel strikes earned it the anger of labor; its resistance to wholesale deportations of radicals aroused the fury of conservatives. Yet the goal of the department and the administration remained exactly what it had always been: to promote cooperation between labor and capital in the hope of advancing the common interests of both. In two industrial conferences in 1919–20 the administration made one last, unsuccessful attempt to achieve that end.

Even before the war a popular catchphrase among some social scientists, labor leaders, government officials, and businessmen was "industrial democracy." The phrase meant different things to different people, but in general it seemed to imply that workers would to some degree share decision making with management. During the war the notion was touted as a way to reduce labor-management conflict and to increase production, and reports of experiments with similar programs in Great Britain were widely publicized.[30] When the wave of strikes hit the United States in 1919, these vague ideas of industrial democracy acquired a new appeal. As the president said, "We cannot . . . achieve our proper success as an industrial community if capital and labour are to continue to be antagonistic instead of being partners." It was imperative, he concluded, to find a new approach that would lead to "a genuine cooperation and partnership based upon a real community of interest and participation in control."[31]

Early in June 1919, while Wilson was still in Europe, his secretary, Joseph Tumulty, proposed a national labor-management conference to promote cooperation and to lay the basis for a new, liberal program for the Democrats in 1920.[32] After his return, the president called the conference to meet in Washington on 6 October 1919. In his letter inviting delegates, Wilson asked them to "canvass every relevant feature of the present industrial situation," and to "discuss . . . methods . . . of bringing capital and labor into close cooperation."[33]

The sixty-one conferees included the secretaries of labor and interior, fifteen men and women chosen by the AFL, four representing the railroad brotherhoods, five each selected by the United States Chamber of Commerce and the National Industrial Conference Board, two chosen by the Investment Bankers Association of America and two by the railroad managers, three representing farmers' organizations, and twenty-three to speak for "the public." The latter group was particularly interesting, ranging from industrialists John D. Rockefeller, Jr., and Elbert H. Gary on one end to muckraker Ida Tarbell and Socialist John Spargo on the other.[34] Notably missing were representatives of radical labor such as the IWW.

Despite the exclusion of most radicals from the conference, it quickly became obvious that in autumn 1919 any idea of a new industrial order was hopelessly utopian. Current issues such as the steel strike and labor's demand for a recognition of the right of collective bargaining led to endless wrangling, and the conference had no prospect of resolving broader questions. When industry representatives refused any concessions on immediate issues the union men walked out, but their departure only sealed the conference's already inevitable failure.

In fact the two sides had in mind completely incompatible plans for future industrial organization. Union leaders wanted the Department of Labor to encourage the formation of a national labor union and national employer associations in each industry. Conflicts would be adjusted by joint labor-management boards in each industry, with the federal government cooperating in providing information and in making suggestions but not actually controlling or supervising the process. The business delegates, in contrast, rejected unionization completely, calling for a national open-shop rule, and proposed instead a system of "shop councils" that would give workers in each factory a forum in which to air grievances but that would not have the power to call strikes or to take part in management decisions.[35] Although each group claimed to want a new, cooperative industrial order, they disagreed on every important issue; and after two weeks of acrimonious debate, the meeting adjourned without the delegates passing a single resolution.

The failure of the industrial conference reveals that after almost seven years of effort the administration was perhaps even further from achieving harmonious industrial relations than it had been at the outset. Understandably, administration leaders did not want to draw that conclusion, so they decided to make another effort to find an acceptable plan for industrial organization. During November Tumulty and Secretary Wilson worked on plans for a second industrial conference, which met in Washington on 1 December 1919. Believing that a major reason for the failure of the first meeting was block voting by business and labor, the organizers excluded representatives of trade associations and labor unions from the second conference and instead invited only seventeen representatives of "the public." Most of them, like vice-chairman Herbert Hoover, came from the group of "business ideologues and dreamers" who had staffed the wartime bureaucracy and shared the dream of a new industrial democracy.[36]

Chaired by Secretary Wilson, the second conference, unlike the first, shunned publicity by meeting in executive session and avoided current issues in the hope of finding fundamental cures for industrial conflict. Not surprisingly, given the wartime experience of many participants, they turned to the War Industries Board as a model for their proposals. In late December they produced a preliminary plan that called for the creation of a National Industrial Tribunal made up of three representatives each from the public, business, and labor and appointed by the president for six-year terms, and they proposed creating regional boards of adjustment along similar lines. Despite their titles, these bodies were not to be courts. Submission of industrial disputes to them would be entirely voluntary. If the local board failed to solve a dispute the case could be appealed to the National Industrial Tribunal, but its powers were restricted to investigating and making recommendations.[37]

The conference's preliminary report seems harmless in retrospect, but many people found fault with it. The AFL attacked what sounded to them like a threat of compulsory arbitration that might deprive unions of the right to strike, and a number of reformers criticized the plan as dealing only with the symptoms of industrial conflict, not with its causes. When the conference reconvened on 12 January 1920 it therefore called a number of witnesses to describe more radical plans for the democratization of industry, and in particular it concentrated on what was called the Rockefeller Plan.[38]

The Rockefeller Plan had been developed by W. L. Mackenzie King of Canada for the Rockefeller Foundation in 1915 after the Colorado coal strike. It proposed the creation of "shop committees" in which labor and management would meet continuously to work out differences. King conceived the plan as an evolutionary step toward full unionization, but most of the two hundred businesses that had adopted it by 1919 used the shop committees only as safety valves to vent worker discontent and to avert unionization. At most, these businesses were willing to accept only "company unions," which had no affiliation with external organizations and were generally under management's thumb. Enthusiastic as many liberals were about the theory of employee participation in corporate governance, the conference found it impossible to draft a specific proposal that would avoid the antiunion bias implicit in the shop committees.[39]

The conference's final report, published in March, made some cosmetic changes in the draft to allay labor's fears and endorsed the labor principles of the Treaty of Versailles (the forty-hour week, equal pay for men and women, and the limitation of child labor); but labor leaders remained suspicious that the shop-committee plan was actually "a subtle weapon directed against the union."[40] Like the peace conference, the second industrial conference assumed that democratization and publicity would cure conflicts. Like the ill-fated peace treaty its report failed to address basic causes of conflict; in the end, the conference report, like the treaty, died. A Senate committee held hearings on it between April and May 1920, but no legislation came from the hearings and thereafter the report was forgotten. President Wilson was too ill to do anything about it, and the recession of the Red Scare and the crushing of the 1919 strikes relieved the public's sense of urgency about the issue. By that time many businessmen had realized that the friendly relations between government and business and the cooperation between competitors engendered during the war need not evolve toward a partnership with labor but could be used instead to destroy unions entirely. Labor leaders, who had never thought much of the shop-committee proposal anyway, willingly dropped it to concentrate on trying to keep the labor movement alive in the hostile environment of the 1920s.[41]

Ironically, the efforts of the Wilson administration to strengthen labor and to promote a new industrial democracy of cooperation between labor and capital had almost the opposite effect from what the president originally had sought. Although union membership in the United States grew by 85 percent between 1913 and 1920 and by 96 percent between 1915 and 1920 and though average hours worked per week fell and wages rose, labor was in many ways worse off by the end of the period than it had been at the beginning.[42]

Although the administration demonstrated a new sensitivity to labor's interests, it did not generally win management over to its position. Especially during the war, business made larger gains than labor as a result of the relaxation of the antitrust laws, the growth of trade associations, and the discovery by businessmen of an effective and publicly acceptable union-busting technique in the shop-committee plan. In June 1919 Tumulty warned the president that he could see "growing steadily from day to day, under our very eyes, a movement that, if it is not checked, is bound to express itself in an attack upon everything that we hold dear."[43] From the standpoint of liberals, not the least of the tragedies of President Wilson's illness during the last year and a half of his administration was his inability to see and avert the growth of this cancer that threatened to abort the industrial democracy he had worked to bring to birth.

The administration also suffered a similar failure to meet the needs of farmers in the postwar period. When the war ended in November 1918 the Agriculture Department was torn between a realistic recognition that the recovery of European farmers and the restoration of world trade would curtail American farm sales overseas and a natural desire to continue wartime activities that were helping farmers to increase production. As early as summer 1917 departmental leaders were becoming concerned that guaranteed prices were leading to overproduction and to the displacement of tenant farmers who provided essential agricultural labor.[44] By the beginning of 1919 the department was anticipating a catastrophic drop in farm prices and urging farmers to reduce production and to diversify crops.[45] At the same time, however, Agriculture officials fought as hard as they could against budget reductions that would force cutbacks in extension work and in scientific research intended to assist farmers in increasing production.[46] Secretary Houston complained that wartime food administrator Herbert Hoover had been inconsistent, one moment saying that farmers should go slowly in increasing production and the next warning that food shortages might occur, but precisely the same thing might have been said about all of postwar agricultural policy.[47]

Regardless of who was to blame for the overproduction that loomed in 1919, everyone in the administration realized that it would be politically dangerous to permit a catastrophic price collapse as well as terribly unfair to urge farmers to produce to the utmost for patriotic reasons and then leave them to suffer when they did what they were asked. Accordingly, Hoover lobbied Congress vigorously on behalf of a bill to grant a credit to the allies of $100 million for the postwar purchase of American agricultural products, and Secretary of the Treasury Carter Glass extended additional credits to foreign countries on the dubious ground that bolshevism represented a military threat that could be stopped by food. Using these funds, Hoover persuaded the European nations to buy additional American products at inflated wartime prices; but as the Food Administration was phased out during spring 1919, he lost his power to support the foreign market for American products. In 1920 prices plunged catastrophically. On 1 June 1920 the average price of all American crops was 24 percent higher than in 1919; by 1 November the average price was 33 percent lower than in that year. "The very foundation of our Nation—the stability of our agriculture—is threatened," declared Secretary Edwin T. Meredith, who had succeeded Houston in February 1920 when the latter moved to the Treasury Department.[48]

At this moment when Agriculture Department officials believed that farmers were facing a major disaster Secretary of the Interior Franklin K. Lane came up with a scheme that seemed likely to worsen the situation materially. Part of Lane's proposal included the development of suburban "garden homes" to permit urban dwellers to move out of apartments, but his most controversial suggestion was that the government should open up abandoned and public lands to returning veterans and provide low-cost financing for land purchases and improvements.[49] Like many others who had been making similar proposals during the war, Lane sought both to provide for the needs of returning veterans and to promote rural life, which he regarded as morally and physically healthier than life in the cities. His proposal drew support from prominent businessmen, political leaders, landowners, labor organizations, and reformers who shared his "country life" values. A number of bills were introduced in Congress to implement his idea or others similar to it, but farmers and their supporters were alarmed.[50]

Privately, Secretaries Houston and Meredith regarded Lane's "hastily evolved soldier settlement scheme" as a crackpot idea. The nation, Houston remarked with considerable understatement, "is not now suffering from a lack of farmers and underproduction of farm products." But publicly he was more restrained, perhaps because the president said he thought the project might be desirable.[51] In his annual report for 1919 Houston paid lip service to the concerns of people who were worried about the high cost of agricultural products or who believed that land resources were being wasted if left unused. He warned, however, that "the inelasticity of demand for farm products sets a very decided limit at a given time to the increase of population and capital profitably employed in agriculture." In his opinion the nation needed "not a 'back to the land' propaganda, but an acceleration of the movement for improvement of the countryside which [would] render the abandonment of farms unnecessary and the expansion of farming inevitable." Draining swamps and irrigating deserts would be costly, he warned, and would bring new lands into production just at the beginning of "the period of competition which is to be expected with the return of normal world conditions." The following year Secretary Meredith said even more bluntly that "present conditions do not seem to justify a policy of encouraging and stimulating the extension of the farm area."[52]

The opposition of farmers and the Agriculture Department to Lane's proposal quickly doomed it. Popular support for it had been based largely on a patriotic desire to do something for the returning veterans; but when farmers objected, it became clear that the most ardent advocates of the idea were actually large landowners and speculators.[53] Like other projects for a planned "reconstruction" after the war, the idea of veterans' colonization was blocked by the opposition of special interests, by the general resistance within the administration to long-term control and planning of the economy, by the president's absorption with issues of foreign policy, and by the growing realization that reconstruction plans that seemed attractive on the surface had a way of becoming too complex and controversial to be implemented. Thus in the end the administration simply left reconstruction to take care of itself.

In general, administration leaders regarded overproduction not as a basic problem of American agriculture but as a temporary condition to be overcome by more aggressive salesmanship. A special agricultural commission that Secretary Houston sent to Europe in August 1918 was to report on current Allied needs and to look into postwar market prospects for American goods. The commission's report urged that foreign-market forecasting become a regular departmental function.[54] That recommendation was included in the secretary's annual report for 1920, but in practice both Houston and Meredith stressed the development of domestic rather than foreign markets as the principal solution to farmers' problems.[55]

In a letter to Henry C. Wallace, then editor of *Wallace's Farmer* and soon to become secretary of agriculture in the Harding administration, Secretary Meredith summed up the administration's attitude: "I feel that it is not a question of holding down production but that the answer to the problem is in seeing that the farmer gets right prices for what he produces and satisfactory conditions for production."[56] Despite the experiences of the war and the postwar agricultural depression, the administration's faith in a system based on small, individual producers remained unshaken.

Facing a drop in the Index of Agricultural Prices from 170 in April to 80 in December of 1920, farmers were understandably less enthusiastic about the administration's prescriptions.[57] During the third session of the Sixty-seventh Congress, from 6 December 1920 to 4 March 1921, farm supporters pushed through bills to revive the War Finance Corporation and subsidize exports and to enact a tariff on agricultural products. On the advice of Houston and Meredith, Wilson vetoed both, but Congress passed the War Finance Corporation bill over his veto. That autumn a group of western and southern farmers presented their demands for relief personally to Houston and Meredith during a hastily arranged conference.[58] Although the farmers were not yet sure of exactly what they wanted, this meeting and the organization of the Farm Bureau Federation in 1919 and the Farm Bloc in 1920 showed that many of them were moving away from individualism toward advocacy of governmental regulation of production.[59]

By the beginning of the 1920s farmers felt betrayed. They had responded to the administration's exhortations to increase production and then found the government unwilling to use its power to relieve the postwar crisis of overproduction and falling prices. In their view, the machinery to solve the problem existed, but the politicians would not use it and were dismantling it as rapidly as possible. In the next decade, as farmers began to organize once again, they would come to see the programs the Wilson administration had devised to strengthen small, independent farmers as susceptible to being turned into something quite different—a structure that could regulate and control the market-place in the interests of large, commercial agriculture.

In the last year and a half of its dealings with industry, labor, and agriculture, the Wilson administration revealed a paralysis comparable to that of the president. Leaderless, the administration fought within its own ranks, proved unable to resolve conflicts in the national economy, and failed to institutionalize any of the new approaches to managing and directing the national economy that had evolved before and during the war. Businessmen, on the other hand, were quick to see that war-time arrangements could serve their interests; and they fought effectively to take advantage of the government's relaxed attitude toward consolidation and to deny labor any significant role in the new order. The treaty was the most famous casualty of the administration's col-lapse, but in the long run failures to plan reconstruction and to consoli-date and build upon prewar and wartime reforms were at least equally serious. Domestically as well as in foreign policy the nation paid a heavy price for its lack of a plan to deal with presidential incapacity.

As the administration stumbled toward its end, the United States took its decennial census and reflected on the state of its health. The census revealed that the nation's population was now over 106 million and that for the first time more than half of those people lived in urban communities of 2,500 or more. That shift alarmed some people and was one of the causes of the back-to-the-land movement of the postwar pe-riod, but others rejoiced at the progress of modernization, symbolized by the 750,000 Model-T Fords sold in 1919 at just over $500 apiece or by the 600 million times that Americans went to the movies in 1920. And indeed there seemed to be little cause for concern. Church membership continued to grow at just about the same rate as the population, and the beginning of Prohibition on 17 January 1920 promised a new era of mo-rality. Rural Americans enjoyed one last great victory in August 1919 when Congress passed the repeal of wartime daylight-savings time over President Wilson's veto.[60]

Nevertheless, there were abundant signs that times were changing. Women could vote for the first time in the presidential election of 1920, and in that year they made up nearly half of all students enrolled in college. Many had gone to work outside the home for the first time during the war; and if they often lost their jobs to returning male veterans, the war left them a new legacy of freedom that was reflected in new, freer clothing, greater use of cosmetics, more access to methods of birth control, and public cigarette-smoking. Even more striking were the changes that came to black Americans, who seized the opportunity offered by the war to begin to escape the poverty of the South. In 1910 nearly 90 percent of all blacks lived in the South, but during the war a half million of them moved north to the cities, doubling the number who lived outside the boundaries of the old Confederacy. In the 1920s this exodus would help to produce the Harlem Renaissance, a remarkable flowering of African-American culture centered in New York. The unfortunate other side of the story, however, was a nationalization of racism, with race riots in twenty-six cities and towns across the country in 1919 that killed at least 120 people, a significant increase in the number of lynchings, and a mushrooming growth of a revived Ku Klux Klan.[61]

Prominent among the concerns of Americans in 1920 was the high cost of living. Since 1914, a quart of milk had gone from nine to fourteen cents, butter from thirty-two to sixty-one cents a pound, eggs from thirty-four to sixty-two cents a dozen, and sirloin steak from twenty-seven to forty-two cents a pound. The cost of living was 77 percent above prewar levels in 1919, 105 percent in 1920. Rents sky-rocketed, and with the return of the soldiers, there was a serious housing shortage.[62]

But the terrifying influenza pandemic, which in combination with pneumonia killed 479,000 Americans in 1918 and 189,000 in 1919, seemed to be on the wane. Astonishingly contagious, resistant to every known medication, and particularly deadly to men of military age, the flu overwhelmed the United States Public Health Service's meager resources and killed more than 25,000 soldiers and sailors in the United States and more than 9,000 in France between the beginning of September 1918 and the armistice two months later. Since the only safeguard that anyone could find against the spread of the epidemic was to advise people to avoid crowds, the flu had a devastating effect on the war. Government offices and factories went on staggered shifts to reduce rush-hour crowds. Draft calls, military training, and shipment of soldiers to France were cut back drastically, and absentee rates at civilian factories threatened to bring war production to a halt. Fortunately, the armistice relieved the military aspects of the crisis. Had the war continued through 1919, as the epidemic did, all of the belligerents would have had a difficult time keeping their war efforts going.[63] Happily, it did not. In 1920 the epidemic ended as abruptly as it had begun, and within a few years most people did not even remember that the disease had killed more than ten times as many Americans as German bullets.

Just as Americans seemingly had forgotten the flu epidemic by 1920, so they seemed also to have lost their interest in reform. The Republican presidential candidate that year was perfectly suited to their mood. Ohio Senator Warren Gamaliel Harding was handsome and genial but no match for Wilson, either in morals or in intellect. William Gibbs McAdoo described him acidly:

> He was a speechmaker; he spoke on every convenient occasion in a big, bow-wow style of oratory. He would use rolling words which had no application to the topic at hand, and his speeches left the impression of an army of pompous phrases moving over the landscape in search of an idea. Sometimes these meandering words would actually capture a struggling thought and bear it triumphantly, a prisoner in their midst, until it died of servitude and overwork.[64]

The idea caught up in the march of Harding's rhetoric during the 1920 campaign was "normalcy," by which he meant normality, or a return to conditions as he fancied they had been before the war and before the last twenty years of progressive reform. His goal, he admitted frankly, was to turn back the clock to a simpler time when the United States generally avoided international involvement and the government left Americans alone to get on with their business. Although the word might not have been in the dictionary, the idea was certainly in the minds of a majority of Americans. Despite the smallest voter turnout to date, Harding won over 60 percent of the popular vote and swept the electoral college, 404 to 127.[65]

On 4 March 1921 Wilson struggled into morning coat and gray trousers for his last official function, the inauguration of his successor. A slumped and frail figure, he rode in an open car to the Capitol with the president-elect and then rode up to the President's Room in a freight elevator because he could not climb steps. He signed a few last bills passed by the expiring session of Congress and then, unable to walk to the reviewing stand for Harding's inaugural, slipped away to drive back to the White House. Few people in the crowd noticed his absence.

After leaving the presidency the Wilsons lived a reclusive life in a house on S Street that Edith said had been presented to Wilson by friends. His health did not improve much, and his days were passed in listening as Edith read to him, in taking rides in the White House Pierce Arrow that he had purchased from the government when he left office, or in attending an occasional baseball game, where his car parked on the outfield grass so that he could watch in seclusion. A few visitors came to see him, but he had little to say to them.

In November 1923 friends persuaded him to give a short Armistice Day talk over the newly popular radio, and he limped through it, prompted constantly by Edith. The "great war for democracy and right" had been "fought and won," he said, only to have the victory "forever marred and embittered for us by the shameful fact that when the victory was won . . . we turned our backs on our associates and refused to bear any responsible part in the administration of peace." Nevertheless, he concluded, there was still time to "retrieve the past" by "resolving to put self-interest away and once more formulate and act upon the highest ideals and purposes of international policy."[66]

The next day, a crowd of veterans gathered across the street from his house, and he struggled outside to say a few words to them. "I am not one of those that have the least anxiety about the triumph of the principles I have stood for," he said with a surprisingly firm voice. "I have seen fools resist Providence before, and I have seen their destruction, as will come upon these again, utter destruction and contempt. That we shall prevail is as sure as that God reigns."[67]

In December the Wilsons quietly celebrated Woodrow's sixty-seventh birthday, but a month later he began to fail rapidly. At 11:15 on Sunday morning, 3 February 1924, he died, and three days later he was buried in a small chapel of the new National Cathedral. All across the country and around the world millions mourned the passing of the Moses who had seen the vision of the promised land from the mountain but had not lived to enter it.

In his last public talk, on the steps of his S Street house, Wilson had once again evoked the central themes of his presidency—that individuals could be inspired to set aside their selfish, personal interests to seek the good of all and that God was working out his plan for the world through the progress of the United States. Just as in this instance he urged America to take up its role of service in the world, so at home he had asked business, labor, and farmers to subordinate private satisfaction to the building of a cooperative, harmonious society. Yet paradoxically, at the same time that he evoked a vision of a new, collective consciousness he sought also to create new opportunities for small farmers, individual workers, new businesses, and, in the international world, small nations. The tension that thus existed in his ideals between the individual and the community was never resolved; but it must be noted that if the concept presents logical problems, it also enabled Wilson to imagine a world in which opportunities would abound for every person or state yet commitment to common interests would transcend selfishness, and society as a whole would be happy and unified. Appealing at any time, that dream seemed realizable to many Americans of the early twentieth century because they regarded resources and opportunities for growth as unlimited. World power, prosperity, happiness, and social justice would come automatically, provided everyone had confidence and worked together for the common good; Adam Smith was to be turned upside down.

Not all of Wilson's contemporaries shared his optimism about the possibilities of the future, and subsequent generations have gradually been forced to confront increasing competition for dwindling resources. Nevertheless, the desire to combine individual satisfaction and collective benefits, national aspirations and international cooperation remains seductive, even if attaining those goals seems no more within reach today than in Wilson's time.

NOTES

PREFACE

1. *Where the Buck Stops: The Personal and Private Writings of Harry S. Truman*, ed. Margaret Truman (New York: Warner Books, 1989), p. 15; Robert K. Murray and Tim H. Blessing, *Greatness in the White House: Rating the Presidents, Washington through Carter; Final Report, the Presidential Performance Study* (University Park: Pennsylvania State University Press, 1988).

2. John Milton Cooper, Jr., *Pivotal Decades: The United States, 1900–1920* (New York: W. W. Norton, 1990), p. 365.

3. Shakespeare, *Othello*, act 5, sc. 2.

CHAPTER 1
THEORY AND PRACTICE, 1856–1912

1. For Wilson's youth, see especially John M. Mulder, *Woodrow Wilson: The Years of Preparation* (Princeton, N.J.: Princeton University Press, 1978); Alexander L. George and Juliette L. George, *Woodrow Wilson and Colonel House: A Personality Study* (New York: John Day, 1956); and Arthur S. Link, *Wilson: The Road to the White House* (Princeton, N.J.: Princeton University Press, 1947). A brief biography is Kendrick A. Clements, *Woodrow Wilson: World Statesman* (Boston: Twayne Publishers, 1987).

2. My analysis of Wilson's political thought is much indebted to Niels Aage Thorsen, *The Political Thought of Woodrow Wilson, 1875–1910* (Princeton, N.J.: Princeton University Press, 1988), which now supersedes such standard works as William Diamond, *The Economic Thought of Woodrow Wilson* (Baltimore:

Johns Hopkins University Press, 1943), and James Kerney, *The Political Education of Woodrow Wilson* (New York: Century, 1926).

3. A religious talk, 4 July 1902, in *The Papers of Woodrow Wilson*, ed. Arthur S. Link et al., 62 vols. to date (Princeton, N.J.: Princeton University Press, 1966-), 12, *1900-1902* (1972), p.:475 (hereafter cited as *PWW*).

4. Wilson's notes for an address on patriotism, 16 Jan. 1898, ibid., 10, *1896-1898* (1971), p. 365; Thorsen, *Political Thought*, pp. 5, 167, 238; Wilson's 5 June 1917 speech to Confederate veterans quoted in Richard J. Bishirjian, "Croly, Wilson, and the American Civil Religion," *Modern Age* 23 (Winter 1979): 36.

5. Frances Wright Saunders, *Ellen Axson Wilson: First Lady between Two Worlds* (Chapel Hill: University of North Carolina Press, 1985).

6. See, for example, the passage from *Congressional Government*, PWW, 4, *1885* (1968), pp. 29-30.

7. Thorsen, *Political Thought*, p. 218. For a different point of view, see Sondra R. Herman, *Eleven against War: Studies in American Internationalist Thought, 1898-1921* (Stanford, Calif.: Hoover Institution Press, 1969), p. 183.

8. Wilson's shorthand diary, 19 June 1876; draft of a speech on "The Union," [15] Nov. 1876, PWW, 1, *1856-1880* (1966), pp. 143, 226-28.

9. "Cabinet Government in the United States," *International Review* 7 (Aug. 1879), ibid., pp. 493-510.

10. Ibid., p. 494; Thorsen, *Political Thought*, pp. 31-3.

11. "The Modern Democratic State," 1 Dec. 1885, PWW, 5, *1885-1888* (1968), pp. 83-84.

12. A lecture on "Democracy," 5 Dec. 1891, ibid., 7, *1890-1892* (1969), p. 347; "The Study of Administration," *Political Science Quarterly* 2 (July 1887), ibid., 5:368-70.

13. Memorandum on leadership, 5 May 1902, ibid., 12:365.

14. "The Ideal Statesman," 30 Jan. 1877, ibid., 1:243.

15. An unpublished letter to the editor, ca. 21 Mar. 1881, ibid., 2, *1881-1884* (1967), pp. 33-40.

16. From *Constitutional Government* (1908), ibid., 18, *1908-1909* (1974), p. 148.

17. Address in St. Paul, 25 May 1911, ibid., 23, *1911—1912* (1977), p. 88.

18. "The Study of Administration," ibid., 5:369.

19. Wilson to Ellen Axson, 24 Feb. 1885, ibid., 4:287.

20. Ibid., 14, *1902-1903* (1972), pp. 170-74.

21. "The Study of Administration," ibid., 5:362-63; "Responsible Government under the Constitution," *Atlantic Monthly* 57 (Apr. 1886), ibid., p. 107.

22. "The Study of Administration," ibid., p. 371.

23. Notes for lectures on administration, 3 Feb-10 Mar. 1890, ibid., 6, *1888-1896* (1969), p. 485.

24. Woodrow Wilson, *Congressional Government: A Study in American Politics* (Boston: Houghton, Mifflin, 1885), p. 254.

25. Peri E. Arnold, *Making the Managerial Presidency: Comprehensive Reorgan-*

ization Planning, 1905–1980 (Princeton, N.J.: Princeton University Press, 1986), pp. 29–38, 42–49; Paolo E. Coletta, *The Presidency of William Howard Taft* (Lawrence: University Press of Kansas, 1973), pp. 130–32.

26. Preface to the 1900 edition of *Congressional Government*, xi.

27. *Woodrow Wilson, Constitutional Government in the United States* (New York: Columbia University Press, 1908), p. 60.

28. Ibid., p. 68.

29. Ibid., pp. 66–67, 76.

30. Ibid., pp. 73, 77, 70–71. For discussion of Wilson's role in defining the presidency as the voice of the people, see Jeffrey K. Tulis, *The Rhetorical Presidency* (Princeton, N.J.: Princeton University Press, 1987), and Stephen E. Ponder, "Executive Publicity and Congressional Resistance, 1905–1913: Congress and the Roosevelt Administration's PR Men," *Congress and the Presidency* 13 (Autumn 1986): 177–86.

31. Thorsen, *Political Thought*, pp. 209–10.

32. *The State: Elements of Historical and Practical Politics: A Sketch of Institutional History and Administration* (Boston: D. C. Heath, 1889), quoted in *PWW*, 6:306; Thorsen, *Political Thought*, pp. 188–89.

33. An address on patriotism to the Washington Association of New Jersey, 23 Feb. 1903, *PWW*, 14:366.

34. "Education and Democracy," 4 May 1907, ibid., 17, *1907–1908* (1974), p. 135 (the order of phrases has been reversed).

35. Thorsen, *Political Thought*, 191–93; Robert W. Cherny, *A Righteous Cause: The Life of William Jennings Bryan* (Boston: Little, Brown & Co., 1985), esp. pp. 199–201; David Sarasohn, *The Party of Reform: Democrats in the Progressive Era* (Jackson: University of Mississippi Press, 1989).

36. Wilson to Ellen Louise Axson, 30 Oct. 1883, *PWW*, 2:501.

37. Address to the Virginia Society of New York, 30 Nov. 1904, ibid., 15, *1903–1905* (1973), p. 548; Wilson to Adrian Joline, 29 Apr. 1907, ibid., 17:124.

38. David W. Hirst, *Woodrow Wilson, Reform Governor: A Documentary Narrative* (Princeton, N.J.: Van Nostrand, 1965); John F. Reynolds, *Testing Democracy: Electoral Behavior and Progressive Reform in New Jersey, 1880–1920* (Chapel Hill: University of North Carolina Press, 1988).

39. George L. Record quoted in Arthur S. Link, "Woodrow Wilson in New Jersey," in *The Higher Realism of Woodrow Wilson and Other Essays*, ed. Arthur S. Link (Nashville, Tenn.: Vanderbilt University Press, 1971), p. 54.

40. "An Annual Message to the Legislature of New Jersey," 9 Jan. 1912, *PWW* 24, *1912* (1977), p. 19.

41. Wilson to David Benton Jones, 27 June 1910, ibid., 20, *1910* (1975), p. 543.

42. Arthur S. Link, *Wilson: The New Freedom* (Princeton, N.J.: Princeton University Press, 1956), pp. 94–95; Stockton Axson Memoir (in the possession of Arthur S. Link), "Social Disposition and Habits."

43. John Milton Cooper, Jr., *The Warrior and the Priest: Woodrow Wilson and*

Theodore Roosevelt (Cambridge, Mass.: Belknap Press of Harvard University Press, 1983), p. 172.

44. Link, *Wilson: The New Freedom*, p. 73.

CHAPTER 2
1912

1. [Edward M. House], *Philip Dru, Administrator: A Story of Tomorrow, 1920–1935* (New York: B. W. Huebsch, 1912), p. 1.

2. For perceptive comment on the novel, see Christopher Lasch, *The New Radicalism in America, 1889–1963: The Intellectual as a Social Type* (New York: Knopf, 1965), pp. 228–34.

3. Neil A. Wynn, *From Progressivism to Prosperity: World War I and American Society* (New York: Holmes & Meier, 1986), p. 6.

4. John Milton Cooper, Jr., *Pivotal Decades: The United States, 1900–1920* (New York: W.W. Norton & Co., 1990), p. 5.

5. Wynn, *From Progressivism to Prosperity*, pp. 15–17.

6. Ibid., pp. 2–3.

7. Ernest May, *American Imperialism: A Speculative Essay* (New York: Atheneum, 1968), pp. 3–11, 192–96.

8. Speech of 12 Aug. 1919, to U.S. Senate, quoted in *An American Primer*, ed. Daniel Boorstin, 2 vols. (Chicago: University of Chicago Press, 1966), 2:786.

9. Burton I. Kaufman, *Efficiency and Expansion: Foreign Trade Organization in the Wilson Administration, 1913–1921* (Westport, Conn.: Greenwood, 1974), pp. 3–7.

10. For contrasting views of the role of progressive reformers in the activist foreign policy of the early twentieth century, see William E. Leuchtenburg, "Progressivism and Imperialism: The Progressive Movement and American Foreign Policy, 1898–1916," *Mississippi Valley Historical Review* 39 (Dec. 1952): 483–504, and John M. Cooper, Jr., "Progressivism and American Foreign Policy: A Reconsideration," *Mid-America* 51 (Oct. 1969): 260–77.

11. William Graebner, *The Engineering of Consent: Democracy and Authority in Twentieth-Century America* (Madison: University of Wisconsin Press, 1987), p. 39. Graebner's specific allusion here is to 1917, but the observation is no less true of the earlier period, as he makes clear elsewhere.

12. Ibid., p. 3.

13. Cooper, *Pivotal Decades*, pp. 11–12.

14. Quoted in Tony Freyer, "The Sherman Antitrust Act, Comparative Business Structure, and the Rule of Reason: America and Great Britain, 1880–1920," *Iowa Law Review* 74 (July 1989): 1013.

15. Thurman Arnold, *The Folklore of Capitalism* (New Haven, Conn.: Yale University Press, 1937), pp. 217–18.

16. Woodrow Wilson, *A History of the American People*, 5 vols. (New York: Harper, 1902), 5:212–13.

17. Richard L. McCormick, *The Party Period and Public Policy: American Poli-*

tics from the Age of Jackson to the Progressive Era (New York: Oxford University Press, 1986), p. 342.

18. Wynn, *From Progressivism to Prosperity*, p. 4.

19. Arthur S. Link and Richard L. McCormick, *Progressivism* (Arlington Heights, Ill.: Harlan Davidson, 1983), p. 99.

20. McCormick, *The Party Period*, p. 332.

21. James Weinstein, *The Corporate Ideal in the Liberal State, 1900-1918* (Boston: Beacon Press, 1968), pp. ix-x.

22. Link and McCormick, *Progressivism*, pp. 343-46; Louis Galambos and Joseph Pratt, *The Rise of the Corporate Commonwealth: U.S. Business and Public Policy in the Twentieth Century* (New York: Basic Books, 1988), pp. 43-70.

23. Link and McCormick, *Progressivism*, pp. 21, 69.

24. Don S. Kirschner, *The Paradox of Professionalism: Reform and Public Service in Urban America, 1900-1940* (Westport, Conn.: Greenwood, 1986).

25. McCormick, *The Party Period*, pp. 222-23, summarizes and cites much of the recent research on this topic.

26. Wynn, *From Progressivism to Prosperity*, pp. 17-18.

27. Ibid., p. 18.

28. Robert W. Cherny, *A Righteous Cause: The Life of William Jennings Bryan* (Boston: Little, Brown & Co., 1985), p. 200.

29. Quoted in John Milton Cooper, Jr., *The Warrior and the Priest: Woodrow Wilson and Theodore Roosevelt* (Cambridge, Mass.: Belknap Press of Harvard University Press, 1983), p. 29.

30. Ibid., pp. 69-70, 76-86; Arthur S. Link, *Woodrow Wilson and the Progressive Era, 1910-1917* (New York: Harper & Bros., 1954), pp. 2-3.

31. Cooper, *Warrior and Priest*, p. 115.

32. George E. Mowry, *The Era of Theodore Roosevelt, 1900-1912* (New York: Harper & Row, 1958), pp. 271-72.

33. A speech at Osawatomie, Kans., 31 Aug. 1910, in *The Works of Theodore Roosevelt, Memorial Edition*, ed. Hermann Hagedorn, 20 vols. (New York, Charles Scribner's Sons, 1924-25), *Social Justice and Popular Rule: Essays, Addresses, and Public Statements Relating to the Progressive Movement (1910-1916)*, 19:24-25, 27.

34. Ibid., p. 25.

35. A speech at Denver, 29 Aug. 1910, in Theodore Roosevelt, *The New Nationalism* (New York: Outlook Co., 1910), p. 55.

36. Address at the Progressive party convention, 6 Aug. 1912, *Works*, 19:358.

37. David Sarasohn, *The Party of Reform: Democrats in the Progressive Era* (Jackson: University of Mississippi Press, 1989), pp. 3-118.

38. Cooper, *Warrior and Priest*, pp. 181-83.

39. Ibid., pp. 185-86; Arthur S. Link, *Wilson: The Road to the White House* (Princeton, N.J.: Princeton University Press, 1947), pp. 431-65.

40. Speech at Chicago, 6 Aug. 1912, Roosevelt, *Works*, 19:391, 381.

41. Ibid., p. 388.

42. Address at Buffalo, N.Y., 2 Sept. 1912, *The Papers of Woodrow Wilson*, ed.

Arthur S. Link et al., 62 vols. to date (Princeton, N.J.: Princeton University Press, 1966–), 25, *1912* (1978), p. 73 (hereafter cited as *PWW*).

43. Benjamin J. Klebaner, "Potential Competition and the American Antitrust Legislation of 1914," *Business History Review* 38 (Summer 1964): 163–85; David Benton Jones to Wilson, 13 July 1912, *PWW*, 24, *1912* (1977):549.

44. Quoted in Wynn, *From Progressivism to Prosperity*, p. 20.

45. Address at Wilmington, Del., 17 Oct. 1912, *PWW*, 25:427. See also Wilson to Brandeis, 27 Sept. 1912, ibid., p. 272.

46. Weinstein, *Corporate Ideal*, pp. 161–67.

47. Cooper, *Warrior and Priest*, p. 205; Tim Taylor, *The Book of Presidents* (New York: Arno Press, 1972), p. 328.

48. Cooper, *Warrior and Priest*, pp. 206–7.

49. Sarasohn, *The Party of Reform*, pp. 149–51.

50. Walter Dean Burnham, *Critical Elections and the Mainspring of American Politics* (New York: Norton, 1966).

51. James MacGregor Burns, *Presidential Government: The Crucible of Leadership* (Boston: Houghton Mifflin Co., 1965), pp. 202–5; Sarasohn, *Party of Reform*, pp. 192–238.

52. Cooper, *Warrior and Priest*, pp. 212–13.

CHAPTER 3

MAJOR DOMESTIC ISSUES, 1913–1916

1. An address to the General Assembly of Virginia and the City Council of Richmond, 1 Feb. 1912, *The Papers of Woodrow Wilson*, ed. Arthur S. Link et al., 62 vols. to date (Princeton, N.J.: Princeton University Press, 1966–), 24, *1912* (1977), pp. 108, 116 (hereafter cited as *PWW*).

2. Ibid., p. 108. The order of phrases has been changed.

3. Ibid., p. 116.

4. Quoted in Arthur S. Link, *Wilson: The New Freedom* (Princeton, N.J.: Princeton University Press, 1956), p. 94.

5. John J. Broesamle, *William Gibbs McAdoo: A Passion for Change, 1863–1917* (Port Washington, New York: Kennikat Press, 1973).

6. David Lawrence, *The True Story of Woodrow Wilson* (New York: George H. Doran Co., 1924), p. 75.

7. Martin J. Sklar, "Woodrow Wilson and the Political Economy of Modern United States Liberalism," *Studies on the Left* 1:3 (1960): 28; A. Howard Mencely, "William Cox Redfield," in *Dictionary of American Biography*, ed. Dumas Malone, (New York: Charles Scribner's Sons, 1935), 8:442.

8. An address on the tariff to the National Democratic Club of New York, 3 Jan. 1912, *PWW*, 23, *1911–1912* (1977), p. 641.

9. Marc Karson, *American Labor Unions and Politics, 1900–1918* (Carbondale: Southern Illinois University Press, 1958), pp. 70, 121–22. The two Wilsons were not related.

10. Bryan to Wilson, 25 Dec. 1912; Edward M. House to Wilson, 22 Nov.

1912; Abbott Lawrence Lowell to Wilson, 9 Nov. 1912; House diary, 18 Dec. 1912, all in *PWW*, 25, *1912* (1978), pp. 622, 558, 535, 610–11; House diary, 13 Feb. 1913, *PWW*, 27, *1913* (1978), p. 110.

11. John M. Blum, *Joe Tumulty and the Wilson Era* (Boston: Houghton Mifflin, 1951).

12. An address to the Commercial Club of Chicago, 11 Jan. 1913; an inaugural address, 4 Mar. 1913, *PWW*, 27:34, 151.

13. House diary, 26 Feb. 1913, quoted in Link, *Wilson: The New Freedom*, p. 27.

14. Woodrow Wilson, *Constitutional Government in the United States* (New York: Columbia University Press, 1908), p. 142.

15. See Jeffrey Tulis, *The Rhetorical Presidency* (Princeton, N.J.: Princeton University Press, 1987).

16. James MacGregor Burns, *Presidential Government: The Crucible of Leadership* (Boston: Houghton Mifflin, 1965), p. 198.

17. Notes for a speech opposing the protective tariff, ca. 23 Sept. 1882; testimony before the Tariff Commission, 23 Sept. 1882, *PWW*, 2, *1881–1884* (1967), pp. 139–43; a speech accepting the Democratic nomination in Sea Girt, New Jersey, 7 Aug. 1912, ibid., 25:8, 11.

18. Page to Wilson, 5 Nov. 1912, ibid., 25:515–17, 567n.3.

19. *The Cabinet Diaries of Josephus Daniels, 1913–1921*, ed. E. David Cronon (Lincoln: University of Nebraska Press, 1963), p. 25 (8 Apr. 1913); an address on tariff reform to a joint session of Congress, 8 Apr. 1913, *PWW*, 27:269–70.

20. A news report (from the *New York World*, 10 Apr. 1913), 9 Apr. 1913, *PWW*, 27:278.

21. Remarks at a press conference, 11 Apr. 1913, ibid., p. 285.

22. Remarks at a press conference, 26 May 1913, and a statement on tariff lobbyists, 26 May 1913, ibid., pp. 472, 473.

23. Remarks at a press conference, 29 May 1913, ibid., pp. 483–84.

24. All quotations in this paragraph may be found in Frank Burdick, "Woodrow Wilson and the Underwood Tariff," *Mid-America* 50 (Oct. 1968): 280–83.

25. For the debate over "corporate liberalism," see Sklar, "Woodrow Wilson and the Political Economy of Modern United States Liberalism," pp. 17–47; Sklar, *The Corporate Reconstruction of American Capitalism, 1890–1916: The Market, the Law, and Politics* (Cambridge: Cambridge University Press, 1988); James Weinstein, *The Corporate Ideal in the Liberal State, 1900–1918* (Boston: Beacon Press, 1968); Louis Galambos and Joseph Pratt, *The Rise of the Corporate Commonwealth: U.S. Business and Public Policy in the Twentieth Century* (New York: Basic Books, 1988); Robert Wiebe, *Businessmen and Reform: A Study of the Progressive Movement* (Cambridge, Mass.: Harvard University Press, 1962); Ellis W. Hawley, "The Discovery and Study of a 'Corporate Liberalism,'" *Business History Review* 52 (Autumn 1978): 309–20; Alan L. Seltzer, "Woodrow Wilson as 'Corporate Liberal': Toward a Reconsideration of Left Revisionist Historiography," *Western Political Quarterly* 30 (June 1977): 183–212.

26. An interview on the banking and currency bill, 23 June 1913, *PWW*, 27:565.

27. Senator Furnifold McLendel Simmons to Wilson, 2 Sept. 1913, *PWW*, 28, *1913* (1978), p. 247; Link, *Wilson: The New Freedom*, pp. 191-93.

28. Joseph Patrick Tumulty to Wilson, 2 Sept. 1913; two telegrams to Tumulty from Wilson, 2 Sept. 1913, *PWW*, 28:247-48.

29. Remarks upon signing the tariff bill, 3 Oct. 1913, ibid., p. 351.

30. See ibid., p. 352n.1.

31. An address to the Commercial Club of Chicago, 11 Jan. 1913, ibid., 27:33. For the "money monopoly" phrase, see, inter alia, a speech to the State Federation of Democratic Clubs, Harrisburg, Pa., 15 June 1911, ibid., 23:157.

32. House to Wilson, 28 Nov. 1912, ibid., 25:564.

33. Link, *Wilson: The New Freedom*, pp. 199-200.

34. House diary, 8 Jan. 1912, *PWW*, 27:21; Sean Davis Cashman, *America in the Age of the Titans: The Progressive Era and World War I* (New York: New York University Press, 1988), pp. 127-28.

35. William Jennings Bryan and Mary Baird Bryan, *The Memoirs of William Jennings Bryan* (Chicago: John C. Winston Co., 1925), p. 370; House diary, 19 May 1913, *PWW*, 27:457.

36. Brandeis to Wilson, 14 June 1913, ibid., pp. 520-21.

37. An address on banking and currency reform to a joint session of Congress, 23 June 1913, ibid., pp. 572-73.

38. Bryan to Carter Glass, 22 Aug. 1913, quoted in Glass, *An Adventure in Constructive Finance* (Garden City, New York: Doubleday, Page & Co., 1927), p. 139.

39. Ibid., 167.

40. Remarks upon signing the Federal Reserve bill, 23 Dec. 1913, *PWW*, 29, *December 2, 1913-May 5, 1914* (1979), pp. 63-66.

41. Sklar, *Corporate Reconstruction of America*, pp. 422-24 (quotation on p. 422). In contrast, see James Livingston, *Origins of the Federal Reserve System: Money, Class, and Corporate Capitalism, 1890-1913* (Ithaca, N.Y.: Cornell University Press, 1986), pp. 233-34, passim. For a summary of the terms of the act, see Cashman, *America in the Age of the Titans*, pp. 128-30.

42. Wilson to Newton Diehl Baker, 5 Mar. 1915, *PWW*, 32, *January 1-April 16, 1915* (1980), p. 324.

43. See his remarks upon signing the rural credits bill, 17 July 1916, ibid., 37, *May 9-August 7, 1916* (1981), pp. 427-28. For a further discussion of the genesis of the Federal Land Bank Act, see chap. 4 of this book.

44. Wilson to Joseph Patrick Tumulty, 24 Jan. 1914, *PWW*, 29:170; Wilson to Charles Samuel Jackson, 24 July 1916, ibid., 37:469; Walter I. Trattner, "The First Federal Child Labor Law (1916)," *Social Science Quarterly* 50 (Dec. 1969): 507-24.

45. Josephus Daniels to Wilson, 16 July 1916; Alexander Jeffrey McKelway to Wilson, 17 July 1916, *PWW*, 37:428-30; Blum, *Progressive Presidents*, pp. 78-79;

Arthur Walworth, *Woodrow Wilson*, 2d rev. ed. (New York: Pelican Books, 1965), 2: 56–57.

46. Woodrow Wilson, *The State* (Boston: D. C. Heath, 1897 [originally published 1889]), p. 663.

47. On child labor, see Wilson to Alexander Jeffrey McKelway, 15 Aug. 1912; the platform of the New Jersey Democratic party, 1 Oct. 1912 (probably written by Wilson), *PWW*, 25:30, 306. On the right of unionization, see his address to working men in Fall River, Mass., 26 Sept. 1912, ibid., pp. 262–64. For his general statement on social justice, see his Labor Day address in Buffalo, N.Y., 2 Sept. 1912, ibid., p. 71.

48. *The State*, pp. 647, 651 (emphasis in original).

49. Oswald Garrison Villard to Robert Hayne Leavell, 15 May 1913, *PWW*, 27:442; Wilson to Villard, 21 Aug. 1913, ibid., 28:202. For a more charitable later view by a black leader, see "Document: W. E. B. DuBois' Impressions of Woodrow Wilson," by Kenneth M. Glazier, *Journal of Negro History* 58 (Oct. 1973): 452–59.

50. Wilson to Villard, 29 Aug. 1913, *PWW*, 28:245; Wilson to Howard Allen Bridgman, 8 Sept. 1913, ibid., pp. 265–66.

51. Joel Williamson, *The Crucible of Race: Black-White Relations in the American South since Emancipation* (New York: Oxford University Press, 1984); Henry Blumenthal, "Woodrow Wilson and the Race Question," *Journal of Negro History* 48 (Jan. 1963): 1–21. For an appraisal of the administration's racial policies as they operated in the Agriculture Department, see chap. 4 of this book.

52. Quoted in Angie Debo, *A History of the Indians of the United States* (Norman: University of Oklahoma Press, 1970), p. 265.

53. Franklin K. Lane to John H. Wigmore, 8 Mar. 1913, in *The Letters of Franklin K. Lane: Personal and Political*, ed. Anne Wintermute Lane and Louise Herrick Wall (Boston: Houghton Mifflin, 1922), p. 132; *Reports of the Department of the Interior for the Fiscal Year Ended June 30, 1913* (Washington, D.C.: GPO, 1914), 2:4; *Reports . . . Interior, 1920* (Washington, D.C.: GPO, 1920), 2:8.

54. Debo, *History of the Indians*, p. 283.

55. A Labor Day address in Buffalo, N.Y., 2 Sept. 1912, *PWW*, 25:73.

56. Jerrold G. Van Cise, *The Federal Antitrust Laws*, 3d ed. (Washington, D.C.: American Enterprise Institute for Public Policy Research, 1983), p. 7.

57. An annual message to Congress, 2 Dec. 1913, *PWW*, 29:7.

58. An address on antitrust legislation to a joint session of Congress, 20 Jan. 1914, ibid., pp. 156–57.

59. Ibid., p. 153. A helpful, brief summary of the Clayton Act, on which this is based, is in William Letwin, *Law and Economic Policy in America: The Evolution of the Sherman Antitrust Act* (New York: Random House, 1965), pp. 273–76.

60. David Davenport in the *Springfield Republican*, 11 Oct. 1914, quoted in Link, *Wilson: The New Freedom*, p. 433.

61. House diary, 2 Oct. 1914, *PWW*, 31, *September 6–December 31, 1914* (1979), p. 122.

62. Letwin, *Law and Economic Policy*, p. 276.

63. Brandeis quoted in Melvin I. Urofsky, "Wilson, Brandeis and the Trust Issue, 1912–1914," *Mid-America* 49 (Jan. 1967): 21.

64. Ibid., pp. 26–27. Compare with Link, *Wilson: The New Freedom*, p. 438.

65. Wilson to Senator Charles Allen Culberson, 30 July 1914, *PWW*, 30, *May 6–September 5, 1914* (1979), p. 320.

66. George Rublee, "Memorandum Concerning Section 5 of the Bill to Create a Federal Trade Commission," enclosed in Franklin K. Lane to Wilson, 10 July 1914, quoted in Seltzer, "Woodrow Wilson as 'Corporate Liberal,'" p. 199, and summarized in *PWW*, 30:274–75n.1. For the later history of the FTC, see G. Cullom Davis's argument in "The Transformation of the Federal Trade Commission, 1914–1929," *Mississippi Valley Historical Review* 49 (Dec. 1962): 437–55.

67. Seltzer, "Woodrow Wilson as 'Corporate Liberal,'" pp. 200–201.

68. Richard A. Posner, "A Statistical Study of Antitrust Enforcement," *Journal of Law and Economics* 13 (Oct. 1970): 366, 369, 381.

69. Seltzer, "Woodrow Wilson as 'Corporate Liberal,'" pp. 201–4. Wilson's remark about "real competition" was made in Sept. 1913 and is quoted in ibid., p. 202. For a more critical interpretation of McReynolds's antitrust record, see John M. Blum, *The Progressive Presidents: Roosevelt, Wilson, Roosevelt, Johnson,* (New York: Norton, 1980), pp. 76–77.

70. Thomas Watt Gregory to Wilson, 5 Oct. 1917; Wilson to Gregory, 10 Oct. 1917, *PWW*, 44, *August 21–November 10, 1917* (1983), pp. 313, 347.

71. Seltzer, "Woodrow Wilson as 'Corporate Liberal,'" pp. 205–6; William H. Becker, *The Dynamics of Business-Government Relations: Industry and Exports, 1893–1921* (Chicago: University of Chicago Press, 1982), pp. 153–55; Michael J. Hogan, *Informal Entente: The Private Structure of Cooperation in Anglo-American Economic Diplomacy 1918–1928* (Columbia: University of Missouri Press, 1977), p. 8.

CHAPTER 4
THE DEPARTMENT OF AGRICULTURE

1. Woodrow Wilson, *Constitutional Government in the United States* (New York: Columbia University Press, 1908), p. 67.

2. David F. Houston, *Eight Years with Wilson's Cabinet, 1913 to 1920,* 2 vols. (Garden City, N.Y.: Doubleday, Page & Co., 1926), 1:89.

3. Arthur S. Link, "David Franklin Houston," in *Dictionary of American Biography,* 11, sup. 2, ed. Robert Livingston Schuyler and Edward T. James (New York: Charles Scribner's Sons, 1958), p. 321.

4. Houston, *Eight Years,* 1:17–20.

5. Wilson to Edward Mandell House, 7 Feb. 1913, *The Papers of Woodrow Wilson,* ed. Arthur S. Link et al., 62 vols. to date (Princeton, N.J.: Princeton University Press, 1966–), 27, *1913* (1978), pp. 102–103 (hereafter cited as *PWW*); Page to Wilson, 27 Nov. 1912, quoted in Burton J. Hendrick, *The Life and Letters of Walter Hines Page,* 2 vols. (Garden City, N.Y.: Doubleday, Page & Co., 1923), 1:114–15.

6. Houston, *Eight Years*, 1:38.

7. Link, "David Franklin Houston," p. 321.

8. Russell Lord, *The Wallaces of Iowa* (Boston: Houghton Mifflin, 1947), p. 192.

9. See Hendrick, *Life and Letters, Page*, 1:84, 112–13; John Milton Cooper, Jr., *Walter Hines Page: The Southerner as American, 1855–1918* (Chapel Hill: University of North Carolina Press, 1977), pp. 206–14, 225–29.

10. Willard W. Cochrane, *The Development of American Agriculture: A Historical Analysis* (Minneapolis: University of Minnesota Press, 1979), pp. 104–5; Wayne D. Rasmussen, "The People's Department: Myth or Reality?" *Agricultural History* 64 (Spring 1990): 294.

11. Cooper, *Walter Hines Page*, pp. 235–46; Lord, *Wallaces of Iowa*, pp. 204–5; Theodore Saloutos, *Farmer Movements in the South, 1865–1933* (Berkeley: University of California Press, 1960), pp. 213–19.

12. Quoted in Murray R. Benedict, *Farm Policies of the United States, 1790–1950: A Study of Their Origin and Development* (New York: Octagon Books, 1966), p. 152.

13. David F. Houston to T. W. Bickett (N.C. attorney general), 1 Aug. 1916; an untitled memorandum on the achievements of the Agriculture Department, 1913–16, 1 Aug. 1916; Memorandum Regarding the Establishment of the Office of Markets and Rural Organization, enclosed in Charles J. Brand (chief of the Office of Markets) to J. A. Osoinach (Office of Assistant Secretary), 2 Dec. 1916; "Agriculture: Summary, 1913–1916, August 7, 1916," all in Records of the Office of the Secretary of Agriculture, entry 17, General Correspondence, drawer 161, "Work of the Department of Agriculture, 1916," RG16, National Archives, Washington, D.C. (hereafter cited as Agriculture Department, General Correspondence [ADGC]); Houston, *Eight Years*, 1:205–6; Gladys L. Baker, Wayne D. Rasmussen, Vivian Wiser, Jane M. Porter, *Century of Service: The First 100 Years of the United States Department of Agriculture* (Washington, D.C.: Centennial Committee, U.S. Department of Agriculture, 1963), pp. 64–69.

14. Wilson's inaugural address, 4 Mar. 1913, *PWW*, 27:150; Houston, *Eight Years*, 1:200; Report of the Secretary, in *Annual Reports of the Department of Agriculture for the Year Ended June 30, 1913* (Washington, D.C.: GPO, 1914), pp. 20–33.

15. Houston, *Eight Years*, 1:201; Francis Butler Simkins, "Asbury Francis Lever," in *Dictionary of American Biography*, 11, Supplement 2:379–80; Assistant Secretary B. T. Galloway to Dr. A[lfred] C[harles] True (head of Office of Experiment Stations, 1893–1915), 22 Mar. 1913, drawer 143, "Lever Bill, 1913"; Galloway to Wallace Buttrick (General Education Board), 26 Apr. 1913, drawer 74, "Demonstration Work, 1912–13," ADGC.

16. An annual message to the legislature of New Jersey, 14 Jan. 1913, *PWW*, 27:150–51.

17. For the history of the demonstration program, see J. A. Evans (head of the Office of Extension Work in the South, 1920–21), "The Farmers' Cooperative Demonstration Work," no date, drawer 74, "Demonstration Work, 1912–13";

"Special Report of the Farmers' Cooperative Demonstration Work, 1913, to the Committee on Agriculture, House of Representatives," 5 Feb. 1914, drawer 131, ADGC; Gladys Baker, *The County Agent* (Chicago: University of Chicago Press, 1939), p. 28; Saloutos, *Farmer Movements*, pp. 225–28. For the funding of the work in 1912–13, see table in drawer 143, "Lever Bill, 1913, ADGC." For the history of the Lever bill of 1912, see B. T. Galloway to Dean E. J. Kyle, School of Agriculture, College Station, Tex., 2 Jan. 1913 [1914], drawer 144, "Lever Bill, 1913," ibid.

18. Houston, *Eight Years*, 1:200. For a more detailed but equally bleak description by a modern scholar, see William H. Harbaugh, "Farmers, County Agents, and the Conservation Movement," in *The Wilson Era: Essays in Honor of Arthur S. Link*, ed. John Milton Cooper, Jr., and Charles Neu (Arlington Heights, Ill.: Harlan Davidson, 1991), pp. 123–55.

19. William L. Bowers, *The Country Life Movement in America, 1900–1920* (Port Washington, N.Y.: Kennikat Press, 1974), pp. 65, 88–89.

20. See the anonymous "Memorandum," 17 Feb. 1912, drawer 144, "Lever Bill, 1912," ADGC; *The Cabinet Diaries of Josephus Daniels, 1913–1921*, ed. E. David Cronon (Lincoln: University of Nebraska Press, 1963), p. 32.

21. B. T. Galloway to Wallace Buttrick, 26 Apr. 1913, drawer 74, "Demonstration Work"; Galloway to Lever, 28 July 1913, drawer 143, "Lever Bill, 1913"; Galloway to Smith, 31 July 1913, drawer 123, "Bill, 1913"; Galloway to Professor W. D. Thompson (chairman, Executive Committee of American Agricultural Colleges and Experimental Stations), 2 Sept. 1913, drawer 144, "Lever Bill, 1913," ADGC.

22. B. T. Galloway to Hoke Smith, 5 Sept. 1913, drawer 143, "Lever Bill, 1913"; Houston to Lever, 17 Sept. 1913, drawer 123, "Bills, 1913"; chart showing differences between 1912 and 1913 Lever bills, 18 Aug. 1913, drawer 143, "Lever Bill, 1913," ADGC.

23. For an excellent account of the struggle in the Senate, see Dewey W. Grantham, *Hoke Smith and the Politics of the New South* (Baton Rouge: Louisiana State University Press, 1958), pp. 259–63. See 38 Stat. 372 for the text of the act. On the matter of racial discrimination in the act, see also Jane Addams, Herbert Parsons, Moorfield Storey, Oswald Garrison Villard, and other members of the board of directors of the Chicago chapter of the NAACP to Wilson, 4 May 1914, drawer 417, "Lever Bill, 1914, May–Dec," ADGC; Saloutos, *Farmer Movements*, pp. 230–32.

24. Harbaugh, "Farmers," p. 134. Note also that the average salary for county agents more than doubled between 1914 and 1919, from $1,200 to $2,450. See Baker, *County Agent*, p. 176.

25. Report of the secretary, *Annual Reports of the Department of Agriculture for the Year Ended June 30, 1916* (Washington, D.C.: GPO, 1917), p. 11.

26. Harbaugh, "Farmers," pp. 132–38.

27. Washington to Houston, 4 Aug. 1914; Houston to Washington, 10 Aug. 1914, drawer 417, "Lever Bill, 1914, May–Dec," ADGC.

28. Houston to McKeown, 26 Feb. 1915, box 1, "Negroes, 1918"; "Number of Cooperative Extension Employees, 1921," in ibid., "Negroes, 1921," ADGC.

29. Baker, *County Agent*, pp. 159, 201.

30. Chicago branch of NAACP to Houston, 12 Sept. 1913; Acting Secretary Galloway to Judge Edward Osgood Brown (one of the signers of the 12 Sept. letter), 14 Oct. 1913, box 1, "Negroes, July–Dec. 1913," ADGC. Some of the department's personnel records did not identify employees by race. See, for example, Acting Forester James B. Adams to R. M. Reese, chief clerk of the department, 17 July 1914, in "Negroes, 1914," ibid. As of Aug. 1914 the department had 447 black employees, all of whom except about 40 seem to have been laborers, clerks, or maids. Most blacks, including those with such responsible jobs as chemists and inspectors, were in the Bureau of Animal Husbandry or the Bureau of Plant Husbandry. See "Statement Showing the Colored Employees by Classes and Salaries in the Department of Agriculture" (ca. 14 Aug. 1914), in ibid. As of the end of 1918, restrooms in the Agriculture Department building apparently were not segregated. See Mrs. [?] Johnston to Chief Clerk R. M. Reese, 30 Nov. 1918, and Reese to Johnston, 7 Dec. 1918, in "Negroes, 1918," ibid.

31. Untitled memorandum, 1913, box 1, "Negroes, July–Dec. 1913," ibid.

32. Assistant Secretary R[aymond] A[llen] Pearson to Giles B. Jackson, 16 May 1917, box 1, "Negroes, 1917," ibid.

33. Ibid.; Secretary E[dwin] T[homas] Meredith to Major R. R. Moton (principal, Tuskegee Institute), 21 Aug. 1920, "Negroes, 1920," ibid.

34. T. D. Walton (acting Extension director, Tex.) to Bradford Knapp (chief, Office of Extension Work in the South), 31 Dec. 1918, forwarded by Knapp to Houston, Jan. 15, 1919; E. L. Blacksheer (a black assistant state agent, Tex.) to Knapp, 23 Mar. 1919, forwarded by Knapp to Houston, 25 Apr. 1919, box 1, "Negroes, 1919," ibid.

35. Wilson's annual message to Congress, 2 Dec. 1913, *PWW*, 29, *December 2, 1913–May 5, 1914* (1979), p. 6; Houston quoted in Baker et al., *Century of Service*, p. 75.

36. Baker et al., *Century of Service*, pp. 74–75.

37. Ibid., p. 501; report of the secretary, *Annual Reports . . . Agriculture . . . , 1916*, p. 5.

38. Report of the secretary, *Annual Reports . . . Agriculture . . . , 1916*, p. 3.

39. Report of the secretary, *Annual Reports of the Department of Agriculture for the Year Ended June 30, 1915* (Washington, D.C.: GPO, 1916), pp. 3–7.

40. Baker et al., *Century of Service*, pp. 76–77; Houston to Elliot F. Goodwin (secretary, U.S. Chamber of Commerce), 3 Feb. 1919, drawer 285, "Agricultural Department Work, 1919," ADGC; Assistant Secretaries Clarence Ousley and R. A. Pearson to Houston, 12 July 1918, drawer 103, "Committee, Agricultural, Sent to Europe, 1918," ibid.

41. Assistant Secretary Carl Vrooman to Houston, 20 Oct. 1918, drawer 103, "Committee, Agricultural, Sent to Europe, 1918," ibid.

42. Edward J. Robbins to Senator Arthur Capper, 15 Apr. 1920, enclosed in

Capper to Meredith, 16 Apr. 1920; Meredith to Capper, 24 Apr. 1920, drawer 498, "Exports, 1920," ibid.

43. Houston, *Eight Years*, 1:206.

44. Baker et al., *Century of Service*, pp. 77–79.

45. Francis G. Caffey (department solicitor) to Assistant Secretary B. T. Galloway, 12 Feb. 1914; Charles J. Brand (chief, Office of Markets) to Galloway, 19 Feb. 1914; Galloway to Lever, 11 Mar. 1914, drawer 393, "Cotton Grades," ADGC; Houston to Lever, 23 Apr. 1914, "Cotton Futures, 1914," ibid.

46. Houston to Lever, 23 Apr. 1914, drawer 393, "Cotton Futures, 1914," ibid.

47. Clipping from New York *Economic World*, 18 Dec. 1915, attached to memorandum by Charles J. Brand, 12 Nov. 1916, drawer 73, "Cotton Futures, 1915"; memorandum by Brand, 24 Sept. 1914, drawer 392, "Cotton Futures, 1914," ibid.

48. *PWW*, 27:150.

49. There is no full account of the development of the land banks, but see Arthur S. Link, *Wilson: Confusions and Crises, 1915–1916* (Princeton, N.J.: Princeton University Press, 1964), pp. 345–50; Clarence Ousely [Ousley], "The Beginning of Rural Credit," *Outlook* 113 (June 28, 1916): 511–14; Saloutos, *Farmer Movements*, pp. 221–23.

50. 26 Nov. 1913. Quoted in Baker et al., *Century of Service*, p. 87.

51. Wilson to Carter Glass, 12 May 1914, *PWW*, 30, *May 6–September 5, 1914* (1979), p. 24.

52. Link, *Wilson: Confusions and Crises*, pp. 347–49; the Odell quotation is on p. 347.

53. Statement showing total appropriations for department for last ten years; statement showing total number of employees in department by years from 1910; also, reports from each bureau, division, or office, 1 May 1920, drawer 453, "Agriculture Department Work, 1920," ADGC.

54. Report of the secretary, *Annual Reports . . . Agriculture . . . , 1913*, pp. 53–54.

55. Report of the secretary, *Annual Reports of the Department of Agriculture for the Year Ended June 30, 1917* (Washington, D.C.: GPO, 1918), pp. 3–5; Houston, *Eight Years*, 1:256–57; Wilson to William Julius Harris, 7 Feb. 1917, and Harris to Wilson, 12 Feb. 1917, *PWW*, 41, *January 24–April 6, 1917* (1983): pp. 146–48, 205–6.

56. Baker et al., *Century of Service*, pp. 88–89; form letter from secretary to editors, 3 Apr. 1917, drawer 441, "National Defense: 2-Food, 1917, April 1–14"; "Conference on Agricultural Situation, St. Louis, Mo., April 10, 1917," ADGC; Wilson, "An Appeal to the American People," 5 Apr. 1917, Wilson to Asbury Francis Lever, 16 May 1917, *PWW*, 42, *April 7–June 23, 1917* (1983), pp. 73–74, 301, and 301 n.1.

57. William Frieburger, "War Prosperity and Hunger: The New York Food Riots of 1917," *Labor History* 25 (Spring 1984): 217–39.

58. William Clinton Mullendore, *History of the United States Food Administration, 1917–1919* (Stanford, Calif.: Stanford University Press, 1941), pp. 4–7.

59. Wilson to Newton D. Baker, 16 Feb. 1917, *PWW*, 41:226 n.1.; report of the secretary, *Annual Reports . . . Agriculture . . . , 1917*, p. 7. According to Josephus Daniels, who was a member of the Council of National Defense, the invitation was sent to Hoover on 7 April rather than on 5 April. Cronon, *Daniels Diaries*, p. 130.

60. Charles J. Brand (chief, Bureau of Markets) to Assistant Secretary Galloway, 17 Apr. 1917, entry 201, B. T. Galloway file, box 5, "Brand, C. J.," RG 16; minutes of Interbureau Committee on National Defense, 9 Apr. 1917, box 11, "Minutes," ibid.; memorandum on "Conference on Agricultural Situation, St. Louis, Mo., April 10, 1917," drawer 44, "National Defense: 2-Food, 1917, April 1–14,"; Houston to Dr. E. S. Haswell, 18 May 1917, drawer 446, "National Defense: 2-Food, 1917, May 15–31," ADGC.

61. Herbert Hoover memorandum to Council of National Defense, 13 May 1917, drawer 445, "National Defense: 2-Food, 1917, May 1–14," ADGC; Frank M. Surface and Raymond L. Bland, *American Food in the World War and Reconstruction Period: Operations of the Organizations under the Direction of Herbert Hoover, 1914 to 1924* (Stanford, Calif.: Stanford University Press, 1931), p. 15; Baker et al., *Century of Service*, p. 89.

62. Dr. A[lonzo] E. Taylor (assistant to secretary) to Houston, 8 May 1917, drawer 445, "National Defense: 2-Food, 1917, May 1–14," ADGC. See also Norman Hapgood to Houston, 18 Apr. 1917, drawer 442, "National Defense: 2-Food, 1917, April 15–18"; Houston to M. Burrell (Canadian minister of Agriculture), 12 May 1917, drawer 445, "National Defense: 2-Food, 1917, May 1–14," ibid.

63. Hoover, Memorandum to Council of National Defense, 13 May 1917, p. 9, drawer 445, "National Defense: 2-Food, 1917, May 1–14," ibid.

64. Surface and Bland, *American Food in the World War*, p. 15; report of the secretary, *Annual Reports . . . Agriculture . . . , 1917*, pp. 7–9.

65. Report of the secretary, *Annual Reports . . . Agriculture . . . , 1917*, pp. 7–8.

66. Hoover to Houston, 8 Aug. 1917, drawer 307, "Work of the Department of Agriculture, 1917," ADGC.

67. David Burner, *Herbert Hoover: A Public Life* (New York: Knopf, 1979), p. 102.

68. Ibid., p. 103; memorandum by Norman B. Beecher (counsel to oil Director, U.S. Fuel Administration) and Mark L. Requa (general director, Oil Division, U.S. Fuel Administration), 23 Jan. 1919, Records of the Department of Interior, Office of the Secretary of Interior, Central Classified File, 1907–36; sec. 1, Administrative; "1–53, Council of National Defense; Box 115, General, Part 6, Nov. 6, 1918–Aug. 7, 1919," RG 48, National Archives, Washington, D.C. (hereafter cited as DICCF).

69. Mullendore, *History of the United States Food Administration*, pp. 60, 48,

319; Hoover's remarks before a conference of agricultural speakers, 20 Mar. 1918, drawer 250, "Speech, 1918," ADGC.

70. Tom G. Hall, "Wilson and the Food Crisis: Agricultural Price Control during World War I," *Agricultural History* 47 (Jan. 1973): 25-26.

71. Ibid., pp. 31-33, 44-46.

72. Quoted in ibid., p. 34.

73. Cronon, *Daniels Diaries*, p. 334; David Burner, *The Politics of Provincialism: The Democratic Party in Transition, 1918-1932* (New York: Knopf, 1967), pp. 36-37.

74. Baker et al., *Century of Service*, pp. 89-91; Houston, *Eight Years*, 1:329-46; Baker, *County Agent*, p. 42.

CHAPTER 5
INDUSTRIAL DEMOCRACY

1. For an excellent brief analysis of the development of Wilson's ideas about labor, see Manfred F. Boemeke, "The Wilson Administration, Organized Labor, and the Colorado Coal Strike, 1913-1914" (Ph.D. diss., Princeton University, 1983), especially chapter 2, "Woodrow Wilson and Organized Labor," pp. 42-110. Unless otherwise noted, the following discussion of the evolution of Wilson's ideas is based on Boemeke.

2. Ibid., pp. 42-61; an address in Bayonne, N.J., 1 Nov. 1910, *The Papers of Woodrow Wilson*, ed. Arthur S. Link et al., 62 vols. to date (Princeton, N.J.: Princeton University Press, 1966-   ) 21, *1910* (1976), p. 491 (hereafter cited as *PWW*).

3. From the *New York Times*, 29 Aug. 1912, ibid., 25, *1912* (1978), p. 58.

4. Quoted in Graham Adams, Jr., *Age of Industrial Violence: The Activities and Findings of the United States Commission on Industrial Violence* (New York: Columbia University Press, 1966), p. 25.

5. Ibid., pp. 30-51. The Gompers quotation is on p. 51.

6. Ibid., pp. 52-53.

7. Ibid., pp. 214-23, 227-29.

8. The NCF was organized in 1900 by Ralph Easley. For its history, see Marguerite Green, *The National Civic Federation and the American Labor Movement, 1900-1925* (Washington, D.C.: Catholic University of America Press, 1956).

9. Quoted in Roger W. Babson, *W. B. Wilson and the Department of Labor* (New York: Brentano's, 1919), p. 124; Marc Karson, *American Labor Unions and Politics, 1900-1918* (Carbondale: Southern Illinois University Press, 1958), pp. 29-41.

10. Babson, *W. B. Wilson*, pp. 127-28; Samuel Gompers to the Executive Council of the AFL, 21 Dec. 1912, *PWW*, 25:614-15.

11. Report of the secretary, 31 Dec. 1913, *Reports of the Department of Labor, 1913* (Washington, D.C.: GPO, 1914), pp. 7, 8, 68; Boemeke, "Wilson Administration," 104-5. For figures on union membership, see Leo Wolman, *The Growth of American Trade Unions, 1880-1923* (New York: National Bureau of Economic Research, 1924), pp. 73, 33.

12. *Reports of the Department of Labor, 1913,* p. 14.

13. John Lombardi, *Labor's Voice in the Cabinet: A History of the Department of Labor from Its Origin to 1921* (New York: Columbia University Press, 1942), p. 97.

14. Ibid., pp. 98–104; *Reports of the Department of Labor, 1915* (Washington, D.C.: GPO, 1916), p. 11; *Reports of the Department of Labor, 1917* (Washington, D.C.: GPO, 1918), pp. 11, 43; *Reports of the Department of Labor, 1919* (Washington, D.C.: GPO, 1920), pp. 27–29.

15. Lombardi, *Labor's Voice,* pp. 105–9.

16. *Reports of the Department of Labor, 1918* (Washington, D.C.: GPO, 1919), p. 232 (the order of phrases has been reversed).

17. Babson, *W. B. Wilson,* p. 191.

18. *Reports of the Department of Labor, 1918,* p. 232. See also, ibid., *1917,* p. 160.

19. See the president's address to the General Assembly of Virginia and the City Council of Richmond, 1 Feb. 1912, *PWW,* 24, *1912* (1977), p. 108.

20. Lombardi, *Labor's Voice,* pp. 109–14; Boemeke, "Wilson Administration," pp. 111–233.

21. Boemeke, "Wilson Administration," p. 150.

22. Ibid., pp. 151–77.

23. Ibid., pp. 187–219.

24. Ibid., pp. 219–33; H. M. Gitelman, *Legacy of the Ludlow Massacre: A Chapter in American Industrial Relations* (Philadelphia: University of Pennsylvania Press, 1988).

25. Karson, *American Labor Unions,* pp. 82–89; John S. Smith, "Organized Labor and the Government in the Wilson Era, 1913–1921: Some Conclusions," *Labor History* 3 (Fall 1962): 266–75.

26. Karson, *American Labor Unions,* pp. 75–78; Smith, "Organized Labor," pp. 272–74. For further discussion of the Clayton Act, see chap. 3 of this book.

27. Arthur S. Link, *Wilson: Confusions and Crises, 1915–1916* (Princeton, N.J.: Princeton University Press, 1964), pp. 321–27, 356–62; Link, *Wilson: Campaigns for Progressivism and Peace, 1916–1917* (Princeton, N.J.: Princeton University Press, 1965), pp. 39–42, 56–65, 83–92, 124–30; James Weinstein, *The Decline of Socialism in America, 1912–1925* (New York: Monthly Review Press, 1967), pp. 105–6.

28. Quoted in Granville Hicks, *John Reed: The Making of a Revolutionary* (New York: Benjamin Blom, 1968), p. 223.

29. Compare Melvyn Urofsky, *Big Steel and the Wilson Administration: A Study in Business-Government Relations* (Columbus: Ohio State University Press, 1969), p. xii, with Walter Dean Burnham, "The System of 1896: An Analysis," in Paul Kleppner et al., *The Evolution of American Electoral Systems* (Westport, Conn.: Greenwood, 1981), p. 148.

30. See Robert D. Cuff, "Woodrow Wilson's Missionary to American Business, 1914–1915: A Note," *Business History Review* 43 (Winter 1969): 545–51.

31. Alexander M. Bing, *War-Time Strikes and Their Adjustment* (1921; reprint, New York: Arno Press, 1971), p. 293.

32. *Reports of the Department of Labor, 1917*, p. 43; ibid., *1918*, p. 33.

33. Lombardi, *Labor's Voice*, pp. 187, 189.

34. Ibid., pp. 179–80, 191–92.

35. Ibid., pp. 194–98.

36. For the Army Appropriations Act of 29 Aug. 1916, which created the Council, see Records of the Department of Interior, Office of the Secretary of Interior; Central Classified File (hereafter cited as DICCF), 1907–36; sec. 1, Administrative; "1–53, Council of National Defense, Box 114, General, Aug. 29, 1916–May 19, 1917," RG 48, National Archives, Washington, D.C.; Keith W. Olson, *Biography of a Progressive: Franklin K. Lane, 1864–1921* (Westport, Conn.: Greenwood, 1979), p. 140.

37. Michael E. Parrish, *Felix Frankfurter and His Times: The Reform Years* (New York: Free Press, 1982), pp. 102–3.

38. For conflicting opinions of the failure or success of the PMC, see Parrish, *Felix Frankfurter*, pp. 87–95 (failure), and Lombardi, *Labor's Voice*, pp. 210–22 (success).

39. Franklin D. Roosevelt, "Report of the Inter-Departmental Committee Called by Council of National Defense to Consider Labor Problems," box 115, "Labor (Domestic & Foreign), Pt. 2, Nov. 3, 1917–May 8, 1919," DICCF.

40. Parrish, *Felix Frankfurter*, pp. 103–4. On the War Industries Board, see Robert D. Cuff, *The War Industries Board: Business-Government Relations during World War I* (Baltimore: Johns Hopkins University Press, 1973).

41. Lombardi, *Labor's Voice*, pp. 242–44; Bing, *War-Time Strikes*, pp. 297–300; Valerie Jean Conner, *The National War Labor Board: Stability, Social Justice, and the Voluntary State in World War I* (Chapel Hill: University of North Carolina Press, 1983), p. 23.

42. Lombardi, *Labor's Voice*, pp. 234, 244.

43. Ibid., pp. 246–49; Conner, *National War Labor Board*, pp. 27–30; Babson, *W. B. Wilson*, pp. 211–13; *Reports of the Department of Labor, 1918*, pp. 95–102, 107.

44. *Reports of the Department of Labor, 1918*, p. 101.

45. Ibid., pp. 115–18; Parrish, *Felix Frankfurter*, pp. 105–14; Lombardi, *Labor's Voice*, p. 259.

46. Lombardi, *Labor's Voice*, p. 252; Bing, *War-Time Strikes*, pp. 120–25.

47. *Reports of the Department of Labor, 1918*, pp. 107–8.

48. Conner, *National War Labor Board*, p. 158.

49. Bing, *War-Time Strikes*, pp. 121–22.

50. Weinstein, *Decline of Socialism*, p. 132.

51. Conner, *National War Labor Board*, pp. 183–86.

52. Robert D. Cuff, "Business, the State, and World War I: The American Experience," in *War and Society in North America*, ed. J. L. Granatstein and R. D. Cuff (Toronto: Thomas Nelson & Sons, 1971), p. 6.

53. Ibid., pp. 9–19; Cuff, *War Industries Board*, pp. 4–6. Bernard Baruch summarized the goals of the business reformers in a proposed plank for the 1920 Democratic platform. See Jordan A. Schwarz, *The Speculator: Bernard M.*

Baruch in Washington, 1917–1965 (Chapel Hill: University of North Carolina Press, 1981), p. 215.

54. David M. Kennedy, *Over Here: The First World War and American Society* (New York: Oxford University Press, 1980), pp. 127–28.

55. Cuff, *War Industries Board*, pp. 113–47.

56. House diary, 17 Jan. 1918, quoted in Seward W. Livermore, *Politics Is Adjourned: Woodrow Wilson and the War Congress, 1916–1918* (Middletown, Conn.: Wesleyan University Press, 1966), p. 88.

57. Kennedy, *Over Here*, pp. 125–26.

58. Schwarz, *Speculator*, pp. 46–47, 53–63.

59. Bernard M. Baruch, *American Industry in the World War: A Report of the War Industries Board* (New York: Prentice-Hall, 1941), p. 106.

60. Ibid., pp. 132–33. For further discussion of the administration's antitrust policy during the war, see chap. 3 in this book.

61. Cuff, *War Industries Board*, pp. 148–242.

62. *The Cabinet Diaries of Josephus Daniels, 1913–1921*, ed. E. David Cronon (Lincoln: University of Nebraska Press, 1963), p. 158 (28 May 1917); Urofsky, *Big Steel*, pp. 192–234.

63. Urofsky, *Big Steel*, pp. 208–11.

64. Bernard M. Baruch, *Baruch: The Public Years* (New York: Holt, Rinehart & Winston, 1960), p. 67.

65. Quoted in Schwarz, *Speculator*, p. 72.

66. Ibid.; Urofsky, *Big Steel*, pp. 216–19.

67. Urofsky, *Big Steel*, pp. 234–47; Alan L. Seltzer, "Woodrow Wilson as 'Corporate Liberal': Toward a Reconsideration of Left Revisionist Historiography," *Western Political Quarterly* 30 (June 1977): 205–6.

CHAPTER 6

DEVELOPING A FOREIGN POLICY

1. David Healy, *Drive to Hegemony: The United States in the Caribbean, 1898–1917* (Madison: University of Wisconsin Press, 1988), pp. 164–68.

2. Quoted in Ray Stannard Baker, *Woodrow Wilson: Life and Letters*, 8 vols. (Garden City, N.Y.: Doubleday, Page & Co., 1927–39), 4:55.

3. Quoted in Arthur S. Link, *Wilson: The Road to the White House* (Princeton, N.J.: Princeton University Press, 1947), p. 27.

4. An address to the National League of Commission Merchants in New York, 11 Jan. 1912, *The Papers of Woodrow Wilson*, ed. Arthur S. Link et al., 62 vols. to date (Princeton, N.J.: Princeton University Press, 1966–), 24, *1912* (1977), p. 36 (hereafter cited as *PWW*).

5. A news report and an address in New York protesting Russian discrimination against American Jews, 7 Dec. 1911, ibid., 23, *1911–1912* (1977), p. 586.

6. An address at Mary Baldwin Seminary, Staunton, Virginia, 28 Dec. 1912; a message to Democratic rallies, 2 Nov. 1912, ibid., 25, *1912* (1978), pp. 629, 502.

7. Kendrick A. Clements, *William Jennings Bryan: Missionary Isolationist* (Knoxville: University of Tennessee Press, 1982); Robert M. Crunden, *Ministers of Reform: The Progressives' Achievement in American Civilization, 1889–1920* (New York: Basic Books, 1982), pp. 226–29; Healy, *Drive to Hegemony*, pp. 168–70.

8. William H. Becker, *The Dynamics of Business-Government Relations: Industry and Exports, 1893–1921* (Chicago: University of Chicago Press, 1982), pp. 123ff.; Burton I. Kaufman, *Efficiency and Expansion: Foreign Trade Organization in the Wilson Administration, 1913–1921* (Westport, Conn.: Greenwood, 1974); Robert Mayer, "The Origins of the American Banking Empire in Latin America: Frank A. Vanderlip and the National City Bank," *Journal of Inter-American Studies and World Affairs* 15 (Feb. 1973): 6–76.

9. "Dinner of the Pan American Society," *Bulletin of the Pan American Union* 36 (June 1913): 816; Wilson, an address on Latin American policy in Mobile, Ala., 27 Oct. 1913, *PWW*, 28, *1913* (1978), p. 450.

10. *PWW*, 28:451.

11. A statement on relations with Latin America, 12 Mar. 1913, ibid., 27, *1913* (1978), p. 172. The order of phrases has been changed.

12. Healy, *Drive to Hegemony*, pp. 175–79.

13. Bryan to Wilson, 5 Nov. 1913; Wilson to Bryan, 7 Nov. 1913, ibid., 28:491, 505; House diary, 16 Dec. 1914, ibid., 31, *September 6–December 31, 1914* (1979), pp. 469–70; Mark T. Gilderhus, "Pan-American Initiatives: The Wilson Presidency and 'Regional Integration,' 1914–1917," *Diplomatic History* 4 (Fall 1980): 409–23; Gilderhus, *Pan American Visions: Woodrow Wilson in the Western Hemisphere, 1913–1921* (Tucson: University of Arizona Press, 1986).

14. Quoted in Frederick B. Pike, *Chile and the United States, 1880–1962: The Emergence of Chile's Social Crisis and the Challenge to United States Diplomacy* (Notre Dame, Ind.: University of Notre Dame Press, 1963), pp. 144–45.

15. Gilderhus, *Pan American Visions*, pp. 75–77.

16. Healy, *Drive to Hegemony*, pp. 181–82.

17. Remarks to the Princeton Alumni Association of the District of Columbia, 29 May 1914, *PWW*, 30, *May 6–September 5, 1914* (1979), pp. 107–8.

18. Quoted in Charles Willis Thompson to Reuben Adiel Bull, 22 May 1913, ibid., 27:465.

19. *The Cabinet Diaries of Josephus Daniels, 1913–1921*, ed. E. David Cronon (Lincoln: University of Nebraska Press, 1963), pp. 6–7 (reporting cabinet meeting of 11 Mar. 1913); Wilson's press statement on relations with Latin America, 12 Mar. 1913, *PWW*, 27:172 (my emphasis).

20. A report by William Bayard Hale, 18 June 1913, *PWW*, 27:552; Larry D. Hill, *Emissaries to a Revolution: Woodrow Wilson's Executive Agents in Mexico* (Baton Rouge: Louisiana State University Press, 1973), is good on the Hale mission and the activities of other agents sent by Wilson.

21. Arthur S. Link, *Wilson: The New Freedom* (Princeton, N.J.: Princeton University Press, 1956), p. 356.

22. Bryan to Wilson, 22 Oct. 1913; John Lind to Bryan, 23 Oct. 1913; Wilson to Bryan, 24 Oct. 1913, *PWW*, 28:422–23, 428–29, 433. For Anglo-Ameri-

can relations on this issue, see Peter Calvert, *The Mexican Revolution, 1910–1914: The Diplomacy of Anglo-American Conflict* (Cambridge: Cambridge University Press, 1970).

23. Hale to Wilson, 28 Sept. 1913, enclosed in Bryan to Wilson, 29 Sept. 1913; Hale to Wilson, 22 Oct. 1913, *PWW*, 28:341, 423.

24. Hale to Bryan, 5 Nov. 1913, 17 Nov. 1913, 9 P.M., ibid., pp. 545, 561.

25. Sir Cecil Arthur Spring-Rice to Sir Edward Grey, 7 Feb. 1914, ibid., 29, *December 2, 1913–May 5, 1914* (1979), pp. 229–30. The order of phrases has been altered.

26. Ibid., p. 229.

27. The standard account of these events is Robert Quirk, *An Affair of Honor: Woodrow Wilson and the Occupation of Vera Cruz* (Lexington: University of Kentucky Press, 1962). See also Link, *Wilson: The New Freedom*, pp. 395–400.

28. Memorandum for the adjutant general by Maj. Gen. W. W. Wotherspoon, chief of staff, 26 Apr. 1914, enclosed in Secretary of War Lindley M. Garrison to Wilson, 26 Apr. 1914, *PWW*, 29:510.

29. Bryan to Domicio Da Gama and others, 25 Apr. 1914, ibid., pp. 506–7; Link, *Wilson: The New Freedom*, pp. 400–401.

30. An unsigned "confidential memorandum" to the diplomatic representatives of Argentina, Brazil, and Chile, 25 Apr. 1914, *PWW*, 29:507.

31. Wilson to William Charles Adamson, 20 July 1914, ibid., 30:289.

32. Sir Cecil Arthur Spring-Rice to Sir Edward Grey, 7 Feb. 1914, ibid., 29:229.

33. Mark T. Gilderhus, *Diplomacy and Revolution: U.S.-Mexican Relations under Wilson and Carranza* (Tucson: University of Arizona Press, 1977), pp. 20–30.

34. Ibid., pp. 32–35.

35. Arthur S. Link, *Wilson: Confusions and Crises, 1915–1916* (Princeton, N.J.: Princeton University Press, 1964), p. 208.

36. A press release, 10 Mar. 1916, *PWW*, 36, *January 27–May 8, 1916* (1981), p. 287.

37. V. Carranza to E. Arredondo, 11 Mar. 1916, ibid., pp. 313–14 n. 1; Link, *Wilson: Confusions and Crises*, pp. 209–15.

38. Wilson to House, 22 June 1916, *PWW*, 37, *May 9–August 7, 1916* (1981), p. 281.

39. Link, *Wilson: Confusions and Crises*, p. 301.

40. Speaker of the House Champ Clark to Wilson, 13 Mar. 1916, ibid., 36:306–7.

41. A statement for the press, enclosed in Wilson to Lansing, 13 Mar. 1916, ibid., p. 298. For a more critical evaluation of Wilson's motives, see Michael L. Tate, "Pershing's Punitive Expedition: Pursuer of Bandits or Presidential Panacea?" *Americas* 32 (July 1975): 46–71.

42. Remarks to the Princeton Alumni Association of the District of Columbia, 29 May 1914, *PWW*, 30:108.

43. See Barbara Tuchman, *The Zimmermann Telegram* (New York: Viking Press, 1958).

44. Wilson to Gordon Auchincloss, Mexican desk officer, 9 Aug. 1918, quoted in Gilderhus, *Diplomacy and Revolution*, p. 85. For de jure recognition, see ibid., pp. 53–71.

45. U.S. Department of State, *Papers Relating to the Foreign Relations of the United States, 1918* (Washington: GPO, 1930), pp. 706, 577 (hereafter cited as *Foreign Relations*, with date).

46. Gilderhus, *Diplomacy and Intervention*, pp. 96–98; Clifford W. Trow, "Woodrow Wilson and the Mexican Interventionist Movement of 1919," *Journal of American History* 58 (June 1971): 46–72.

47. Gilderhus, *Diplomacy and Revolution*, p. 105.

48. Bryan to Wilson, 27 Mar. 1915; Wilson to Bryan, 31 Mar. 1915, *PWW*, 32, *January 1–April 16, 1915* (1980), pp. 440, 458.

49. Thomas L. Haskell, "Capitalism and the Origins of the Humanitarian Sensibility, pt. 2," *American Historical Review* 90 (June 1985): 556. Haskell's analysis of the antislavery movement in Britain is also relevant to Wilson's interventionism in the Caribbean.

50. Wilson to Bryan, 31 Mar. 1915, *PWW*, 32:458.

51. Wilson to Robert Lansing, 4 Aug. 1915, ibid., 34, *July 21–September 30, 1915* (1980), p. 78.

52. Hans Schmidt, *The United States Occupation of Haiti, 1915–1934* (New Brunswick, N.J.: Rutgers University Press, 1971); Healy, *Drive to Hegemony*, pp. 187–92.

53. Healy, *Drive to Hegemony*, pp. 192–99.

54. Wilson to Bryan, 10 June 1914, enclosing Walker Whiting Vick to Bryan, 30 May 1914, *PWW*, 30:164–65.

55. "To Various Dominican Leaders," 27 July 1914, ibid., p. 309; four memorandums by Jordan Stabler, assistant chief of the Latin American Division of the State Department, 9 and 17 July (two), 20 July 1914, nos. 839.00/1424, 1425, 1451, 1458, in the State Department Decimal Files, National Archives, Washington, D.C.; Arthur S. Link, *Wilson: The Struggle for Neutrality, 1914–1915* (Princeton, N.J.: Princeton University Press, 1960), p. 512.

56. New York *World*, 7–11, 13 Dec. 1914; Bryan to Senator-elect James D. Phelan (who conducted the investigation), 23 Dec. 1914, in James D. Phelan Papers, Bancroft Library, University of California at Berkeley. Phelan's report was published as *Santo Domingo Investigation; Copy of the Report, Findings, and Opinion of James D. Phelan, Commissioner Named by the Secretary of State, with the Approval of the President, to Investigate Charges against the United States Minister to the Dominican Republic* (Washington, D.C.: GPO, 1915).

57. Bryan to Minister James Mark Sullivan [still in office, although under investigation], 12 Jan. 1915, *Foreign Relations, 1915* (Washington, D.C.: GPO, 1924), p. 279.

58. Wilson to Lansing, 26 Nov. 1916, enclosing Lansing to Wilson, 22 Nov. 1916, *PWW*, 40, *November 20, 1916–January 23, 1917* (1982), pp. 81–82. The military government lasted eight years. See Bruce J. Calder, *The Impact of Interven-*

tion: The Dominican Republic during the U.S. Occupation of 1916–1924 (Austin: University of Texas Press, 1984).

59. Lester D. Langley to the editor of *Journal of American History* 72 (Dec. 1985): 766.

60. Francis Burton Harrison, *The Corner-Stone of Philippine Independence: A Narrative of Seven Years* (New York: Century Co., 1922), p. 50.

61. Eugene P. Trani, "Woodrow Wilson, China, and the Missionaries, 1913–1921," *Journal of Presbyterian History* 49 (Winter 1971): 328–51.

62. Bryan to Wilson, 5 Jan. 1913, *PWW*, 27:14; Paul S. Reinsch, *An American Diplomat in China* (Garden City, New York: Doubleday, Page & Co., 1922), p. 63.

63. A statement on the pending Chinese loan, 18 Mar. 1913, *PWW*, 27:192–94.

64. David F. Houston, *Eight Years with Wilson's Cabinet, 1913 to 1920, with a Personal Estimate of the President*, 2 vols. (Garden City, N.Y.: Doubleday, Page & Co., 1926), 1:49.

65. Thomas A. Bailey, "California, Japan, and the Alien Land Legislation of 1913," *Pacific Historical Review* 1 (Mar. 1932): 36–59; Roy Watson Curry, *Woodrow Wilson and Far Eastern Policy, 1913–1921* (New York: Bookman, 1957), pp. 43–65.

66. Paolo E. Coletta, " 'The Most Thankless Task': Bryan and the California Alien Land Legislation," *Pacific Historical Review* 36 (May 1967): 163–87.

67. Clements, *William Jennings Bryan*, pp. 72–74.

68. Quoted in Reinsch, *American Diplomat*, p. 135.

69. Bryan to Reinsch, 4 Nov. 1914, *Foreign Relations, 1914, Supplement* (Washington, D.C.: GPO, 1928), p. 190.

70. Bryan to Viscount Sutemi Chinda, 13 Mar. 1915, ibid., *1915* (Washington, D.C.: GPO, 1924), p. 108.

71. Wilson to Bryan, 24 Mar. 1915, *PWW*, 32:426.

72. Wilson to Bryan, 14 Apr. 1915, ibid., pp. 520–21.

73. Bryan to Chinda, 5 May 1915, ibid., 33, *April 17–July 21, 1915* (1980): pp. 102–4; Bryan to Paul Reinsch, 6 May 1915, 7:00 P.M., *Foreign Relations, 1915*, p. 143.

74. Wilson to Bryan, 10 May 1915, *PWW*, 33:140; *Foreign Relations, 1915*, p. 146.

75. See Wilson to Lansing, 21 June 1918, *PWW*, 48, *May 13–July 17, 1918* (1985), p. 382.

76. Robert Lansing, Memorandum for Viscount Ishii, 6 July 1917, ibid., 43, *June 25–August 20, 1917* (1983), p. 82.

77. Burton F. Beers, *Vain Endeavor: Robert Lansing's Attempts to End the American-Japanese Rivalry* (Durham, N.C.: Duke University Press, 1962), pp. 111–12.

78. *Foreign Relations, 1917* (Washington: GPO, 1926), p. 265.

79. Wilson to Lansing, 7 Nov. 1917, *PWW*, 44, *August 21–November 10, 1917* (1983), p. 530.

80. Translation from the Mantoux minutes of the Council of Four at the

Paris Peace Conference, 27 Mar. 1919, 3:30 P.M., ibid., 56, *March 17–April 4, 1919* (1987), p. 328; Fourteen Points address, 8 Jan. 1918, ibid., 45, *November 11, 1917–January 15, 1918* (1984), p. 537.

81. For a different view, see Frederick S. Calhoun, *Power and Principle: Armed Intervention in Wilsonian Foreign Policy* (Kent, Ohio: Kent State University Press, 1986).

82. Lord Reading to Sir William Wiseman, 12 July 1918, quoted in Betty Miller Unterberger, "Woodrow Wilson and the Russian Revolution," in *Woodrow Wilson and a Revolutionary World*, ed. Arthur S. Link (Chapel Hill: University of North Carolina Press, 1982), p. 72.

83. For the intervention, see George F. Kennan, *Soviet-American Relations, 1917–1920*, 2 vols. (Princeton, N.J.: Princeton University Press, 1956, 1958); John M. Thompson, *Russia, Bolshevism, and the Versailles Peace* (Princeton, N.J.: Princeton University Press, 1967); Betty M. Unterberger, *America's Siberian Expedition, 1918–1920: A Study of National Policy* (Durham, N.C.: Duke University Press, 1956); Unterberger, *The United States, Revolutionary Russia, and the Rise of Czechoslovakia* (Chapel Hill: University of North Carolina Press, 1989); William Appleman Williams, "The American Intervention in Russia, 1917–1920," *Studies on the Left* 3 (Fall 1963): 24–48; Carl J. Richard, " 'The Shadow of a Plan': The Rationale behind Wilson's 1918 Siberian Intervention," *Historian* 49 (Nov. 1986): 64–84.

CHAPTER 7
NEUTRALITY AND WAR, 1914–1917

1. J. M. Winter, *The Experience of World War I* (New York: Oxford University Press, 1989), pp. 121–22.

2. Wilson to Mary Hulbert, 23 Aug. 1914, Mary Eloise Hoyt to Wilson, 11 Aug. 1914, *The Papers of Woodrow Wilson*, ed. Arthur S. Link et al., 62 vols. to date (Princeton, N.J.: Princeton University Press, 1966–) 30, *May 6–September 5, 1914*, p. 437 (hereafter cited as *PWW*).

3. Arthur S. Link, *Wilson: The Struggle for Neutrality, 1914–1915* (Princeton, N.J.: Princeton University Press, 1960), p. 5–6.

4. An address, 18 Aug. 1914, *PWW*, 30:393–94.

5. A Jackson Day address at Indianapolis, 8 Jan. 1915, ibid., 32, *January 1–April 16, 1915* (1980), p. 41.

6. At a meeting on the evening of 6 Jan. 1915, ibid., p. 53 n.1.

7. Bryan to Wilson, 10 Aug. 1914, ibid., 30:372–73; Bryan to J. P. Morgan & Co., 15 Aug. 1914, *Papers Relating to the Foreign Relations of the United States, 1914, Supplement* (Washington, D.C.: GPO, 1928) (hereafter cited as *Foreign Relations*, with date).

8. Robert Lansing's memorandum of conversation with the president, 23 Oct. 1914, *PWW*, 31, *September 6–December 31, 1914* (1979), pp. 219–20.

9. Lansing to Wilson, 6 Sept. 1915, ibid., 34, *July 21–September 30, 1915* (1980), p. 421. For the failure of the 1915 loan, see Link, *Wilson: The Struggle for Neutrality*, pp. 627–28.

10. Bryan to Ambassador Walter Hines Page [in London] and other ambassadors, 6 Aug. 1914, *Foreign Relations, 1914, Sup.*, p. 216.

11. Department of State, *Papers Relating to the Foreign Relations of the United States, 1909* (Washington, D.C.: GPO, 1914), pp. 320-33.

12. John W. Coogan, *The End of Neutrality: The United States, Britain, and Maritime Rights, 1899-1915* (Ithaca, N.Y.: Cornell University Press, 1981), pp. 104-47.

13. Arthur S. Link, *Woodrow Wilson and the Progressive Era, 1910-1917* (New York: Harper, 1954), p. 154.

14. For detailed discussions of these problems, see Link, *Wilson: Struggle for Neutrality*, pp. 74-104.

15. Lansing to Wilson, 27 Sept. 1914, *PWW*, 31:86.

16. House diary, 27 Sept. 1914, ibid., p. 87.

17. House diary, 28 Sept. 1914, ibid., pp. 91-93; Spring-Rice to Sir Edward Grey, no. 66, 28 Sept. 1914, ibid., pp. 97-98.

18. Coogan, *End of Neutrality*, pp. 178-81.

19. Quoted in Link, *Wilson: Struggle for Neutrality*, pp. 113, 114.

20. Spring-Rice to Grey, 29 Sept. 1914, *PWW*, 31:100.

21. House diary, 30 Sept. 1914, ibid., pp. 108-9; Spring-Rice to Grey, 1 Oct. 1914, ibid., pp. 117-18.

22. Grey of Fallodon, *Twenty Five Years, 1892-1916*, 2 vols. (New York: Frederick A. Stokes Co., 1925), 2:107.

23. Lansing to Wilson, 21 Oct. 1914; Wilson to Lansing, 21 Oct. 1914, enclosing draft of Lansing to Page (sent 22 Oct.), *PWW*, 31:197-98.

24. Lansing to Wilson, 20 Oct. 1914, ibid., pp. 188-89.

25. Grey, *Twenty Five Years*, 2:107.

26. See *Foreign Relations, 1914, Sup.*, p. ix.

27. Wilson to House, 23 Oct. 1914; Page to Bryan, 15 Oct. 1914, 20 Oct. 1914, 11 P.M., *PWW*, 31:214, 160, 195.

28. Coogan, *End of Neutrality*, pp. 194-208.

29. Ibid., pp. 210-11.

30. Wilson to House, 9 July 1914, *PWW*, 30:264.

31. Wilson to House, 29 Jan. 1915, ibid., 32:158. For the autumn's peace efforts and House's decision to go to Europe, see Patrick Devlin, *Too Proud to Fight: Woodrow Wilson's Neutrality* (London: Oxford University Press, 1974), pp. 228-51.

32. Edith Bolling Galt to Wilson, 26 Aug. 1915, *PWW*, 34:338.

33. Devlin, *Too Proud to Fight*, p. 255-63.

34. Draft of a note to Germany, 6 Feb. 1915, *PWW*, 32:194-95.

35. Bryan to Wilson, 2 Apr. 1915, enclosing Lansing to Bryan, 2 Apr. 1915, ibid., pp. 464-66.

36. Wilson to Bryan, 3 Apr. 1915, ibid., pp. 468-69.

37. Lansing to Bryan, 3 May 1915; Bryan to Wilson, 5 May 1915, ibid., 33, *April 17-July 21, 1915* (1980), pp. 54, 106-7.

38. Wilson to Edith Galt, 9 May 1915, P.M.; an address in Philadelphia to newly naturalized citizens, 10 May 1915, ibid., pp. 137, 149.

39. Draft of the first *Lusitania* note, ca. 11 May 1915, ibid., pp. 156–57, 158.

40. Link, *Wilson: Struggle for Neutrality*, pp. 383–84.

41. William G. McAdoo, *Crowded Years* (Boston: Houghton Mifflin, 1931), p. 336.

42. See Devlin, *Too Proud to Fight*, pp. 305–7, 468–71.

43. Ibid., pp. 307–8, 319–25.

44. Ibid., pp. 325–34.

45. John Whiteclay Chambers II, *To Raise an Army: The Draft Comes to Modern America* (New York: Free Press, 1987), p. 75.

46. Quoted in Devlin, *Too Proud to Fight*, p. 361. See also Chambers, *To Raise an Army*, pp. 104, 107–17; Link, *Wilson: Struggle for Neutrality*, pp. 590–93.

47. Link, *Wilson: Struggle for Neutrality*, pp. 130–31.

48. Ibid., pp. 594–616.

49. Devlin, *Too Proud to Fight*, p. 247; George W. Egerton, *Great Britain and the Creation of the League of Nations: Strategy, Politics and International Organization, 1914–1919* (Chapel Hill: University of North Carolina Press, 1978), pp. 25–26.

50. Egerton, *Great Britain and the Creation of the League*, pp. 27–28.

51. House diary, 8 Oct. 1915, *PWW*, 35, *October 1, 1915–January 27, 1916* (1980), pp. 43–44.

52. Wilson to House, 18 Oct. 1915, enclosing revised draft of House to Grey, 17 Oct. 1915, ibid., pp. 80–82; Egerton, *Great Britain and the Creation of the League*, p. 28.

53. A copy of the House-Grey Memorandum, as initialed on 22 Feb. 1916, is in *PWW*, 36, *January 27–May 8, 1916* (1981), p. 180 n.2. For the insertion of the additional "probably," see House diary, 6 Mar. 1916, ibid., p. 262.

54. Devlin, *Too Proud to Fight*, pp. 384, 431–38.

55. Ibid., pp. 384–86.

56. Ibid., pp. 438–42, 445–47.

57. Quoted in ibid., p. 446.

58. Bernstorff to House, 14 Apr. 1916, enclosed in House to Wilson, 15 Apr. 1916; draft of note to Germany, enclosed in Wilson to Lansing, 17 Apr. 1916 (sent 18 Apr. 1916), *PWW*, 36:486–87, 490–96.

59. Arthur S. Link, *Wilson: Confusions and Crises, 1915–1916* (Princeton, N.J.: Princeton University Press, 1964), pp. 256–70.

60. Wilson's draft of a note to Germany, 7 May 1916, *PWW*, 36:650.

61. Lansing to Wilson, 23 June 1916, ibid., 37, *May 9–August 7, 1916* (1981), pp. 287–88; notes on Wilson's "Basis of Peace," 7 Feb. 1917, enclosed in Lansing to Wilson, 8 Feb. 1917, ibid., 41, *January 24–April 6, 1917* (1983), p. 163. For various interpretations of the conference, see Edward B. Parsons, *Wilsonian Diplomacy: Allied-American Rivalries in War and Peace* (St. Louis: Forum Press, 1978), pp. 3–7; Carl P. Parrini, *Heir to Empire: United States Economic Diplomacy, 1916–1923* (Pittsburgh, Pa.: University of Pittsburgh Press, 1969), pp. 15–22; Burton I. Kaufman, *Efficiency and Expansion: Foreign Trade Organization in the Wilson*

Administration, 1913–1921 (Westport, Conn.: Greenwood, 1974), pp. 165–76; David M. Kennedy, *Over Here: The First World War and American Society* (New York: Oxford University Press, 1980), pp. 308–11.

62. Wilson to House, 23 July 1916, *PWW*, 36:467.

63. Ibid., pp. 113–14, 116. See also Wilson's campaign addresses at Omaha on 5 Oct., at Indianapolis on 12 Oct., and at Shadow Lawn, N.J., on 14 Oct., ibid., 38, *August 7–November 19, 1916* (1982), pp. 348, 418, 437.

64. See Joseph Patrick Tumulty to Wilson, 16 May 1916, ibid., 37:58–60.

65. Wilson to House, 29 May 1916, ibid., p. 118.

66. Devlin, *Too Proud to Fight*, pp. 490–95.

67. Arthur S. Link, *Wilson: Campaigns for Progressivism and Peace, 1916–1917* (Princeton, N.J.: Princeton University Press, 1965), pp. 1–16.

68. Link, *Wilson: Campaigns for Progressivism*, pp. 4–6.

69. Ibid., p. 102.

70. Devlin, *Too Proud to Fight*, pp. 524–33; Link, *Wilson: Campaigns for Progressivism*, pp. 93–164; David Sarasohn, *The Party of Reform: Democrats in the Progressive Era* (Jackson: University of Mississippi Press, 1989), pp. 192–238.

71. Kathleen Burk, *Britain, America and the Sinews of War, 1914–1918* (Boston: George Allen & Unwin, 1985), pp. 5, 6.

72. Devlin, *Too Proud to Fight*, p. 518.

73. Draft of a peace note, ca. 25 Nov. 1916, *PWW*, 40, *November 20, 1916–January 23, 1917* (1982), pp. 70–74.

74. Henry Pomeroy Davison to Wilson, 25 Nov. 1916; from the diary of Charles Sumner Hamlin, 25 Nov. 1916; Wilson to William Procter Gould Harding, with enclosed draft of statement, 26 Nov. 1916; from the Hamlin diary, 27 Nov. 1916; Harding to Wilson, enclosing revised statement, 27 Nov. 1916; Wilson to Harding, Nov. 27, 1916; Wilson to House, 24 Nov. 1916, ibid., pp. 75–80, 87–88, 62–63.

75. Memorandum by Robert Lansing, 14 Dec. 1916; House diary, 14 Dec. 1916, ibid., pp. 234–36, 237–41.

76. Wilson to House, 19 Dec. 1916, ibid., p. 276.

77. House diary, 26 Nov. 1916; an appeal for a statement of war aims, 18 Dec. 1916; House to Wilson, 20 Dec. 1916; House diary, 20 Dec. 1916, ibid., pp. 84, 274, 293–94, 304–5.

78. Quoted in Link, *Wilson: Campaigns for Progressivism*, p. 222.

79. See *PWW*, 40:306–11, especially Wilson to Lansing, 21 Dec. 1916, p. 307 n.1.

80. See Lansing to Wilson, 24 Dec. 1916; House diary, 23 Dec. 1916, 4 Jan. 1917, ibid., pp. 326–27, 408–9; Devlin, *Too Proud to Fight*, pp. 598–99.

81. House diary, 3 Jan. 1917, *PWW*, 40:403–4.

82. House diary, 11 Jan. 1917; Wilson to Lansing, 12 Jan. 1917; address to the Senate, 22 Jan. 1917, ibid., pp. 445–47, 536–39; Devlin, *Too Proud to Fight*, pp. 595–97.

83. Page to Lansing for the president, 20 Jan. 1917, *PWW*, 40:532.

84. Franklin K. Lane to George Whitfield Lane, 3 Feb. 1917, ibid., 41:183–84.

85. Robert Lansing's memorandum on the severance of diplomatic relations with Germany, 4 Feb. 1917; House diary, 1 Feb. 1917, ibid., pp. 123, 87.

86. Winter, *Experience of World War I*, pp. 102–3.

87. House diary, 4 Mar. 1917; Wilson's second inaugural address, 5 Mar. 1917, *PWW*, 41:332, 332–35.

88. See Franklin K. Lane to George Whitfield Lane, 9 Feb. 1917, ibid., p. 184.

89. See the accounts of the cabinet meeting on 20 Mar., one by Lansing, the other by Josephus Daniels, in ibid., pp. 441, 445.

90. Lansing to Wilson, 19 Mar. 1917, ibid., pp. 425–27.

91. Accounts of the cabinet meeting of 20 Mar. 1917, by Lansing and Josephus Daniels, ibid., pp. 436–45.

92. Address to a Joint Session of Congress, 2 Apr. 1917, ibid., pp. 519–27.

93. Quoted in Devlin, *Too Proud to Fight*, p. 684.

94. War message, *PWW*, 41:523–24 (the order of phrases has been changed).

95. Ibid., p. 527.

CHAPTER 8
THE WAR, 1917–1918

1. Peter Fearon, *War, Prosperity and Depression: The U.S. Economy, 1917–45* (Lawrence: University Press of Kansas, 1987), pp. 3, 7, 11. The figure for wartime credits to the Allies is given as £7.3 billion rather than $7.3 billion—plainly a typographical error.

2. An address to a joint session of Congress, 2 Apr. 1917, *The Papers of Woodrow Wilson*, ed. Arthur S. Link et al., 62 vols. to date (Princeton, N.J.: Princeton University Press, 1966–), 41, *January 24–April 6, 1917*, p. 522 (hereafter cited as *PWW*).

3. Ibid., p. 522; John Whiteclay Chambers II, *To Raise an Army: The Draft Comes to Modern America* (New York: Free Press, 1987), p. 153.

4. Ibid., pp. 74–85, 153–54. Edward M. Coffman, *The War to End All Wars: The American Military Experience in World War I* (New York: Oxford University Press, 1968), p. 55.

5. Coffman, *War To End All Wars*, pp. 3, 8.

6. Quoted in David M. Kennedy, *Over Here: The First World War and American Society* (New York: Oxford University Press, 1980), p. 18.

7. Quoted in ibid., p. 144.

8. Ibid., pp. 147–49; Chambers, *To Raise an Army*, pp. 134–42.

9. Quoted in Chambers, *To Raise an Army*, p. 164.

10. A proclamation drafted by the Office of the Secretary of War for the president, as amended by Wilson, enclosed in Newton D. Baker to Wilson, 1

May 1917, *PWW*, 42, *April 7–June 23, 1917* (1983), p. 181. The proclamation was issued on 18 May.

11. Ibid.; Chambers, *To Raise an Army*, pp. 171–77, and Kennedy, *Over Here*, pp. 152–54.

12. Coffman, *War to End All Wars*, p. 29.

13. Ibid.; Kennedy, *Over Here*, pp. 155–66; Chambers, *To Raise an Army*, pp. 210–34.

14. Coffman, *War to End All Wars*, pp. 29–31.

15. Ibid., pp. 31–33.

16. Ibid., pp. 33–42, 129.

17. Address in St. Louis on preparedness, 3 Feb. 1916, *PWW*, 36, *January 27–May 8, 1916* (1981), pp. 120, 118. The order of the phrases has been reversed.

18. Coffman, *War to End All Wars*, pp. 90–92.

19. Quoted in ibid., p. 87.

20. Quoted in ibid., pp. 94–95. For Anglo-American naval cooperation, see David F. Trask, *Captains and Cabinets: Anglo-American Naval Relations, 1917–1918* (Columbia: University of Missouri Press, 1973).

21. Coffman, *War to End All Wars*, pp. 95–100.

22. See, for example, Wilson's acceptance speech, 7 Aug. 1912, and a speech to the Commercial Club in Omaha, 5 Oct. 1912, *PWW*, 25, *1912* (1978), pp. 15–16, 341–42.

23. Burton I. Kaufman, *Efficiency and Expansion: Foreign Trade Organization in the Wilson Administration, 1913–1921* (Westport, Conn.: Greenwood, 1974), pp. 165–76, 124–29; Kennedy, *Over Here*, pp. 301–4.

24. Jeffrey J. Safford, "Edward Hurley and American Shipping Policy: An Elaboration on Wilsonian Diplomacy, 1918–1919," *Historian* 35 (Aug. 1973): 568–86.

25. Kennedy, *Over Here*, p. 169.

26. Ibid., pp. 169–70.

27. Wilson to House, 21 July 1917, *PWW*, 43, *June 25–August 20, 1917* (1983), p. 238 (emphasis in original); Wilson to Newton Baker, 4 Feb. 1918, ibid., 46, *January 16–March 12, 1918* (1984), p. 237.

28. Kennedy, *Over Here*, pp. 171–75.

29. Chambers, *To Raise an Army*, p. 203.

30. Kennedy, *Over Here*, pp. 94–95; Christopher Lasch, *The New Radicalism in America, 1889–1963, The Intellectual as a Social Type* (New York: Knopf, 1965), p. 237. See also chaps. 4 and 5 in this book.

31. An undated memorandum by George Creel, enclosed in Josephus Daniels to Wilson, 11 Apr. 1917; Robert Lansing, Newton D. Baker, and Josephus Daniels to Wilson, 13 Apr. 1917, *PWW*, 42:39, 55. For the best description of the origin of the CPI, see Stephen Vaughn, *Holding Fast the Inner Lines: Democracy, Nationalism, and the Committee on Public Information* (Chapel Hill: University of North Carolina Press, 1980), pp. 3–22.

32. Quoted in ibid., p. 20.

33. Ibid., p. 234. See also William Graebner, *The Engineering of Consent: Democracy and Authority in Twentieth-Century America* (Madison: University of Wisconsin Press, 1987), pp. 42–45.

34. John Milton Cooper, Jr., *Pivotal Decades: The United States, 1900–1920* (New York: W. W. Norton, 1990), p. 298; Kennedy, *Over Here*, p. 77.

35. Sinclair to Wilson, 22 Oct. 1917, enclosed in Wilson to Joseph Patrick Tumulty, 30 Oct. 1917, *PWW*, 44, *August 21–November 10, 1917* (1983), pp. 469–70.

36. Quoted in Kennedy, *Over Here*, p. 76.

37. Ibid., pp. 77–78.

38. Wilson to Burleson, 11 Oct. 1917; Burleson to Wilson, 16 Oct. 1917, *PWW*, 44:358, 390.

39. Wilson to Joseph Patrick Tumulty, 18 Sept. 1918, ibid., 51, *September 14–November 8, 1918* (1985), pp. 55–56, 55 n.1.

40. Quoted in Kennedy, *Over Here*, p. 81.

41. For a full account, see Joan M. Jensen, *The Price of Vigilance* (Chicago: Rand McNally, 1968).

42. Wilson to Gregory, 4 June 1917, *PWW*, 42:446.

43. Jensen, *Price of Vigilance*, pp. 188–234, passim; Cooper, *Pivotal Decades*, pp. 299, 303–5; Kennedy, *Over Here*, pp. 82–83.

44. Kennedy, *Over Here*, pp. 83–86; Cooper, *Pivotal Decades*, pp. 300–2.

45. John F. McClymer, *War and Welfare: Social Engineering in America, 1890–1925* (Westport, Conn.: Greenwood, 1980), p. 168.

46. Ibid., pp. 168–69; Cooper, *Pivotal Decades*, p. 307.

47. Quoted in John A. Thompson, *Reformers and War: American Progressive Publicists and the First World War* (Cambridge: Cambridge University Press, 1987), p. 212.

48. Baker and Pinchot both quoted in Thompson, *Reformers and War*, p. 183.

49. Wilson's address to Congress, 2 Apr. 1917, *PWW*, 41:522; McAdoo quoted in Kennedy, *Over Here*, p. 107.

50. Charles Gilbert, *American Financing of World War I* (Westport, Conn.: Greenwood, 1970), pp. 91, 68, 227, 229.

51. Ibid., p. 224.

52. Ibid., p. 227; Wilson's address to Congress, 27 May 1918, *PWW*, 48, *May 13–July 17, 1918* (1985), p. 164; Seward W. Livermore, *Politics Is Adjourned: Woodrow Wilson and the War Congress, 1916–18* (Middletown, Conn.: Wesleyan University Press, 1966), pp. 134–37.

53. Gilbert, *American Financing*, pp. 224, 197, 214.

54. Ibid., p. 221.

55. For further discussion of the details of the voluntary system in the mobilization, see chaps. 4 and 7 in this book.

56. Fearon, *War, Prosperity and Depression*, pp. 7–15.

57. Glenda Riley, *Inventing the American Woman: A Perspective on Women's History* (Arlington Heights, Ill.: Harlan Davidson, 1986), pp. 183–88.

58. Quoted in Cooper, *Pivotal Decades*, p. 308.

59. Wilson quoted in memorandum of interview by the duke of Devonshire, governor general of Canada, enclosed in Wilson to Tumulty, 23 Jan. 1918, *PWW*, 46:81. For the influence of Ellen Axson Wilson and the president's daughters, see Frances Saunders, *Ellen Axson Wilson: First Lady between Two Worlds* (Chapel Hill: University of North Carolina Press, 1985).

60. Riley, *Inventing the American Woman*, pp. 191–96.

61. Wilson's "Statement to the American People," 26 July 1918, is in *PWW*, 49, *July 18–September 13, 1918* (1985), pp. 97–98. For warnings about black unrest, see George Creel to Wilson, 17 June 1918, and Newton D. Baker to Wilson, 1 July 1918, ibid., 48:341–42, 475–76. General accounts of the racial situation during the war are in Kennedy, *Over Here*, pp. 279–84; Chambers, *To Raise an Army*, pp. 222–26; and Joel Williamson, *The Crucible of Race: Black-White Relations in the American South since Emancipation* (New York: Oxford University Press, 1984), pp. 392–95.

62. See the excerpt from the diary of Raymond Blaine Fosdick, 8 Dec. 1918, *PWW*, 53, *November 9, 1918–January 11, 1919* (1986), pp. 340–41.

63. See an address to a joint session of Congress, 27 May 1918, *PWW*, 48:164.

64. Address, 25 Oct. 1918, *PWW*, 51:382.

CHAPTER 9
THE PEACEMAKER

1. *The Papers of Woodrow Wilson*, ed. Arthur S. Link et al., 62 vols. to date (Princeton, N.J.: Princeton University Press, 1966–   ), 40, *November 20, 1916–January 23, 1917*, pp. 535–38 (hereafter cited as *PWW*).

2. Memorandum by Sidney Edward Mezes, David Hunter Miller, and Walter Lippmann, drafted in early Dec. 1917 but only examined with care by Wilson and House on 4 Jan. 1918; Wilson's Fourteen Points address, ibid., 45, *November 11, 1917–January 15, 1918* (1984), pp. 459–74, 534–35. See also N. Gordon Levin, *Woodrow Wilson and World Politics: America's Response to War and Revolution* (New York: Oxford University Press, 1968), pp. 50–51.

3. *PWW*, 45:537–38.

4. From the diary of Dr. Cary T. Grayson, 8 Dec. 1918, ibid., 53, *November 9, 1918–January 11, 1919* (1986), pp. 336–37.

5. For a critique of Wilson's decision to go to Europe, see Robert H. Ferrell, *Woodrow Wilson and World War I, 1917–1921* (New York: Harper & Row, 1985), pp. 136–37.

6. The text of the German note of 6 Oct. is in *PWW*, 51, *September 14–November 8, 1915* (1985), p. 253. For the background of the German peace offer, see Klaus Schwabe, *Woodrow Wilson, Revolutionary Germany, and Peacemaking, 1918–1919: Missionary Diplomacy and the Realities of Power*, trans. Rita Kimber and Robert Kimber (Chapel Hill: University of North Carolina Press, 1985), pp. 30–39.

7. Schwabe, *Revolutionary Germany*, pp. 39–43.

8. For the evolution of the note of 8 Oct. see *PWW*, 51:263–65.

9. Inga Floto, *Colonel House in Paris: A Study of American Policy at the Paris Peace Conference 1919* (Princeton, N.J.: Princeton University Press, 1980), pp. 36–38; Schwabe, *Revolutionary Germany*, pp. 50–55.

10. House diary, 15 Oct. 1918, *PWW*, 51:342.

11. Ibid., pp. 418–19.

12. For speculations on the meaning of the note, see among others, Schwabe, *Revolutionary Germany*, pp. 58–72; Floto, *Colonel House*, pp. 38–42.

13. Memorandum by Wiseman, ca. 16 Oct. 1918, *PWW*, 51:347–52. For Wiseman's importance, see Wilton B. Fowler, *British-American Relations, 1917–1918: The Role of Sir William Wiseman* (Princeton, N.J.: Princeton University Press, 1969).

14. Floto, *Colonel House*, pp. 44–60.

15. House to Wilson, 5 Nov. 1918, *PWW*, 51:594.

16. Floto, *Colonel House*, p. 60; Keith L. Nelson, "What Colonel House Overlooked in the Armistice," *Mid-America* 51 (April 1969): 75–91.

17. Quoted in Arno J. Mayer, *Political Origins of the New Diplomacy, 1917–1918* (New Haven, Conn.: Yale University Press, 1959), p. 194.

18. Quoted in ibid., p. 226.

19. *PWW*, 42, *April 7–June 23, 1917* (1983), p. 503; Mayer, *Political Origins*, p. 229.

20. Quoted in Mayer, *Political Origins*, pp. 247–48.

21. Annual message on the state of the union, 4 Dec. 1917, *PWW*, 45:196.

22. Address to a joint session of Congress, 8 Jan. 1918, ibid., p. 537.

23. For discussion of allied intervention in Russia in 1918–1920, see chapter 6 in this book.

24. Victor S. Mamatey, *The United States and East Central Europe, 1915–1918: A Study in Wilsonian Diplomacy and Propaganda* (Princeton, N.J.: Princeton University Press, 1957), p. 346.

25. Quoted in ibid., p. 347.

26. Address to a joint session of Congress, 11 Nov. 1918, *PWW*, 53:42.

27. Quoted in Mamatey, *United States and East Central Europe*, p. 349.

28. Grayson diary, 25 Mar. 1919; Lloyd George's secret memorandum, 25 Mar. 1919, *PWW*, 56, *March 17–April 4, 1919* (1987), pp. 247, 262. Marshal Foch proposed a military solution to the problem. See his memorandum, 27 Mar. 1919, ibid., pp. 314–15.

29. Wilson to House, 2 Sept. 1917, *PWW*, 44, *August 21–November 10, 1917* (1983), pp. 120–21.

30. The standard history of the Inquiry is Lawrence E. Gelfand, *The Inquiry: American Preparations for Peace, 1917–1919* (New Haven, Conn.: Yale University Press, 1963).

31. Quoted in Floto, *Colonel House in Paris*, p. 61.

32. Ibid., pp. 65–68; Arthur Walworth, *Wilson and His Peacemakers: American Diplomacy at the Paris Peace Conference, 1919* (New York: W. W. Norton, 1986), pp. 7–11.

33. Ibid., pp. 47–48.

34. Thomas A. Bailey, *Woodrow Wilson and the Lost Peace* (New York: Macmillan, 1944), p. 25.

35. Walworth, *Wilson and His Peacemakers*, pp. 1–2.

36. Raymond Blaine Fosdick diary, 14 Dec. 1918, *PWW*, 53:385.

37. Floto, *Colonel House in Paris*, p. 69.

38. House diary, 14 Dec. 1918, *PWW*, 53:389.

39. George Juergens, *News from the White House: The Presidential-Press Relationship in the Progressive Era* (Chicago: University of Chicago Press, 1981), pp. 206–11, 234–36.

40. See Lord Derby to Arthur James Balfour, 22 Dec. 1918, *PWW*, 53:470–72. For a different interpretation, see Lloyd Ambrosius, *Woodrow Wilson and the American Diplomatic Tradition: The Treaty Fight in Perspective* (New York: Cambridge University Press, 1987), p. 52.

41. Hankey's notes of a meeting of the Council of Ten, 30 Jan. 1919, 11 A.M., *PWW*, 54, *January 11–February 7, 1919* (1986), pp. 350–54.

42. Wilson to House, 21 July 1917, *PWW*, 43, *June 25–August 20, 1917* (1983), p. 238 (the order of phrases has been reversed).

43. Protocol of Plenary Session, 25 Jan. 1919, *PWW*, 54:266 (the order of phrases has been reversed).

44. For details, see Warren F. Kuehl, *Seeking World Order: The United States and International Organization to 1920* (Nashville, Tenn.: Vanderbilt University Press, 1969).

45. Ibid., pp. 224–26.

46. Thomas J. Knock, "Woodrow Wilson and the Origins of the League of Nations" (Ph.D. diss., Princeton University, 1982), pp. 140–201.

47. George W. Egerton, *Great Britain and the Creation of the League of Nations: Strategy, Politics and International Organization, 1914–1919* (Chapel Hill: University of North Carolina Press, 1978), pp. 8–13.

48. William Graves Sharp to Robert Lansing, 10 Jan. 1917, *PWW*, 40:439.

49. Egerton, *Great Britain and the Creation of the League*, pp. 53–61 (the quotation is on p. 61).

50. Ibid., pp. 65–69.

51. House to Wilson, enclosing House to Lord Robert Cecil, 25 June 1918; Wilson to House, 8 July 1918, *PWW*, 48, *May 13–July 17, 1918* (1985), pp. 424–26, 549.

52. House to Wilson, enclosing his suggestion for "a Covenant for a League of Nations," 16 July 1918, *PWW*, 48:630–37.

53. House diary, 15 Aug. 1918; Wilson to House, enclosing draft of covenant, 7 Sept. 1918, *PWW*, 49, *July 18–September 13, 1918* (1985), pp. 265–68, 466–71.

54. Kuehl, *Seeking World Order*, pp. 260–64. But see also Ambrosius, *Woodrow Wilson*, pp. 44–45.

55. Frankfurter to Manley Hudson, 13 Jan. 1918, quoted in Michael E. Par-

rish, *Felix Frankfurter and His Times: The Reform Years* (New York: Free Press, 1982), p. 115.

56. A brief, convenient summary of the work of the Commission is Kuehl, *Seeking World Order*, pp. 270–71. See also Egerton, *Great Britain and the Creation of the League*, pp. 127–38.

57. The covenant as described here is the amended version incorporated in the final Treaty of Versailles, not that presented by Wilson to the conference in February. A full text is conveniently available in the Appendix of Walworth, *Wilson and His Peacemakers*, pp. 563–70.

58. Address to the third plenary session of the peace conference, 14 Feb. 1919, *PWW*, 55, *February 8–March 16, 1919* (1986), p. 175.

59. Report in the *New York Times*, 27 Feb. 1919, ibid., p. 275.

60. Address at the Metropolitan Opera House, New York City, 4 Mar. 1919, ibid., p. 419.

61. Floto, *Colonel House*, p. 103.

62. Ibid., pp. 118–19; Levin, *Woodrow Wilson and World Politics*, pp. 123–25.

63. Floto, *Colonel House*, pp. 119–22; Wilson to House, ca. 23 Feb. 1919; Wilson to Lansing, 23 Feb. 1919, noon, *PWW*, 55:229–30, 231.

64. Floto, *Colonel House*, pp. 124–26.

65. See Vance Criswell McCormick diary, 2 Mar. 1919; memorandum by Sidney Mezes [?], 11 Mar. 1919, *PWW*, 55:387, 475–77 and n.1.

66. Floto, *Colonel House*, pp. 145–46.

67. Ibid., pp. 152–53, 158.

68. For a more positive interpretation of House's role in this critical period, see Walworth, *Wilson and His Peacemakers*, pp. 145–62, 175–80.

69. Ray Stannard Baker diary, 15 Mar. 1919, *PWW*, 55:531.

70. Floto, *Colonel House*, 169; David Hunter Miller diary, 18 Mar. 1919; Taft to Wilson, 18, 21 Mar. 1919, *PWW*, 56:75–81, 83, 157–59.

71. Lord Robert Cecil diary, 18 Mar. 1919; House diary, 1 Apr. 1919, *PWW*, 56:81, 517.

72. Henry Wickham Steed to House, enclosing draft of proposal for temporary occupation of Saar Basin, 1 Apr. 1919, *PWW*, 56:515–17.

73. Memorandum by Jan Christian Smuts, 31 Mar. 1919; memorandum by John Foster Dulles, 1 Apr. 1919; Vance Criswell McCormick diary, 1 Apr. 1919, *PWW*, 56:480–82, 498–99, 501.

74. Bert E. Park, "The Impact of Wilson's Neurologic Disease during the Paris Peace Conference," in Appendix, *PWW*, 58, *April 23–May 9, 1919* (1988), pp. 619–20.

75. Edwin A. Weinstein, *Woodrow Wilson: A Medical and Psychological Biography* (Princeton, N.J.: Princeton University Press, 1981), pp. 340–42.

76. Ibid., pp. 339–40, 342–44.

77. Ray Stannard Baker diary, 8 Apr. 1919, *PWW*, 57, *April 5–22, 1919* (1987), p. 140.

78. Arthur Walworth, *America's Moment, 1918: American Diplomacy at the End of World War I* (New York: W. W. Norton, 1977), pp. 156–66.

79. Wilson's memorandum presented to Orlando, 14 Apr. 1919, *PWW*, 57:344.

80. Statement on the Adriatic question, 23 Apr. 1919, *ibid.*, 58:8.

81. Walworth, *Wilson and His Peacemakers*, pp. 345–51, 356–58, 549–52.

82. Minutes of a meeting of the League of Nations Commission, 11 Apr. 1919, 8:30 P.M., *PWW*, 57:261.

83. Ibid., pp. 261, 263–64. Compare, however, with the slightly different transcript printed on pp. 268–70.

84. On these events, see chap. 5 in this book.

85. Lansing to Wilson, 22 Apr. 1919, *PWW*, 57:597.

86. Minutes of a meeting of the Council of Four, 22 Apr. 1919, 11:30 A.M., ibid., pp. 605–6.

87. Ray Stannard Baker diary, 25 Apr. 1919, ibid., 58:143.

88. Memorandum by Balfour, 27 Apr. 1919, ibid., pp. 175–76.

89. Memorandum by Lansing, 28 Apr. 1919; Ray Stannard Baker diary, 29 Apr. 1919; Tasker H. Bliss to Wilson, 29 Apr. 1919; Cary T. Grayson diary, 30 Apr. 1919, House to Wilson, 29 Apr. 1919, ibid., pp. 185, 214, 232–34, 244–45, 228.

90. Wilson to Tumulty, 30 Apr. 1919, ibid., p. 273.

91. Minutes of a meeting of the Council of Four, 2 June 1919, 4 P.M., ibid., 60, *June 1–17, 1919* (1989): pp. 23–27.

92. Minutes of a discussion with the American delegation, 3 June 1919, ibid., p. 67.

93. Walworth, *Wilson and His Peacemakers*, pp. 416–27, and also, 403–5.

94. Notes of a meeting of the Council of Four, 13 June 1919, 11:00 A.M., *PWW*, 60:495–96.

95. Grayson diary, 23 June 1919, ibid., 61, *June 18–July 25, 1919* (1989), p. 79.

96. For firsthand accounts of the signing, see Grayson diary, 28 June 1919; Lansing's memorandum, 28 June 1919; William Linn Westermann's diary, 28 June 1919; and House diary, 28 June 1919, ibid., pp. 302–6, 321–28, 328–32, 332–33.

97. See, for example, his remarks at a press conference on 27 June 1919, in ibid., pp. 242, 245.

98. Wilson to George Davis Herron, 28 Apr. 1919, ibid., 58:204.

99. Bailey, *Woodrow Wilson and the Lost Peace*, p. 312.

100. Eric F. Goldman, *Rendezvous with Destiny: A History of Modern American Reform*, rev. ed., abridged (New York: Vintage, 1956), pp. 209–13.

CHAPTER 10
PEACE

1. Tumulty to Wilson, 30 Apr. 1919, *The Papers of Woodrow Wilson*, ed. Arthur S. Link et al., 62 vols. to date (Princeton, N.J.: Princeton University Press, 1966–), 58, *April 23–May 9, 1919*, p. 244 (hereafter cited as *PWW*); Tumulty to

Wilson, ca. 4 June, 16 June 1919, ibid., 60, *June 1-17, 1919* (1989) pp. 145, 610–11; Edward M. House diary, 29 June 1919, ibid., 61, *June 18-July 25, 1919* (1989) pp. 354–55; Wilson to Lansing, 24 May 1919, ibid., 59, *May 10-31, 1919* (1988) pp. 470–71.

2. Address to the Senate, 10 July 1919, ibid., 61:436, 434, 428–29, 426.

3. Two reports in the *New York Times*, 11 July 1919, ibid., pp. 424–26, 437–38.

4. Ashurst diary, 11 July 1919, ibid., pp. 445–46.

5. McAdoo to Wilson, 11 July 1919, ibid., p. 459.

6. Quoted in William C. Widenor, *Henry Cabot Lodge and the Search for an American Foreign Policy* (Berkeley: University of California Press, 1980), p. 176.

7. Ibid., p. 208.

8. Ibid., pp. 297, 316.

9. Ralph Stone, *The Irreconcilables: The Fight against the League of Nations* (Lexington: University of Kentucky Press, 1970).

10. Thomas A. Bailey, *Woodrow Wilson and the Great Betrayal* (New York: Macmillan, 1945), pp. 53–69. For an analysis of the "mild reservationists," see Herbert F. Margulies, *The Mild Reservationists and the League of Nations Controversy in the Senate* (Columbia: University of Missouri Press, 1989).

11. Report of Wilson's meetings with senators in the *Washington Post*, 18 July 1919; Sir William Wiseman to Arthur James Balfour, 18 July 1919; Wiseman to House, 19 July 1919, *PWW*, 61:515–17, 541–43, 561–62.

12. Charles Thaddeus Thompson's report of a press conference, 27 June 1919; news report from the *New York Times*, 11 July 1919, ibid., pp. 251–52, 437.

13. See, for example, Wilson's remarks in a press conference on 10 July 1919, ibid., p. 422–23.

14. Minutes of a meeting of the Council of Four, 25 June 1919, 4 P.M.; Stanley K. Hornbeck to the American Commissioners, 25 June 1919, ibid., pp. 155, 175–76.

15. Lloyd Ambrosius, *Woodrow Wilson and the American Diplomatic Tradition: The Treaty Fight in Perspective* (New York: Cambridge University Press, 1987), 172.

16. From the Covenant of the League as adopted on 28 Apr. 1919, *PWW*, 58:191.

17. From his speech presenting the treaty to the Senate, 10 July 1919, ibid., 61:433 (emphasis added).

18. See the article, "35 to Block League" in the *Washington Post*, 20 July 1919, ibid., pp. 563–65. On Wilson's health, see the news stories in ibid., pp. 562–63, 569–70, 578–79, 599.

19. See the draft of Wilson to Lodge, 14 Aug. 1919, and Tumulty to Wilson, 15 Aug. 1919, in ibid., 62, *July 26-September 3, 1919* (1990) (used in typescript by courtesy of the editors). For the Wilson-Hitchcock conference, see the article in the *New York Times*, 16 Aug. 1919, p. 1.

20. Exposition of the League to the Foreign Relations Committee, 19 Aug. 1919, *The Public Papers of Woodrow Wilson: War and Peace; Presidential Messages, Ad-*

dresses, and Public Papers, 1917–1924 (authorized ed.), ed. Ray Stannard Baker and William E. Dodd, 2 vols. (New York: Harper & Bros., 1927), 1:574–80.

21. Ibid., p. 579. The order of phrases has been reversed.

22. Margulies, *Mild Reservationists*, pp. 50–58.

23. Quoted in ibid., p. 75.

24. Widenor, *Henry Cabot Lodge*, p. 342.

25. Cary T. Grayson, *Woodrow Wilson: An Intimate Memoir* (New York: Holt, Rinehart & Winston, 1960), pp. 94–95.

26. Speech at Columbus, Ohio, 4 Sept. 1919, Baker and Dodd, *Public Papers*, 1:591–92, 594.

27. Speech at the Coliseum, St. Louis, 5 Sept. 1919, ibid., pp. 636, 638–39, 640.

28. At Convention Hall, Kansas City, Mo., 6 Sept. 1919, ibid., 2:10.

29. At auditorium, St. Paul, Minn., 9 Sept. 1919, ibid., p. 78.

30. At auditorium, Portland, Oreg., 15 Sept. 1919, ibid., p. 213; at Pueblo, Colo., 25 Sept. 1919, ibid., p. 400.

31. Hofstadter's phrase, "paranoid style," is used by Ambrosius, *Woodrow Wilson and Diplomatic Tradition*, p. 180. For Wilson's claim that the League would make the treaty work, see his speech at Bismarck, N.Dak., 10 Sept. 1919, in Baker and Dodd, *Public Papers*, 2:95.

32. At the auditorium, St. Paul, Minn., 9 Sept. 1919, ibid., p. 72.

33. Ibid., p. 84.

34. At Bismarck, N.Dak., 10 Sept. 1919, ibid., p. 93. The order of phrases has been altered.

35. At Billings, Mont., 11 Sept. 1919, ibid., p. 108.

36. At Bismarck, N.Dak., 10 Sept. 1919, ibid., p. 96.

37. At the Opera House, Helena, Mont., 11 Sept. 1919, ibid., pp. 130–31.

38. At the Armory, Tacoma, Wash., 13 Sept. 1919, ibid., p. 169.

39. At Hotel Portland, Portland, Oreg., 15 Sept. 1919, ibid., p. 197.

40. Grayson, *Woodrow Wilson: Memoir*, pp. 96–98; Weinstein, *Woodrow Wilson: A Medical and Psychological Biography* (Princeton, N.J.: Princeton University Press), p. 355.

41. Grayson diary, 26 Sept. 1919, *PWW*, 63, *September 4, 1919–November 5, 1919* (forthcoming) pp. 518–19 (used in page proofs by courtesy of the editors); statement by Dr. Grayson (undated, probably between 2 Oct. and 20 Oct. 1919) for Dr. Francis X. Dercum, ibid., 64, *November 6, 1919–February 7, 1920* (forthcoming), pp. 507–10 (used in page proofs by courtesy of the editors); Grayson, *Woodrow Wilson: Memoir*, pp. 99–100. There is some inconsistency among Grayson's various accounts of the 25 Sept. episode. His report to Dr. Dercum, however, recently discovered by the editors of *PWW*, is probably the most authoritative.

42. Edith Bolling Wilson, *My Memoir* (Indianapolis: Bobbs-Merrill, 1938), pp. 284–85.

43. Memorandum of an examination of Wilson by Dr. Francis X. Dercum on 2 Oct. 1919, enclosed in Dercum to Grayson, 20 Oct. 1919, *PWW*, 64:500–503.

These medical records, recently found in Dr. Grayson's papers by the editors, give us for the first time a precise account of Wilson's condition by the leading expert of the day.

44. David F. Houston, *Eight Years with Wilson's Cabinet, 1913 to 1920, with a Personal Estimate of the President*, 2 vols. (Garden City, N.Y.: Doubleday, Page & Co., 1926), 2:38; Grayson's statement, 15 Oct. 1919, *PWW*, 64:497–99.

45. Weinstein, *Woodrow Wilson: Medical Biography*, p. 360; Grayson, *Woodrow Wilson: Memoir*, p. 53.

46. Bert E. Park, "The Aftermath of Wilson's Stroke," *PWW*, 64:525–28 (the order of phrases has been altered).

47. Ibid., pp. 525–28. For Grayson's resignation proposal, see the references to the diaries of John W. Davis and Ray Stannard Baker in ibid., p. 363n.1.

48. Park, "Aftermath," p. 527.

49. E. B. Wilson, *My Memoir*, p. 289.

50. Weinstein, *Woodrow Wilson: Medical Biography*, pp. 365–66.

51. Widenor, *Henry Cabot Lodge*, pp. 342–43.

52. Speech at Tabernacle, Salt Lake City, Utah, 23 Sept. 1919, Baker and Dodd, *Public Papers*, 2:350, 349.

53. Ambrosius, *Woodrow Wilson and Diplomatic Tradition*, pp. 180–86.

54. The Lodge reservations, in both their November 1919 and March 1920 forms, may be found in Bailey, *Great Betrayal*, pp. 387–93.

55. Grayson, *Woodrow Wilson: Memoir*, pp. 102–3. Grayson records this conversation as taking place on 17 Nov. and may be correct.

56. Margulies, *Mild Reservationists*, pp. 173–75.

57. Quoted in Weinstein, *Woodrow Wilson: Medical Biography*, p. 362; E. B. Wilson, *My Memoir*, pp. 296–97.

58. Wiseman to Arthur James Balfour, 18 July 1919, *PWW*, 61:542.

59. The Wilson reservations are given, together with Hitchcock's, which were based on Wilson's, in Bailey, *Great Betrayal*, pp. 393–94.

60. Alexander L. George and Juliette L. George, *Woodrow Wilson and Colonel House: A Personality Study* (New York: John Day Co., 1956), pp. 118–19.

61. Ambrosius, *Woodrow Wilson and Diplomatic Tradition*, p. 290.

62. Bailey, *Great Betrayal*, pp. 172–73, 185, 275. For an argument that Wilson really sought compromise with opponents in the Senate, see Kurt Wimer, "Woodrow Wilson Tries Conciliation: An Effort that Failed," *Historian* 25 (Aug. 1963): 419–38.

63. Weinstein, *Woodrow Wilson: Medical Biography*, pp. 357–59; Bert Edward Park, *The Impact of Illness on World Leaders* (Philadelphia: University of Pennsylvania Press, 1986), pp. 44–60.

64. See Tumulty's original, error-filled draft of this message, 6 Jan. 1920, Secretary Houston's corrected draft of 7 Jan., and the message Wilson actually sent on 8 Jan. *PWW*, 65, *February 28, 1920–July 31, 1920* ([forthcoming] used in galley proofs by courtesy of the editors).

65. Bailey, *Great Betrayal*, pp. 214–15; Kurt Wimer, "Woodrow Wilson's Plan for a Vote of Confidence," *Pennsylvania History* 28 (July 1961): 279–93.

66. Two memorandums by Cary Travers Grayson, 25 Mar. 1920; Charles Lee Swem shorthand diary, 17 May 1920, *PWW*, 65.

67. Joseph Tumulty to Edith Wilson, 23 Mar. 1920; two memorandums by Cary Travers Grayson, 13 and 14 Apr. 1920; desk diary of Robert Lansing recording conversation with Attorney General A. Mitchell Palmer, 14 Apr. 1920, ibid.

68. Two memorandums by Carter Glass, 16 and 19 June 1920; memorandum by Homer S. Cummings, 18 Jan. 1929, ibid.

69. Weinstein, *Woodrow Wilson: Medical Biography*, pp. 366–68; Kurt Wimer, "Woodrow Wilson and a Third Nomination," *Pennsylvania History* 29 (April 1962): 193–211.

70. Quoted in Weinstein, *Woodrow Wilson: Medical Biography*, p. 369.

CHAPTER 11
AFTER THE WAR

1. For an example of the abrupt termination of wartime controls, see Richard L. Lael and Linda Killen, "The Pressure of Shortage: Platinum Policy and the Wilson Administration during World War I," *Business History Review* 56 (Winter 1982): 545–58.

2. Clarkson to Secretary of Interior Franklin K. Lane, 25 Mar. 1918; Wilson to Clarkson, 26 Mar. 1918, Records of the Department of Interior, Office of the Secretary of Interior, Central Classified File (DICCF) box 114, "1–53, Council of National Defense, Genl., pt. 4, Nov. 21, 1917–May 7, 1918."

3. Clarkson to Lane, 20 Aug. 1918, box 401, "1–201, Reconstruction, Genl., pt. 1, May 16, 1918–Dec. 30, 1918," ibid.

4. An annual message on the state of the union, 2 Dec. 1918, *The Papers of Woodrow Wilson*, ed. Arthur S. Link et al., 62 vols. to date (Princeton, N.J.: Princeton University Press, 1966–), 53, *November 9, 1918–January 11, 1919*, p. 278 (hereafter cited as *PWW*); Gompers to Wilson, 27 Nov. 1918, and Wilson to Gompers, 27 Nov. 1918, ibid., pp. 217–20; Clarkson to Lane, 9 Dec. 1918, enclosing Dec. 1918 "Bulletin of the National City Bank of New York," box 115, "1–53, Council of National Defense, Genl., pt. 6, Nov. 6, 1918–Aug. 7, 1919," DICCF.

5. Burl Noggle, *Into the Twenties: The United States from Armistice to Normalcy* (Urbana: University of Illinois Press, 1974), pp. 33–34.

6. For Secretary Wilson's proposals, see *Reports of the Department of Labor, 1915* (Washington, D.C.: GPO, 1916), pp. 44–45; ibid., *1916* (Washington, D.C.: GPO, 1917), pp. 70–73; ibid., *1917* (Washington, D.C.: GPO, 1918), p. 153; ibid., *1919* (Washington, D.C.: GPO, 1920), p. 303; Roger W. Babson, *W. B. Wilson and the Department of Labor* (New York: Brentano's, 1919), pp. 225–27.

7. Noggle, *Into the Twenties*, pp. 55–56; Robert D. Cuff, *The War Industries Board: Business-Government Relations during World War I* (Baltimore: Johns Hopkins University Press, 1973), pp. 242–43.

8. Noggle, *Into the Twenties*, pp. 31–33, 36–45.

9. Arthur S. Link, "World War I," in John A. Garraty, *Interpreting American*

History: Conversations with Historians, 2 vols. (New York: Macmillan, 1970), 2: 137.

10. Noggle, *Into the Twenties*, pp. 46-47.

11. Wilson to Anna Howard Shaw, 18 Nov. 1918, *PWW*, 53:118.

12. Quoted in Noggle, *Into the Twenties*, p. 62.

13. Neil A. Wynn, *From Progressivism to Prosperity: World War I and American Society* (New York: Holmes & Meier, 1986), pp. 202-3.

14. Quoted in John Lombardi, *Labor's Voice in the Cabinet: A History of the Department of Labor from Its Origin to 1921* (New York: Columbia University Press, 1942), p. 307.

15. Noggle, *Into the Twenties*, pp. 69-73.

16. Michael E. Parrish, *Felix Frankfurter and His Times: The Reform Years* (New York: Free Press, 1982), p. 118. Parrish is in error in stating that 1919 was the worst year for strikes in American history. For the figures see David M. Kennedy, *Over Here: The First World War and American Society* (New York: Oxford University Press, 1980), p. 262.

17. Lombardi, *Labor's Voice*, pp. 316-17; John S. Smith, "Organized Labor and the Government in the Wilson Era, 1913-1921: Some Conclusions," *Labor History* 3 (Fall 1962): 280-81; Stanley Coben, *A. Mitchell Palmer: Politician* (New York: Columbia University Press, 1963), pp. 176-77.

18. Coben, *A. Mitchell Palmer*, pp. 174-79; Edward Berman, *Labor Disputes and the President of the United States* (New York: Columbia University Press, 1924), pp. 166-81.

19. Berman, *Labor Disputes*, pp. 183-87.

20. Ibid., pp. 170-76; Smith, "Organized Labor," pp. 282-84.

21. Kennedy, *Over Here*, pp. 252-53.

22. Noggle, *Into the Twenties*, pp. 77-80 (quotation on p. 80).

23. Ibid., pp. 80-81.

24. Ibid., pp. 81-83; Kennedy, *Over Here*, pp. 256-58.

25. Kennedy, *Over Here*, pp. 287-89; Frederick Lewis Allen, *Only Yesterday: An Informal History of the Nineteen-Twenties* (New York: Harper & Row, 1931), pp. 49-50.

26. Joan M. Jensen, *The Price of Vigilance* (Chicago: Rand McNally, 1968), pp. 261-62; Kennedy, *Over Here*, pp. 311-13.

27. Kennedy, *Over Here*, pp. 290-92; Robert K. Murray, *Red Scare: A Study in National Hysteria, 1919-1920* (Minneapolis: University of Minnesota Press, 1955), pp. 82-104.

28. Lombardi, *Labor's Voice*, pp. 338-39.

29. Ibid., pp. 341-49. The report is quoted on p. 347. The order of the last two phrases is reversed here.

30. Larry G. Gerber, "Corporatism in Comparative Perspective: The Impact of the First World War on American and British Labor Relations," *Business History Review* 62 (Spring 1988): 99-115; Milton Derber, "The Idea of Industrial Democracy in America, 1898-1915," *Labor History* 7 (Fall 1966): 259-86, and

"The Idea of Industrial Democracy in America, 1915-1935," *Labor History* 8 (Winter 1967): 3-29.

31. A special message to Congress, 20 May 1919, *PWW*, 59, *May 10-31, 1919* (1988), p. 291.

32. A memorandum by Joseph Patrick Tumulty, ca. 4 June 1919, enclosed in Tumulty to Wilson, 4 June 1919, ibid., 60, *June 1-17, 1919* (1989), pp. 145-53.

33. (3 Sept. 1919) U.S. Dept. of Labor, *Proceedings of the First Industrial Conference, October 6 to 23, 1919* (Washington, D.C.: GPO, 1920), p. 5.

34. Ibid., pp. 5-7.

35. Haggai Hurvitz, "Ideology and Industrial Conflict: President Wilson's First Industrial Conference of October 1919," *Labor History* 18 (Fall 1977): 515-23. The chief spokesman for the industry representatives was John D. Rockefeller, Jr. See H. M. Gitelman, *Legacy of the Ludlow Massacre: A Chapter in American Industrial Relations* (Philadelphia: University of Pennsylvania Press, 1988), pp. 315-18.

36. Robert D. Cuff, "Business, the State and World War I: The American Experience," in *War and Society in North America*, ed. J. L. Granatstein and R. D. Cuff (Toronto: Thomas Nelson & Sons, 1971), p. 6; Gary Dean Best, "President Wilson's Second Industrial Conference, 1919-1920," *Labor History* 16 (Fall 1975): 507-9.

37. Best, "President Wilson's Second Industrial Conference," pp. 509-10.

38. Ibid., pp. 510-14; Gitelman, *Legacy of the Ludlow Massacre*, pp. 325-29.

39. Best, "President Wilson's Second Industrial Conference," pp. 514-18; Gitelman, *Legacy of the Ludlow Massacre*, passim.

40. *Report of Industrial Conference Called by the President* (n.p.: 6 March 1920), pp. 8-12.

41. Best, "President Wilson's Second Industrial Conference," pp. 519-20.

42. Gerber, "Corporatism in Comparative Perspective," p. 99; Wynn, *From Progressivism to Prosperity*, p. 107.

43. Tumulty to Wilson, 4 June 1919, *PWW*, 60:153.

44. Clarence Ousley (then assistant to the secretary; he became assistant secretary on 17 Aug. with the passage of the wartime agricultural acts) to Houston, 7 Aug. 1917, Records of the Office of the Secretary of Agriculture, General Correspondence (ADGC), drawer 448, "National Defense: 2-Food, 1917, August-December." On the other hand, see Houston's optimistic assessment in Houston to C. S. Duncan, 15 July 1918, drawer 227, "Reconstruction, 1918," ibid.

45. Bulletin: "Safety First; To Farmers and Business Men in Cotton Territory," 7 Feb. 1919, drawer 327, "Cotton, 1919, January-June"; Houston to Thomas Diamond, 30 Oct. 1919, drawer 391, "Production, 1919"; Robert P. Skinner (American consul-general, London), memorandum, "The Price of Live Hogs in the United States," confidential, 16 Jan. 1919, drawer 391, "Production Committee, 1919," ibid.

46. See *Weekly News Letter* of the Department of Agriculture, 13 Aug., drawer 283, "Agricultural Work of Department, 1919"; speeches by Secretary E.

T. Meredith, 24 February–8 June 1920, drawer 566, "Speeches (Secretary's), 1920," ibid.

47. *The Cabinet Diaries of Josephus Daniels, 1913–1921*, ed. E. David Cronon (Lincoln: University of Nebraska Press, 1963), p. 348 (12 Nov. 1918).

48. David Burner, *Herbert Hoover: A Public Life* (New York: Knopf, 1979), pp. 108–10; Gladys L. Baker, Wayne D. Rasmussen, Vivian Wiser, Jane M. Porter, *Century of Service: The First 100 Years of the United States Department of Agriculture* (Washington, D.C.: Centennial Committee, U.S. Department of Agriculture, 1963), pp. 93–94; report of secretary, *Annual Reports of the Department of Agriculture for the Year Ended June 30, 1920* (Washington, D.C.: GPO, 1921), pp. 11–12.

49. Report of the secretary of the interior, *Reports of the Department of the Interior for the Fiscal Year Ended June 30, 1919* (Washington, D.C.: GPO, 1919), 1:25–32. See also Bill G. Reid, "Proposals for Soldier Settlement during World War I," *Mid-America* 46 (July 1964): 172–86; Reid, "Franklin K. Lane's Idea for Veterans' Colonization, 1918–1921," *Pacific Historical Review* 33 (November 1964): 447–61; and Reid, "Agrarian Opposition to Franklin K. Lane's Proposal for Soldier Settlement, 1918–1921," *Agricultural History* 41 (April 1967): 167–79.

50. Reid, "Agrarian Opposition," pp. 168–70.

51. David F. Houston, *Eight Years with Wilson's Cabinet, 1913 to 1920*, 2 vols. (Garden City, N.Y.: Doubleday, Page & Co., 1926), 1:351.

52. Houston's remarks are quoted from report of secretary, *Annual Reports . . . Agriculture . . . , 1919* (Washington, D.C.: GPO, 1920), pp. 18–21; Meredith's from report of secretary, *Annual Reports . . . Agriculture . . . , 1920*, p. 24. By contrast, note Houston's endorsement of the promotion of farm settlement in his 1918 report, published before the proposals for veterans' colonization were made. See report of secretary, *Annual Reports . . . Agriculture . . . , 1918* (Washington, D.C.: GPO, 1919), pp. 45–49.

53. Reid, "Agrarian Opposition," pp. 178–79.

54. "Report of the Agricultural Commission to Europe," [1918] drawer 320, "Committee, Agricultural, Sent to Europe"; Assistant Secretary G. J. Christie to L. C. Corbett (Bureau of Plant Industry), 14 Nov. 1918, drawer 227, "Reconstruction, 1918," ADGC.

55. Report of secretary, *Annual Reports . . . Agriculture . . . , 1920*, pp. 13–14.

56. Meredith to Wallace, 18 June 1920, drawer 452, "Agriculture Department Work, 1920, January to June," ADGC.

57. Henry C. Dethloff, "Edwin T. Meredith and the Interregnum," *Agricultural History* 64 (Spring 1990): 186.

58. Baker, et al., *Century of Service*, pp. 98–100.

59. Morton Rothstein, "Farmer Movements and Organizations: Numbers, Gains, Losses," *Agricultural History* 62 (Summer 1988): 178; Fred A. Shannon, *American Farmers' Movements* (New York: D. Van Nostrand, 1957), pp. 84–87.

60. Noggle, *Into the Twenties*, pp. 152–78.

61. Ibid.

62. Allen, *Only Yesterday*, pp. 5-6; Wesley M. Bagby, *The Road to Normalcy: The Presidential Campaign and Election of 1920* (Baltimore: Johns Hopkins University Press, 1962), p. 22.

63. See Alfred W. Crosby, *America's Forgotten Pandemic: The Influenza of 1918* (New York: Cambridge University Press, 1989).

64. William Gibbs McAdoo, *Crowded Years* (Boston: Houghton Mifflin, 1931), pp. 388-89.

65. John Milton Cooper, Jr., *Pivotal Decades: The United States, 1900-1920* (New York: W. W. Norton, 1990), pp. 371-72; Bagby, *Road to Normalcy*, pp. 157-67.

66. *The Public Papers of Woodrow Wilson: War and Peace; Presidential Messages, Addresses and Public Papers, 1917-1924* (authorized ed.), ed. Ray Stannard Baker and William E. Dodd, 2 vols. (New York: Harper & Bros., 1921), 2:540-41.

67. Quoted in Gene Smith, *When the Cheering Stopped: The Last Years of Woodrow Wilson* (New York: William Morrow, 1964), pp. 231-32.

BIBLIOGRAPHICAL ESSAY

This essay is divided into two parts: a section describing primary and secondary sources used throughout the book and a section of chapter bibliographies that discuss sources of particular importance to individual chapters. Sources noted in the first section are not repeated in the chapter bibliographies, and individual works that may be relevant to several chapters are generally discussed under the heading of the chapter where they first appear.

PRIMARY SOURCES

Documentary sources for the Wilson administration are abundant. Wilson's own papers are in the Library of Congress, but most researchers will now find that *The Papers of Woodrow Wilson*, ed. Arthur S. Link et al., 62 vols. to date (Princeton, N.J.: Princeton University Press, 1966–   ), not only provides virtually all essential information in the manuscript collection but supplements the papers with documents culled from many other sources both in the United States and abroad and provides as well invaluable additional information in footnotes and short essays on various topics. A microfilm edition of the Wilson Papers, prepared by the Library of Congress, is also available. *The Public Papers of Woodrow Wilson*, ed. Ray Stannard Baker and William E. Dodd, 6 vols. (New York: Harper & Bros., 1925–27), is now useful only for the last months of Wilson's presidency and the last years of his life, for which the volumes of the new edition have not yet been published.

Other documentary collections in the Library of Congress that are of particular importance to the Wilson administration are the papers of Newton D. Baker, Ray Stannard Baker, William Jennings Bryan, Albert S. Burleson, Bainbridge Colby, Josephus Daniels, Thomas Watt Gregory, Gilbert M. Hitchcock, Robert Lansing, William Gibbs McAdoo, Theodore Roosevelt, William Howard Taft, and Joseph Tumulty. Elsewhere, the Edward M. House Papers at Yale University Library, the Walter Hines Page Papers and David Houston Papers at Harvard University Library, the Lindley M. Garrison Papers at Princeton University Library, and the William B. Wilson Papers at the Pennsylvania Historical Society in Philadelphia are also significant.

The diary of Wilson's physician, Cary Grayson, and an unpublished memoir by his brother-in-law, Stockton Axson, are both in the possession of Arthur S. Link at Princeton, and he has been generous in allowing researchers to examine both, as well as in publishing excerpts from them in the *Papers*.

In the National Archives, the records of the various departments of the administration and those of such special agencies as the War Industries Board and the Committee on Public Information provide an enormous amount of information on the workings of the administration. Published annual reports of the departments are also important as are the *Congressional Record* and the Department of State's *Papers Relating to the Foreign Relations of the United States* for this period, including the special volumes in that series, *The Lansing Papers, 1914–1920*, 2 vols. (Washington, D.C.: Government Printing Office, 1939–40), and the thirteen volumes on the Paris Peace Conference (1942–47).

MEMOIRS, DIARIES, AND PUBLISHED CORRESPONDENCE

Wilson left no memoirs, but many of those associated with his administration did. Among those used for this study are Bernard Baruch, *Baruch: The Public Years* (New York: Holt, Rinehart & Winston, 1960); William Jennings Bryan and Mary Baird Bryan, *The Memoirs of William Jennings Bryan* (Chicago: John C. Winston Co., 1925); E. David Cronon, ed., *The Cabinet Diaries of Josephus Daniels, 1913–1921* (Lincoln: University of Nebraska Press, 1963); Josephus Daniels, *The Wilson Era: Years of Peace, 1910–1917* and *Years of War, 1917–1923* (Chapel Hill: University of North Carolina Press, 1944, 1946); Carter Glass, *An Adventure in Constructive Finance* (Garden City, N.Y.: Doubleday, Page & Co., 1927); Cary T. Grayson, *Woodrow Wilson: An Intimate Memoir* (New York: Holt, Rinehart & Winston, 1960); Grey of Fallodon, *Twenty Five Years, 1892–1916*, 2 vols. (New York: Frederick A. Stokes Co., 1925); Francis Burton Harrison, *The Corner-Stone of Philippine Independence: A Narrative of Seven Years* (New York: Century, 1922); Mary Hulbert, *The Story of Mrs. Peck: An Autobiography* (New York: Milton, Balch & Co., 1933); *The Letters of Franklin K. Lane: Personal and Political*, ed. Anne Wintermute Lane and Louise Herrick Wall (Boston: Houghton Mifflin, 1922; Robert Lansing, *War Memoirs* (Indianapolis: Bobbs-Merrill, 1925); William Gibbs McAdoo, *Crowded Years* (Boston: Houghton Mifflin, 1931); Paul Reinsch, *An American Diplomat in China* (Garden City, N.Y.: Doubleday, Page & Co., 1922); and Joseph Tumulty, *Woodrow Wilson as I Know Him* (Garden City, N.Y.: Doubleday, Page, & Co., 1921). Special mention should be made of the stolid but valuable memoirs of Secretary of Agriculture David F. Houston, *Eight Years with Wilson's Cabinet, 1913 to 1920, with a Personal Estimate of the President*, 2 vols. (Garden City, N.Y.: Doubleday, Page & Co., 1926), and of the important but unreliable volumes edited by Charles Seymour, *The Intimate Papers of Colonel House*, 4 vols. (Boston: Houghton Mifflin, 1926–28). *The Letters of Theodore Roosevelt*, ed. Elting E. Morison, 8 vols. (Cambridge, Mass.: Harvard University Press, 1951–54), is excellent, while for Roosevelt's speeches, readers should consult Hermann Hagedorn, ed., *The Works of Theodore Roosevelt, Memorial Edition*, 20 vols. (New York: Charles Scribner's Sons, 1924–25).

WILSON'S OWN WORKS

Like Theodore Roosevelt, Wilson was a prolific author on many subjects, and a full bibliography of his works would be lengthy. Books important for this study include *Congressional Government: A Study in American Politics* (Boston: Houghton Mifflin, 1885); *Constitutional Government in the United States* (New York: Columbia University Press, 1908); *Division and Reunion, 1829–1889* (New York: Longmans, Harper, 1902); *A History of the American People*, 5 vols. (New York: Harper, 1902); *The State: Elements of Historical and Practical Politics: A Sketch of Institutional History and Administration* (Boston: D. C. Heath, 1889 [1897]). Important and relevant articles are "Cabinet Government in the United States," *International Review* 7 (August 1879):146–63; "Committee or Cabinet Government?" *Overland Monthly*, 2d ser., 3 (January 1884):17–33; "The Study of Administration," *Political Science Quarterly* 2 (July 1887):197–222; "The Making of the Nation," *Atlantic Monthly* 80 (July 1897):1–14; "The Reconstruction of the Southern States," *Atlantic Monthly* 87 (January 1901):1–15; "Politics (1857–1907)," *Atlantic Monthly* 100 (November 1907):635–46; "The Road Away from Revolution," *Atlantic Monthly* 132 (August 1923):145–46.

BIOGRAPHIES OF WILSON

For many years the standard biography of Wilson was Ray Stannard Baker, *Woodrow Wilson: Life and Letters*, 8 vols. (Garden City, N.Y.: Doubleday, Page & Co., 1927–39). Based upon research in Wilson's papers and on Baker's personal acquaintance with the president and written in a pleasant and readable style, these volumes are still valuable. Modern students of Wilson, however, can now rely on the far more thorough research and judicious judgments of Arthur S. Link, whose five-volume biography, *Wilson* (Princeton, N.J.: Princeton University Press, 1947–65), carries the story through the American declaration of war in April 1917. With its progress suspended for twenty-five years while Link served the scholarly community by editing *The Papers of Woodrow Wilson*, which are now nearing completion, we may hope that if Link does not himself finish the biography someone else will take up the task. In the meantime, the fullest modern biography is Arthur Walworth's Pulitzer Prize winning *Woodrow Wilson*,

2 vols., (2d rev. ed., New York: Pelican, 1965; 3d ed., New York: Norton, 1978). Two important new biographies of Wilson appeared too late to be consulted in the preparation of this volume: August Hecksher, *Woodrow Wilson* (New York: Scribner's 1991), and J. W. Schulte Nordholt, *Woodrow Wilson: A Life for World Peace* (Berkeley: University of California Press, 1991).

A series of shorter works by Arthur S. Link centering on Wilson include *Woodrow Wilson and the Progressive Era, 1910–1917,* (New York: Harper & Bros., 1954; rev. ed., 1963); *Woodrow Wilson: A Brief Biography* (Cleveland, Ohio: World, 1963); and *Woodrow Wilson: Revolution, War, and Peace* (Arlington Heights, Ill.: AHM, 1979), a much-revised version of his *Wilson the Diplomatist: A Look at His Major Foreign Policies* (1957). A collection of Link's essays in *The Higher Realism of Woodrow Wilson and Other Essays* (Nashville, Tenn.: Vanderbilt University Press, 1971) provides interpretive insights and detailed analyses of specific aspects of his career, and a collection of essays by various Wilson scholars who gathered at Princeton in 1989 to honor Link also offers new analyses. It is edited by John Milton Cooper, Jr., and Charles Neu and is entitled *The Wilson Era: Essays in Honor of Arthur S. Link* (Arlington Heights, Ill.: Harlan Davidson, 1991). Link's reflections on Wilson's role during World War I are outlined in John A. Garraty, *Interpreting American History: Conversations with Historians,* 2 vols. (New York: Macmillan, 1970).

Especially notable among the many brief biographies of Wilson by other authors are John Morton Blum, *Woodrow Wilson and the Politics of Morality* (Boston: Little, Brown, 1956) and the section on Wilson in his *Progressive Presidents: Roosevelt, Wilson, Roosevelt, Johnson* (New York: Norton, 1980), and John A. Garraty, *Woodrow Wilson: A Great Life in Brief* (New York: Knopf, 1956). Kendrick A. Clements, *Woodrow Wilson: World Statesman* (Boston: Twayne Publishers, 1987) is a recent one-volume biography. *Woodrow Wilson and a Revolutionary World,* ed. Arthur S. Link (Chapel Hill: University of North Carolina Press, 1982), contains excellent essays on aspects of Wilson's foreign policy by various experts.

John Milton Cooper, Jr.'s dual biography, *The Warrior and the Priest: Woodrow Wilson and Theodore Roosevelt* (Cambridge, Mass.: Belknap Press of Harvard University, 1983), compares historically the two men who were so often linked in the minds of contemporaries. For those who seek to burrow into Wilson's own mind, several books invite comparison. *Woodrow Wilson and Colonel House: A Personality Study* (New York: John Day, 1956) by Alexander L. George and Juliette L. George depicts Wilson as waging a futile lifelong battle to escape his father's domineering influence by trying to control people and events. In contrast, Edwin Weinstein argues in *Woodrow Wilson: A Medical and Psychological Biography* (Princeton, N.J.: Princeton University Press, 1981) that Wilson's sometimes erratic behavior was the result of cerebrovascular illness rather than of psychological impairment. Further refinements of this interpretation have also been advanced by Bert E. Park in *The Impact of Illness on World Leaders* (Philadelphia: University of Pennsylvania Press, 1986) and in an essay, "The Impact of Wilson's Neurologic Disease during the Paris Peace Conference," in the appendix of volume 58 of *The Papers of Woodrow Wilson,* where an essay by Weinstein, "Woodrow Wilson's Neuropsychological Impairment and the Paris Peace Conference," and one by James F. Toole, "Some Observations on Wilson's Neurologic Illness," may also be found. Park, Weinstein, the Georges, and the editors of the *Papers* have for several years engaged in a vigorous debate about these issues, although some of the problems may be settled by new medical documents and expert commentaries on them now being published in volume 64 of the *Papers*. No one, however, has bothered to refute the lamentably shallow and inadequate psychological study of Wilson by Sigmund Freud and William C. Bullitt, *Thomas Woodrow Wilson: Twenty-Eighth President of the United States: A Psychological Study* (Boston: Houghton Mifflin, 1967); its hostile tone reflects Bullitt's disillusionment more than Freud's desire to understand.

GENERAL WORKS

There are a number of excellent biographies of men important to the Wilson administration. John Morton Blum's *Joe Tumulty and the Wilson Era* (Boston: Houghton Mifflin, 1951) is a sympathetic portrait of Wilson's private secretary and closest political adviser. Wilson's son-in-law and secretary of the treasury, William Gibbs McAdoo, is well depicted by John J. Broesamle, *William Gibbs McAdoo: A Passion for Change, 1863-1917* (Port Washington, N.Y.: Kennikat Press, 1973). Secretary of State Bryan has attracted a number of good biographers in recent years; Paolo E. Coletta's *William Jennings Bryan*, 3 vols. (Lincoln: University of Nebraska Press, 1964-69) gives the fullest account of his life, but Robert W. Cherny, *A Righteous Cause: The Life of William Jennings Bryan* (Boston: Little, Brown, 1985), and LeRoy Ashby, *William Jennings Bryan: Champion of Democracy* (Boston: Twayne Publishers, 1987) are good, short treatments. Bryan's role in foreign policy is discussed in Kendrick A. Clements, *William Jennings Bryan: Missionary Isolationist* (Knoxville: University of Tennessee Press, 1982). Stanley A. Coben's *A. Mitchell Palmer: Politician* (New York: Columbia University Press, 1963) is a hard-eyed look at the major leader of the Red Scare of 1919.

John Milton Cooper, Jr.'s, *Walter Hines Page: The Southerner as American, 1855-1918* (Chapel Hill: University of North Carolina Press, 1977) explores the career of one of the most important southern influences on the early Wilson administration; later, as ambassador to England, Page lost Wilson's confidence. In contrast to Cooper's study, Burton J. Hendrick's *The Life and Letters of Walter Hines Page*, 2 vols. (Garden City, N.Y.: Doubleday, Page & Co., 1923) is much less analytical, but it is still useful for its lengthy excerpts from Page's letters.

Other biographies of administration figures are of varying quality. Thomas Hartig's *Robert Lansing: An Interpretive Biography* (New York: Arno Press, 1982) is disappointing, and Lansing still needs a good, full biography. On the other hand, Keith Olson's *Biography of a Progressive: Franklin K. Lane, 1864-1921* (Westport, Conn.: Greenwood, 1979) is perceptive despite the lack of a substantial body of Lane papers upon which to draw. Michael Parrish's *Felix Frankfurter and His Times: The Reform Years* (New York: Free Press, 1982) is solid. When Charles Neu completes his biography of Edward M. House it will fill a large hole in the literature of the administration; in the meantime, we must content ourselves with the Georges' study of House's relationship with Wilson, with Seymour's uncritical *Intimate Papers*, and with Rupert Norval Richardson's sycophantic *Colonel Edward M. House: The Texas Years, 1858–1912* (Abilene, Tex.: Abilene Printing and Stationary Co., 1964). On Secretary of War Newton D. Baker, see either Frederick Palmer, *Newton D. Baker: America at War*, 2 vols. (New York: Dodd, Mead & Co., 1931), or the newer Daniel R. Beaver, *Newton D. Baker and the American War Effort, 1917–1919* (Lincoln: University of Nebraska Press, 1966).

Wilson's influential first wife has thus far attracted only one biographer, but fortunately she is an able one. Frances Saunders's *Ellen Axson Wilson: First Lady between Two Worlds* (Chapel Hill: University of North Carolina Press, 1985) is a sensitive account of an outstanding woman. Edith Bolling Galt Wilson, on the other hand, has several biographies, of which Ishbel Ross, *Power with Grace: The Life of Mrs. Woodrow Wilson* (New York: Putnam's, 1975), is perhaps the best.

A number of general works on the period helped to fill in the context of this study. These include Sean Davis Cashman, *America in the Age of the Titans* (New York: New York University Press, 1988); John Milton Cooper, Jr., *Pivotal Decades: The United States, 1900–1920* (New York: W. W. Norton, 1990); Robert M. Crunden, *Ministers of Reform: The Progressives' Achievement in American Civilization, 1889–1920* (New York: Basic Books, 1982); Lewis L. Gould, *Reform and Regulation: American Politics, 1900–1916* (New York: Wiley, 1978); Ellis W. Hawley, *The Great War and a Search for a Modern Order: A History of the American People and Their Institutions, 1917–1933* (New York: St. Martin's Press, 1979); Paul Kleppner et al., *The Evolution of American Electoral Systems* (Westport, Conn.: Greenwood, 1981); Christopher Lasch, *The New Radicalism in America, 1889–1963: The Intellectual as a Social Type* (New York: Knopf, 1965); Arthur S. Link and Richard L. McCormick, *Progressivism* (Arlington Heights, Ill.: Harlan Davidson, 1983); John F. McClymer, *War and Welfare: Social Engineering in America, 1890–1925* (Westport, Conn.: Greenwood, 1980); David F. Noble, *America by Design: Science, Technology, and the Rise of Corporate Capitalism* (New York: Knopf, 1979); Robert Wiebe, *Businessmen and Reform: A Study of the Progressive Movement* (Cambridge, Mass.: Harvard University Press, 1962); and Neil A. Wynn, *From Progressivism to Prosperity: World War I and American Society* (New York: Holmes & Meier, 1986). A classic and still delightful social history of the period is Mark Sullivan, *Our Times: The United States, 1900–1925*, 6 vols. (New York: Scribner's Sons, 1927–35).

James MacGregor Burns, in *Presidential Government: The Crucible of Leadership* (Boston: Houghton Mifflin, 1965), credits Wilson with extremely effective leadership of Congress, while Jeffrey K. Tulis, *The Rhetorical Presidency* (Princeton, N.J.: Princeton University Press, 1987), argues that Wilson transformed the presidency, making it the central focus of the federal government and the locus of public expectations about government. Richard J. Fenno's *The President's Cabinet: An Analysis in the Period from Wilson to Eisenhower* (Cambridge, Mass.: Harvard University Press, 1959) emphasizes the degree to which Wilson depended on his cabinet to run the government on a day-to-day basis.

In recent years a number of historians have argued that the Wilson era saw the culmination of a movement toward "corporate liberalism" in which the modern corporation came to dominate the business world and benignly paternalistic corporate leaders moved to control government. Martin J. Sklar suggested this interpretation in "Woodrow Wilson and the Political Economy of Modern United States Liberalism," in *Studies on the Left* 1,3 (1960): 17–47, and a number of historians have explored aspects of his thesis in the years since. These include Alfred D. Chandler, Jr., *The Visible Hand: The Management Revolution in American Business* (Cambridge, Mass.: Belknap Press of Harvard University, 1977); Louis Galambos and Joseph Pratt, *The Rise of the Corporate Commonwealth: U.S. Business and Public Policy in the Twentieth Century* (New York: Basic Books, 1988); Larry G. Gerber, "Corporatism in Comparative Perspective: The Impact of the First World War on American and British Labor Relations," *Business History Review* 62 (Spring 1988): 93–127; William Graebner, *The Engineering of Consent: Democracy and Authority in Twentieth-Century America* (Madison: University of Wisconsin Press, 1987); Samuel Haber, *Efficiency and Uplift: Scientific Management in the Progressive Era, 1890–1920* (Chicago: University of Chicago Press, 1964); Ellis W. Hawley, "The Discovery and Study of a 'Corporate Liberalism,'" *Business History Review* 52 (Autumn 1978): 309–20; David F. Noble, *America by Design: Science, Technology, and the Rise of Corporate Capitalism* (New York: Knopf, 1979); and James Weinstein, *The Corporate Ideal in the Liberal State, 1900–1918* (Boston: Beacon Press, 1968). My interpretation of the Wilson administration has been most influenced by Martin J. Sklar's recent book, *The Corporate Reconstruction of American Capitalism, 1890–1916: The Market, the Law, and Politics* (Cambridge: Cambridge University Press, 1988), which refines his earlier argument, making it more subtle and accounting for problems ignored in the 1960 article. Those problems have been pointed out trenchantly by critics of the corporatist thesis, including Alan L. Seltzer, "Woodrow Wilson as 'Corporate Liberal': Toward a Reconsideration of Left Revisionist Historiography," *Western Political Quarterly* 30 (June 1977):183–212, and William H. Becker, *The Dynamics of Business-Government Relations: Industry and Exports, 1893–1921* (Chicago: University of Chicago Press, 1982), among others.

CHAPTER 1
THEORY AND PRACTICE, 1856–1912

The standard study of Wilson's youth and education is now John M. Mulder, *Woodrow Wilson: The Years of Preparation* (Princeton, N.J.: Princeton University Press, 1978). It supersedes Henry Wilkinson Bragdon, *Woodrow Wilson: The Academic Years* (Cambridge, Mass.: Belknap Press of Harvard University Press, 1967), and George C. Osborn, *Woodrow Wilson: The Early Years* (Baton Rouge: Louisiana State University Press, 1968).

The evolution of Wilson's political thought has been analyzed perceptively by Niels Aage Thorsen, *The Political Thought of Woodrow Wilson, 1875–1910* (Princeton, N.J.: Princeton University Press, 1988), but readers may also wish to consult some earlier, specialized studies. William Diamond, *The Economic Thought of Woodrow Wilson* (Baltimore: Johns Hopkins University Press, 1943), James Kerney, *The Political Education of Woodrow Wilson* (New York: Century, 1926), Harley Notter, *The Origins of the Foreign Policy of Woodrow Wilson* (Baltimore: Johns Hopkins University Press, 1937), and Sondra R. Herman, *Eleven against War: Studies in American Internationalist Thought, 1898–1921* (Stanford, Calif.: Hoover Institution Press, 1969), are all still useful. Richard Stillman, "Woodrow Wilson and the Study of Administration: A New Look at an Old Essay," *American Political Science Quarterly* 67 (June 1973): 582–88, examines the topic less thoroughly than Thorsen, but neither really exhausts it. Peri E. Arnold, in *Making the Managerial Presidency: Comprehensive Reorganization Planning, 1905–1980* (Princeton, N.J.: Princeton University Press, 1986), gives Wilson credit for pioneering the study of administration but points out that as president he did not make administrative reorganization a priority. Richard J. Bishirjian's interesting article, "Croly, Wilson, and the American Civil Religion," *Modern Age* 23 (Winter 1979): 33–38, assisted me in understanding an aspect of Wilson's thought.

Because few records seem to have survived from Wilson's governorship of New Jersey, historians have not been able to analyze his gubernatorial career as thoroughly as they would have liked. David Hirst's *Woodrow Wilson, Reform Governor: A Documentary Narrative* (Princeton, N.J.: Van Nostrand, 1965) is generally complimentary to Wilson, but the value of progressive reforms of the period is sharply questioned by John F. Reynolds, *Testing Democracy: Electoral Behavior and Progressive Reform in New Jersey, 1880–1920* (Chapel Hill: University of North Carolina Press, 1988).

For Wilson's presidential predecessors, see Lewis L. Gould, *The Presidency of Theodore Roosevelt* (Lawrence: University Press of Kansas, 1990), George E. Mowry, *The Era of Theodore Roosevelt, 1900–1912* (New York: Harper & Row, 1958), and Paolo E. Coletta, *The Presidency of William Howard Taft* (Lawrence: University Press of Kansas, 1973). An argument that Roosevelt originated the "rhetorical presidency" is advanced by Stephen E. Ponder in "Executive Publicity and Congressional Resistance, 1905–1913: Congress and the Roosevelt Administration's PR Men," *Congress and the Presidency* 13 (Autumn 1986): 177–86, but Tulis notes that Roosevelt never used public opinion to put pressure on Congress as Wilson later did. Roosevelt's reform program as he prepared for the 1912 election is set out in his book, *The New Nationalism* (New York: Outlook Co., 1910).

CHAPTER 2
1912

Two recent books focus on the election of 1912. Francis L. Broderick, in *Progressivism at Risk: Electing a President in 1912* (Westport, Conn.: Greenwood, 1989), tells the story in brisk, vigorous prose, arguing as most historians have that Wilson owed his election to the split in the Republican party. David Sarasohn, however, takes a revisionist position in *The Party of Reform: Democrats in the Progressive Era* (Jackson: University of Mississippi Press, 1989). In this persuasive book he argues that by 1912 the Democrats had become a united "party of reform" with a clear program and that it was the voters' positive preference for this program rather than the negative effect of the Republican split that led to Wilson's victory. Somewhat more problematical is Sarasohn's speculation that Wilson's majority in 1916 would have been larger without the war. Sarasohn's work at least indirectly challenges some of Walter Dean Burnham's conclusions in his classic, *Critical Elections and the Mainspring of American Politics* (New York: Norton, 1966).

For a popular view of conditions in the country as Wilson took office, see Paul M. Angle, *Crossroads: 1913* (Chicago: Rand McNally, 1963). Edward M. House's anonymous novel, *Philip Dru, Administrator: A Story of Tomorrow 1920-1935*, (New York: B. W. Huebsch, 1912), sets out the reforms the colonel hoped to secure through Wilson and reveals an apocalyptic vision of what might happen if reform were blocked. For the situation in regard to antitrust legislation, see Tony Freyer, "The Sherman Antitrust Act, Comparative Business Structure, and the Rule of Reason: America and Great Britain, 1880-1920," *Iowa Law Review* 74 (July 1989): 991-1017; the ineffectual nature of existing antitrust legislation is scathingly described by Thurman Arnold, *The Folklore of Capitalism* (New Haven, Conn.: Yale University Press, 1937). For public attitudes about the corporations, see Richard L. McCormick, *The Party Period and Public Policy: American Politics from the Age of Jackson to the Progressive Era* (New York: Oxford University Press, 1986). The ambivalent goals of progressives are ably set forth in Don S. Kirschner, *The Paradox of Professionalism: Reform and Public Service in Urban America, 1900-1940* (Westport, Conn.: Greenwood, 1986).

Background on the rise of America to world power in this period may be found in Ernest May, *American Imperialism: A Speculative Essay* (New York: Atheneum, 1968), and in a famous article by William E. Leuchtenburg, "Progressivism and Imperialism: The Progressive Movement and American Foreign Policy, 1898-1916," *Mississippi Valley Historical Review* 39 (December 1952): 483-504, but see also John Milton Cooper, Jr.'s, modifications of Leuchtenburg's thesis, "Progressivism and American Foreign Policy: A Reconsideration," *Mid-America* 51 (October 1969): 260-77.

CHAPTER 3
MAJOR DOMESTIC ISSUES, 1913-1916

Wilson's tariff-reform programs are traced in Frank Burdick, "Woodrow Wilson and the Underwood Tariff," *Mid-America* 50 (October 1968): 272-90; Benjamin J. Klebaner, "Potential Competition and the American Antitrust Legislation of 1914," *Business History Review* 38 (Summer 1964): 163-85; Robert Murray, "Public Opinion, Labor, and the Clayton Act," *Historian* 21 (May 1959): 255-70; Melvin Urofsky, "Wilson, Brandeis and the Trust Issue, 1912-1914," *Mid-America* 49 (January 1967): 3-28; G. Cullom Davis, "The Transformation of the Federal Trade Commission, 1914-1929," *Mississippi Valley Historical Review* 49 (December 1962): 437-55; Richard A. Posner, "A Statistical Study of Antitrust

Enforcement," *Journal of Law and Economics* 13 (October 1970); William Letwin, *Law and Economic Policy in America: The Evolution of the Sherman Antitrust Act* (New York: Random House, 1965); and Jerrold G. Van Cise, *The Federal Antitrust Laws*, 3d ed. (Washington, D.C.: American Enterprise Institute for Public Policy Research, 1983). On the Federal Reserve Act, James Livingston, *Origins of the Federal Reserve System: Money, Class, and Corporate Capitalism, 1890-1913* (Ithaca, N.Y.: Cornell University Press, 1986), presents a corporatist interpretation.

Wilson's skill in dealing with Congress during his early years in office is documented in Marshall E. Dimock, "Woodrow Wilson as Legislative Leader," *Journal of Politics* 19 (February 1957): 3–19. The influence of the South on the administration and on progressive reform is discussed in Richard M. Abrams, "Woodrow Wilson and the Southern Congressmen, 1913-1916," *Journal of Southern History* 22 (November 1956): 417-37; Arthur S. Link, "The South and the New Freedom: An Interpretation," *American Scholar* 20 (Summer 1951): 314–24; and, Dewey Grantham, "Southern Congressional Leaders and the New Freedom, 1913-1917," *Journal of Southern History* 13 (November 1947): 439-59. More recently, Grantham has analyzed in depth the importance of the South to the development of progressivism in *Southern Progressivism: The Reconciliation of Progress and Tradition* (Knoxville: University of Tennessee Press, 1983).

One aspect of the New Freedom obviously influenced by southern attitudes was racial policy. Overviews of that topic are Henry Blumenthal, "Woodrow Wilson and the Race Question," *Journal of Negro History* 48 (January 1963): 1-21, and Joel Williamson, *The Crucible of Race: Black-White Relations in the American South since Emancipation* (New York: Oxford University Press, 1984). A surprising evaluation of Wilson and racial policy by a leading black militant is found in Kenneth M. Glazier, "Document: W. E. B. DuBois' Impressions of Woodrow Wilson," *Journal of Negro History* 58 (October 1973): 452-59. A standard history of native Americans is Angie Debo, *A History of the Indians of the United States* (Norman: University of Oklahoma Press, 1970).

Wilson's move to the Left as the election of 1916 approached has been noted in a number of places. See, for example, Walter I. Trattner, "The First Federal Child Labor Law (1916)," *Social Science Quarterly* 50 (December 1969): 507-24. The only full book on the election, however, is disappointingly unanalytical. See S.D. Lovell, *The Presidential Election of 1916* (Carbondale: Southern Illinois University Press, 1980). For the role of the Left in this election, see Granville Hicks, *John Reed: The Making of a Revolutionary* (New York: Benjamin Blom, 1968), and James Weinstein, *The Decline of Socialism in America, 1912-1925* (New York: Monthly Review Press, 1967).

CHAPTER 4
THE DEPARTMENT OF AGRICULTURE

A detailed account of the Agriculture Department's policies and organization, but little analysis of the reasons for its actions, can be found in the department's centennial history: Gladys L. Baker, Wayne D. Rasmussen, Vivian Wiser, and Jane M. Porter, *Century of Service: The First 100 Years of the United States Department of Agriculture* (Washington, D.C.: Centennial Committee, U.S. Department of Agriculture, 1963). General accounts of American farm policy and farmers' opinions include Murray R. Benedict, *Farm Policies of the United States, 1790–1950: A Study of Their Origin and Development* (New York: Octagon Books, 1966); William L. Bowers, *The Country Life Movement in America, 1900–1920* (Port Washington, N.Y.: Kennikat Press, 1974); Willard W. Cochrane, *The Development of American Agriculture: A Historical Analysis* (Minneapolis: University of Minnesota Press, 1979); Theodore Saloutos, *Farmer Movements in the South, 1865–1933* (Berkeley: University of California Press, 1960); Fred A. Shannon, *American Farmers' Movements* (New York: D. Van Nostrand, 1957); Wayne D. Rasmussen, "The People's Department: Myth or Reality?" *Agricultural History* 64 (Spring 1990): 291–99; and Morton Rothstein, "Farmer Movements and Organizations: Numbers, Gains, Losses," *Agricultural History* 62 (Summer 1988): 161–81.

Aspects of the Wilson administration's policies and the farmers' reactions to them are dealt with in Gladys L. Baker, *The County Agent* (Chicago: University of Chicago Press, 1939); Dewey Grantham, *Hoke Smith and the Politics of the New South* (Baton Rouge: Louisiana State University Press, 1958); Clarence Ousley, "The Beginning of Rural Credit," *Outlook* 113 (June 28, 1916): 511–14; and Russell Lord, *The Wallaces of Iowa* (Boston: Houghton Mifflin, 1947).

CHAPTER 5
INDUSTRIAL DEMOCRACY

The attainment of "industrial democracy," in which labor and capital were supposed to cooperate toward the common good, was a central thrust of the Wilson administration. For the origin and evolution of the idea, see Milton Derber, "The Idea of Industrial Democracy in America, 1898–1915" and "The Idea of Industrial Democracy in America, 1915–1935," *Labor History* 7 (Fall 1966): 259–86, and 8 (Winter 1967): 3–29.

In the prewar period such harmony seemed far away. See, for example, Graham Adams, Jr., *Age of Industrial Violence: The Activities and Findings of the United States Commission on Industrial Violence* (New York: Columbia University Press, 1966); Manfred F. Boemeke, "The Wilson Administration, Organized Labor, and the Colorado Coal Strike, 1913–1914" (Ph.D. diss., Princeton University, 1983); and H. M. Gitelman, *Legacy of the Ludlow Massacre: A Chapter in American Industrial Relations* (Philadelphia: University of Pennsylvania Press, 1988).

For the status of labor at this point, see Marguerite Green, *The National Civic Federation and the American Labor Movement, 1900–1925* (Washington, D.C.: Catholic University of America Press, 1956); Marc Karson, *American Labor Unions and Politics, 1900–1918* (Carbondale: Southern Illinois University Press, 1958); Philip Taft, *The AF of L in the Time of Gompers* (New York: Harper & Row, 1957); and Leo Wolman, *The Growth of American Trade Unions, 1880–1923* (New York: National Bureau of Economic Research, 1924). The Wilson administration, with the organization of the Department of Labor, opened a new chapter in labor-governmental relations. For a commonly accepted appraisal of that relationship, see John S. Smith, "Organized Labor and the Government in the Wilson Era, 1913–1921: Some Conclusions," *Labor History* 3 (Fall 1962): 265–86. Less well known than the Smith essay, but a much more thorough and important study is John Lombardi, *Labor's Voice in the Cabinet: A History of the Department of Labor from Its Origin to 1921* (New York: Columbia University Press, 1942). The only published biography of Labor Secretary Wilson is the admiring one by an assistant, Roger W. Babson, *W. B. Wilson and the Department of Labor* (New York: Brentano's, 1919), but see Wilhelm Clarke's dissertation, "William B. Wilson: The First Secretary of Labor" (Ph.D. diss., Johns Hopkins University, 1967).

CHAPTER 6
DEVELOPING A FOREIGN POLICY

A number of historians believe that the Wilson administration marked a culmination of tendencies in American foreign policy toward paternalistic interventionism. As Thomas L. Haskell has recently argued in two articles dealing with the origins of the British antislavery movement, it may well be that the rise of capitalism brought both the desire and the ability to reform the world. See Haskell, "Capitalism and the Origins of the Humanitarian Sensibility," *American Historical Review* 90 (April, June 1985): 339–61, 547–66. If that is true, then the policies of the Wilson administration in much of the world may be very like those earlier followed by Great Britain in the nineteenth century and may come from similar sources.

Most American historians, however, have been less concerned with the ultimate origins of Wilson's policies than with their immediate sources and effects. Frederick S. Calhoun, in *Power and Principle: Armed Intervention in Wilsonian Foreign Policy* (Kent, Ohio: Kent State University Press, 1986), argues that any instinct to reform the world on Wilson's part was limited by a realistic understanding of the problems and limitations of using armed force. Some historians such as Lloyd Gardner, however, have seen in the remarkable number of interventions during the Wilson administration evidence of a desire to inhibit change and to maintain a world economic and political order comfortable for the United States. See, for example, Gardner's *Safe for Democracy: Anglo-American Responses to Revolution, 1913–1921* (New York: Oxford University Press, 1984) or Samuel F. Wells, Jr.'s, "New Perspectives of Wilsonian Diplomacy: The Secular Evangelism of American Political Economy," *Perspectives in American History* 6 (1972): 389–419. For a sharp critique of this point of view, readers should examine Lloyd Ambrosius, "The Orthodoxy of Revisionism: Woodrow Wilson and the New Left," *Diplomatic History* 1 (Summer 1977): 199–214.

Latin America was a particular focus of Wilsonian foreign policy, and though the administration's aims were often idealistic, it also had more concrete goals. One statement of the administration's point of view may be seen in Secretary of State Bryan's remarks to the Pan American Union in 1913; see, "Dinner of the Pan American Society," *Bulletin of the Pan American Union* 36 (June 1913):

816. But Mark Gilderhus and David Healy point out, in *Pan American Visions: Woodrow Wilson in the Western Hemisphere, 1913-1921* (Tucson: University of Arizona Press, 1986) and in *Drive to Hegemony: The United States in the Caribbean, 1898-1917* (Madison: University of Wisconsin Press, 1988), that idealism and self-interest went hand in hand. Some of the pragmatic realities of Wilsonian policy have been explored by Mark Gilderhus in "Pan-American Initiatives: The Wilson Presidency and 'Regional Integration,' 1914-1917," *Diplomatic History* 4 (Fall 1980): 409-23 and by Burton I. Kaufman in "United States Trade and Latin America: The Wilson Years," *Journal of American History* 28 (February 1962): 342-63, "The Organizational Dimension of United States Economic Foreign Policy, 1900-1920," *Business History Review* 46 (Spring 1972): 17-44, and *Efficiency and Expansion: Foreign Trade Organization in the Wilson Administration, 1913-1921* (Westport, Conn.: Greenwood, 1974). A similar viewpoint, less subtly argued, is in Joseph Tulchin, *Aftermath of War: World War I and United States Policy toward Latin America* (New York: New York University Press, 1971). Specifics of American economic expansionism are examined in Robert Mayer, "The Origins of the American Banking Empire in Latin America: Frank A. Vanderlip and the National City Bank," *Journal of Inter-American Studies and World Affairs* 15 (February 1973): 6-76; and a sample of the Latin American reaction may be found in Frederick B. Pike, *Chile and the United States, 1880-1962: The Emergence of Chile's Social Crisis and the Challenge to United States Diplomacy* (Notre Dame, Ind.: University of Notre Dame Press, 1963).

The Mexican Revolution was one of the first foreign crises the Wilson administration had to face and remained one of its most lasting problems. The best overview of the topic is Mark T. Gilderhus, *Diplomacy and Revolution: U.S.-Mexican Relations under Wilson and Carranza* (Tucson: University of Arizona Press, 1977). For other aspects of the Mexican imbroglio, see Peter Calvert, *The Mexican Revolution, 1910-1914: The Diplomacy of Anglo-American Conflict* (Cambridge: Cambridge University Press, 1970); P. Edward Haley, *Revolution and Intervention: The Diplomacy of Taft and Wilson with Mexico, 1910-1917* (Cambridge, Mass.: MIT University Press, 1970); Larry D. Hill, *Emissaries to a Revolution: Woodrow Wilson's Executive Agents in Mexico* (Baton Rouge: Louisiana State University Press, 1973); Friedrich Katz, *The Secret War in Mexico: Europe, the United States, and the Mexican Revolution* (Chicago: University of Chicago Press, 1972); Robert Quirk, *An Affair of Honor: Woodrow Wilson and the Occupation of Vera Cruz* (Lexington: University of Kentucky Press, 1962); Robert Freeman Smith, *The United States and Revolutionary Nationalism in Mexico, 1916-1932* (Chicago: University of Chicago Press, 1972); and Barbara Tuchman, *The Zimmermann Telegram* (New York: Viking Press, 1958). Useful articles include Kendrick A. Clements, "Woodrow Wilson's Mexican Policy, 1913-1915," *Diplomatic History* 4 (Spring 1980): 113-36; Michael L. Tate, "Pershing's Punitive Expedition: Pursuer of Bandits or Presidential Panacea?" *Americas* 32 (July 1975): 46-71; and Clifford W. Trow, "Woodrow Wilson and the Mexican Interventionist Movement of 1919," *Journal of American History* 58 (June 1971): 46-72.

Wilsonian diplomacy in Haiti and the Dominican Republic has been roundly criticized by historians. See, for example, David Healy, *Gunboat Diplo-macy in the Wilson Era: The U.S. Navy in Haiti, 1915–1916* (Madison: University of Wisconsin Press, 1976); Hans Schmidt, *The United States Occupation of Haiti, 1915–1934* (New Brunswick, N.J.: Rutgers University Press, 1971); and Bruce J. Calder, *The Impact of Intervention: The Dominican Republic during the U.S. Occupa-tion of 1916–1924* (Austin: University of Texas Press, 1984). The American minis-ter to the Dominican Republic was accused of corruption and after much stall-ing removed from office. The incident is noteworthy because, as far as I can determine, this was the only hint of corruption to blemish the administration. The report of the investigation was printed as *Santo Domingo Investigation: Copy of the Report, Findings, and Opinion of James D. Phelan, Commissioner Named by the Secretary of State, with the Approval of the President, to Investigate Charges against the United States Minister to the Dominican Republic* (Washington, D.C.: Government Printing Office, 1915).

The administration's policy in Asia showed similar tendencies to its Latin American policy but was necessarily more restrained because of distance and the presence of strong rivals for dominance. Standard accounts are Roy Watson Curry, *Woodrow Wilson and Far Eastern Policy, 1913–1921* (New York: Bookman, 1957), and Tien-yi Li, *Woodrow Wilson's China Policy, 1913–1917* (New York: Twayne Publishers, 1952). Jerry Israel's *Progressivism and the Open Door: America and China, 1905–1921* (Pittsburgh, Pa.: University of Pittsburgh Press, 1971) ar-gues a strong connection between selfish and idealistic motives throughout the period. One source of the administration's idealism is suggested by Eugene P. Trani, "Woodrow Wilson, China, and the Missionaries, 1913–1921," *Journal of Presbyterian History* 49 (Winter 1971): 328–51. For the Japanese-American conflict over California's alien land law, which poisoned relations throughout the pe-riod, see Thomas A. Bailey, "California, Japan, and the Alien Land Legislation of 1913," *Pacific Historical Review* 1 (March 1932): 36–59, and Paolo E. Coletta, " 'The Most Thankless Task': Bryan and the California Alien Land Legislation," *Pacific Historical Review* 36 (May 1967): 209–30. With the beginning of World War I the Japanese saw a chance to expand their power in China. On American ef-forts to restrain them, see Burton F. Beers, *Vain Endeavor: Robert Lansing's At-tempts to End the American-Japanese Rivalry* (Durham, N.C.: Duke University Press, 1962).

Wilson described Soviet-Western relations as the "acid test" of Western ide-alism, and most historians agree that the West failed the test, although they dis-agree about why. Various views of the question are expressed by George F. Ken-nan, "Russia and the Versailles Conference," *American Scholar* 30 (Winter 1960–61): 13–42; Victor S. Mamatey, *The United States and East Central Europe, 1915–1918: A Study in Wilsonian Diplomacy and Propaganda* (Princeton, N.J.: Princeton University Press, 1957); John M. Thompson, *Russia, Bolshevism, and the Versailles Peace* (Princeton, N.J.: Princeton University Press, 1967); Betty M. Unterberger, *America's Siberian Expedition, 1918–1920* (Durham, N.C.: Duke Uni-versity Press, 1956), *The United States, Revolutionary Russia, and the Rise of Czecho-slovakia* (Chapel Hill: University of North Carolina Press, 1989), and "Woodrow

Wilson and the Bolsheviks: The 'Acid Test' of Soviet-American Relations," *Diplomatic History* 11 (Spring 1987): 71–90; and William Appleman Williams, "The American Intervention in Russia, 1917–1920," *Studies on the Left* 3 (Fall 1963): 24–48. A convenient summary of the contending interpretations is Carl J. Richard, " 'The Shadow of a Plan': The Rationale behind Woodrow Wilson's 1918 Siberian Intervention," *Historian* 49 (November 1986): 64–84.

CHAPTER 7
NEUTRALITY AND WAR, 1914–1917

There are many good studies of American policy during the period of neutrality at the beginning of World War I. A seminal interpretation of Wilson's wartime policy as an effort to create a liberal-capitalist world order is N. Gordon Levin, *Woodrow Wilson and World Politics: America's Response to War and Revolution* (New York: Oxford University Press, 1968). Among the best studies of the neutrality period specifically are: John W. Coogan, *The End of Neutrality: The United States, Britain, and Maritime Rights, 1899–1915* (Ithaca, N.Y.: Cornell University Press, 1981); John Milton Cooper, Jr., *The Vanity of Power: American Isolationism in the First World War, 1914–1917* (Westport, Conn.: Greenwood, 1969); Patrick Devlin, *Too Proud to Fight: Woodrow Wilson's Neutrality* (London: Oxford University Press, 1974); Ernest May, *The World War and American Isolation, 1914–1917* (Cambridge, Mass.: Harvard University Press, 1959); Jeffrey J. Safford, *Wilsonian Maritime Diplomacy, 1913–1921* (New Brunswick, N.J.: Rutgers University Press, 1978); and Charles Seymour, *American Diplomacy during the World War* (Baltimore: Johns Hopkins University Press, 1934).

Economic ties between the United States and the Allies are described in Kathleen Burk, *Britain, America and the Sinews of War, 1914–1918* (Boston: George Allen & Unwin, 1985), and the economic reversal of positions by Britain and the United States is analyzed in John Milton Cooper, Jr., "The Command of Gold Reversed: American Loans to Britain, 1915–1917," *Pacific Historical Review* 45 (May 1976): 209–30. Mira Wilkins, *The Maturing of Multinational Enterprise: American Business Abroad from 1914 to 1970* (Cambridge, Mass.: Harvard University Press, 1974) has a solid account of the economic impact of the war on American business. Edward B. Parsons, in *Wilsonian Diplomacy: Allied-American Rivalries in War and Peace* (St. Louis: Forum Press, 1978), deals disappointingly with an important topic; better is Carl P. Parrini, *Heir to Empire: United States Economic Diplomacy, 1916–1923* (Pittsburgh, Pa.: University of Pittsburgh Press, 1969). Lawrence Martin, on the other hand, treats well the difficult problem of *Peace without Victory: Woodrow Wilson and the British Liberals* (Port Washington, N.Y.: Kennikat, 1973). The devastating impact of war on Britain is clearly indicated in J.M. Winter, *The Experience of World War I* (New York: Oxford University Press, 1989). Secretary of State Robert Lansing's ambiguous role in the American policy of neutrality is described in Daniel M. Smith, *Robert Lansing and American Neutrality, 1914–1917* (Berkeley: University of California Press, 1958).

CHAPTER 8
THE WAR, 1917–1918

On the history of the draft in World War I, see John Whiteclay Chambers II, *To Raise an Army: The Draft Comes to Modern America* (New York: Free Press, 1987). The standard history of American participation in the war is Edward M. Coffman, *The War to End All Wars: The American Military Experience in World War I* (New York: Oxford University Press, 1968), but a particularly vivid picture of the military aspects of the war may also be found in Robert H. Ferrell, *Woodrow Wilson and World War I, 1917–1921* (New York: Harper & Row, 1985), which is also excellent on other topics. Two books by David F. Trask are valuable in understanding other aspects of American war policy. They are: *Captains and Cabinets: Anglo-American Naval Relations, 1917–1918* (Columbia: University of Missouri Press, 1973) and *The United States in the Supreme War Council: American War Aims and Inter-Allied Strategy, 1917–1918* (Middletown, Conn.: Wesleyan University Press, 1961). Wilton B. Fowler's *British-American Relations, 1917–1918: The Role of Sir William Wiseman* (Princeton, N.J.: Princeton University Press, 1969) describes how Wiseman became, like House, an important if unusual channel of communication between Washington and the Allies. Such channels were important because, although leaders on both sides denied it publicly, a good deal of commercial rivalry existed between the Americans and their European Allies. See, for example, Jeffrey J. Safford, "Edward Hurley and American Shipping Policy: An Elaboration on Wilsonian Diplomacy, 1918–1919," *Historian* 35 (August 1973): 568–86.

Maintaining national unity was seen by the administration as vital. The massive propaganda effort that they mounted is well described by Stephen Vaughn in *Holding Fast the Inner Lines: Democracy, Nationalism, and the Committee on Public Information* (Chapel Hill: University of North Carolina Press, 1980); the even more extreme activities of citizen groups that sought to enforce conformity are discussed by Joan M. Jensen in *The Price of Vigilance* (Chicago: Rand McNally, 1968) and by William Preston, Jr., in *Aliens and Dissenters: Federal Suppression of Radicals, 1903–1933* (Cambridge, Mass.: Harvard University Press, 1963). Among the most ardent members of the administration in suppressing all dissent was Post Office Secretary Burleson; see Donald Johnson, "Wilson, Burleson, and Censorship in the First World War," *Journal of Southern History* 28 (February 1962): 46–58. Governmental and private excesses aroused others to defend civil liberties. See Paul L. Murphy, *World War I and the Origin of Civil Liberties in the United States* (New York: W. W. Norton, 1980).

Although most reformers feared that war would disrupt or end chances of reform, some saw it as an opportunity to press reforms. On this topic, see John A. Thompson, *Reformers and War: American Progressive Publicists and the First World War* (Cambridge: Cambridge University Press, 1987). Two groups that of course gained from the war were women and Prohibitionists, both of whom were able to gain long-sought constitutional amendments. For the triumph of the suffrage movement, see Glenda Riley, *Inventing the American Woman: A Per-*

spective on Women's History (Arlington Heights, Ill.: Harlan Davidson, 1986), and Christine Lunardini and Thomas J. Knock, "Woodrow Wilson and Woman Suffrage: A New Look," *Political Science Quarterly* 95 (Winter 1980–81): 655–71. James H. Timberlake chronicles the success of Prohibition in *Prohibition and the Progressive Movement, 1900–1920* (New York: Atheneum, 1970).

Policy for wartime economic mobilization is a complex and important topic; the best place to start is with David M. Kennedy, *Over Here: The First World War and American Society* (New York: Oxford University Press, 1980). Valerie Jean Conner, *The National War Labor Board: Stability, Social Justice, and the Voluntary State in World War I* (Chapel Hill: University of North Carolina Press, 1983), gives an excellent overview of labor policies. Contemporary accounts that provide useful detail are Edward Berman, *Labor Disputes and the President of the United States* (New York: Columbia University Press, 1924) and Alexander M. Bing, *War-Time Strikes and Their Adjustment* (1921; reprint, Arno Press, New York: 1971). More general modern accounts are Jerold E. Brown and Patrick D. Reagan, *Voluntarism, Planning, and the State: The American Planning Experience, 1914–1916* (Westport, Conn.: Greenwood, 1988); Peter Fearon, *War, Prosperity and Depression: The U.S. Economy, 1917–45* (Lawrence: University Press of Kansas, 1987); and H. M. Gitelman, "Being of Two Minds: American Employers Confront the Labor Problem, 1915–1919," *Labor History* 25 (Spring 1984): 189–216. The political aspects of wartime economic policies are explored in Seward W. Livermore, *Politics Is Adjourned: Woodrow Wilson and the War Congress, 1916–1918* (Middletown, Conn.: Wesleyan University Press, 1966).

Whether the administration's attempts to work cooperatively rather than antagonistically with business as well as with labor were successful depends on the point of view. For an enthusiastic account, see Bernard Baruch, *American Industry in the World War: A Report of the War Industries Board* (New York: Prentice-Hall, 1941), but a radically different conclusion is reached by Paul A. C. Koistinen, "The 'Industrial-Military Complex' in Historical Perspective: World War I," *Business History Review* 38 (Summer 1964): 378–403. A standard biography of Bernard Baruch is Jordan A. Schwarz, *The Speculator: Bernard M. Baruch in Washington, 1917–1965* (Chapel Hill: University of North Carolina Press, 1981). For other studies that range between these two extremes, see William J. Breen, *Uncle Sam at Home: Civilian Mobilization, Wartime Federalism, and the Council of National Defense* (Westport, Conn.: Greenwood, 1984); Robert D. Cuff, *The War Industries Board: Business-Government Relations during World War I* (Baltimore: Johns Hopkins University Press, 1973); J. L. Granatstein and Robert D. Cuff, eds., *War and Society in North America* (Toronto: Thomas Nelson & Sons, 1971); Robert D. Cuff, "Woodrow Wilson's Missionary to American Business, 1914–1915: A Note," *Business History Review* 43 (Winter 1969): 545–51; Robert D. Cuff, "Harry Garfield, the Fuel Administration, and the Search for a Cooperative Order during World War I," *American Quarterly* 30 (Spring 1978): 39–53; Robert D. Cuff and Melvin Urofsky, "The Steel Industry and Price-Fixing during World War I," *Business History Review* 44 (Autumn 1970): 291–306; Robert F. Himmelberg, "The War Industries Board and the Antitrust Question in November 1918," *Journal of*

American History 52 (June 1965): 59-74; K. Austin Kerr, "Decision for Control: Wilson, McAdoo, and the Railroads, 1917," *Journal of American History* 54 (December 1967): 550-60; Richard L. Lael and Linda Killen, "The Pressure of Shortage: Platinum Policy and the Wilson Administration during World War I," *Business History Review* 56 (Winter 1982): 545-58; and Melvin Urofsky, *Big Steel and the Wilson Administration: A Study in Business-Government Relations* (Columbus: Ohio State University Press, 1969). Charles Gilbert, *American Financing of World War I* (Westport, Conn.: Greenwood, 1970), is a straightforward account of its topic from which some conclusions about the actual impact of the administration's policies on taxation and borrowing can be deduced.

Activities of the wartime Food Administration are described by participants in William Clinton Mullendore, *History of the United States Food Administration, 1917-1919* (Stanford, Calif.: Stanford University Press, 1941) and in Frank M. Surface and Raymond L. Bland, *American Food in the World War and Reconstruction Period: Operations of the Organizations under the Direction of Herbert Hoover, 1914 to 1924* (Stanford, Calif.: Stanford University Press, 1931). A brief but considerably more skeptical account is in David Burner, *Herbert Hoover: A Public Life* (New York: Knopf, 1979), but probably the full description of the Food Administration and Hoover's role in it must await the publication of the third volume of George Nash's biography of Hoover. The seriousness of the food crisis of 1917 and the administration's reaction to it are described in William Frieburger, "War Prosperity and Hunger: The New York Food Riots of 1917," *Labor History* 25 (Spring 1984): 217-39 and in Tom G. Hall, "Wilson and the Food Crisis: Agricultural Price Control during World War I," *Agricultural History* 47 (January 1973): 25-46. The impact of agricultural policy on the crucial election of 1918 is analyzed by David Burner in *The Politics of Provincialism: The Democratic Party in Transition, 1918-1932* (New York: Knopf, 1967) and in "The Breakup of the Wilson Coalition of 1916," *Mid-America* 45 (January 1963): 18-35.

CHAPTER 9
THE PEACEMAKER

Klaus Schwabe, in *Woodrow Wilson, Revolutionary Germany, and Peacemaking, 1918-1919: Missionary Diplomacy and the Realities of Power*, trans. Rita Kimber and Robert Kimber (Chapel Hill: University of North Carolina Press, 1985), has described masterfully German-American relations at the end of the war. On the American side, preliminary negotiations were handled largely by Colonel House, who sometimes failed to grasp the requirements of the situation, as Keith L. Nelson pointed out in an article, "What Colonel House Overlooked in the Armistice," *Mid-America* 51 (April 1969): 75-91, and Inga Floto later discussed in devastating detail in *Colonel House in Paris: A Study of American Policy at the Paris Peace Conference 1919* (Princeton, N.J.: Princeton University Press, 1980).

Arno J. Mayer was one of the first to suggest that American peace policy was intended to compete for world leadership with the ideas of the Bolsheviks.

See *Political Origins of the New Diplomacy, 1917–1918* (New Haven, Conn.: Yale University Press, 1959) and *Politics and Diplomacy of Peacemaking: Containment and Counterrevolution at Versailles, 1918–1919* (New York: Vintage, 1969). A more traditional interpretation of American aims is presented in Arthur S. Walworth, *America's Moment, 1918: American Diplomacy at the End of World War I* (New York: W. W. Norton, 1977). On Wilson's preparations for the conference, see Lawrence E. Gelfand, *The Inquiry: American Preparations for Peace, 1917–1919* (New Haven, Conn.: Yale University Press, 1963).

Wilson's adversarial relations with the press and the question of whether secrecy during the peace conference served American ends are analyzed in George Juergens, *News from the White House: The Presidential-Press Relationship in the Progressive Era* (Chicago: University of Chicago Press, 1981), Kenneth W. Thompson, ed., *The Presidents and the Press* (Washington, D.C.: University Press of America, 1988), and James D. Startt, "The Uneasy Partnership: Wilson and the Press at Paris," *Mid-America* 52 (January 1970): 55–69.

For the origins of the idea of the League of Nations, see Warren F. Kuehl, *Seeking World Order: The United States and International Organization to 1920* (Nashville, Tenn.: Vanderbilt University Press, 1969). Thomas J. Knock, in "Woodrow Wilson and the Origins of the League of Nations" (Ph.D. diss., Princeton University, 1982) and in his forthcoming book, tentatively entitled *To End All Wars: Woodrow Wilson and the League of Nations*, offers valuable new insights into Wilson's development of the idea. The American movement for the creation of a league to enforce peace is described in Ruhl J. Bartlett, *The League to Enforce Peace* (Chapel Hill: University of North Carolina Press, 1944), and the British side is well covered by George W. Egerton, *Great Britain and the Creation of the League of Nations: Strategy, Politics and International Organization, 1914–1919* (Chapel Hill: University of North Carolina Press, 1978), and Seth P. Tillman, *Anglo-American Relations at the Paris Peace Conference of 1919* (Princeton, N.J.: Princeton University Press, 1961). Other aspects of Allied-American relations at, before, and after the peace conference are examined by Michael J. Hogan, *Informal Entente: The Private Structure of Cooperation in Anglo-American Economic Diplomacy, 1918–1928* (Columbia: University of Missouri Press, 1977), and his "Informal Entente: Public Policy and Private Management in Anglo-American Petroleum Affairs, 1918–1924," *Business History Review* 48 (Summer 1974): 187–205; Melvyn P. Leffler, *The Elusive Quest: America's Pursuit of European Stability and French Security* (Chapel Hill: University of North Carolina Press, 1979); A. Lentin, *Lloyd George, Woodrow Wilson and the Guilt of Germany: An Essay in the Prehistory of Appeasement* (Baton Rouge: Louisiana State University Press, 1984); and Keith L. Nelson, *Victors Divided: America and the Allies in Germany, 1918–1923* (Berkeley: University of California Press, 1975).

Thomas A. Bailey's *Woodrow Wilson and the Lost Peace* (New York: Macmillan, 1944) presents a strong version of the traditional interpretation of Wilson's role at the peace conference as the struggle of American idealism against European realism. A similar argument is presented by Arthur Walworth in *Wilson and His Peacemakers: American Diplomacy at the Paris Peace Conference, 1919* (New York: W.

W. Norton, 1986), which is the best available one-volume account of the American role at the conference. A number of writers at the time and since have argued, however, that Wilson must bear at least a share of blame for the ensuing disaster. Most recently, Lloyd Ambrosius, in *Woodrow Wilson and the American Diplomatic Tradition: The Treaty Fight in Perspective* (New York: Cambridge University Press, 1987), argues persuasively that Wilson's failure resulted less from European intransigence than from the president's attempt to combine incompatible goals of international interdependence and American unilateralism. And in *Rendezvous with Destiny: A History of Modern American Reform* (rev. ed., abridged, New York: Vintage, 1956), Eric Goldman also suggests that the problems of the peace could be traced as much to contradictions within the Fourteen Points as to European resistance. Paul Gordon Lauren, among others, has pointed out that the Japanese demand for a racial-equality clause in the treaty revealed a marked limitation to Wilsonian idealism; see "Human Rights in History: Diplomacy and Racial Equality at the Paris Peace Conference," *Diplomatic History* 2 (Summer 1978): 257–78. By far the most sweeping attack on Wilsonian diplomacy, however, is John Maynard Keynes's famous diatribe, *The Economic Consequences of the Peace* (New York: Harcourt, Brace & Howe, 1920), in which he predicted the failure of the treaty and blamed it entirely on Wilson's impracticality. Etienne Mantoux, in *The Carthaginian Peace: Or, the Economic Consequences of Mr. Keynes* (New York: Scribner's, 1952), took sharp exception to Keynes's interpretation but has not succeeded in driving Keynes's argument out of textbooks and popular accounts of the period.

CHAPTER 10
PEACE

Thomas A. Bailey's *Woodrow Wilson and the Great Betrayal* (New York: Macmillan, 1945) is a standard account of the treaty ratification fight, which finds most virtue on Wilson's side. More recent accounts, however, have explored the roles of opponents of the treaty and suggested that they, too, had rational positions. See, for example, Herbert F. Margulies, *The Mild Reservationists and the League of Nations Controversy in the Senate* (Columbia: University of Missouri Press, 1989), Ralph Stone, *The Irreconcilables: The Fight against the League of Nations* (Lexington: University of Kentucky Press, 1970), and, especially, the fine study by William Widenor, *Henry Cabot Lodge and the Search for an American Foreign Policy* (Berkeley: University of California Press, 1980). Briefer but also thoughtful is James E. Hewes, Jr., "Henry Cabot Lodge and the League of Nations," *Proceedings of the American Philosophical Society* 114 (August 1970): 245–55. The disenchantment of some of Wilson's most ardent early supporters is described in Stuart I. Rochester, *American Liberal Disillusionment in the Wake of World War I* (University Park: Pennsylvania State University Press, 1975).

Wilson's increasingly frantic and unrealistic poststroke attempts to find some way to secure American membership in the League have been cataloged in a series of articles by Kurt Wimer: "Woodrow Wilson and a Third Nomination," *Pennsylvania History* 29 (April 1962): 193–211, "Woodrow Wilson Tries Conciliation: An Effort That Failed," *Historian* 25 (August 1963): 419–38, "Woodrow Wilson's Plan for a Vote of Confidence," *Pennsylvania History* 28 (July 1961): 279–93; and "Woodrow Wilson's Plans to Enter the League of Nations through an Executive Agreement," *Western Political Quarterly* 11 (December 1958): 800–812.

CHAPTER 11
AFTER THE WAR

Most of the issues of the immediate postwar period of course had their origins during the war. Many of the works cited under Chapter 9 are equally relevant to this period.

After the war the administration made one last effort to achieve industrial democracy through a pair of national conferences. The record of the first one was published by the Department of Labor as *Proceedings of the First Industrial Conference, October 6 to 23, 1919* (Washington, D.C.: Government Printing Office, 1920), that of the second as *Report of Industrial Conference Called by the President* (n.p.: 6 March 1920). On the first conference, see Haggai Hurvitz, "Ideology and Industrial Conflict: President Wilson's First Industrial Conference of October 1919," *Labor History* 18 (Fall 1977): 509–24; the second is covered by Gary Dean Best, "President Wilson's Second Industrial Conference, 1919–1920," *Labor History* 16 (Fall 1975): 505–20.

Wartime and postwar Agriculture Department policies are discussed in Henry C. Dethloff, "Edwin T. Meredith and the Interregnum," *Agricultural History* 64 (Spring 1990): 182–90 and in Bill G. Reid's three articles, "Agrarian Opposition to Franklin K. Lane's Proposal for Soldier Settlement, 1918–1921," *Agricultural History* 41 (April 1967): 167–79, "Franklin K. Lane's Idea for Veterans' Colonization, 1918–1921," *Pacific Historical Review* 33 (November 1964): 447–61, and "Proposals for Soldier Settlement during World War I," *Mid-America* 46 (July 1964): 172–86.

Black Americans gained little from wartime reforms and often became victims of the wartime frenzy. See, for example, Elliott M. Rudwick, *Race Riot at East St. Louis, July 2, 1917* (Carbondale: Southern Illinois University Press, 1964); William H. Tuttle, Jr., *Race Riot: Chicago in the Red Summer of 1919* (New York: Atheneum, 1970); and Robert L. Zangrando, *The NAACP Crusade against Lynching, 1909–1950* (Philadelphia: Temple University Press, 1980).

Two largely forgotten epidemics—one of disease and the other of fear—had an enormous impact on the administration during and just after the war. For the former, see Alfred W. Crosby, *America's Forgotten Pandemic: The Influenza of 1918* (New York: Cambridge University Press, 1989); for the latter, see Robert K. Murray, *Red Scare: A Study in National Hysteria, 1919–1920* (Minneapolis: University of Minnesota Press, 1955).

For the last days of the administration and Wilson's illness and last years, see Wesley M. Bagby, *The Road to Normalcy: The Presidential Campaign and Election of 1920* (Baltimore: Johns Hopkins University Press, 1962); Burl Noggle, *Into the Twenties: The United States from Armistice to Normalcy* (Urbana: University of Illinois Press, 1974); and an especially charming book, Gene Smith, *When the Cheering Stopped: The Last Years of Woodrow Wilson* (New York: William Morrow, 1964). Frederick Lewis Allen's delightful look at the 1920s, *Only Yesterday: An Informal History of the Nineteen-Twenties* (New York: Harper & Row, 1931), has lost none of its appeal with the passage of time. The consensus among Americans that Wilson belongs among their greatest presidents is documented in Robert K. Murray and Tim H. Blessing, *Greatness in the White House: Rating the Presidents, Washington through Carter; Final Report, the Presidential Performance Study* (University Park: Pennsylvania State University Press, 1988).

INDEX

291

Clements, Kendrick
    A., 1939-

The presidency of
Woodrow Wilson.

$14.95

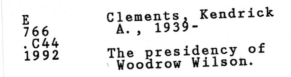

DATE			